JACKSON SCHOOL PUBLICATIONS
IN INTERNATIONAL STUDIES

JACKSON SCHOOL PUBLICATIONS
IN INTERNATIONAL STUDIES

Senator Henry M. Jackson was convinced that the study
of the history, cultures, political systems, and languages of
the world's major regions was an essential prerequisite for wise
decision making in international relations. In recognition of
his deep commitment to higher education and advanced
scholarship, this series of publications has been established
through the generous support of the Henry M. Jackson
Foundation, in cooperation with the Henry M. Jackson School
of International Studies, and the University of Washington Press.

*The Crisis of Leninism and the Decline of the Left:*
*The Revolutions of 1989*

EDITED BY DANIEL CHIROT

*Sino-Soviet Normalization and Its International Implications, 1945–1990*

BY LOWELL DITMER

*Contradictions:*
*Artistic Life, the Socialist State, and the Chinese Painter Li Huasheng*

BY JEROME SILBERGELD
WITH GONG JISUI

*The Found Generation:*
*Chinese Communists in Europe during the Twenties*

BY MARILYN A. LEVINE

*Rules and Rights in the Middle East: Democracy, Law, and Society*

EDITED BY ELLIS GOLDBERG,
RESAT KEŞABA, AND JOEL S. MIGDAL

*Can Europe Work?*
*Germany and the Reconstruction of Postcommunist Societies*

EDITED BY STEPHEN HANSON
AND WILLFRIED SPOHN

*Marxist Intellectuals and the Chinese Labor Movement:*
*A Study of Deng Zhongxia (1894–1933)*

BY DANIEL Y. K. KWAN

*Essential Outsiders:*
*Chinese and Jews in the Modern Transformation*
*of Southeast Asia and Central Europe*

EDITED BY DANIEL CHIROT
AND ANTHONY REID

*Days of Defeat and Victory*

BY YEGOR GAIDAR

*The Production of Hindu-Muslim Violence in Contemporary India*

BY PAUL R. BRASS

*Modern Clan Politics:*
*The Power of "Blood" in Kazakhstan and Beyond*

BY EDWARD SCHATZ

*Serbia since 1989:*
*Politics and Society under Milošević and After*

EDITED BY SABRINA P. RAMET
AND VJERAN PAVLAKOVIĆ

*Boris Yeltsin and Russia's Democratic Transformation*

BY HERBERT J. ELLISON

*The New Woman in Uzbekistan:*
*Islam, Modernity, and Unveiling under Communism*

BY MARIANNE KAMP

# *The* NEW WOMAN
# *in* UZBEKISTAN

## *Islam, Modernity, and*
## *Unveiling under Communism*

# MARIANNE KAMP

*UNIVERSITY OF WASHINGTON PRESS*

*SEATTLE & LONDON*

Publication of this book was made possible in part by the
Jackson School Publications Fund, established through the generous
support of the Henry M. Jackson Foundation and other donors,
in cooperation with the Henry M. Jackson School of
International Studies and the University of Washington Press.

University of Washington Press
PO Box 50096, Seattle, WA 98145, USA
www.washington.edu/uwpress

Library of Congress Cataloging-in-Publication Data
Kamp, Marianne.
The new woman in Uzbekistan : Islam, modernity,
and unveiling under communism / Marianne Kamp.
p. cm. — (Jackson School publications in international studies)
Includes bibliographical references and index.
ISBN 0-295-98644-1 (alk. paper) ISBN 13: 978-0-295-98644-9
1. Women—Uzbekistan—History.
2. Women—Uzbekistan—Social conditions.
I. Title.  II. Series.
HQ1735.27.K36 2006
305.48'8943250904—dc22      2006015767

*Cover:* The unveiling ceremony of Tursun Otajonova,
an activist in the Hujum. Kokand Museum photo.

# CONTENTS

# ACKNOWLEDGMENTS

THIS BOOK WOULD HAVE BEEN impossible without the aid of Professor Doctor Dilarom A. Alimova of the Institute of History, Uzbekistan Academy of Sciences. She enabled me to gain access to institutions in Uzbekistan, opened her own home to me repeatedly in the years since I first met her, and dispelled many of my preconceived ideas about Uzbek women. In her unofficial role as an advisor on my research she directed me to sources, and she introduced me to her mother, Rahbar-oi, whose oral history plays a central role in this book. I am very thankful to Rahbar-oi and to all of the women who shared their life stories with me; their names are listed in the bibliography.

I owe thanks to Professors John Perry, Sheila Fitzpatrick, and Robert Dankoff from the University of Chicago, who were patient with my slow pace in writing, and who, with outside reader Erika Loeffler, provided careful, thoughtful, and critical comments on this work.

Friends and acquaintances aided my research in Uzbekistan in many ways: Theresa Truax gave me companionship and back-up in many of the oral history interviews; Ikrom Nugmanxo'jaev and Saodat Xolmatova helped me to gain a more nuanced understanding of issues and phrases that came up in interviews, and many others facilitated interviews, introducing me to the most interesting elderly women they knew.

These include Aziza and Vera Nouritova, Vita Semeniuta, Jo'ra Boltaev, Shavkat Boltaev, Mamlakat Madalieva, Dilarom and Abduhamid Dunyarov, Aziz and Shoira Ibrohimov, Akbar Samadov, Nozim Habibullaev, Saidakbar Ag'zamxo'jaev, Mavjuda Habibullaeva, Ra'no Faizullaeva, Zamira Asadova, Tursun-Ali Valiev, Nodira Baghramova, Timur Valiev, Shahnoza Gayupova, and Ortaqali Utanov. The staff of the Uzbekistan State Archive reading room in Tashkent always provided the best research environment possible, not only fulfilling my myriad document orders, but also providing me with tea and hospitality. The staff of the Bukhara and Namangan affiliates of the Uzbekistan State Archive were likewise helpful and hospitable. My thanks are also due to Rinat Shigabudinov for frequent help in locating rare documents and publications.

IREX (International Research Exchange) supported my research, and funding came from Whitman College's Perry Grant, from the University of Wyoming's Basic Research Grant, the College of Arts and Sciences, and the Caitlin Long Excellence fund. The University of Michigan's Middle East and North African Studies Center and Center for Russian and East European Studies gave me a job, intellectual support, and access to the University of Michigan library early in this project.

Many colleagues have read and commented on sections of this work. My heartiest thanks are for those who have read versions of the book manuscript and took time to comment and to offer suggestions: Adeeb Khalid, Shoshana Keller, Katie Thorsos, my sister Elizabeth Graham, Paula Michaels, and the two other anonymous readers of the manuscript for the University of Washington Press. I also thank the University of Washington Press editors Michael Duckworth and Mary Ribesky for their encouragement, and in particular, Julie van Pelt, for her careful copyediting.

It was only after a few years of work on this project that I became aware that part of my interest in women and unveiling arose from stories that my mother, Velma Frey Kamp, told me about leaving home for college, removing her Mennonite head covering, cutting her religiously sanctioned long hair, and replacing conservative Mennonite dress with fashions sewn from Vogue patterns. I am grateful to her and to my father, Charles Kamp, for instilling in me the love of learning and for encouraging curiosity about the world.

And finally, thanks to Michael Brose, for love, support, and companionship over the many years it took me to write this book, and to Elaine Shangguan Brose, our daughter, thanks to whom, life is half honey.

# A NOTE ON
# TRANSLITERATION
# AND ABBREVIATIONS

ALL TRANSLATIONS ARE BY THE
author. Abbreviations in the text and notes are spelled out or briefly
defined where they first appear and are also included in the glossary.
These include: Communist Party of Uzbekistan (CPUz), and Uzbekistan
State Archive (Uz. St. Arch.).

Uzbek (O'zbek) names, regardless of period or source text, are
spelled according to the 1996 Uzbek Latin alphabet, with some exceptions. Uzbek names are represented with Russian transliteration only
in quoted material and in bibliographic citations, where I include Uzbek
spelling in brackets. Russian names are transliterated according to the
Library of Congress system, except when there is a widely accepted standard English spelling (Moscow, not Moskva, in the text). I use Uzbek,
not O'zbek, as the most familiar international form of the ethnic name.
Place names in Uzbekistan appear in their Uzbek form unless another
form is widely familiar and consistently spelled in English: thus Uzbekistan (not O'zbekiston), Tashkent (not Toshkent), Bukhara (not Buxoro),
Kokand (not Qo'qon), Khiva (not Xiva). I have chosen the simplest
form, Fargana, rather than the inconsistant transliteration from Russian, Fergana/Ferghana or the Uzbek form Farg'ona. Words that relate
to Islam, if they are commonly used in English, are spelled in their simplest transliteration from Arabic (not from Uzbek or Russian)—Sharia,

rather than Shariah or Shari`ah or Shariat, and Quran, rather than Koran or Qur`an. The index and glossary include some alternate spellings.

In the 1920s, Uzbek was codified by Soviet linguists (including Uzbek scholars) as a language separate from other closely related Central Asian Turkic languages. Before the 1920s, the written Turkic language of oasis Central Asia was called Turki (and known to western scholars as Chagatay). Turki was written in Arabic script. By the early twentieth century, Central Asian writers began to modify the ways they wrote, decreasing attention to the "proper" spelling of words borrowed from Arabic, and in particular downplaying the differences among ت and ط; ث, س, and ص; and ذ, ز, ض, as well as adding vowels or diacriticals to express Uzbek pronunciations. In the early 1920s, many of these changes to the Arabic script became formalized, even as a committee for a new alphabet was working at adopting a modified Latin alphabet. The Latin alphabet was introduced in 1926, but was not widely used until 1930. After 1930, it underwent continual revision, with some Cyrillic letters replacing earlier choices. In 1940, Uzbek was abruptly assigned a Cyrillic alphabet, which in 2005 was still commonly used. In 1993, independent Uzbekistan adopted a new Latin alphabet and then modified it in 1996; as of 2005, the 1996 Latin alphabet was taught in schools and was used by youth and in some media.

Western scholars have used numerous solutions to the quandary of representing Uzbek words in Latin script. Although many use the phonetic representation of Uzbek that Professor Edward Allworth worked out, I chose to use the 1996 Uzbek Latin alphabet. There is no perfect solution to transliteration, but the 1996 Uzbek Latin alphabet is fairly transparent. It enables the reader who knows Uzbek in its earlier forms to recognize earlier spellings. However, in references and in discussion of pre-1917 literature, I use a more generic Persian transliteration without diacriticals for some Turkic language journal articles, especially Tatar journals, even though this introduces some inconsistencies. There are also several references from the 1930s that reflect the 1930s version of the Uzbek Latin alphabet.

| LATIN | CYRILLIC | |
|---|---|---|
| a | А | as in apple or as in ah |
| b | Б | b |
| ch | Ч | as in chair |
| d | Д | d |
| e | Э, Е | as in end |
| f | Ф | f |
| g | Г | as in gum |
| g' | Г | no equivalent; a guttural gh |
| h | Х | as in hi |
| i | И | as in it or meet |
| j | Ж | as in jam; in words borrowed from Russian, zh |
| k | К | k |
| l | Л | l |
| m | М | m |
| n | Н | n |
| o | О | as in hot |
| o' | Ў | similar to boat |
| p | П | p |
| q | Қ | no equivalent; a k made from the back of the throat |
| r | Р | rolled r |
| s | С | s |
| sh | Ш | as in shirt |
| t | Т | t |
| u | У | as in room |
| v | В | pronounced either as English v or English w, depending on dialect |
| x | Х | as in Scottish loch |
| y | Й, И | consonant as in yeast; vowel as in many |
| z | З | z |
| ' | Ъ | (Arabic `ayn), following a vowel, either lengthens the vowel or inserts a glottal stop |

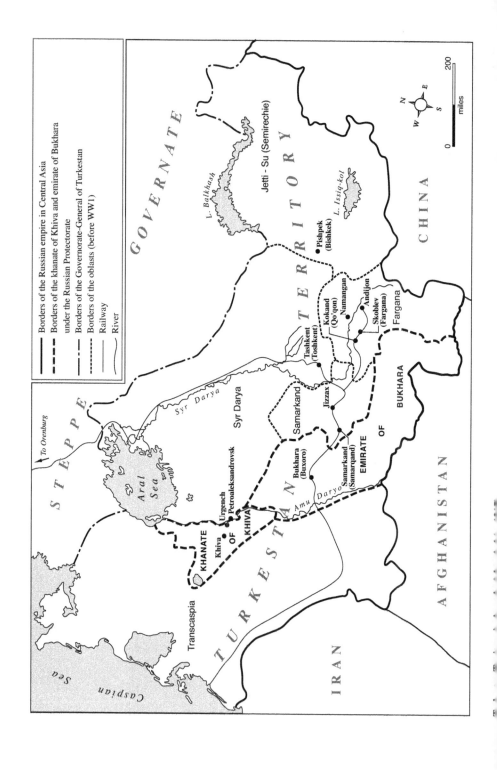

STEPPE GOVERNATE

TERRITORY

Jetti - Su (Semirechie)

L. Balkhash

L. Issiq-kol

CHINA

Pishpek (Bishkek)

Namangan

Andijon

Kokand (Qo'qon)

Skoblev (Fargana)

Fargana

Tashkent (Toshkent)

Jizzax

Samarkand

BUKHARA

OF

Syr Darya

Syr Darya

EMIRATE

Samarkand (Samarqand)

Bukhara (Buxoro)

Amu Darya

To Orenburg

Aral Sea

Petroaleksandrovsk

Urgench

KHANATE OF KHIVA

Khiva

AFGHANISTAN

Transcaspia

TURKESTAN

IRAN

Caspian Sea

Borders of the Russian empire in Central Asia

Borders of the khanate of Khiva and emirate of Bukhara under the Russian Protectorate

Borders of the Governorate-General of Turkestan

Borders of the oblasts (before WW1)

Railway

River

N
W E
S

0        200
miles

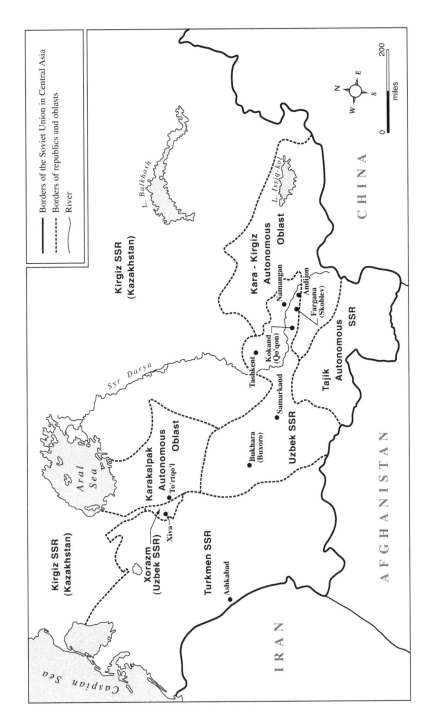

Soviet Socialist Republic, 1925

**Legend:**
Borders of the Soviet Union in Central Asia
Borders of republics and oblasts
River

Kirgiz SSR (Kazakhstan)

Kara - Kirgiz Autonomous Oblast

L. Balkhash

L. Issiq-kol

CHINA

Namangan
Andijon
Farg'ana (Skoblev)

Tashkent

Kokand (Qo'qon)

Tajik Autonomous SSR

Syr Darya

Samarkand

Uzbek SSR

Bukhara (Buxoro)

Aral Sea

Karakalpak Autonomous Oblast
To'rtqo'l

Xorazm (Uzbek SSR)
Xiva

Kirgiz SSR (Kazakhstan)

Turkmen SSR

Ashkabad

Caspian Sea

IRAN

AFGHANISTAN

N
W E
S

0    200
miles

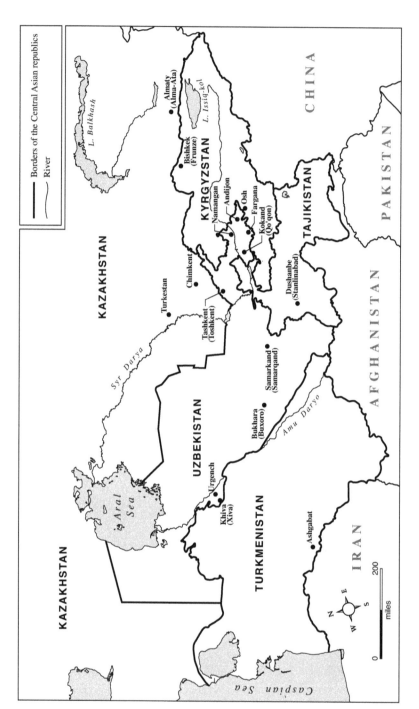

Uzbek Soviet Socialist Republic and independent Uzbekistan (post-1959 borders)

# THE NEW WOMAN
# IN UZBEKISTAN

# INTRODUCTION

$I$N UZBEKISTAN IN 1927, THOU-
sands of Uzbek women responded to the Communist Party's call for
public demonstrations of their liberation and embrace of rights by throwing off their *paranjis* and *chachvons* (body and face veils). This campaign,
the Hujum (attack or assault), can be seen as a turning point for women
in Central Asia and as a turning point in the development of Soviet
Uzbekistan. As a starting point, the Hujum gives evidence of a sudden
initiation of Stalinist methods of transformation. On the other hand,
as the end of an era the Hujum must be seen a moment when Jadid
discourses about Muslim women's rights became subordinated to the
Communist Party's approach to both women's rights and social transformation. Overt and politically motivated violence against women grew
in response to the state's increasing coercive power. Persuasion lost
importance; ultimately force became the state's instrument for creating consent.

A history that is concerned with processes and the development of
the Soviet state, such as works by Gregory Massell and Douglas Northrop,
may begin with the Hujum.[1] My work, however, is concerned with the
lives of Uzbek women and thus begins earlier, when those lives became
visible. Uzbek and other Central Asian women became objects of observation when the Russian conquest of Central Asia brought foreign gov-

ernment officials, travelers, and ethnographers to the region. Colonialism itself created a newly self-conscious literary class of Central Asian men who wrote about and criticized their own society. Like modernizing reformers elsewhere in the Islamic world, the Central Asian reformers (Jadids) turned their attention to the "improvement" of women, calling for women's education and changes in social practices that kept women in seclusion. A few urban Central Asian women responded to these critiques by writing about their own lives and conditions and calling for increased education. These small but significant moves preceded the October 1917 Bolshevik revolution and had nothing to do with Communist social transformation programs. However, after the revolution, the relationship between indigenous reform and Communist transformation was complex, and Uzbek women who desired change sought support from an unpopular and violent government. The Communist Party promised women liberation, but its strategies met violent responses that put "liberated" Uzbek women at risk for their lives.

This volume's central concern is the experience of Uzbek women in this period of transformation, from the early twentieth century into the 1930s. A number of Soviet historians and Western historians have written about the Soviet state's and Communist Party's attempts to change life radically for Central Asian women.[2] My research differs in several significant ways: First, women's experiences and their actions receive more emphasis than the state's or the Communist Party's programs. Second, in trying to find women's experience, this work draws on sources that present Uzbek women's thoughts: Uzbek women's published writings from the 1920s and 1930s, oral histories that I conducted with elderly women in Uzbekistan in the early 1990s, and published memoirs and autobiographies. Third, this work is explicitly comparative, examining what was unique about the Soviet experiment in Central Asia by comparing programs and outcomes in Uzbekistan with similar efforts to modernize women in Turkey and Iran. I am not convinced that the Soviet experiment was unique, either as a fulfillment of the ideology of Communism or as a totalitarian empire; rather, the Soviet Union was one of numerous twentieth century experiments in ruthless modernization. And finally, this work seeks out continuities that span the 1917 divide, in ideas about women and their transformation.

In basing my study of Uzbek women on Uzbek-language sources rather than Russian-language government and Party documents, I see Uzbeks in an active contest with each other to define their identity and trajectory instead of viewing Russians as actors (the colonizers) and Uzbeks as acted upon or resisting (the colonized). The conflict featured in this work began as one between Jadids and conservatives over women's reform and continued into the Hujum, when the successors of each tendency battled over women's veiling.

In his pioneering work, *The Surrogate Proletariat: Moslem Women and Revolutionary Strategies in Soviet Central Asia, 1919–1929,* Gregory Massell examines the Communist Party's motivations for and methods of trying to change the lives of Muslim women in Central Asia. Through an exhaustive reading of published works in Russian, as well as western scholarship and travel accounts, Massell reconstructs the shifting emphases of Party strategy as it attempted to engineer a women's revolution. Massell's work thus portrays Central Asia through the lens of Russian speakers in the Party, a limitation that he acknowledges: "we know little indeed about the Central Asian cadres, the men and women who were heavily involved in the events dealt with in this study . . . only in a handful of cases do we know anything at all about the first generation of native Central Asian female cadres . . . except that they tended to be orphans, runaway child-brides, young widows, or divorcées."[3] Massell's work has been widely used among scholars of Soviet history as an in-depth study of the Party's implementation of a social engineering scheme.

Douglas Northrop, in *Veiled Empire,* builds on Massell's work but reexamines the whole topic of the Party's efforts to transform Uzbek women, basing his research on the archives of the Women's Division of the Communist Party and of the Central Asian Bureau (CAB) of the Communist Party, as well as on newspapers and other published sources of the time. He argues that the Soviet Union was a colonial empire, one where Bolsheviks tried to transform daily cultural practices and gender relations against the wishes of most Uzbeks, who responded as colonial subjects by using the weapons of the weak. Northrop agrees with Massell's basic assertion that the Communist Party started the unveiling campaign because it saw Central Asian women as potential substitutes for a proletariat, believing that if the Party offered them liberation, they would become loyal transformers of society. He then outlines the ways that this vision failed: through the "complex social and subaltern strategies pursued by individual Uzbek men and women in dealing with an alien state . . . [ranging] from apparent support to active opposition, from studied obliviousness to passive resistance to the spreading of gossip and rumors."[4] What emerges is a careful, nuanced look at a variety of Uzbek social responses to Soviet laws and the Party's unveiling campaign. However, because Northrop uses primarily Party sources and Russian-language published sources, and because he only uses post-1930 Uzbek-language sources, the Uzbek side of this conflict is compressed; the competing voices and lively arguments among Uzbeks in the 1920s about identity and modernity are eliminated, and Uzbeks appear to be unified in their anticolonialism. My examination of Uzbek publications from the early twentieth century and up to 1929, when censorship became much more strict, sees Uzbeks as not as objects of Russian colonialism, but as the primary actors in a multisided struggle. In this struggle, women became symbols for both modernist transformation and for tradition, and some women managed to make their own voices heard.

The Uzbek feminist activist Marfua To'xtaxo'jaeva, in her work *Between the Slogans of Communism and the Laws of Islam*, combines interviews with women about their family history with a review of Uzbek scholarship on women. She asks why the promised Soviet transformation of women's lives was only partially successful, and where it did change matters, why it did not necessarily improve life for women. Listening to women's stories, she observes that "the Soviet period brought changes which had both positive and negative impacts on women, while at the same time also failing to change many of the most fundamental aspects of their daily lives."5 The stories that women told to To'xtaxo'jaeva, and those that elderly Uzbek women told me about their lives, help to answer a question that I address: why did the Party's efforts in some spheres, such as education, make an extraordinary impact, while Party ideas about marriage and family, although made into law, only gradually and partially change Uzbek society?

## A COMPARATIVE CONTEXT: WOMEN IN THE ISLAMIC WORLD

Uzbek women's lives in the twentieth century were shaped by a political context, that of the Russian empire and the Soviet Union, and by a hybrid cultural context, that of an Islamic world under colonial domination. While the Soviet Union created what Uzbekistan became economically and politically, until the 1930s the Soviet Union was not the sole factor in shaping ideas and ideologies in Uzbekistan. Central Asian intellectual and religious exchanges with the Islamic world, in the movement of scholars, publications, and pilgrims, increased in the late tsarist period and continued at high rates until the end of the 1920s. Central Asian ideas about society and social change in the early twentieth century formed in response to colonialism, but also in interaction with other Islamic societies.

Literacy rates give a sense of the affects of the Soviet model of development in Uzbek women's lives. By 1959, Soviet statistics claimed that 97 percent of women between ages nine and forty-nine in Uzbekistan were literate, leaving only 3 percent below age fifty illiterate.[6] Such levels of literacy for men or women, though inflated, remained beyond imagining in the neighboring states of Pakistan and Afghanistan even in the year 2000. In 1955, Turkey's rate of female literacy for those over age fifteen was 21 percent; in Iran in 1976, 24 percent.[7] In both Turkey and Iran, female literacy and education rates rose substantially in the last two decades of the twentieth century, but in the early twenty-first century they still do not approach Soviet Uzbekistan's achievement of full literacy.

The point is that, protestations that Uzbekistan's women suffered under Soviet rule notwithstanding, socialism clearly benefited these women, if such things as education are viewed as a social and individual good. One can argue that statistics in the Soviet Union were falsified, so that reality differs substantially from image, or one could protest that the costs of Soviet-style modernization, in its suppression of freedom of thought and religion, were so great that any benefits in health or education are paltry by comparison. But the comparison reveals how much Uzbek women's lives changed in the socialist decades. Life might have been otherwise, but it was not, and the Soviet system of the 1920s and 1930s set Uzbek women's lives on a path rather far removed from that of Muslim women in neighboring countries in the same time period.

The literature in English on women in Central Asia is limited to a few works, but scholarship concerning women in other Islamic societies is broad and deep, and it poses questions for this volume. Does Islam as a religion shape the lives of Muslim women in similar ways? Are there commonalities among Islamic societies that exist because of a connection to Islam, rather than because of similar economic and political conditions? Certainly Islam has basic religious texts that express ideas about women's roles, ideas that may be seen as norms. However, Islam does not create a specific historical destiny for gender relations, which instead vary with the influence of culture, politics, and social and economic change. Similar ideas and processes concerning change emerged in both Central Asia and the Middle East in the late nineteenth and early twentieth centuries, but the source of similiarity rests not solely or even primarily in Islam. Rather the common experience of colonial domination by Europeans, and the networks of intellectual exchange between Muslims in the Middle East and the Russian empire through the press and through travel for trade and education, brought about similar responses. Ideas about the "reform of women" that emerged in the Egyptian colonial context traveled to Russia's Muslims, and ideas about the nation emerging among Tatars spread among Turks.

Historian Stephen Kotkin addresses the question of comparability of the Soviet Union with other states in an essay on "the interwar conjucture." He argues that, like the Soviet Union, between the First and Second World Wars many states made modernity their goal and expressed it through state intervention and the creation of the welfare state, as well as through mass politics, mass production, and mass consumption. States competed to rid themselves of "backwardness" and to embrace the idea of the new, the modern, by mobilizing the population in unprecedented ways. In this sense, he argues, the interwar Soviet Union can be compared to its contemporaries, including both liberal and illiberal regimes.[8] Laura Engelstein summarizes this understanding: "The Soviet Union is but one variation on a general cultural-political type: the modern state with its invasive but extra-institutional techniques that organize, control, constrain and promote social activity, while shaping productive life." Engelstein notes that this approach reduces attention to the ways the Soviet Union differed from other modern states, while others argue that the ideology of the Soviet Union set it apart from most other modern states.[9] This question—whether the Soviet Union can be compared with other states, or must be examined either sui generis or in comparison only with other "totalitarian" states—divides historians of the Soviet Union.

When examining the question through the lens of Uzbekistan in the 1920s and 1930s, both comparability and incomparability with the experience of other states are apparent. Some authors see the experience of Uzbekistan and the other Central Asian republics as a direct continuation of Russian colonialism, while others examine the differences between Soviet and other colonialisms.[10] Women's history, the focus of this work, presents one way of approaching comparability. Among the many tasks taken on by states that sought to become "modern," changing women's status and social roles was significant, both symbolically and instrumentally. In the competition for recognition as modern, interwar states touted their policies on women. In striving to penetrate and transform the lives of citizens, interwar states created policies aimed at shaping women and thus also shaping families. In many states, women took on greater public roles than they had previously, and many strove to use government attention to achieve their own goals.[11] This work argues that some of the experiences of Uzbek women were comparable to that of women in other states, perhaps even more so than to experiences of women elsewhere in the Soviet Union.

In the pre–World War I period, Turkestan (of which the southern provinces became part of Uzbekistan) was a Russian colony; Bukhara and Khiva (parts of which also became Uzbekistan) were Russian protectorates. The processes of change that shaped colonies elsewhere, especially in the Middle East and South Asia, also affected Russian Central Asia. Ellen Fleischmann notes some of these—"shifts in power between rural and urban elites, increased commercialization of agriculture, . . . accelerating integration into the world market, and the effects of Western industrialization on local economies . . ."—and she links these phenomena to changing social ideas about women's roles.[12] As Adeeb Khalid shows, Central Asian intellectual links to the Middle East remained strong in the colonial period.[13] It is not surprising, then, that attention to "the woman question" and "the reform of women" arose in prewar Turkestan, as it did elsewhere in response to colonization, drawing on ideas that spread from other Islamic societies.

Had there been no Bolshevik revolution, had Central Asia become independent in some way, as other colonial territories of other empires eventually did, the trajectories that Turkestani society in general and women in particular followed would probably have resembled those of other Islamic societies in the Middle East and South Asia more closely, where ideas about the reform of women that had impact on some elites and members of the nationalist middle classes were weakly supported by governments and did not result in sweeping change. But there was a Bolshevik revolution, and Central Asia remained attached to Russia. The particularities of the Soviet system shaped Uzbekistan, its society, its economy, its political life, and the lives of Uzbek women, creating significant distances from the experiences of neighboring states.

I argue that prerevolutionary ideas for the reform of women gained ground in Uzbekistan because many of those who espoused them joined the Communist Party and were able to harness state power behind their modernizing agenda. However, there are also striking similarities in the ways women experienced change in Uzbekistan, Turkey, and Iran in the 1920s and 1930s. I argue that similarities arose from the role that governments took in changing society and in attempting to disestablish the institutions and legal authority of Islam. However, Uzbekistan's leadership, as part of the Soviet Union, had far greater coercive force at its disposal than even the ruthless Mustafa Kemal Atatürk had, and certainly more than Reza Shah of Iran.

I compare Uzbekistan, Turkey, and Iran to illuminate some of the methods and motives of the modern state in transforming women, but the difference between Uzbekistan as a part of the Soviet Union and Turkey and Iran as independent states is crucial. The coercive power and reach of the state is important in explaining the biggest difference between the experience of Uzbek women in the rush to modernity and that of Iranian or Turkish women. Namely, Uzbek women were murdered in large numbers by Uzbek men who opposed the state's efforts to transform women and who opposed women's participation in those changes. While both Iran and Turkey experienced some social turmoil arising from government attempts to change women's roles and unveil them, neither witnessed such a murder wave.

Uzbekistan was a constituent republic of the Soviet Union. The government actions and Communist Party policies that drastically changed the economic base, the political structure, and culture transformed the lives of women all over the Soviet Union in very determined and intentional ways.[14] But the impact of those transformations differed, because the cultural and economic base on which they were enacted varied considerably. Policy planners of the 1920s tried to consider differences arising from Islamic society and the realities of Central Asian culture and geography so that while policies were broadly similar for the whole union, they were not uniform. Similar efforts did not produce identical results, and the lives of most Uzbek women, even when confronted with the state's interventions, remained in many ways quite unlike the lives of the union's Europeans.[15] Although the Soviet context explains much, comparisons with women outside the union can help to illuminate what in the Soviet experience was distinctive and what was not.

## POWER, AGENCY, AND RESISTANCE

The event that historians have seen as defining Uzbek women's experience of the Soviet Union was the Hujum. Hujum—assault or attack—

was the name that the Communist Party gave to its campaign, beginning in 1927, to change Uzbek women's lives rapidly, to bring them into
public life, paid work, education, and membership in the Party. The
Hujum had a key symbol: unveiling. In 1927 and for some years after-
ward, the Communist Party called on Uzbek women to remove the
paranji and chachvon, a combination head-and-body covering robe with
horsehair face veil. Tragically, many women were murdered for unveiling. Fearing violence, thousands of women resumed wearing their paranjis and chachvons, abandoning them years later.

These dramatic moments drew the attention of Soviet and American historians not to the actions of women per se, but to the actions of
the Party/state upon women. For several decades of Soviet historians,
whose work might be exemplified by Rakhima Aminova's *October Revolution and the Liberation of Women in Uzbekistan*, the actions of the Party
provided a cohesive narrative framework within which to discuss how
Uzbek women's lives had improved under Soviet rule. For American
scholar Gregory Massell, an examination of the Party's approaches and
decisions regarding women in Central Asia provide deep insight not
into women's lives, but into the workings of the Soviet system. Shoshana
Keller emphasizes women's victimization as the result of the Party's
program, the Hujum. Douglas Northrop uses the Communist Party
archives to explore not only the Party and state's initiatives, but also
resistance from Uzbeks, Party members, and non-Party members; he
regards the Hujum as a colonial project and Uzbek resistance to unveiling as anticolonial resistance. Northrop concludes that the project was
an "utter and abject failure—at least in the 1920s and 1930s—to
achieve the intended metamorphosis of Uzbek society by transforming local gender relations."[16] These accounts all rely for their sources
primarily on documents produced by the Communist Party itself, its
Russian-speaking Women's Division agents, or the local functionaries
of Soviet government and the police. What they lack is an attention to
women's subjectivity.

Women's subjectivity and agency, women's ability to act and do, are
at the core of women's history. As Lata Mani observes in her exploration
of colonial representations of women and *sati* (when a Hindu widow
dies by casting herself upon her husband's funeral pyre as a sign of devotion), accounts in which women are always represented and never represent themselves "foreclose any possibility of women's agency," so that
"women in this discourse remain eternal victims."[17]

This book is about Uzbek women and is based on the words of Uzbek women. This is a quest for agency in a context of coercion and limitation. Margot Badran, in her exploration of Egyptian feminism, focuses on "middle and upper-class women assuming agency—the capacity to exercise their will, to determine the shape of their own lives, and to partake in the shaping of their culture and society."[18] Women's agency may seem unproblematic (though it is not) in the context of liberal regimes and relative freedom, but it obviously questionable when women have few choices because of poverty or because of oppressive state or patriarchal systems. Joan Scott argues that in any case, subjects "are not unified, autonomous individuals exercising free will, but rather subjects whose agency is created through situations and statuses conferred on them. Being a subject means being 'subject to definite conditions of existence . . .' These conditions enable choices, though they are not unlimited."[19] In presenting Uzbek women as agents, I stress that Soviet political life placed very serious limitations on women's actions and on men's actions, and that Uzbek society also placed enormous constraints on women's choices.

Conceptually, agency may be linked to resistance, but it is not limited to resistance. Agency refers to the ability to make decisions and act on one's own behalf: those decisions may appear as compliance or resistance, but the subject's own thought and decision is the central concern. This does not mean that subjects can act effectively; the results of action are unpredictable.[20] In Uzbekistan, to borrow Keller's words, women were "trapped between state and society" in the Hujum.[21] On one hand, the Party/state pressured women to unveil in public; on the other hand, families often tried to force women to remain veiled. In this context, what is resistance and what is compliance?

Historians of the Soviet Union have made much of evidence of ordinary peoples' resistance to the state,[22] but resistance is not only resistance to the state; women's resistance is most often recognized in a struggle against patriarchal social norms. In Rosalind O'Hanlon's words, literature that portrays communal resistance may "disguise the extent to which these 'communities' may themselves be fractured by relations of power, with gender prominent among them."[23] Research simply does not support a unified Central Asia resisting a Hujum imposed by imperialistic Bolsheviks; there was no unity among Uzbeks, who were divided by prerevolution loyalties and ideologies, as well as by class and gender. Compliance too, involves decision and strategizing. Women may "active[ly] collu[de] in the reproduction of their own subordination."[24] In Uzbekistan, if women resisted state pressure, they complied with social pressure, and vice versa.

While feminist scholars explore agency in discussing women's lives, it should be emphasized that all subjects, male and female, may exercise agency, making decisions in contexts where society and politics limit choice but also make choice possible. Uzbek men's actions in the 1920s were if anything more multifaceted and complex than women's because they had a greater realm of choices. Some joined the Party, some supported the Soviets' social changes, some opposed those changes, and some tried to create alternatives to the Party's hegemony. "'Resistance masculinity'" may be "not only a form of resistance against race and class oppression, but also a means of oppressing women."[25] Those Uzbeks who chose to murder women for unveiling were not victims of Russian colonialism; they were agents who decided to enact their opposition to the Soviet state and to the ideas of the Uzbek reformers (whom the Soviets had empowered) through violence against women.

## UZBEKISTAN AND UZBEK WOMEN

The Soviet project included incorporating the diverse ethnic groups of the former Russian empire into a union by emphasizing and supporting their differentiation into "nations." Soviet citizens who would participate in the new union came with national identification as well as class identification, and in many of the republics national identification was much stronger than class. Before the revolution, urban and sedentary speakers of Turkic languages in Russian Turkestan, Bukhara, and Xorazm (Khiva) were most often identified as Sarts, Uzbeks, or Turks. But in the early 1920s, the Soviet Union's Nationalities Bureau encouraged the use of Uzbek as an inclusive term, and in 1924 mapped out Uzbekistan as the homeland of Uzbeks (some of whom had been Sarts or Turks until the 1920s).[26] The structures through which the newly expanded national group "Uzbeks" encountered the Bolshevik government were devised in Moscow. The Provisional Government, established after the February Revolution of 1917, established voting rights for all—men and women, all nationalities and classes—in one of its first proclamations. The Bolsheviks—especially several women Bolsheviks—made women's participation in the Party and in the new government a significant goal.[27] Turkestan was dragged into the revolution and was reeled back into the renewed empire through a multi-sided struggle that lasted several years. Women had not been important to any plans laid in Turkestan; rather, the emphasis on their newly awarded status as citizens and their duties as participants came from revolutionary Russia.

But from the beginning of Bolshevik power in Turkestan, citizenship was gendered, Party membership was gendered, and the expectations for citizen participation were gendered. Ordinary patterns of Uzbek speech required that if a speaker wanted to speak to all of society, both men and women, the word "women" had to be articulated. Uzbek society was thoroughly gender-segregated. To include women in new state projects, organizers needed to create structures to deal with them separately from men. Thus, people who had been doubly marginalized in the imperial period—as subjects without rights in a colony of the Russian empire and as women in a patriarchal society[28]—suddenly occupied a new category, Uzbek women, endowed with political rights of citizens. The Women's Division of the Communist Party gradually gave Uzbek women and other "backward, Eastern women" more and more attention, and the state structures forming in Uzbekistan took active interest in women.[29] This book concerns the ways that Uzbek women articulated their own identities, using veiling and unveiling as well as many other strategies to define what being Uzbek would mean.[30]

SOURCES: ORAL HISTORIES, ARCHIVES, PUBLICATIONS

Oral histories conducted in 1992–1993, with women who lived through the teens, 1920s, and 1930s, provide a substantial portion of the source material for this book.[31] I found interview subjects by snowballing, that is, using networks of friends and acquaintances to make connections with willing elderly women. I carried out most of my research in the cities of Tashkent, Bukhara, Namangan, and Kokand, so urban women's experiences play a much larger role in this book than rural women's experiences. However, in a subsequent oral-history project concerning collectivization in Uzbekistan, carried out between 2001 and 2004, a team of researchers conducted 120 interviews in seven rural regions of Uzbekistan, and transcripts from those interviews inform my comments on unveiling in rural regions.[32] Most of the 1992–1993 interviewees were elderly Uzbek women, and I carried out the interviews in Uzbek. I also interviewed several Tajik and Tatar women, as well as one Bukharan Jewish woman and one Turkestan-born Russian woman; I conducted most of those interviews in Russian.

Oral history gives voice to at least some Uzbek women, something that Soviet archives cannot do, though the range of voices is limited by the accident of the subject's longevity, as well as by the whims of snowballing. I also draw on published autobiographies of Uzbek women. The oral histories, though different from Soviet autobiography because they include negative accounts, criticisms, and discussion of religion, are formulaic, just as Soviet autobiographies are, in part because narrators who lived through the Soviet period had specific models for presenting their lives, and because I, the interviewer, only asked certain questions.[33]

My recording of life stories from ordinary Uzbek women is not an effort to locate the "liberal subject" in Soviet society or to establish "popular memory" among Uzbeks.[34] According to oral historian Trevor Lummis, the popular memory school argues that "memory cannot simply be a memory of life as it was, but that anyone's memory must be selectively distorted by the class power behind the projection of these images. In other words 'memory' is constructed from past and present ideology and is not a recalled impression of 'things as they were.'" Lummis disagrees with this reasoning, arguing that "the individual oral history accounts from the memories of those who actually lived that experience are very different from 'popular' presentations."[35] In my own oral interviews, I sought both the general and the unique, the common stories about unveiling and social change in the 1920s as well as the moments that were specific to one person's life. In previous work I have examined the ways that dominant narratives and historical moments shaped the ways women told their life stories, and yet I conclude with Lummis that while each subject's interpretation of her life changes over time, her remembrance of particular events generally remains stable and does reflect what she experienced decades ago.[36]

Individual stories permit an exploration of the spectrum of responses to Soviet transformation schemes. Each life story differs, but it can be inferred that themes and experiences that are repeated in many life stories are somewhat representative of the experiences of a generation. Examining a group of life stories together allows me to explore both details that shed light on women's agency and to construct the general outlines of urban Uzbek women's lives in the 1920s.

Articles by and about women from the periodicals that Uzbeks were most likely to read, *Yangi Yo'l, Yer Yuzi, Ma'orif va O'qituvchi,* and *Qizil O'zbekiston,* also provide sources for this research. In the 1920s, Uzbek speakers and Russian speakers had limited access to one another's worlds.[37] Uzbeks and Russians generally could not speak each other's languages, with the exception of some young, well-educated, Uzbek Party members. Uzbek women, even urbanites, were likely to learn Russian only if they fell on hard times and went to work for Russians. With few exceptions, rural people did not see or interact with Russians.[38]

In order to enter the mental world of Uzbek women, Uzbek-language sources from the 1920s and 1930s are essential reading, while Russian sources, including the majority of Party documents, reveal largely what Russian speakers said to each other about Uzbek women. Russians had been writing about Uzbek women for some fifty years, ever since the Russian conquest of Central Asia, but their work was usually based on interaction with male translators. By the 1920s, the Party had a Women's Division in which Russian/European women could interact directly with Uzbek women, but only a few participants were adequately bilingual; translators were still necessary. The vast majority of rural Uzbeks were illiterate in any language in the 1920s. Among urban Uzbeks, literacy rates were typically 25 percent for men, and 5 percent for women. Russians in Uzbekistan had much higher literacy rates: 80 percent for urban men and 60 percent for urban women. But Russians made up only about 7 percent of Uzbekistan's five million people. Thus, even in the 1920s, with low literacy rates among Uzbeks, most of Uzbekistan's publications were in Uzbek, because Uzbeks vastly outnumbered Russians and literate Uzbeks usually only read Uzbek.[39]

For those who were literate, the language that they read shaped the borders of their world. For example, in 1928 Russian teachers in Xorazm, Uzbekistan, lived in the Soviet Union, reading the Central Asian Bureau's Russian-language newspaper, *Pravda Vostoka,* which was published in Tashkent, and various journals that were published in Russia. At the same time, Turkic-speaking teachers in Xorazm lived in Uzbekistan, reading Uzbek-language newspapers that were published in Tashkent and Samarkand and nothing from the larger union.[40] Likewise, some of my interviewees read Uzbek publications like *Yer Yuzi, Qizil O'zbekiston,* and *Yangi Yo'l,* but none read Russian papers. Uzbek-language publications carried significantly different perspectives from Russian language publications, however careful the censors were about ideology. While the historian can assume that some male Uzbek Party members did read Russian in this period, a historian studying Uzbek women needs to find their words in Uzbek-language publications.

I also used the Uzbekistan State Archives in Tashkent, Namangan, and Bukhara and archives of the Communist Party of the Soviet Union's Central Asian Bureau (in Moscow), especially files concerning the activities of the Women's Division of the Communist Party.

OVERVIEW

Chapter 1 sets the socioeconomic context of colonial Russian Turkestan and Bukhara and explains why it was that even though many aspects of Central Asian life changed dramatically under Russian rule, women's lives continued largely unchanged. Chapter 2 introduces the Jadid movement, a movement of Islamic reform in Central Asia, and explores Jadid ideas about the reform of women. This exploration helps to explain the trajectories and parameters of reformist thought about women, which themselves laid the groundwork for Uzbek women activists' concepts even when these women were working for the Communist Party Women's Division. Chapter 3 outlines the political transformation from colonial Russian Turkestan into Soviet Uzbekistan and examines the Soviet state's approach to changing women's roles in society by comparing Soviet Uzbekistan in the 1920s with republican Turkey.

The focus of chapter 4, women's education, allows a discussion of ideological continuities before and after 1917 and argues that Jadid approaches to education for girls were not eradicated, but rather expanded through the creation of the Soviet educational system in Uzbekistan. Chapter 5 focuses on the first Uzbek women's journal, *Yangi Yo'l*, discussing the lives of some of its editors, reviewing the journal's emphases, and comparing and contrasting the journal's version of the New Woman with the better-known Soviet understanding of women's liberation. I argue that the journal synthesized Communist and Jadid concerns and approached change for women rather conservatively, hoping to appeal to a conservative Uzbek public.

Chapters 6, 7, and 8 all deal with unveiling. Chapter 6 establishes that unveiling was debated by Jadids before the revolution and that some early Uzbek activist women saw veiling as incompatible with their vision of the New Woman's life. These women unveiled before the Communist Party decided to promote unveiling as its strategy for cultural revolution. Chapter 7 examines the Hujum, the Party's campaign for radically changing women's situation in Central Asia by ending seclusion. In this chapter I stress that the Hujum involved both choice and force. Chapter 8 questions the causes of the murder wave that the Hujum triggered. Uzbek men murdered unveiled Uzbek women in alarmingly high numbers; the effect of their actions, I argue, was to reinforce women's subordination by terrorizing women into reveiling.

Chapter 9 looks at the continued efforts for unveiling in Uzbekistan, especially in rural communities in the 1930s, and asks about the longer-term consequences of Soviet modernization for women's lives. Finally, in the conclusion I return to a discussion of resistance and agency, and I briefly address the new religious veiling in postindependence Uzbekistan.

☙ 1 ☙

# RUSSIAN COLONIALISM
# IN TURKESTAN
# AND BUKHARA

In 1993, I WANDERED INTO AN
antiques shop in Bukhara and found a photo, a sepia-tinted image from
the second decade of the twentieth century, with "Marseilles" lettered
at the bottom. The photo pictured a man in a European suit with a
dandy's haircut. Anvar, the shopkeeper, said this was his grandfather, a
Bukharan merchant who traveled to Europe for trade and recorded his
journey with this photo. Eventually Anvar invited me to interview his
grandmother, Muattar S. (b. 1899, Bukhara), the wife of that international merchant.[1] Muattar's life story suggests some of the changes that
Russian colonialism wrought in Central Asia, but mainly demonstrates
the continuities of Central Asian women's lifestyles amid economic and
political change.

Muattar grew up in a family closely connected to the final two
Bukharan emirs. Her father once served as a leading judge for the emirate. As a child, Muattar often went to the emir's palace with her stepmother, a nursemaid. The daughter of a wealthy and educated father,
Muattar began studying at age seven with a woman religious teacher who
taught her the Quran and the prayers.[2] When she was about sixteen,
she was given in an arranged marriage to a Bukharan merchant, a man
twenty-two years her senior. She had two children, both of whom died,
and her husband died in 1917. Muattar then became the second wife

Paranji-clad women, Bukhara, undated. Ark Museum reprint, Bukhara.

of her first husband's nephew, who was also a merchant. He was the dandy who appeared in the old photo. Muattar and her co-wife lived in one large home, staying together even after their husband died.

Although Muattar's father was a high-ranking official in the emir's government, her older brothers became involved with the Jadid movement, which called for educational, social, and political reform in Central Asia.[3] Emir Alimxon suppressed the Jadids and exiled Muattar's two brothers. Her father made an appeal to the emir on their behalf, but the emir exiled her father. Revolution swept the emir and his court away in 1920.

Before the Bolshevik revolution, Muattar felt the influence of Russian colonialism and Central Asian response indirectly. Russian economic ties made her husband's business expand and made possible his trip to Marseilles. Her brothers and husband all responded to Russian imperialism and the winds of change in Bukhara, the former joining the Jadid movement and the latter donning European garb. But Muattar lived much as her female ancestors did, exposed only to traditional education, not to the Jadid education of her brothers; and she was married young, by arrangement, and became a second wife. Colonialism reached into every Central Asian's life, but women's segregation and seclusion meant that its impact on them was indirect.

## RUSSIAN COLONIALISM IN TURKESTAN AND BUKHARA

Uzbekistan did not exist as such before 1924. Uzbekistan was one of a number of Soviet "union republics" that was designed by the Soviet Nationalities Commissariat, an entity within the Bolshevik government of the Soviet Union. Stalin, the head of the commissariat, believed that Central Asia needed territorial divisions in order to allow "nationalities"— groups that shared a language, culture, history, and land area—to develop their identity within a polity that they dominated numerically. Nothing in Central Asia fit Stalin's clear-cut theory, however. The major ethnic groups of Central Asia spoke several languages and dialects that fall within two major linguistic groups, Turkic and Persian. They had a variety of lifestyles—nomadic, sedentary agricultural, and urban. And they referred to themselves in terms that could designate tribe, religion (Muslim), or something closer to modern concepts of ethnicity. The places discussed in this chapter—cities and regions in the Bukharan emirate and in the southern provinces of Russian Turkestan, namely Fargana, Syr Darya (Tashkent), and Samarkand—all became part of Uzbekistan after 1924, and the majority of their inhabitants would be designated Uzbeks.[4] However, reflecting prerevolutionary usage, this chapter refers to the city dwellers and farmers of Central Asia as Turkestanis, the name that Central Asian reformers most often used.

The Russian conquest of Central Asia began in the 1700s, with Russia's gradual assumption of control over the Kazakh steppe. By 1854, Russian forces established forts at Verny (Almaty) and other towns that now form the southern border of Kazakhstan. Russian merchants, travelers, and ambassadors collected information that would facilitate conquest of the khanates of Khiva and Kokand and the emirate of Bukhara.[5] In 1865, Russian forces attacked and seized Tashkent, the commercial center of the Kokand Khanate, and by 1876 they defeated the armies of Kokand, Bukhara, and Khiva. The Russian Interior Ministry chose to incorporate the lands of Kokand, as well as bits of Bukhara and Khiva, into a single province—Turkestan—to be ruled by a Russian governor-general. Most of Bukhara and most of Khiva were left to the internal control of their respective emir and khan, with Russia in charge of foreign relations. Uzbekistan was formed from parts of these three entities, and hence encompassed two rather different recent legacies—protectorate rule in Bukhara and Khiva and direct colonial rule in Turkestan.

Russians thought of Central Asia as the dark and backward corner of the empire, a place for them to civilize.[6] But Central Asia, like most other places on earth, was not stagnant before the Russians arrived, and it continued to change after they took control. In the late nineteenth century, hardly any place in the world was impervious to the goods and the pressures from core colonial states. Colonization could only intensify those interactions and turn gradual and selective adoption of new objects and ideas into rapid and coerced material and social change.

Until the revolution, currents of social and political change in sedentary Central Asia flowed slowly, but the economy of Turkestan, and to a lesser extent of Bukhara and Khiva, was transformed in the Russian colonial period (1865–1917).[7] The imperial government actively promoted cotton cultivation in southern Turkestan, built railroads joining the old Silk Road cities to Russia's central metropolis, and changed laws to expand private land ownership. These factors led to growing commerce, increasing wealth, and strong economic relations between the empire's center and its Central Asian periphery. However, modes of governance that encouraged the assimilation of elites elsewhere in the empire were not implemented to the same degree in Turkestan, and for the vast majority of Turkestan's population, Russians remained strangers.[8] Barriers of religion, language, and lifestyle separated colonizer from colonized, while Russian attitudes of European superiority and Turkestani concerns with contamination contributed to those walls.

Mingling took place in certain urban workplaces and markets, which were male spaces. Uzbeks and other indigenous Central Asians took active measures to keep women separated from all that was Russian. The veil that urban Central Asian women wore became a sign of identity as well as a physical barrier placed between the woman and the foreigner. Muattar's second husband had traveled to Europe for trade and pleasure before World War I, and Muattar herself was aware of political and social change through her elder brothers, but she was not an active participant. Male Bukharan merchants and Jadids might adopt Western dress as a sign of their identification with social change, but Muattar wore a paranji from age seven until 1928, when representatives of Soviet power forced her to remove it.

## LEGAL CHANGES

The policies that the first governors-general established in Russia's new Turkestan territory minimized the empire's direct administration of the lives of "natives," but made several fundamental legal changes that had significant impact on the lives of ordinary men and women. These related to the legal status of imperial subjects, to slavery, and to land ownership. Those immigrant settlers who came from Russia to Turkestan were considered Russian citizens, subject to Russian law; this meant that Russian settlers were also liable to conscription into the tsar's armies. Turkestanis were granted citizenship only on an individual and exceptional basis; they were not equal to Russian citizens in rights or responsibilities and were not subject to military conscription. Turkestanis were subject to Sharia (Islamic law) and customary law in civil matters, but were under the authority of the governor-general's Russian courts in criminal cases.[9] The governor-general outlawed slavery in Turkestan and included abolition of slavery in the treaties that the defeated Bukharan emir and Khivan khan were forced to sign. Slave trading ended rapidly in Turkestan and decreased significantly in Bukhara and Khiva, finally ending in the 1880s when the Russian armies conquered the Turkmens.

In 1886, new laws in Turkestan changed land tenure, increasing the percentage of cultivated lands that were directly heritable and alienable. After the colonial authorities toyed with the idea of introducing Russian-style collective ownership, agricultural land, except *waqf* land (land belonging to Islamic charitable endowments), was registered to the person who farmed it, who gained the right to sell his property. Bukhara retained a system of landownership influenced by Islamic law, with a large variety of landholding and ownership categories, where small farmers were often tenants on large estates. Land law in the various parts of Russian Central Asia diverged, with capitalist concepts of property dominating in southern Russian Turkestan.[10]

Under the Russian colonial administration, Muslim women's legal rights were largely unchanged. Leaving Sharia in place was, to the minds of some Russian administrators like N. S. Lykoshin, exemplary of Russian broad-mindedness and tolerance of other religions, and it followed long-established Russian imperial practices.[11] Muslims went to elected *qazis* to seek justice in matters of family and personal status, while they turned to Russian courts for justice in criminal matters. Islamic law, as practiced in Turkestan and elsewhere, gave men more rights than women in matters of marriage and divorce.[12] Islamic law permitted a wife to initiate divorce in limited cases, such as abandonment. By contrast, husbands had unrestricted rights to unilateral divorce; however, if a man initiated divorce, he might have to pay his wife delayed *mahr* (marriage gift), and he could not demand repayment of *qalin* (bridewealth, or bride-price) money.[13] Many factors restrained wives from seeking divorce, no matter how unpleasant their marriage circumstances. There was strong social and family pressure for women to stay married and disapproval of divorced women. A wife who initiated divorce would not receive delayed mahr, and her family might be forced to repay qalin to her husband. She also knew that unless her family accepted her return, she might be left destitute. Further, men could take up to four wives while women could have only one husband at a time.

But Turkestanis were subject to Russian law in criminal cases. Sharia penalties for adultery (whipping or stoning) could no longer be exercised. The Russian administration allowed the Islamic court to levy fines, but not to sentence the guilty to corporal punishment, prison, or death.[14] In some cases, murders in the name of honor may have taken the place of Sharia retribution for adultery. For example, the Turkestan provincial newspaper reported in 1874 that a Muslim man from Ura Tepe, having found his wife in the arms of her lover, murdered them both and then went to the authorities to confess.[15] However, Validimir Petrovich Nalivkin and M. Nalivkina, Russian ethnographers writing in the 1880s, suggested that extramarital affairs were not uncommon for women or men in the Fargana Valley and that divorce, not murder or legal recourse, was the typical response to a woman's extramarital sexual relations.[16] It remains unclear whether Russia law and reduction of Sharia court competence made a significant difference to women's lives in Russian Central Asia. Major legal change would come in the Soviet period, when Islamic courts were abolished and new civil and criminal codes established.

When Russian armies conquered Central Asia, they announced slavery's end, but the trade stopped only when slave traders were prevented from obtaining captives and providing them to a willing, clandestine market. Persian slaves, captured and traded by Turkmens, were most numerous in Bukhara and Khiva and worked in agriculture, while Dungans, Chinese-speaking Muslims from Kuldja and Kashgar, served in the homes of the rich in the Fargana Valley.[17] Some freed slaves returned to their homelands, but those who were kidnapped as children were likely to remain in Russian Central Asia. The Nalivkins observed that Dungan women slaves in the Fargana Valley, especially those taken as children, had few choices: "women slaves almost all remained in place, because they either were married to workers and servants of their former owners, or they were too young to begin an independent life."[18]

Nowhere in Central Asia was the presence of slaves very large, and so the ending of slavery did not affect society broadly. However, when discourses of women's equality began to emerge in Central Asia circa 1910, writers and activists used slavery as a metaphor for woman's status, pointing to her lack of rights in family and society. While such language was common in worldwide feminist discourse, slogans that told Uzbek women to cast off the chains of slavery were expressed to a society where there were still living ex-slaves.

## ECONOMIC CHANGES

In addition to social and governmental innovations, Russian colonialism brought rapid economic change. While the Central Asian khanates had centuries-old trade relations with Russia, their incorporation into the Russian empire changed the internal economy of Central Asia dramatically. No longer centering on itself, Central Asia became a raw-material-producing periphery to an empire with distant economic centers, as well as a land targeted for colonial immigration. To what extent the Russian empire was similar to or different from other contemporaneous empires is a matter of debate.[19] However, it is undeniable that in Central Asia Russia used military conquest to gain lands that had no historic or cultural association with Russia, ruled those lands using military governors and emergency regulations, applied law differently than elsewhere in the empire, directed the economy toward increased cotton production for the benefit of industrial enterprises located in the Russian heartland, and had no interest in integrating Central Asians or making them citizens equal to other Russian citizens. The Russian government encouraged investments in infrastructure, such as irrigation canals and railroads, that would facilitate production of raw materials and their shipment to Russia, but the government made laws preventing investment in industry. Thus, while Turkestan became host to 204 of Russia's 220 cotton-cleaning mills, the law prohibited building factories that would turn cleaned cotton into cloth. Instead, most of the cleaned cotton was shipped to the fabric manufacturers of central Russia.[20]

While Russia seized herding lands in Turkestan from nomads and turned them over to Russian peasant colonists to develop agriculture (a policy that severely harmed Kazakhs in northern Turkestan), the imperial policy on agricultural lands in Turkestan was not to expropriate, but rather to expand, especially to increase cotton growing. The amount of land planted with cotton increased exponentially between 1865 and 1913.[21] Cotton was planted both on lands previously irrigated and sown with other crops and on lands opened to agricultural production by new irrigation projects. Central Asia *dehqons* (farmers), funded with credit from Russian banks, devoted more of their labor and land to cash crops.[22] Agricultural stations experimented with varieties of cotton seed, and eventually American upland cotton replaced native seed varieties. Russian and Central Asian investors established cotton-ginning factories that drew rural Central Asians to the cities and into the Russian economic system as hired laborers.[23]

Growth in the textile sector, in both cotton and silk, meant that the time women spent working in the cash economy increased significantly. In general, women carried out the most labor-intensive and least financially rewarding aspects of cotton production, and the same was true of silk. Women's participation in field labor varied by region and crop. In 1872, before cotton's economic dominance, the Russian ethnographer A. D. Grebenkin observed that in Uzbek villages in the Zarafshan valley, women did almost all of the fieldwork. The Nalivkins reported that in the Fargana Valley's agricultural communities women worked in the fields only for the cotton and melon harvests.[24] Cotton-ginning mills hired Russian and Central Asian men, and occasionally women, as laborers. Central Asian families retained a portion of the cleaned cotton fiber for personal or small-scale production of cloth, woven on nonmechanized looms. Women spun raw cotton into thread. Both men and women wove cotton; women produced the cheapest grade of cloth.

Rural and village women raised silkworms and reeled thread from cocoons. Raising silkworms was a temporary occupation, taking several months of springtime labor. It thus was not recorded in statistics on primary occupation, although production of silkworms provided a significant portion of the cash income of many dehqon families. Men dominated silk dying and weaving. Both men and women sewed clothing, and women specialized in embroidery.

Very few Central Asian women were employed either in factories or workshops, but the 1897 census found that in Fargana province, more than 10 percent of native women had spinning, weaving, or sewing as their main occupation.[25] Men carried out most of the market transactions related to textiles; only a few women would appear in the bazaar to sell their own hand-spun thread, although some women sold their products directly to other households.[26]

As gross production of cotton and silk increased, the amount of women's labor devoted to these activities increased. Understandings of gender roles did not change; both men and women continued to think of women as homemakers, not earners of income.

CULTURAL CHANGES IN THE WORLD OF MEN

Economic change alone does not determine what kinds of cultural change may emerge in colonial situations. Male Central Asians, using vastly improved transportation and communications, strengthened their connections with other Muslims and became familiar with ideas of reform that were spreading in the Middle East and the Asian subcontinent. They also encountered Russians and Russian institutions. Like people under colonial rule elsewhere, Central Asians responded to colonial rule with a mixture of adaptation, resistance, and reform. The reform movement best known to scholars of early twentieth century Central Asia, the Jadid movement, grew through interaction with Ottoman and Tatar reform movements and through involvement in some Russian colonial institutions, especially schools.[27] Individuals who identified with the Jadid movement in Central Asia were largely from urban settings, and came from families of merchants or the *ulama* (the Muslim religious scholars).

For urban men, interaction with Russians might take place in everyday life. Some urban Uzbek families chose to send at least one son to the primary level Russian-native schools, and to Russian gymnasia for high-school education.[28] Some urban Central Asian men worked in factories and on railroads with Russian laborers, and a few joined unions. Wealthier Uzbeks could gain social distinction from the Russian colonial order, occasionally being granted Russian citizenship and participating in public activities with Russians. Philanthropic organizations drew members from both colonizer and colonized; in 1895, for example, Samarkand's division of the Turkestan Philanthropic Society listed a number of Central Asian men within a predominantly Russian membership, as did the Red Cross.[29]

However, while there was interaction, there was also discrimination and distance. Central Asian men responded to the disparaging attitudes of Russian colonizers in varied ways. Some strove to become more like Russians, by studying the Russian language, adopting Russian dress, and finding ways to work for the administration. Many utterly rejected all things Russian, struggled to keep their lives separate from Russians and their ways, and criticized Central Asians who seemed too eager to please their colonial rulers; and a few rose up violently against Russian rule. The Jadids struggled between these poles. Like reformers in other colonial situations in the Islamic world, they called for learning from their rulers, acquiring their knowledge, but also defining their own identities in contrast to Russian and European models. In Bukhara, the complexities of Jadidism were even greater than in Russian Turkestan, since members of the movement saw the downfall of their society, and hence its need for change, in the emir's misrule as well as in Russian colonial domination of the protectorate. Muattar's father, an Islamic judge and scholar, raised two sons who joined the Jadid movement. They apparently drew on reformist ideas to criticize the emir (not Russian colonialism), and were exiled to Siberia (due to colonialism).

What was true of urban Central Asian men, who might encounter Russians and the direct influences of colonialism in a variety of settings, was not at all the case for Central Asian women, who lived in intentional and de facto separation from the Russian-dominated public realm. Although her brothers were Jadids and her father was their supporter, Muattar's life did not differ from that of most women in Bukhara or Turkestan. Jadids first raised their voices to call for the reform of education and politics, and rather later began to see the reform of women as important to their larger goals.

## SEPARATE SPACES, SEPARATE CULTURES

In colonial Turkestan, most urban Turkestani women, and some rural sedentary women, veiled by covering themselves from head to toe in a robe, the "collar" of which rested on the top of the head and the sleeves of which dangled uselessly and decoratively down the back. This robe, ordinarily made of blue and grey striped cotton, is known in Uzbek as the paranji. It had an accompanying face veil of woven horsehair, known as the chachvon.[30] By the early twentieth century, the paranji was the dominant mode of veiling among urban and agriculturalist Tajiks and Uzbeks and remained so until the late 1920s campaign against veiling.[31] The paranji, which women only wore when they left their houses, separated its wearers from all others on the streets, made them anonymous, and kept them hidden from male and foreign eyes when they left seclusion.

Courtyard walls, more than veils, embodied the barrier between Turkestani and colonizer. Turkestanis reproduced family culture within spaces that were not open to outsiders. The spatial and social organization of urban and village women's lives included scarcely any events or settings in which they would interact with non-Turkestanis. The physical layout of cities in Turkestan, Bukhara, and Khiva tended toward segregation. Newcomers from Russia settled in "new cities" which were either joined to older urban areas, as in Tashkent, or were entirely separate from their older counterparts, as with Bukhara and Kagan.[32] In new cities, streets were laid out and buildings designed in colonial style, while in old cities Turkestanis resided in homes surrounded by courtyard walls along narrow, unpaved streets.

In the early twentieth century, many Central Asians lived in spaces separated by gender. According to customs expressed in and explained by Islamic law, adult males and adult females who were not of the same family were not to interact, an arrangement designed to prevent unapproved sexual relations and protect family honor—that is, women's sexual purity. City and town dwellers who could afford to do so built homes where the domestic buildings, with rooms for sleeping, cooking, and work, surrounded two courtyards: the *tashkari*, or outer court, and the *ichkari*, or inner court.[33] Women lived and did much of their work, such as raising children, cooking, sewing, embroidering, spinning, raising fowl, and feeding silkworms, in the ichkari, where the courtyard was open to the sky and might include a garden and fruit trees. Women and children slept and ate in the ichkari, and women entertained female guests there. The tashkari included the primary, gated entrance to the household complex, a reception room for male guests, and perhaps a workshop or a stable. When there were no guests, men slept and ate with their families in the ichkari. The degree of gender separation varied with wealth, religiosity, region, and available space. In poor urban households, and in many rural homes, there was only one room and one courtyard, and thus no opportunity for a gendered separation of space. While adult men and women observed these gendered boundaries, children and servants were less restricted.[34]

Boys and girls, and children of different ethnic groups, could play on the streets together until they reached ten to twelve years of age. Around this time a girl was given her first paranji, symbolizing and enforcing her entrance into the gender-segregated adult world.[35] After this she went out only with permission, wearing her veil and accompanied by a family member. She spent time with women, learning to cook, sew, spin, and embroider. She entered the religious and ritual life of women, which might include saying the five daily prayers at home and participating in gatherings where an *otin*, a female religious teacher, recited the Quran and called on female saints. She attended parties for female friends who were getting married and joined in other women's life-cycle gatherings. Eventually a marriage was arranged for her.[36]

There was hardly any intersection between an urban or village Muslim woman's life and the public sphere, unless poverty drove her to work outside the home. Even the need to earn money did not necessarily mean that she would leave her courtyard; most women who earned a living through textile manufacture spun cotton or wove cloth at home, as participants in cottage industry. In rare instances, women found work in factories. It was easier for a woman to find work as a domestic servant, but this put her in the morally compromising situation of interacting with nonfamily men.[37] Working in cottage industry provided women with some income, but did not expose them to a wider world. Rural women lived with fewer spatial restrictions, but they also rarely participated in activities outside the family. Muattar's husband traveled to France by train to sell goods and see the world, but as was the case for almost every Uzbek woman in prerevolution Turkestan and Bukhara, Muattar's family courtyard and neighborhood described the boundaries of her life.

In Bukhara, Khiva, and Turkestan, Jadids began to turn attention to women in 1910, calling for reform in family life and in the raising of daughters. Although Muattar's life exemplified continuities, women in other Jadid families saw significant changes that are outlined in the following chapters.

## 2

# JADIDS AND THE
# REFORM OF WOMEN

$\mathbf{I}$N THE EARLY TWENTIETH CEN-
tury, a few Jadid reformers in Central Asia opened modern school programs for girls, and many discussed the necessity of "reforming" women
to become better partners for men in the project of remaking their society. Their discussions of women's reform drew on ideas that circulated
in the larger Islamic world, and especially among Tatars in Russia. I argue
that the concepts they focused on became the base for Uzbek ideas about
"women's liberation" in the early years of the Soviet experiment. By this
I mean that although the Communist Party Women's Division would
do its best to spread the Party's views on male-female equality and
women's roles in the socialist state, the ideas for changing women's roles
that most profoundly shaped Uzbek activists, whether male or female,
expressed continuity with Jadid thought far more than a deep reflection
of Bolshevik agendas.

Before the revolution brought Communist Party ideas about transforming women, there was already a lively discussion about educating
and reforming Muslim women in Central Asia. No one who wrote about
Uzbek women before the revolution was satisfied with them as they were.
Central Asian Jadid men wrote that women's lack of education kept the
nation from improving itself. Russians saw Uzbek women's ignorance
as emblematic of Central Asian backwardness. Central Asian religious

scholars saw women as devoted to superstition rather than to right practices. To Tatars, Uzbek women seemed deprived of normal life.

Bolsheviks began promoting unveiling in 1927, thinking of it as a method for shaking up Uzbek society and winning Uzbek women to the Soviet government's side.[1] They were latecomers; Jadids began discussing unveiling around 1910 (see chapter 6). But in Jadid thought, the most important way that women could be changed, and thus bring change to all of Turkestani society, was through modern education. As a few Central Asian women became associated with the Jadid movement, they too championed teaching girls to read and write in their native language, believing that educated mothers could contribute to a Turkestani cultural revival.

Many of the Communist Party's Uzbek members had been associated with the Jadid movement. Adeeb Khalid notes that Jadid failures to influence Central Asian society "brought home to them the importance of the state as an agent of change."[2] Before the revolution, they wanted to bring about change in marriage and family life, in the training of girls, and in the roles women would play in society, all in the name of becoming *jadid*, meaning new, or modern. After the revolution, they joined the Party with the understanding that it would empower them to carry out reform, and they brought into the Party their own ideas about the significance of transforming women. Muslims of Russia who discussed ideas of freedom, rights, progress, and reform in the colonial period have often been referred to as Westernizers or Russifiers, with the implication that their impetus toward change came from their contact with Europe and Russia. However, Khalid argues convincingly that, while the Jadid reformers of Turkestan promoted the study of Russian, most of them owed their intellectual formation to their travels in the Islamic world and to reading Arabic, Persian, and Turkish books, including translations of European works. Their reformist ideas were connected to emerging discourses in the larger Islamic world.[3]

The people of Turkestan responded to Russian colonial rule not as a single body united by common identity and goals, but rather—as in much of the rest of the colonized world—with widely opposing analyses of the problem and the solution. There are broad parallels in the structure of responses to colonialism throughout the world in the late nineteenth and early twentieth centuries; as Partha Chatterjee suggests, discourses of reform and of preservation, of modernization and of authenticity, all turned attention to women.[4]

Ideas for reforming women were directly linked to discourses about restoring the *millat* (nation), a concept itself undergoing change in early twentieth-century Turkestan. In the nineteenth century, the meaning of millat had expanded from a legal denotation for a minority religious community to encompass ideas of ethnic group, majority religious group, and nation. In Russia, when Muslims wrote about "our millat," they referred to a religiously defined community and increasingly an ethnolinguistically defined community, a nation that was not a state and that was considered in conscious reference to other millats—especially Russians, who were the power holders in the state. When Muslims in the Russian empire wrote of "the progress of our millat" they were concerned with the progress of Muslims in Russia and sometimes with particular groups of Muslims. In Central Asia, Jadids often defined their millat as "Turkestani," an identity that could include all Turkic and Tajik speakers of Central Asia.[5]

Turkestani Muslims did not agree among themselves about how they could restore their nation, or about reforming women. Their divisions were similar to those found in late nineteenth and early twentieth century Egypt, where Beth Baron demonstrates that Muslim women who contributed to discussions of reform wrote "as Modernists or Islamists": "Both groups argued within the context of Islam, with the intention of revitalizing and strengthening religion, and both condemned certain Western influences and excesses . . . Modernists sought expansion in the realm of education and reform in marriage and divorce laws. Islamists, on the other hand, sought enforcement of Islamic laws, including women's right to education, but encouraged women to learn the law to know their rights, not to modify them."[6]

The belief that their millat had been left behind and was in danger of disappearing, while others in Russia were clearly making progress, motivated Jadids in Central Asia to call for women's reform. The millat had been left behind through ignorance; education would bring progress. Most Central Asian Jadids wrote in Islamic idiom, and argued for some sort of renewal of Islam, through purer practice, stripped of "superstition," and more compatible with their progressive values. Their assertions provoked many in the religious establishment to a spirited defense of Islamic learning and practice, a defense that saw piety, not progress, as the goal of Islamic society. Both Jadids and conservatives in Central Asia articulated positions that continued to shape the postrevolution debate over Uzbek women.

Tatar writings about women in general and Turkestani women in particular are featured in this chapter, because Tatars mediated knowledge between Central Asia and Russia. Tatars were interpreters for the Russian administration of Turkestan, for emissaries and travelers. Because scholars writing about Central Asia in the nineteenth and twentieth centuries usually use Russian- and European-language sources, Tatars and their crucial role in creating images of Central Asia remain unnoticed. Tatars were not neutral channels of information; they were trying to establish themselves as enlighteners for Turkestanis. Tatar men and women interacted directly with Uzbek and other Central Asian women, studying them and making them targets for their educational mission. Tatars and Turkestanis shared a written language and read each other's ideas about reform. Until the 1920s, Russians, including the Bolsheviks who planned strategies for Central Asia, learned about Turkestan's women largely from Tatars; and some urban Turkestani women learned about progress and rights from Tatars as well as from Central Asian Jadids.

Tatar women activists opened schools for girls in Turkestan, and they reported on their project in the pages of *Suyum Bike*, a Tatar women's journal published in Kazan. When Tatar women compared themselves to Turkestani women, they regarded themselves as cultured and educated, and believed uncultured, uneducated Turkestani women needed their words of enlightenment. Just as the Russian intelligentsia made Russian peasants their counterpart in a discourse of cultured Self and backward Other, and went to the countryside to bring enlightenment, Tatar women and men went to the women of Turkestan and Bukhara.

In addition to opening girls' schools, Tatar reformers in Samarkand established women's societies, hoping to attract local Muslim women. The Muslim Women's Association, with its emphasis on lectures and educational meetings for women, provided the first model for the women's associations that would emerge among Turkestan's Muslims after the revolution, and the organization would become part of the local base for the Communist Party Women's Division work in Turkestan.

This chapter examines the competing ideas that Muslims, both Tatars and Turkestanis, conservatives and Jadids, advocated in calling for "the reform of women." Central Asian reformers promoted change in girls' education and in marriage, and although their programs only affected a few urban groups, their ideas would continue to influence policies toward women after the revolution. The following discussion draws on didactic booklets composed by Tatars and Turkestanis and articles from Turkic-language newspaper and journals, including women's journals. The ideas that Turkestani men and Tatar men and women advocated concerning women's education, marriage age, companionate marriage, and women's public roles would shape Uzbek women activists' own programs in the 1920s.

## ONE WOMAN'S CALL FOR REFORM

In 1906, a Central Asian woman from Kokand, Tajie, wrote to the first Turkic-language women's journal in the Russian empire.[7] In her letter she complained about the state of women in Turkestan, using arguments typical of the Jadid press.

TO THE LETTERS DEPARTMENT:

Honored Shafiqa Hanum, we humbly write the following lines . . .

It must be evident to everyone that today in Russia great effort and energy is expended by every people and sect, in learning freedom, rights, progress and reform. It is seen that Muslim women have their own special weekly publication and that they are also capable of writing many letters and contributing articles to many Muslim newspapers, with proposals and recommendations, questions and answers. We have no word for them except: excellent, well done. However, while we thank Muslim women in the center of Russia for their action, we Sartiya[8] women regret that we are not fulfilling our responsibilities to that level.

While others are showing great efforts, we Sartiya Muslim women are regrettably in the condition of a very comfortable sleep, a sleep without any awareness. If only a few lines on the editorial pages of one of the newspapers would say a few words about the ignorance and lack of rights of Sartiya women in comparison with Crimea and Kazan ladies.[9] If our degenerating condition is written of and demonstrated, then in our future we can be made glad by reforms as others are, and we can become a bit more hopeful about coming into possession of our rights.

But will it be? Woe of woes! We are all in need of study and teaching.

We have heard that education is very valuable in your work. Among us there is no valuable effort or action. Our present lack of effort shows that this will also be impossible in the future. We should note that in our days scarcely one of a hundred Sartiya Muslim women knows how to read and write; and the other ninety-nine know no other skill than how to look at strangers while walking under a paranji.

It is possible to say that in this world, there are no Muslim women so deprived of rights as we are. Our men treat us with such oppression that my tongue is impotent to describe and my pen to write. We have no free choice in anything. Many of us live without seeing our spouse for months, even half a year or a year, and some of us, whose husbands oppress us by not providing enough for food and drink, cannot survive unless we turn to prostitution, ruining this life and the next. We, evidently being so despicable, base, deprived of rights, and ignorant, are causing our children to continue after us equally uneducated and deprived of everything. It seems that we want to make our boys and girls, the light of our eyes, our hearts and souls, as weak as ourselves. We are not helping the Noghai women teachers,[10] who, knowing our condition, are sacrificing soul and wealth to open girls' schools for us, [expending] great trouble and labor to open our eyes. On the contrary, it must be acknowledged that our steps have not striven to increase our desire for learning, but have made a mess; the extent of our stupor and our inclination must be acknowledged. While Muslims of the Glorious Quran made great efforts on the path of progress and reform, if we go on sleeping in such a stupor, wasting our lives on useless things like tobacco and water-pipe, let us be aware that someday our names alone among all the Muslim women of the world will deserve to be remembered with hatred in the pages of history. Let us take [their] example, and struggle to reform our condition. Let us send our sons and daughters to the Noghai maktabs to learn.

XO'QANDLI ASHRAF UL-BANAT TAJIE[11]

The letter from Tajie to the editor of *Alem-i Nisvan* is an extremely rare example of a Turkestani woman's published writing from before the revolution. The letter is typical in expressing Jadid concerns about Turkestani society, but is unique in presenting those concerns as women's issues. Tajie described Sart (that is, sedentary Turkestani or

Uzbek) women as lacking in rights and modern education as the only solution to their pitiable situation. Her letter reflects a Jadid emphasis, calling for transforming Islamic education into modes that could compete with modern European education, in order to "awaken" the nation. In the late nineteenth and early twentieth centuries, from Egypt to Iran and India, Muslim women made claims to education by arguing that religion encouraged seeking knowledge and that female education would improve the nation as a whole.[12]

Tajie's new ideas had their source in the networks of the Islamic world and the Turkic press. She referred to the deeds of Muslim women in Russia, but not to Russian women. Russians may have lived next door to her, but she did not acknowledge their existence in her letter, much less look to them for an example of enlightenment. While the Russian administration promoted a "civilizing mission," this was largely directed at Turkestani men who might become local administrative officials.[13] Turkestani girls and women lived in separation from Russian culture, even when Russians moved into their cities. Tajie instead located herself in the milieu of Muslim women; she believed that solutions could emerge from the larger Islamic community, in accordance with the Quran.

In her letter, Tajie revealed her awareness of the possibility of change that was linked to print, education, and ideas of reform and progress. She was cognizant of social problems such as prostitution and of government statistics on women's literacy rates. Women's literacy rates in 1897 averaged less than 1 percent in Turkestan's southern provinces. But with rising prosperity, young girls increasingly attended schools; urban Muslim girls, between the ages of nine and nineteen, had the highest literacy rates among females, reaching 10 percent.[14] Tajie regarded modern schooling as the solution to a host of social problems, from laziness to prostitution, destitution, and the weakness of children and society.

Tajie lived in Kokand, a city that saw a flood of immigrants, including Tatar Muslims, after being linked to the Russian empire's railway system.[15] Kokand's merchants, Russians and Tatars as well as Central Asians, invested in cotton export and grain import, and the city took the lead in banking for Turkestan. By 1900, there were four printing presses in Kokand and numerous bookstores, and a number of new-method (Jadid) schools added to the very large network of *maktabs* and *madrasas*. However, while Kokand's economy flourished, many dehqons lost their land and became seasonal workers; and many families became destitute.[16] Many of Kokand's merchants would travel for months or years for trade, sometimes without making adequate provision for their wives and children.[17]

Tajie claimed that destitute wives who lacked alternatives entered prostitution. The extent of prostitution in Turkestan is difficult to ascertain.[18] Regulation of prostitution followed the Russian army into Central Asia, where some prostitutes were registered and brothels were licensed.[19] The legalized presence of such "houses of tolerance" upset Turkestan's religious leaders and social reformers. Central Asians listed prostitution, along with drinking alcohol, as one of the vices that Russians brought with their conquest. The Russian ethnographers, the Nalivkins, pointed out that Russian law made prostitution obvious to all, noting that many brothels took in runaway women and held them in a sort of debt-slavery, but that some prostitution took the guise of polygyny.[20] The Nalivkins believed women chose prostitution and even gained liberation when their profession was legalized. They linked this to a broader characterization of Central Asian women's active pursuit of sexual adventure, one that emerges periodically in their monograph and that is common to many colonial narratives. By contrast, Tajie, echoing the concerns of Jadid reformers, saw prostitutes as victims, desperate women who had no other means of survival.[21]

Tajie's impressions of prostitution may have arisen from personal knowledge, but other sources are also possible. She may have read articles from the government-sponsored Turkestani-language newspaper, *Turkiston Viloyatining Gazetasi*, in which Jadids, Islamic clergy, and Russian administrators condemned prostitution.[22] Her views may reflect discussions in women's social gatherings, such as the one begun in nineteenth-century Kokand by a group of women poets who recited their new works at such meetings.[23] Tajie's views may also reflect knowledge common among educated families in Kokand. Turkestani women in Kokand did not participate in the male public sphere, but some held gatherings that resembled men's social gatherings known as *gap*, a regular meeting of friends for conversation, feasting, religious instruction, and discussion. Jadids used the gap as a venue for spreading their reformist ideas.[24]

While Tajie's voice is almost unique, she echoed what other Muslim progressives were saying. However, unlike the male Jadid voices calling for the reform of women, Tajie's language was devoid of misogyny.

Her letter reflected a belief that, if given education, women were capable of escaping from and remedying social ills. Two decades later, when Uzbek women were working within the Communist Party Women's Division for the liberation of women, they would articulate exactly the same argument.

## EDUCATING WOMEN

Tajie's language, her assessment of Sart women's condition, and her solution to problems all reflect Jadid discourse. Central Asian Jadids condemned Muslims whose "sleep of ignorance" led to moral corruption, and they presented their own project in terms of awakening, enlightenment, and progress.[25] In Turkestan, Central Asian and Tatar Jadids began with reforming education for Muslim children, opening new schools featuring literacy training and "modern" subjects like history, geography, and science, in addition to Islamic religious education; and they established presses to publicize their ideas.[26]

Abdurauf Fitrat, one of Central Asia's best-known Jadids, published his thoughts on women's roles in an instruction booklet entitled "The Family." Fitrat, like many Muslim reformers of his time, argued that religion demanded that both men and women be educated: "If you refer to the Noble Quran, you see that aside from two or three commands, in all matters the declarations to men and women are the same . . . In light of the fact that every single person carries out religious and worldly duties, women also are required to learn knowledge."[27]

Aware that most of his readers would not agree that girls needed education, Fitrat appealed not only to religion, but also to men's self interest. Men, he wrote, go out of the home to earn a living, and often come home with worries; what they want is an orderly home life. "Women who are knowledgeable and educated fulfill these tasks excellently, and make their husbands content. But husbands who married uneducated and ignorant wives are deprived of this blessing from God."[28] He described the quarrelling of women in the ichkari and their selfish demands on husbands for material goods.

Beyond trying to convince men that educated women made better wives, Fitrat also responded to objections that conservative religious scholars raised against the education of women. One such objection was that a girl who could write might use that skill to communicate with men outside her family and even to arrange forbidden meetings with strangers. Fitrat acknowledged that this was possible, but argued that men, even religious scholars themselves, often misused knowledge, and yet no one suggested that they should therefore be forbidden education.

Fitrat connected his call for girls' education to the destiny of the nation of Turkestan: "It is obvious to all that the condition of our country is ruined, and our future is in danger. Every person must understand that the path we have taken is leading to our destruction. Today or tomorrow we will die out."[29] The degeneration of the nation could only be halted through educational development, and that, Fitrat asserted, required modern education for females: "The remedy is that our children must be brought up to have good character . . . in accord with progress for Islam, so that they can free the religion and their co-religionists from the ravine of tragedy and ruin. In order to achieve this goal, our wives and daughters—the mothers of the millat—must attain education and science, their morals and knowledge must be brought to perfection."[30] Thus, the educated woman would not only be a good spouse, but would bring up the healthy, moral children necessary to the nation's future.

Fitrat's contemporary, Mahmud Xo'ja Behbudi, the publisher of the Samarkand Jadid journal *Oina*, used a different argument for girls' education. He wrote that women's brains were smaller than men's brains, and thus "woman is lower than man in strength, intelligence and feelings. Because of this, Shariat rightly places women lower than men." However, he noted that there were also experiments showing that men's brain function weakened if they did little work, and that if woman is educated, and works, "her blood and brain will also reach perfection."[31] Behbudi's conclusion on the perfectibility of inherently flawed woman was similar to the feminist but misogynist ideas of Egyptian author Qasim Amin, who, while arguing for women's rights, believed that women were morally deficient, but that with education they would become responsible beings.[32] A Tatar woman teacher, Sara Muzafiriya, tried to refute this sort of argument, one that could easily be used to make a case against women's education. She attested that school examinations showed that female brains were not deficient. Education would make women better mothers, she wrote, but the fundamental reason that women should be educated was that education was women's Islamic right and duty.[33]

Modernists like Fitrat drew on earlier Tatar works advocating that girls become educated for the sake of the millat's progress, for improved family life, and for religious renewal. Several Tatar women religious scholars had written tracts to promote educating girls both in reading and writing; Hanifa Khanim argued that girls who knew writing could do useful work, teach children, and write to religious scholars with questions.[34] Similar tracts by Tatar men, such as the Islamic judge Rizauddin Fakhriddin, supported the idea that the well-trained and proper Muslim girl should learn to write.[35] Some years later, Fitrat continued to press this argument for an unconvinced Turkestani audience.

But among the Muslims of the Russian empire, strong voices argued against modern education for girls and against teaching them to write. In the conservative Kazan religious and literary journal *Din va Ma'ishat*, one author argued that the so-called sacrifices that Jadids called for in the name of progress were instead sacrificing the nation to "the knife of the infidel." With their encouragement of girls' writing and mixing of the sexes at dances, Jadids were corrupting Muslim youth.[36]

Likewise, a contributor to the Tashkent newspaper *Turkiston Viloyatining Gazetasi* blamed Jadids for corrupting young girls:

Some call it the evil method [using *usul-i yazid*, in place of *usul-i jadid*, or new method]. You are the reason that some of our unfortunate Muslims have become irreligious. You are the cause for women and girls throwing off the chadra and chachvon that are required by Shariat, and becoming completely uncovered . . . and they stop doing prayers. You say that your wives and daughters have studied with the *usul-i yazid* or the new rule, and learned literacy quickly, and have become informed of God's purposes. Your words are true, but you are the cause of the removal of modesty and honor from an eleven or twelve year old girl, causing pain to a bridegroom's heart. You are the reason that her mother and father have difficulty giving her in marriage, and of her condition on her wedding night.[37]

The suggestion that Jadids were either sexual predators or were encouraging girls' sexual knowledge and experience was inflammatory, and implies the degree of hostility between the opposing sides in the debate over girls' education.

The most conservative writers argued that society was crumbling and that only their own approach, encouraging piety, would preserve the Muslim family. Reformers based their position on the same understanding of society, but asserted that only a reform of women and the family would allow Muslim society to overcome the forces of degeneration. "Great harm, rather than benefit, is caused by women who do not know how to educate children and who cannot teach good virtues."[38]

Both reformers and conservatives expressed anxiety about woman's moral nature and her influence on children. Conservatives responded by calling for male guardianship for all women, making men responsible for securing women's morality through seclusion and limiting contact with outsiders and new ideas. Most Jadids argued instead for turning women into agents of morality, through extensive education. The argument that educated mothers would bring up well-trained children combined religious and modernist emphases: women's moral agency as Muslims bound them to instruct children in moral terms; and knowledge of science and health would enable mothers to care for children physically. However, the close link between education for girls and women's roles as mothers set inherent limits on the types and degree of education to which women could assert rights, and this led to ideas of reforming social roles based on male-female difference rather than equality.[39]

## MARRIAGE, ARRANGED MARRIAGE, AND POLYGYNY

Central Asian Jadids assumed that every girl's destiny was marriage: Islamic ethics held marriage as a moral responsibility for everyone, male or female. Behbudi remarked, "Shariat says marriage is necessary." Fitrat echoed this: "one should know that marrying is necessary for every man who has strength."[40] The purpose of marriage, Fitrat affirmed, was to produce children. The practice of arranged marriage secured this outcome for nearly all women in Turkestan. The 1897 census shows that the majority of girls were first married between the ages of fifteen and nineteen, and that 99 percent of all adult Turkestani women were married at least once. By contrast, while men also attained a 98 percent rate of marriage, the majority were married for the first time when they were between thirty and thirty-nine.[41] In other words, arranged marriage meant early marriage for females and late marriage for males.

Turkestani Jadids did not quarrel with the inevitability of marriage; there were no roles for "old maids" in Central Asian society. Rather, they were concerned that not all men had marriage opportunities. Behbudi and Fitrat both drew on European scientific articles about sexuality to claim that marriage was not only a religious duty, but also physiologically necessary for men: they claimed that refraining from sex after puberty was unhealthy for men and led to moral and social degeneracy.[42] Some writers blamed polygyny for denying some men the chance to marry; others attacked social conventions that were driving up the cost of marriage, especially wedding feasts and dowry. Fitrat, pointing to these costs, commented, "So some of our millat do not take a wife ever, and for this reason our millat's progeny decreases daily."[43]

In novels and plays, some Jadids depicted arranged marriage as a social ill, but in didactic writings, Jadids upheld arranged marriage for girls, focusing their arguments instead on the proper age of marriage and the importance of suitability, compatibility, and the bride's consent.[44] Fitrat saw marriage's first failings arising from lies about the bride or groom's qualities and parents choosing their children's partners based on money and status rather than character. He recommended deeper inquiries into potential matches, but did not think that the potential bride and groom should meet.[45] The avowedly feminist editors of the Tatar women's journal *Suyum Bike* published a proposal from a group of St. Petersburg Tatar women to remove absolute authority over marriage choice from parents by making sure that the bride and groom voiced their own consent to their marriage, rather than allowing representatives to speak for them.[46]

A Tatar author, Fakhr ul-Banat Sibghatulla qizi, described an ideal of companionate marriage, produced by arrangement: "A man and woman are united and live as one body and one soul in the manner demanded by Shariat, so that whatever suffering or hardship comes to one is also laid on the other. That is to say, a husband and wife are each other's life's companion, partners who are never separated." She wrote that this outcome was possible when parents made unselfish arrangements: "It is not a good thing to sell a girl like a sheep or buy her like cattle." Even though she spoke of partnership, Fakhr ul-Banat believed in husbands' authority to restrict their wives: "A husband's rights are great indeed." However, she tempered this inequality with advice that both parties should treat each other with respect and love.[47]

Fitrat tried to bring some aspects of modern, companionate marriage into his image of the ideal, which was still based on Sharia and male guardianship. He wrote that knowledge of the Quran and the world was the most important quality in a wife. She could thus be a partner who could converse with her husband.[48] But even the idea of partnership had its critics among Jadid writers. Fakhriddin wrote, "things like friend-ship and closeness, however firm, are not sufficient in founding a fam-ily . . . a wife is not a partner, but is one's family."[49]

Jadid authors most frequently argued for reforming marriage expenses, rather than marriage itself. However, the writers' concern was not that such expenses for feasting degraded women or harmed the mar-riage relationship, but that extravagant feasts wasted money that might better be spent for education. They protested that men were being forced into massive debt, or priced out of the marriage market. Turkestan's entrance into the cash economy of Russia and the proliferation of cotton- and trade-based fortunes turned some of the customary "gift" exchanges into ostentatious displays of wealth. Fitrat complained that while some men could never marry, the rich could "take new wives every day and divorce the old ones."[50]

The customary gift exchange at marriage included mahr or qalin. Mahr, according to the Quran, is a marriage gift that the groom must make to the bride. Islamic law defined mahr as an initial portion (two-thirds) given at the time of the marriage, and a "delayed" portion (one-third) that the husband gave his wife if he divorced her. Mahr was an urban practice in Central Asia, and it followed the norms of Islamic law. Mahr agreements were written down and became legally binding.[51] Fitrat argued that mahr ought to be a small gift and should signify the groom's and bride's decision to enter marriage. He regarded the large gifts of money given in Bukhara in mahr as one of the reasons that many men were unable to marry.[52]

But it was qalin, usually interpreted as "bride-price," that attracted the most criticism. Qalin was not regulated by Islamic law; it was one of the gift transactions of marriage that came from Turkic custom, and the groom presented it to the bride's father, who was not required to give it to his daughter. There were many other marriage gifts as well: the bride's family gave the groom and his male kin clothing (*sarpo*); the bride's parents gave their daughter a dowry of clothing, jewelry, and house furnishings; the groom gave a gift of money to the bride's mother (*sut puli*); and the groom's family brought large amounts of food for the feast at the bride's home (*yuk berdi*). Each gift had monetary value and all transactions were subject to detailed negotiation. When marriages were arranged between families of similar wealth and status, the value of what each family provided might be equal, but when a wealthy older man offered to make the daughter of a poor man his third wife, qalin might be the only gift and would be large enough to provide incentive for the arrangement. Thus, qalin was criticized; parents who accepted qalin were accused of selling their daughter.[53] Although Russian texts frequently mentioned qalin (using the Russian *kalym*), Jadids, in their booklets on marriage and the family, did not; but Jadids did condemn expensive wedding feasts and "selling a bride."

Because marriage was expensive, and men delayed it to accumulate the necessary wealth, husbands and wives often differed considerably in age.[54] Jadid authors argued that major age differences between marriage partners were a problem; however, they disagreed on the proper age of marriage. The conservative Noghai Mullah seemed to say that girls typically married at age twelve. Tatar Jadids proposed much older ideal ages for first marriage, between eighteen and thirty for women and twenty to forty for men. Fakhriddin asserted that marrying young girls to elderly men resulted in unhealthy children, while Fakhr ul-Banat argued that young women should not marry old men because the women would be unhappy.[55]

The Turkestani Jadid Behbudi discussed marriage age as a question of healthy sexuality. He assured readers that it would be harmful to an adolescent boy to begin sexual activity before "his sexual organ is mature," but that after maturity it was harmful to refrain from sex. Not surprisingly, he did not address the sexual needs of adolescent girls. He discouraged marriage for the very young, because "their children will be deficient . . . and they will become corrupt and a burden to society."[56] He cited European research to suggest that delayed marriage for men contributed to social decay, remarking that most crimes and murders were committed by unmarried men. Likewise, he wrote, unmarried women tended toward criminality and the insane were mainly unmarried and divorced.[57]

Some reformers drew a connection between the expense of marriage, the exclusion of young men from marriage opportunities, and polygyny. That is, polygyny was questioned on androcentric grounds as depriving other men of marriage opportunities. Polygyny was also challenged as an unhappy condition for women, but reformist didactic literature often upheld polygyny. The Egyptian Mufti Muhammad Abduh's teaching, that Quran 4:3 limits, but does not entirely forbid polygyny was spreading among reformists. The verse reads, "If you fear you cannot be equitable to orphan girls (in your charge, or misuse their persons), then marry women who are lawful to you, two, three, or four; but if you fear you cannot treat so many with equity, marry only one, or a maid or a captive. That is better than being iniquitous."[58] Abduh and his followers emphasized the second half of this verse, arguing that one husband could not treat multiple wives with justice and fairness, and thus they interpreted this verse as strongly discouraging polygyny.[59]

Fakhr ul-Banat wrote that a husband could not possibly treat multiple wives equally.[60] But few male reformists concurred. Many Jadids of the Russian empire agreed with Abduh that men should take additional wives only under certain conditions. Fakhriddin interpreted Sharia as permitting multiple wives under conditions such as barrenness or chronic illness of a wife. He regarded divorce as the greater social ill; polygyny was preferable to divorcing barren wives or denying men the right to have offspring.[61]

Fitrat acknowledged that all Turkestanis could see evidence that polygonous marriages were oppressive for women, but he nonetheless argued that Sharia correctly permitted polygony. Marriage was for producing children, so if a husband's first wife could not bear children, he needed to marry another. In addition, Fitrat asserted that because a man's sexual needs had to be satisfied, and could not be when his wife was pregnant or had recently given birth, he should take another wife. He disagreed that Islam insisted on equal love for both wives; the Quran demanded equal provision. But it was natural, he asserted, that a husband would love his younger, prettier wife more, and of course wives would see this as unfair. And so, taking extreme liberties, Fitrat asserted that the Quran told men to continue to treat unloved wives with respect and not to show too much favor to the beloved wife.[62] Fitrat never examined women's needs with any seriousness and did not even support limitations so that anything beyond a man's own conscience would govern how many wives he could take. Although he wrote from his own observation that most polygynous marriages were oppressive to women, men's needs demanded social change in some areas and justified continuities in others.[63]

While in 1915 Fitrat seemed to think that polygyny needed defense, a man named Qaramiyev wrote to *Suyum Bike* to point out the evils of polygyny in Tashkent. He asked how others could ignore the woman taken as a second wife at age fifteen, treated like a servant, and then later divorced, with her children becoming "a sacrifice to someone else's pleasure?" He recognized women's powerlessness to affect their own situation, observing that power was in the hands of community leaders who were sympathetic to men's Sharia right to polygyny and unsympathetic to the injustice done to wives.[64]

By May 1917, Tatar women active in the various branches of the Muslim Women's Association, including those in Central Asia, considered polygyny a serious issue and took a stand on it in the proposals they submitted to the all-Russian Muslim Congresses.[65] A transcript of the women's May congress discussion about polygyny appeared in *Suyum Bike*, with activists taking opposing sides. When Labiba Husainova argued that taking multiple wives should be banned as inherently unjust, Zahida Burnasheva responded that the Quran permits multiple wives, but in limited situations. She pointed to the verse's context—that multiple wives were permitted in a situation where there were many female orphans. Because this was not the case for Muslims in Russia, taking multiple wives was now unnecessary. Fatima Latifa said that men always interpreted this verse to their own advantage, ignoring the necessity of justice; justice would permit taking an additional wife only in the case of barrenness, and others agreed that the practice should be limited.[66]

In December 1917, *Suyum Bike* published a *fatwa* (a legal decision) from the Kazan Spiritual Directorate declaring limits on polygyny. Henceforth, a man who wanted to take a second wife would have to write a request to the local police or have the local imam carry out an inspection to make sure that the requirements of justice were met.[67] This decision clearly emerged from discussions among Russia's Muslim clergy about polygyny. It did not apply to Central Asia, which came under the Orenburg Spiritual Directorate, but it was indicative of the kinds of thought that shaped efforts in the early Soviet period, from 1917 to 1924, to modify Sharia and make it compatible with Soviet law. The Soviet government did not recognize polygyny, but ongoing discussions of law gave Muslims the understanding that Soviet law on marriage was negotiable. In my interviews with elderly Uzbek women, three were married to polygynous husbands during the 1940s to 1960s. In one case, the husband's first wife became paralyzed, and he married a second wife to bring up his children and take care of his first wife. Before marrying, he had local authorities write up a document giving him permission to take a second wife based on his first wife's condition, and he used this to legally marry the second without divorcing the first. While this was contrary to the letter of Soviet law, it seems to reflect the Jadid idea and the Kazan fatwa that polygyny was acceptable, if limited by justice.[68]

In sum, while Muslim reformers tended to speak with one voice when urging education for girls, their views diverged when considering reforms to marriage. Rarely did the word "equality" arise; most writers accepted difference, and advocated reform largely in the interests of men.

## RIGHTS

While most discussions about women focused on education and family life, the Turkic press in Russia also opened the question of rights for women. After the failed revolution of 1905, the Russian emperor Nikolai II agreed to political liberalizations, including establishing a body of elected representatives, the Duma, and increasing freedom of assembly and the press. Revolutionary activism in 1905 took place far from Turkestan, but the changes affected Turkestan, allowing nongovernmental presses to open, new Muslim civic organizations to appear, a few Turkestanis to be elected to the first Duma (though they were barred from successive Dumas), and participation of some Turkestanis in Russia's Muslim congresses. By 1905 there were many women's organizations among Russians active in social issues, women workers' issues, and in seeking voting rights.[69]

The discourse of rights—citizenship, voting, and religious—was ubiquitous in the Russian empire, and Muslim women began to demand rights or the defense of their rights. In 1907, a woman named Najie sent a letter to the Muslim members of the Duma, noting that Sharia gives women many rights, including the right to worship and pray in the mosque, to travel and go on the Hajj, and to participate in trade, and that Muslim women in Instanbul and Egypt were exercising these rights. By contrast, Najie averred, "our men . . . have enclosed us within four walls, hiding us for months and years." She pointed to articles that religious scholars in Russia had published, noting that they seemed intent on further restricting women, and she presented her challenge: "Let the Muslim members who attend the Duma grant Muslim women all rights . . . We are mothers of the nation; we are half of humanity; the progress and purity of the nation depends on us."[70]

The language of rights for Muslim women had two overlapping contexts: political rights in Russia and religious, Islamic rights. Rights could be new, connected to liberal, universalizing ideas of the relationship between citizen and government; or rights were once established through God's revelation, and since degraded and ignored. In the first instance, a right was to be demanded and granted: as Kamila Muzafiriya observed, "rights do not fall from the sky."[71] In the second, rights existed in Islamic law, but they needed to be recognized and defended. Najie's letter reflects aspects of both. She demanded rights for women with reference to Islamic religious and social practice and made no explicit allusion to the political rights of women as citizens. However, she addressed this letter to the Muslim deputies of the Duma, not to a body of religious authorities. She asked them to grant women rights such as pilgrimage and mosque attendance, bolstering her argument not with reference to religious text, but rather to women's role in the nation. By contrast, a member of the Ufa Muslim Women's Association argued not for the granting of rights, but for restoration of rights. She posited a golden age of Islamic rights for women in the distant past, and she interpreted all that followed as decline and corruption. She wrote, "Shariat gives women great rights. But Muslims have reduced them to slavery, rightlessness, kept them inside four walls like possessions, considered them men's servants." Educated women who learned of these rights could demand their restoration.[72]

Many writers asserted that in Sharia, God gave women and men equal rights.[73] Fitrat emphasized that Islamic law made women equal to men in rights and duties, although he recognized that Islamic law gave leadership to men: "Yes, women are the same as us in all rights and duties. So you will say, God has given men leadership, so how can you say women are really equal? Only if leadership means one is higher, but it is really work and labor . . . The Islamic religion . . . has only given to men the service of leadership, that is, has placed men as servants and guardians."[74] A Tatar Jadid, Zakir al-Qadiri, citing a *hadith* to say that education is so obligatory for a woman that she has the right to obtain it even without her husband's permission, argued that girls needed to learn about their rights regarding marriage contracts, alimony, and inheritance.[75] He wrote that Tatar mullahs "who do not know a word of Arabic" declare forbidden to women all sorts of things that are not forbidden, such as speaking in men's presence, studying, gathering for education, going to prayer at the mosque, and showing face and hands.[76]

Those who defended Muslim women's rights based on this interpretation of Sharia knew that their position was contentious, and they often portrayed their opponents as ignorant, as in al-Qadiri's characterization of Tatar mullahs. But there was diversity within the ranks of women's supporters. Fakhr ul-Banat, who opposed polygyny, believed in companionate marriage, and supported education for girls, had difficulty finding equality for men and women in Sharia. She wrote, "It is improper for a woman to visit her neighbors without her husband's permission, and according to Sharia it is not even correct for her to go to her parents without her husband's permission." She argued that the companionship of spouses should ameliorate these restrictions; wives should seek permission, and husbands should grant it. "Are women and girls condemned to sit at home? No. They are people, too. They also can go to their friends and neighbors." She would not assert that Sharia gave women the right to freedom of movement; rather she appealed for their freedom of movement as a normal aspect of human life.[77] By contrast, a contributor to *Suyum Bike* wrote that Europeans believed that Islam held women back from progress, but he contended that it was actually custom and misunderstanding of Islam that deprived women of rights.[78]

Could a defense of women's rights be based on Islamic texts and doctrines? This issue lay at the core of the early twentieth century discourse on women. In their discussions of rights, of marriage, and of education for women, Russia's Muslims demonstrated their close links to currents of thought in the central Islamic lands; similar discussions arose in Egypt, the Ottoman Empire, and India. In the early twentieth century, members of the Russian empire's Muslim millat, whether Tatars or Turkestanis, argued among themselves on the basis of a shared identity as Muslims and framed their arguments about women within this rubric. When the Russian Revolution actually established equal rights for women, Muslim political actors in Turkestan were unprepared to discuss women's rights in the liberal, universalist terms that Russian revolutionaries used, and much less in the socialist terms of the Bolsheviks. Between 1917 and 1924, while Soviet law established equality for women and men, lawmakers in Turkestan tried to negotiate compromise between Sharia-based concepts of rights and Bolshevik concepts, so that until 1924, the legal rights of Turkestani women were uncertain.

Jadids introduced new ideas about women's roles in Turkestani society, building women into their understandings of national reform, by emphasizing the need for girls' education. Tatar women in Russia unveiled, created women's societies, established higher education for women, published books and journals, and debated issues such as polygyny and veiling. Knowledge about Tatar efforts spread in Central Asia both through the press and through the presence of Tatar progressive "missionaries," who reported on and tried to influence the lives of Turkestani women. However, Central Asian Jadidism was conservative by comparison with Tatar thought; even the most progressive Central Asian men, like Fitrat and Behbudi, were reluctant to consider limitations on polygyny, an end to gender segregation, or serious changes in the relative status of men and women in family life. Although the February and October 1917 revolutions changed laws and granted women equality with men, in Uzbekistan the focus of "the reform of women" continued to be the least controversial area, namely education for women. Radical Soviet challenges to Turkestani attitudes toward marriage and family life, by contrast, could not build on a strong base in Jadid thought.

## ❧ 3 ❧

# THE REVOLUTION AND
# RIGHTS FOR UZBEK WOMEN

Iₙ 1916, TURKESTAN WAS A
colony under military administration. In 1924, Uzbekistan was drawn
on a map and declared a Soviet socialist republic, one of six that formed
the Soviet Union.[1] Within eight years a vast political change created both
Soviet citizenship and an Uzbek nation in Central Asia. After the Communist Party consolidated its power and stifled other political parties,
Soviet citizenship was based on a principle of equality and the state constructed its subjects through activism and mobilization. That is, to be a
good Soviet citizen meant to respond actively to government and Party
campaigns for transforming the economy and society. At the same time,
the government of the Soviet Union, by dividing its territory into new
republics based on the Party's particular understanding of the term
"nation," established a new locus of identity and loyalty, as well as a new
field of opportunity, for Central Asian men and women.

Jadid ideas about nation and citizenship—where women's roles were
defined in terms of modern, educated motherhood—were subsumed
under a broader and more invasive Soviet project. Turkestani women
became citizens of Soviet Uzbekistan through processes that linked gender and ethnicity to new public roles. While there were commonalities
to citizenship for everyone in the Soviet Union, the creation of Uzbekistan and campaigns directed at women there made "Uzbek woman" a

category apart from "Soviet woman." In some ways, the nation and state-building processes of 1920s Uzbekistan paralleled many non-Soviet experiences. In this chapter, I compare Uzbek and Turkish measures for turning women into modern citizens during this period. Measures of forced modernization were not unique to the Soviet Union, although in Uzbekistan efforts were backed by a more powerful state than in Turkey.

This chapter sets a context for the following chapters through an overview of the Soviet project for changing government, law, and the relations of the individual to the state in Central Asia. From 1916 to the end of the 1920s, the state's role in Central Asian lives grew enormously. In establishing the Uzbekistan Soviet Socialist Republic, the state itself defined Uzbeks and made establishing public identities and roles for women central to the creation of modern, socialist Uzbeks.

## BREAKING INTO THE PUBLIC

In 1916, Muslim women in cities and towns throughout Turkestan suddenly appeared in riots against the Russian administration. This was unprecedented. There was no tradition of women's rioting in Turkestan; Turkestani women did not appear in public gatherings at all. But they turned out in significant numbers in the uprising against wartime labor conscription.

Throughout the period of Russian rule in Turkestan there were numerous localized uprisings against the Russian authorities. The 1916 uprising was different; triggered by a change in tsarist policy on conscription, the uprising swept across Turkestan and the Steppe Governate (present-day Uzbekistan, Kazakhstan, and Kyrgyzstan), pitting Central Asians against the colonial government and its local, native agents. Some Uzbek historians characterize this uprising as a "national-liberation movement." It was the first mass uprising of Turkestanis against the Russian administration since the conquest, and the first to include women.

Since the Russian conquest of Central Asia, there had been a fundamental difference between natives of Turkestan and the Steppe territories and subjects of any ethnicity who lived in other areas of the empire: Central Asians were not obligated, or asked, to serve in the army. This was a mark of their inequality with Russia's other subjects and of the Russian government's distrust. While other Muslims in the empire—

Tatars, those from the Caucasus, and even a Turkmen regiment—served in the tsar's army in the Great War, Turkestanis did not.[2] World War I affected their lives in other ways: they paid higher taxes, provided more livestock for military requisition, and faced rising prices and a falling living standard. But on June 25, 1916, the Russian government decreed that in Central Asia and the Steppe, native men would be called up to work as laborers behind military lines, where they would dig trenches and graves and would not be given guns or taught to fight. Turkestan was to provide 220,000 men between the ages of nineteen and forty-three. News spread rapidly via telegraph and messengers.[3]

The local administrators from villages and neighborhoods, Turkestani men, were responsible for assembling lists of men and selecting names for the call-up. This perfidy—placing Russian interests ahead of the mil-lat (nation)—was enough to cause outrage, and in some villages local administrators were also accused of taking bribes to remove names from the lists.[4] On July 4, 1916, in Xojand (Fargana Valley), a demonstration against conscription turned violent; protesters attacked the police sta-tion, and four protesters were killed. The next day, a crowd of two thou-sand gathered in Urgut, Samarkand Province; they destroyed lists and killed local administrators. In the next two weeks similar riots took place in villages in Samarkand Province, Fargana Province, and in the cities of Jizzax and Tashkent. In villages, crowds attacked local and Russian administrators, killing them and their families and burning their homes. In cities, crowds attacked police stations.[5]

Reports from Russian administrators frequently noted that demon-strations began when native women gathered and men joined in, stand-ing behind them. In Naimancha, near Kokand, "women . . . were standing in the front rows of the crowd, shouting and interfering with questioning the men." In Gazi-yazlik, a crowd of two thousand men and women marched on the homes of local administrators and killed them.[6] In most cases, men were charged with instigating the riots and with crimes of murder and looting, but in the village of Nizhnii Asht, the adminis-tration also arrested and investigated ten women who were involved in the uprising there, before dropping their cases.[7] A few Uzbek women were sentenced to Siberian imprisonment for their participation.[8]

In Tashkent, a large crowd gathered at the police station in the old city on July 11, 1916. Tikhotskii, the chief of police for old city Tashkent, reported that a meeting of neighborhood officials with the military gov-ernor had been called for 11:00 A.M. but that a dense crowd of women appeared there before 9:00 A.M., protesting the call-up. Soon men joined, and the crowd attacked the police station.[9] As demonstrators broke down the doors of the police headquarters, the police fired shots into the crowd. Eleven protesters were killed, including one woman.[10] Robiya Nosirova, an Uzbek woman who became deeply involved with the Communist Party Women's Division, described this demonstration: "I was also there, in the huge crowd of Uzbek women and poor men, headed toward the building of the Tashkent police headquarters in order to destroy the hated lists of those called up to fulfill labor behind the lines. I remember how a shot from a police pistol killed an Uzbek woman who was in the front row, bravely demanding that they leave her only son and provider."[11]

At this Tashkent demonstration, an Uzbek man tried to convince the women that they should not be demonstrating. Just before he died of his wounds in the hospital, Usta Muhammad Azizxo'jaev told his brother that he told the women that shouting and smashing things was "unmannerly for women," but the crowd of men and women "grabbed him, threw him in the street, and someone in the crowed stabbed him in the side and belly."[12]

The uprising in southern Turkestan was not well organized and lasted only a few weeks. However, it was not spontaneous; typesetters and telegraph operators spread word of the demonstrations, and then calls to rise up roared through mosques and bazaars. Local military governors and other officials were convinced that word of the call-up had spread as soon as it came over the telegraph wires and that plans for opposition were soon laid.[13] Although the call-up had excluded imams, mullahs, and religious teachers, their presence in the lists of those arrested suggests they played a role in inciting the demonstrations. A report from Jizzax named as leaders an ishon (member of the Muslim clergy), an imam, and several of Jizzax's wealthiest landowners, who decided "to proclaim a holy war, and having gathered a mass of the people, to set out to attack Jizzax with the intention of re-conquering it from Russia and forming an independent Bek-dom there."[14]

Unlike the uprisings in the Kazakh and Kyrgyz-dominated Jetti-Su and Issik Kol regions of Turkestan and the Steppe Governate, the demonstrations in Tashkent and in Fargana and Samarkand provinces were not sustained, but were quickly put down by the Russian army, which added a division to enforce military rule. In the Kyrgyz and Kazakh regions, the uprisings were massive and lasting. Nomads who had been dispossessed of lands attacked settlers from Russia, who fought back. The 1916 uprising continued for several months, and its outcomes were still being contested after the February 1917 revolution. In southern Turkestan, the uprisings were brief, and to classify them as a national-liberation movement seems exaggerated. However, the uprising was a new phenomenon: if one could speak of a Turkestani nation (as Jadids did) in 1916, this was the first national uprising—the first to extend beyond one locality and to respond to a common threat.

Turkestani women's participation in the demonstrations was unprecedented and calls for explanation, but source materials only permit guesses. Women's motivations remain unclear: some may have decided to participate; others may have marched because men told them to. The call-up would have deprived Turkestan of many male agricultural workers during harvest season. The military governor of Fargana, Ivanov, wrote that "Muslim women, who were threatened by the fate of being left alone without men's provision," joined the very first demonstrations. He understood their presence as reflecting that "the native woman— the secluded one of the sedentary population of the territory—is in no way capable of any kind of work."[15] Robiya Nosirova's account portrayed one participant's motivation as personal—a mother's plea to keep her son's support—rather than political. But Nosirova's biographer noted that Nosirova organized a group of paranji-clad women to join the demonstration.[16] Edward Sokol commented that the women demonstrators must have had the permission of the men of their families to go out, and this may have been true for many women participants, but still does little to shed light on their decision to break with the norms of seclusion and move aggressively into public, political action. That large numbers of women demonstrated in many towns suggests that they were called on by the agitators at the mosques and bazaars, probably through husbands and other men, to come out in public and make their grievances known. Perhaps some Turkestanis had come to accept the rhetoric that "women are the mothers of the nation," to believe, against decades of practice, that women did have a place in the political life of Turkestan and some right to speak on their own, or the nation's, behalf.

In Russia, women's demonstrations and rebellions, or *babye bunty*, were common in the early twentieth century, from the bread riots preceding the 1905 and 1917 revolutions, to women arming with pitchforks to drive off collectivizers in the 1930s. In addition, Russian women had long been involved in revolutionary groups and organized political activity. While later Soviet historians like Roza Karryeva set the women's movement in Central Asia within the context of the Russian women's movement, there was hardly any evidence of interaction or connection between the Russian women's movement and any activity among Turkestani women before 1919. There were so few agriculturalist Russian settlers in Turkestan that it is a near certainty that no *babye bunty* ever took place among them and that Turkestanis never saw or heard of such a phenomenon.[17] However, in Tashkent in early 1916, working-class Russian and European women rioted against Muslim merchants, accusing them of hording food and overcharging, and they attacked many shops. Some were arrested and served time in jail.[18] It may be that Turkestanis in 1916 suddenly chose to follow a Russian example, but it may also be that they drew examples from neighboring Islamic countries where many Turkestanis had traveled. For instance, during the Iranian Constitutional Revolution of 1906, women participated in public demonstrations—much to the surprise of observers.[19] However, Turkestani agitators may have called women out, judging, as demonstrators in many countries did, that police would be less likely to shoot if women stood in front of men. In any case, this feature of the 1916 uprising—Turkestani women's political action in demonstrating—contrasts strongly with their image as secluded from the public sphere. They went into public, shouted, threw stones, joined in violent attacks, and some were sent to Siberia for their actions. To understand Uzbek women's activism in the 1920s, this moment seems important as an indication that social attitudes about women's roles were changing.

## TURKESTAN 1917 TO UZBEKISTAN 1924

The Russian Revolution of 1917, like so many other significant events in the empire, took place far from Tashkent, but profoundly affected Central Asia. For Russia's citizens who participated, the revolution's goal was to overthrow the rule of the tsar and establish a true parliamentary, constitutional government. Central Asians, however, called the new period *hurriyat*, or freedom, and saw in it a possibility for gaining independence, or at least autonomy. Among the Russian provisional government's first guarantees were individual liberties, including equal rights for women. But Turkestanis who became involved in political matters following the revolution were locked in battle among themselves:

many wanted independence, some in an Islamic state, others in a nationalist, constitutional state, while still others cast their lot with the Bolsheviks. Rights for women, while included in some Turkestani programs, were not a high priority, and women themselves were not involved in setting agendas. Jadids and conservatives continued their divisions over women's roles, with the former arguing that women Turkestani women should be permitted to vote in the summer 1917 elections and conservatives rejecting equality for women on the basis of the Quran.[20]

Events in the period between 1917 and 1924, when the Soviet government redivided territories in Central Asia and established the Uzbekistan Soviet Socialist Republic, were complex. Elsewhere, Civil War from 1918 to 1920 pitted Reds against Whites in a struggle for the right to rule the successor to the Russian empire, but in Turkestan the Red Army fought against secessionists.

After the February Revolution, military rule in Turkestan collapsed; the colonial administration was strong only in major cities and retained little control of rural areas. The colonial administration tried to reformulate itself as a popular, representative government. This would have meant granting Turkestanis proportional representation, something that Russians in the administration were unwilling to do because they would have been entirely overwhelmed and outvoted, not to mention that many were simply chauvinists. However, divisions among Turkestanis between the Jadids, who promoted modernization, and their opponents, who sought a full reinstatement of Sharia, meant that Turkestanis were unable to present a united front against the colonial government. Instead, individuals and groups bargained and negotiated with elements of the colonial government. The colonial government itself was not united; members of all the parties found in Russia were also present among Russians in Turkestan. There were several violent coups within the provisional government in Tashkent, and in mid-October 1917 a group that identified itself as Bolshevik seized control in Tashkent, even before the Bolsheviks carried out their overthrow of the provisional government in Moscow and Petrograd.[21]

The main representative organization for native Turkestanis, the Shura-i Islami Party, cooperated with the provisional government and utterly rejected the Bolsheviks. After a soviet of soldiers' and workers' deputies seized power in Tashkent in September 1917, several hundred leaders of this party and other representatives of Muslim political groups decamped to Kokand, where they announced their own government, the Turkeston Muxtoriyati (Turkestan Autonomy).[22] The Tashkent Soviet, representing the Bolshevik government, sent Red Army forces against Kokand in January 1918 and, in three days of bombardment in February, brought an end to the Turkestan Autonomy and devastated most of the city of Kokand. The Autonomy itself had not been united, stable, or able to draw support from across Turkestan, and just before the Red Army attacked, a Kurbashi, or militia leader, replaced the political leader in an internal coup. When the Autonomy was destroyed, its military forces dispersed, headed into the mountains, and tried to establish links with other regions of Turkestan, as well as calling for support from Afghanistan and Britain. The Soviet government referred to these military groups as Basmachi (raiders, bandits, from *basmoq*, to tread on or trespass), while recent Uzbek historiography calls them Kurbashi (for the militia leaders, though obviously the majority of fighters were not so titled), or Istiqlal Haraqatchilar, freedom fighters.[23]

In 1918, the Soviets set up a few basic institutions of government, building on what was left of the colonial government in the cities, but most of Turkestan faced warfare and instability in the years immediately following the revolution. In Samarkand province, urban and rural populations dropped almost 20 percent between 1917 and 1920, and the amount of planted land also dropped precipitously. There was mass emigration from Turkestan and Bukhara to Afghanistan and other countries until 1927. There was also migration to other regions in Turkestan; Tashkent region grew in population in this period. There was drought and famine in 1917–1918, and some districts may have experienced starvation.[24] In short, there was chaos.

For four years, there was serious competition between the Soviet government and the various Autonomy forces for control of Turkestan. The political leadership of the Autonomy for a time was able to draw on connections with Turkestanis who joined the Soviet government, and the anti-Soviet military effort was dubiously boosted by the renegade Turkish general Enver Pasha's adventurism in 1921 and 1922. The Soviet government initially enhanced popular support for the Basmachis by instigating radical policies, including land confiscation from a few hundred large landowners, grain requisitioning, and the declaration that waqfs would be seized.[25]

National self-determination, a policy meant to attract non-Russians to the Soviet government, was defined as the will of the people as expressed by its leading revolutionary class. Thus, the tiny minority of Turkestanis who worked on railroads, in factories, and served in the Red Army, could form themselves into soviets, or councils, of workers' and soldiers' deputies and declare on behalf of Turkestanis that they supported Soviet power. Anyone who disagreed was obviously not from the leading revolutionary class, and thus had no right to express self-determination on behalf of Turkestanis. National self-determination, then, could only result in the wise choice of union with the Soviet state. Even the term "autonomy" was co-opted by the Soviet state, which renamed Turkestan Territory the Turkestan Autonomous Soviet Socialist Republic (TASSR).

When the Red Army gained the upper hand against Basmachis in any region of Turkestan, soviets of workers' deputies were quickly organized to form the basis of local government and legitimize control from Tashkent. In 1920, the Soviet government's struggle for control of Turkestan became easier after they supported an uprising in Bukhara to overthrow the emir and establish a people's republic. In the four-year existence of the Bukharan People's Republic, its territory ceased to be a haven of support for Basmachis, and its leadership, under Faizulla Xo'jaev, was drawn into ever closer cooperation with the TASSR. The other protectorate, the Khivan Khanate, went through turmoil in this period. A semipopular uprising in 1918, with Bolshevik support, ended the khan's rule and established the People's Republic of Khiva, but there were years of internal warring among numerous parties, who switched sides so often that it would be hard to name them either Soviet partisans or Basmachis. The Soviet government gradually pushed the two people's republics into signing treaties establishing unity with the TASSR. In 1924, the Soviet government drew new borders, uniting parts of Bukhara and Khiva with part of the former Turkestan territory to form Uzbekistan.[26]

By 1920, there was an active Communist Party in Turkestan, one that encompassed conflicting interests. Some Turkestanis saw the Party as a venue for promoting their own national interests, while Russians who had not left behind their colonial views also contended for control. The Party's center, in Moscow, sent the Turkestan Commission to review the situation and to establish Moscow's order and administration. The Turkestan Commission intended "to break up the multinational state structure of the Turkestan ASSR and to redraw its administrative boundaries in conformity with its ethnographic divisions." The commission regarded this policy as essential for ending warfare, which they understood as arising from ethnic differences. If Turkmens and Uzbeks were separated, then war would end in Khiva, they asserted, totally ignoring the political, not ethnic, base for the Basmachi war against the Red Army. The Turkestan Commission asserted that national delimitation would undermine clan divisions and create a situation in which class stratification and socialist development could take place. It would also satisfy an "'elemental longing' of the nationalities to possess their own state."[27] Census workers would determine where particular ethnic groups lived and new territorial boundaries would be established accordingly. On the basis of these maps, the Soviet Nationalities Commissariat drew the borders of Uzbekistan and declared it a Soviet republic in October 1924.

Throughout the Soviet period, anti-Soviet authors charged that the territorial divisions in Central Asia were artificial and that the division was a Communist Party/Russian strategy to end Muslim or Turkic unity and its potential power, and thus keep Central Asia under Soviet/Russian control.[28] Indeed, it is easy to demonstrate that the borders drawn were artificial. Nationality was not the most prominent organizing idea in the early twentieth-century politics of Central Asia, and those who were supposed to be Uzbeks and Tajiks according to the standards of the Nationalities Commission were thoroughly mixed in localities and did not necessarily recognize those ethnonyms as their own, or as the most important element in their political identity. Of course, the previous political territories—Turkestan, Bukhara, and Khiva—also had no inherent, organic unity other than that which was constructed by whatever political entity held power. But the modern nation is a political construct, and while there was no compelling reason that there must be an Uzbekistan, there was also no strong force behind any competing form.

Within Central Asia, several groups contested national delimitation. Some objected to dividing Turkestan and dismantling the idea of a Turkestani nation, encompassing Uzbeks, Sarts, Tajiks, Turkmens, Kazakhs, Kyrgyz, and so on, as the nation had been proposed by Jadids in the early twentieth century (conforming to an existing territory that was defined by Russian conquest). Others opposed particular borders: Tajiks living in Bukhara and Samarkand wanted their region to be Tajikistan; Kazakhs claimed the Tashkent region; Khivans did not want their territory divided between Uzbekistan and Turkmenistan. Francine

Hirsch, in her examination of this policy, argues that "the national-territorial delimitation of Central Asia should not be dismissed as a devious strategy of 'divide and rule' or accepted as proof of the Soviet regime's 'ethnophilia,' but instead should be understood as a manifestation of the Soviet regime's attempts to define a new (and presumably nonimperialistic) model of colonization."[29] Certainly the Bolsheviks considered that dividing Turkestan would reduce the possibility of some sort of anti-Soviet Turk federation,[30] but the territorial delimitation approach was consistent with Soviet nationalities policy toward other ethnic groups and territories.

The status of the newly created Soviet Republic of Uzbekistan vis-à-vis the Soviet center was not the same as Turkestan's relationship to the Russian imperial center had been. Turkestan was very clearly a colony, and its inhabitants were colonial subjects; but the relationship between the inhabitants of Uzbekistan and the Soviet government was supposed to be one of citizenship. While colonial government of Turkestan exercised its authority indirectly and needed a pacified, rather than a mobilized, population, building socialism demanded high rates of citizen participation in the public realm—though not the public sphere in Jürgen Habermas's sense—and operated through direct state intervention in the lives of citizens. The Soviet government and the Uzbekistan Communist Party could carry out their modernizing, socialist project only by recruiting large numbers of activists, by training them in schools and brief courses, and by redistributing them throughout the territory of Uzbekistan.

Although there was opposition to dividing Turkestan into national republics, there was also substantial support. The Soviet nationalities policy of the mid-1920s, by creating entirely new republics, also created a need for government servants from the nationality for whom a republic was created. That is, if Uzbeks needed a state, then the state also needed Uzbeks. The state and the Party invested in schools, theaters, print media, and training for work and government service in national languages and tried to find "natives" who could be promoted to positions of responsibility. Terry Martin refers to this phase in Soviet history as "the affirmative action empire," when the Soviet state retained control over former colonial territories, but did so by consciously creating national cadres.[31] Those Turkestanis who joined the Soviet side early did so not only to enhance their own careers, but because they saw possiblities for national development with Soviet support.

Faizulla Xo'jaev, who was the president of the Bukharan People's Republic (BPR), became one of the prominent advocates for building an Uzbek nation within the Soviet Union. Xo'jaev was involved with the Red Army's attack on Bukhara in 1920, and when the emir fled, Xo'jaev, at age twenty-four, became president. The BPR's constitution included liberal and socialist elements, but the government had neither the power nor the support to speed ahead with reforms. With the national-territorial delimitation in 1924, the BPR ceased to exist, and so did Xo'jaev's presidency.[32] However, Xo'jaev became a member of the newly organized Communist Party of Uzbekistan and was named Chairman of the People's Commissars for Uzbekistan, a post he held into the 1930s.[33] In this office, as head of all government ministries in Uzbekistan, Xo'jaev could promote and implement social reforms that he could only have dreamed of in Bukhara.

Xo'jaev seemingly saw Uzbekistan as a place where Uzbeks could build a modern, progressive nation. Party officials from the Nationalities Commissariat emphasized that national republics were not to be sites of national chauvinism. Republics were to be equal partners in the Soviet Union, not sovereign or independent entities. The national consciousness that was supposed to develop following the establishment of the republics was the first step on the road to true internationalism. But the Uzbekistan Soviet Socialist Republic, like others, was given many of the trappings of the modern nation-state. For example, early in 1925 the Uzbekistan Communist Party approved the formation of a national division of the Red Army, which would be "an inseparable part of the Worker and Peasant Red Army of the USSR" and at the same time would "be a strong step forward in the area of national self-determination of the peoples of Central Asia." There was room for several understandings of relative importance of "inseparable part" and "national self-determination," and Xo'jaev sometimes emphasized the latter in his speeches to the Uzbek public.[34]

The Uzbek-langauge press referred to Uzbekistan as "our country" and gave little attention to the Soviet Union as a locus of identity or loyalty.[35] There had not been an Uzbekistan prior to 1924, though, and defining who was Uzbek was part of the process of creating Uzbekistan. Men and women who earlier may have referred to themselves as Sart, Turk, or Uzbek, were all dubbed Uzbek by the state and were declared to be the people who should participate in state government. Tajik speakers, a large minority in Uzbekistan who might earlier have been identified as Sart or Turkestani, now were, by linguistic criteria, denied the privileges of the majority. Being Uzbek brought rewards.

Benedict Anderson examines the process of national formation in colonial territories, drawing attention to one of the processes that helped create national identities, and his analysis seems apt for Central Asia. He writes that in the Netherlands Indies, as in other colonies, "the twentieth-century colonial school-system brought into being pilgrimages which paralleled longer-established functionary journeys . . . From all over the vast colony, but nowhere outside it, the tender pilgrims made their inward, upward way, meeting fellow-pilgrims from different, perhaps once hostile, villages in primary school; from different ethno-linguistic groups in middle-school; and from every part of the realm in the tertiary institutions of the capital."[36]

Anderson argues that both the circumscribed ascent of native functionaries in colonies and the similarly circumscribed path of modern schooling in the colonies enabled those whose paths were thus delimited to imagine their administrative unit as a nation. The native administrator in India might have gone to the British metropole for education, but his career was to be played out in India; he might be moved laterally within India, but would never become a local administrator in the British Isles. In describing the careers of creole functionaries who may be seen as the inventors of New World nationalisms, Anderson writes, "The apex of his looping climb, the highest administrative centre to which he could be assigned, was the capital of the imperial administrative unit in which he found himself."[37]

Through similar pilgrimages, Central Asians, both men and women, in the newly delineated Uzbekistan Soviet Socialist Republic began to see themselves as Uzbeks. Selected and sent to Tashkent for education and for political meetings, Uzbeks (who may previously have thought of themselves as Sart or Bukharan or Turk) began to imagine and experience a new form of political community in the 1920s. The creation of Uzbekistan was one step in a rather long project that eventually transformed a Russian colony into an independent state (of course, this was not at all the intention of its Soviet creators), one whose borders were simply invented. The movement of people—students, Party members, and government workers—within those borders was an essential component in the invention of Uzbekistan. Throughout the Soviet period,

Uzbeks could expect access to positions and opportunities within Uzbekistan, but did not find doors opened wide within the larger boundaries of the Soviet Union.

A program of Soviet modernity facilitated the process of nation creation. Not content to control territory, the Communist Party of the Soviet Union continually intervened in the lives of its citizens to transform them and their economic structures. A rationale for Soviet development demanded capable workers in every national setting, and so Uzbeks, along with other Soviet citizens, went to Soviet schools and training programs in order to take on the business of running the state and the economy (at least partially). In this context, the state and the Party directed extraordinary effort toward establishing women's legal equality with men in Central Asia and bringing women into active participation in public life.

## MAKING THE NEW WOMAN IN SOVIET UZBEKISTAN AND REPUBLICAN TURKEY

The Soviet Union's program for modernizing women in order to change broader society resembled projects that other states undertook in the 1920s. Republican Turkey, established on the ruins of the Ottoman Empire, undertook many similar measures to change law, family life, and women's roles during the 1920s. Comparing Uzbekistan and Turkey suggests that the transformative measures that Soviet leaders planned were not unique, emerging solely from Communist ideology, but were aspects of modernization that other states also pursued in this period. However, these modernizing changes met a very violent backlash in Uzbekistan, which was not true elsewhere.

Nilüfer Göle argues that women are "a touchstone of modernization."[38] Not only in symbolic ways, but in terms of real social transformation, those who sought to establish the new states—the Turkish Republic and the Soviet Union—saw women's education, labor, and public activity as both signs that would demonstrate the state's modernness and as means to achieve the the state's modernization. For the male leaders of revolutionary change in Turkey and in Uzbekistan, men who had criticized their own societies' social structures, this meant first of all directing the state's attention to factors that were the strongest markers of civilizational backwardness: polygyny, child marriage, and unilateral divorce rights for men, all of which were founded on Islamic law. Throughout the 1920s, both Turks and Soviets sought radical disestablishment of Islamic law and focused on the area where its power was most pervasive, family law. State actions, namely the passage of laws and the implementation of programs affecting women's social roles, emerged from ideological and pragmatic concerns.

State efforts to change women's rights and roles in the 1920s in Turkey and Uzbekistan were intimately linked to both states' modernizing and secularizing projects. Both projects shocked societies that had long assumed that women's roles were defined by Islamic norms. But the scope of change was swifter, broader, and more violent in Uzbekistan, where the state made modernizing women part of a program of sweeping economic change and used a mobilized, activist government and party to push these transformations.

In her discussion of women's emancipation in Turkey, Deniz Kandiyoti points to the importance of state actions, noting that "the political project of the state can act as a major source of discontinuity in the experiences of women in Muslim countries. The state may be a powerful instigator of change through policies that may in some cases represent an onslaught on existing cultural practices."[39] In both Uzbekistan and Turkey, the state's project for modernizing women was instrumentalist: the goal was not to establish women's rights and individual freedoms for their own sake, but to change women's roles for the sake of broad social transformation. The state strove to turn women into educated participants in public life.[40] In Turkey, the nationalist program emphasized a new form of citizenship that its elites referred to as "civilization," by which they meant Westernization, brought about through "social and cultural engineering." Citizenship in the republic was to form "a totally new man by preaching even the rearrangement of private life, or the very life-style of the people."[41] In Uzbekistan, socialist modernization required the participation of all citizens, both men and women, in public life and work, both for the transformation of the citizen's consciousness and to achieve a rapid economic breakthrough.

The new programs for women came from above, from governments that desired to defeat what they saw as backwardness, the source of state weakness in a competitive world. Thus historians writing about the dramatic efforts to change women's position in Uzbekistan and Turkey have often begun not with the women themselves, but with these state projects.[42] It is quite clear from Uzbekistan's experience that laws on family life did not simply translate into life; to become reality, they had to be promoted, taught, and enforced. In *The Surrogate Proletariat*, Gregory Massell examines the means that the Soviet government of Uzbekistan and the Communist Party used to displace the influence of Islamic law and enforce new family law. Douglas Northrop's work points to the ways that Uzbeks resisted these changes and tried to reject the government's program for women's equality in the late 1920s and 1930s.[43] Turkish scholarship presents only an overview of steps toward women's legal equality in Turkey and occasionally mentions that the majority flouted the new laws, but there is no in-depth examination of the Turkish government's approach to making its laws concerning women into reality.[44] Thus, comparisons can be made between the laws that the two modernizing states passed concerning women, but the consequences of those laws are more difficult to compare.

## Changing Laws and Women's Roles

In both revolutionary regimes, Uzbekistan and Turkey, law was seen as an instrument for social change. In explaining Turkey's 1923 Constitution and 1926 secular Code of Civil Law, Göle writes that while "laws have functions to institutionalize cultural change and social consensus in Western countries, their function in Turkey was limited to the determination and acceleration of the modernization process . . . they became the leading force of social change in Turkey. The main object of the civil law was not to 'express' traditions and customs but, rather, to alter those traditions and customs along with the introduction of a new family structure running parallel to the requirements of modernity."[45] In exactly the same way in Soviet Uzbekistan, law was not designed to institutionalize social changes, but rather to force society to change. Law was the state's primary tool for bringing change to family life in Turkey and in Soviet Uzbekistan. In neither place was new, modernizing law based on common practice or representative of the preferences of the majority.[46]

While the most significant legal changes for women in Republican Turkey were enacted by the Grand National Assembly at once in 1926, as discussed below, legal changes in Uzbekistan were piecemeal. Between 1917 and 1924, in the TASSR's early legal reforms, there were compromises between Soviet revolutionary legal ideas and Sharia. After 1924, most of the legal codes were based on Soviet codes designed in Moscow and were modified to address the particularities of Uzbek life.

In December 1917, the Bolsheviks promulgated a decree establishing state control of marriage. Marriages would be legal only if conducted in a civil ceremony. Marrying parties had to be present and give consent to marriage voluntarily. The minimum age for marriage was set at sixteen for women and eighteen for men. Marriage partners could not be in another existing marriage, thus effectively refusing recognition to polygynous marriage.[47] But family law emanating from Leningrad or Moscow had dubious validity in the TASSR, because the TASSR government considered it necessary that a code of civil law should conform to the particular customs of native nationalities. The TASSR's commissions on family law drew up new recommendations between 1920 and 1924. These law commissions continued the Russian imperial tradition that Muslims be judged by Muslim "People's Judges" while non-natives went to European judges, and that Muslim marriage and divorce conform to Sharia and custom.[48] Believing that family laws could not be changed all at once and made effective, the state allowed religious courts to continue to exist until 1927, but circumscribed their scope, empowered the secular People's Courts more fully, and allowed Muslims to choose to take their cases to the People's Courts rather than the Muslim courts. Judges in the People's Courts included many who were first madrasa trained, and then gradually retrained in Soviet law.

The state tried to limit the effectiveness of Muslim courts, but only after the establishment of the Uzbekistan Soviet Socialist Republic did the government begin to construct comprehensive secular legislation. Massell writes that "in their norms, forms, procedures, and personnel, and in their massive and detailed concentration on sexual equality, Soviet initiatives in Central Asia were meant to pose a fundamental challenge to the structure and life syle of local communities."[49] As in Turkey, the Party/state intended to use law to change life.

The 1928 Uzbekistan Code on Family, Marriage and Child-Support established that only marriages registered in the ZAGS (the civil registry) would be recognized, though preexisting marriages were valid. Those marrying had to appear at the registry, show evidence that they met the minimum age standard, and could not be in an existing marriage. Divorce was available on demand, either by consent or by a petition from one of the marriage partners, but divorce would only be recognized through a court proceeding. This law was specific to Central Asia and was meant to end the Islamic practice of male unilateral divorce.[50] A spouse who was not capable of work was entitled to three years of alimony from a working spouse upon divorce.[51] The Criminal Code of 1926 criminalized polygyny, the marriage of minors, marriage by coercion, and the payment of qalin (brideprice).[52]

The central modernizing laws of the Turkish Civil Law Code of 1926 established Turkey's secularism and directly uprooted Islamic family law. While there were earlier legal reforms affecting family law, such as the 1917 law giving wives the ability to refuse husbands the right to take second wives,[53] the 1926 Turkish civil code swept away Islamic law entirely. Canan Aslan writes that "the relationship between women's emancipation and secularization policies could be better comprehended by taking into consideration the fact that emancipating women from Islamic practices was actually a serious blow to religion via an attack on what was considered to be Islam-inspired social and political norms and conduct."[54] The commission charged in 1923 with creating a civil code first based that code on existing practice, with some modifications, meaning that Sharia was largely upheld. However, the proposed code was subject to public discussion, and Halide Edip led the voices of women who criticized the code. In 1925, Mustafa Kemal Atatürk appointed a new committee, which instead of modifying existing practice, chose to adapt the Swiss civil code for Republican Turkey.[55] "The major accomplishment of the Civil Law, for the purposes of a modern state, was the establishment of state control over the institution of the family."[56]

The Turkish civil code established that only civil weddings would be recognized as legal; religious ceremonies could take place but would not be recognized by the state. The code banned polygyny, established seventeen as the lowest marriageable age for women and eighteen for men, gave women the right to civil divorce, ended the Islamic freedom of unilateral divorce for men, and equalized inheritance for sons and daughters.[57] However, as many scholars have observed, the code did not make women and men equal. The husband was designated head of the household, and a wife could only work with her husband's permission. According to law, a wife was responsible for housework, and "serve[d] as the assistant and consultant to her husband to pursue the happiness of the family."[58] Details of the divorce statutes made divorce more difficult for women than men.

Unlike Turkish law, Uzbek Soviet law did not articulate separate responsibilities or roles for husband and wife; women and men were equal under the law in every way, except for limitations on women's work in heavy labor and women's maternity-leave rights. The new laws aimed not only to establish women's equality, but also to attack the privileged position and power of those whom the Soviet order deemed its class enemies: the clergy and the wealthy. Because law was seen as an instrument of social revolution, the Party and the state actively, even aggressively, pursued enforcement. The Code of Family Law was adopted in 1928 after two years of public discussions held at workplaces, soviets, and party organizations. The discussions brought feedback that changed the laws only slightly, but their real purpose was to make the Uzbek public aware of the new code of law.[59]

Uzbek women activists from the Women's Division of the Communist Party were given the task of publicizing and popularizing Uzbekistan's new laws through public and individual talks with women, through articles in women's and general publications, by bringing women plaintiffs to court and advocating on their behalf, and by encouraging women to become judges. Women's Division activists also promoted women's knowledge and use of their right to vote and be elected by organizing election meetings for women, inviting women to attend representatives' meetings where they learned about law and about the public positions they could hold,[60] and by bringing women into Party organizations. In addition, the Party tried forcing its members to comply with new laws by making examples of those who flouted the law, purging them from the Party rolls and putting on trial those who broke the law by, for example, paying qalin.

The Turkish and Uzbek approaches to law and social change differed in their rapidity and enforcement. Turkey simply shut down its religious courts and replaced them with state courts. Historians have not explained where the state found the judges for the new courts and how thoroughly these judges enforced the new laws. Uzbekistan allowed two systems to exist for several years and focused on drawing women to the new courts by making clear that only the new courts would uphold the new, equalizing laws; if a woman wanted an easy Soviet divorce, she would need to turn to the new court.

Turkey popularized laws through example and enforced them, at least somewhat, in the cities. Members of the People's Democratic Party (men) were supposed to follow the example of Mustafa Kemal Atatürk and his close associates in bringing wives into public, encouraging daughters to become educated, and drawing women into poltical parties when they were granted the right to vote. Uzbekistan's measures for popularizing and enforcing law were more thorough and far-reaching. Party members, both rural and urban, were to set examples in the treatment of women and faced strong government pressure to cooperate. Perhaps more importantly, collectivization allowed the state and the Party to establish surveillance in rural areas; by the early 1930s, representatives of the state were present throughout rural Uzbekistan and were charged with reporting violations of family law as well as other laws.

There is evidence that both Turks and Uzbeks disregarded the new laws. From Douglas Northrop's studies, it is apparent that government representatives found many violations of family law in Uzbekistan in the 1930s, including many cases of polygyny and underage marriage, extremely widespread payment of qalin, as well as hundreds of cases of rape, murder, and abuse of women. Northrop characterizes these violations as "massive," but his footnotes tend to portray numbers in the hundreds. He reasons that the violations that were found and prosecuted are probably only the "tip of the iceberg," and that most violations went unreported. Alternatively, the widespread reporting of violations may reveal something of the presence of the Soviet state and the seriousness of many of its representatives in enforcing the new laws. State functionaries carried out audits on the record books of local marriage registries to find underage marriages, for example.[61]

By contrast, in Turkey, there is clear evidence that at least one aspect of the new marriage law, legal registry, was breached far more often than it was upheld for several decades. Under Turkish law, only children of marriages registered in the state's secular system were considered legitimate. Whether because these offices were not present in villages, or because marrying parties were unacquainted with the civil code, or because they chose not to observe the law, Turks gave birth to children whom the state considered illegitimate. The numbers were so large that the government periodically passed special laws to recognize these children as legitimate. In thirty years, between the Civil Code of 1926 and the passage of a special recognition law in 1956, the state had recognized a legal status for 7,724,419 such children, this in a population that was only about 25,000,000 in 1956. In other words, vast numbers of Turkish children were born in marriages that did not conform to Turkish law.[62] Evidence on Turks' adherence to other new laws, such as equal inheritance and the ban on polygyny, is simply lacking.

By comparison, it seems that Uzbekistan's mechanisms for enforcing compliance with the law, including surveillance, the presence of government agencies, and an active program of prosecuting violators, were much stronger than those mechanisms in Turkey. The shock of modernization is not necessarily in the passage of laws but in the programs to enforce them.

## Political Equality

In Russia, women's right to vote and be elected equally with men were declared in 1917, following the February Revolution, and these rights were upheld by the Bolsheviks after the October Revolution. Limitations on franchise were connected to social class, not gender. While the provisional government was in control of Tashkent in 1917, the Shura-i Islami Party debated whether women should be given the right to vote, indicating that they did not accept the law on women's equality emanating from St. Petersburg. After the Bolshevik takeover in Turkestan, the TASSR's early legal codes confirmed women's right to vote and be elected, but in practice few Uzbek women knew about or exercised this right until the late 1920s.

In Turkey, women's enfranchisement began with the right to vote in local elections in 1930 and was made complete in 1934 with the right to vote for and be elected to the Grand National Assembly.[63] Although Turkey enfranchised women later than Uzbekistan did, Turkish women had a longer history of political activism and participation than women in Uzbekistan. During the late Ottoman period, women formed associations for the defense of their rights and the government appointed a woman, Halide Edip, as education minister.[64] In the early republican period, activist women agitated for equal rights and formed the Women People's Party.[65] The Turkish Women's Federation argued for women's voting rights and labor protections from 1924 until 1935. The government fully enfranchised women in 1934, and eighteen women were selected for parliamentary seats. Turkish scholar Şirin Tekeli argues that Atatürk saw enfranchising women as part of presenting a modern face to other countries and as a way of showing the differences between his regime and the regimes of European facism.[66]

In Uzbekistan, women's initiation into political life followed enfranchisement, rather than preceding it. After the October Revolution, it was the job of the Women's Division to recruit Uzbek women into Communist Party activism and participation in elections and local government. The Women's Division encouraged women's participation through separate women's meetings related to local elections and by holding conferences for women representatives. Local women's meetings elected representatives, who were given all-expenses-paid trips to regional centers to participate in conferences where they were taught their rights and instructed in how to join the Party or run for elections. Women were granted the right to vote when Central Asia was brought under Communist control, but were slow to exercise that right. A few women participated in soviets from the time of their formation, and in Uzbek state and Party leadership from the time Uzbekistan was formed. Uzbek women were made aware of Turkish women's political activism through newspapers; features on Halide Edip were used to promote women's activism in Uzbekistan.[67] All political activity for Uzbek women was organized and promoted through the Women's Division of the Communist Party.

In the 1920s, the leaders of Republican Turkey and of the Soviet Union, including its constituent republic Uzbekistan, were committed to the idea of creating a modern state, and ending what they saw as backwardness, by implementing a new vision of state control and social construction. In both states, the government created new levers of control over ordinary life, through law, bureaucracy, and documentation. The role of women themselves in creating or supporting the nation's modernizing project was minimal; in Turkey and Uzbekistan, small women's movements had preceeded the 1920s reforms, but were not the primary actors who brought about change in the 1920s. Rights for women were not adopted in either place by popular mandate; in both places, a radical new vision of the state clashed with the desires of many from the elite and the ordinary people. However similar the choices made in family law or the emphasis on women's public roles, there are also salient differences: Turkey's transformation in the 1920s was self-contained. Uzbekistan was changed largely by directive from Moscow, with interpretation from local actors. In Turkey, Mustafa Kemal Atatürk's stacking of the Grand National Assembly enabled his ideas, including nearly equal rights for women, to prevail against "the conservative forces" of the Sharia Ministry.[68] After the Communists gained control in Central Asia, new laws adopted in Uzbekistan in the 1920s were more radically egalitarian than those of Turkey. In both cases, though, laws that established civil marriage and created secular regulation of family life were primary indicators of the state's commitment to "modern" family and social life.

By the 1930s, the coercive power in these two one-party states increased, and the government's need to attract the support of women and to persuade the public of the necessity of modernizing women decreased, leaving women with symbols and images, but very slow real change. Some Turkish scholars have argued that in Turkey, women's rights were promoted for the benefit of society, not for the benefit of the individual, and this resulted in the emphasis on external changes while discourses and gender roles in families remained fairly untouched. Marfua To'xtaxo'jaeva makes a similar argument about the results of the Soviet modernization program: that while it did create equality in work and education (those areas that benefit society), discourses and gender roles remained largely unchanged in the Soviet period.[69]

While some Turkestani women showed glimmers of interest in public events by participating in the 1916 anticonscription demonstrations, in the early Soviet period women in Turkestan were more acted upon by a state that began to establish their legal and political equality than they were actors in their own story. Why the state chose the measures it did, I argue, has much to do with Soviet ideas of making women, and society as a whole, "modern." In 1924, when the Soviet state divided Central Asia into five union and autonomous republics, Uzbekistan and the other republics were given new tasks: to turn their "titular nationalities" into mobilized participants in building a modern, socialist, national entity. Women were as integral as men to the "national republic," as new, interchangeable citizens who would staff a growing, modernizing Uzbek pseudostate.

By comparing the legal and political efforts to create equality for women in Uzbekistan with those in Turkey, I emphasize that many features of Soviet transformation in the 1920s were not uniquely Soviet, nor were they primarily directed at turning women into a "surrogate proletariat."[70] Rather, the similarity between efforts made by both Turkey and the Soviet Union supports Stephen Kotkin's thesis, that Soviet modernization, with its emphasis on mass politics and mass participation and efforts to rid the country of "backwardness," was similar to the projects launched by many other states in the period between the world wars.[71] To understand why many Uzbek women themselves embraced the state's project in the 1920s, it is crucial to explore the ways that Soviet modernity in Central Asia built on Jadid modernity and to examine Uzbek women's own discourses about becoming "new women."

## ⁓ 4 ⁓

# THE OTIN AND
# THE SOVIET SCHOOL

$I$N THE YEARS LEADING TO THE
1917 revolutions, Jadid modernity in the form of desacralized schooling, a didactic press, and societies for enlightenment had little chance
of swaying the Turkestani masses without government support. Soviet
modernity in the form of modern and ideologically socialist schooling, a pedantic press, and government-controlled social organizations,
joined a fragile Jadid base to powerful Party resources. Mass education
was even more important in the Communist Party's agenda for social
transformation than it had been in Jadid programs. In Turkestan,
Islamic education was widely available in the cities and towns, to girls as
well as to boys, both before the revolution and until the Party repressed
Islamic institutions in 1927. However, neither Jadids nor Communists
had much respect for traditional Islamic education. Neither saw any
value in the otin, the woman who taught Quran recitation, prayer, and
literacy to girls in Turkestan and Bukhara.

Rahbar-oi Olimova, an Uzbek woman born in Tashkent in 1908, first
studied with her grandmother before going through a series of Jadid
and Soviet schools. When I asked her whether her grandmother was an
otin, she qualified the term: "My grandmother, . . . my father's mother,
gathered the children, the girls, from the neighborhood and gave them
lessons. [By otin do you mean] a simple otin, the kind who recites

[Quran]? Not that kind. She did not like them. But she was an educated otin, one who educated the people."[1]

This chapter provides context for Rahbar-oi's comment, in which the otin is affirmed and denied, stripped of her religious role, and justified as an educator. First, otins are discussed—their roles in Turkestani society and their training. More importantly, this chapter explores a transition from traditional Islamic education to Jadid education and from Jadid schooling to Soviet schooling. Jadids tried to replace the otin, associated with rote learning and superstition, with the *mu'allima*, or woman teacher who was trained in modern educational theories. The Soviet school built on the Jadid approach, and in the 1920s the otin's roles divided. The otin either became a teacher in the secular state system or a practitioner of communally necessary but publicly derided religious functions in the gendered world of Central Asian Islamic piety.

## THE OTIN AND TRADITIONAL EDUCATION

In the gender-segregated Muslim society of Turkestan and Bukhara, the otin provided both education and religious leadership to women. Central Asian women did not attend the mosque: they recited prayers at home, and attended gatherings for prayer and recitation with neighborhood women for holidays and life-cycle events. These were led by the otin.[2]

The otin's other role was to instruct the young. In the nineteenth and early twentieth centuries, Central Asian boys and girls could receive a basic, formal religious education from a *domla*, a male teacher who taught in a *maktab* (Islamic school), or from an otin, a female teacher who usually taught in her home. The otin was educated in Islamic religious texts and in the classics of Central Asian literature, and she instructed children in prayer, Quran recitation, and these texts. The content of a girl's education with the otin was equal to a boy's education with a domla, and both otin and domla could teach boys and girls together, though this was unusual.

Men's and women's religious knowledge and practice generally remained separate. Otins formed their own chains of knowledge transmission, and in gatherings involving religious practice, women's separation from men allowed the creation of women's religious authority. However, women's religious knowledge and authority could not compete with male authority. Girls did not attend the madrasa (Islamic college), and there are no accounts of women who attained degrees as religious scholars among Central Asians, although some Tatar women did.[3] A well-educated otin was qualified to lead women's prayers and recite religious texts for women's gatherings, but she did not have access to the topics of madrasa learning, such as law, logic, and philosophy, and she could not hold religious authority over men.

It is difficult to find out much about the history of the otin; there are very few records about otins before the early twentieth century. Some continuity between the roles of women in shamanic Turkic practice and that of the otin might be posited; certainly there remains an overlap between otin and folk-healer among Tajiks and Uzbeks.[4] At least one nineteenth-century chain of otins can be established because of their contributions to poetry. Dilshod Otin of Kokand (c. 1800–1905/6), the daughter of a poet, became a poet and otin. Her husband's mother was an otin; Dilshod may have studied with her. She noted in her memoir, "I could read without glasses until age eighty-eight, and ran a maktab. I had a maktab for fifty years, had twenty-three (female) students at the middle and higher level, and made 891 girls literate." Among Dilshod's students was Anbar Otin (Kokand, 1870–1906), who became an otin and a poet.[5] Anbar's father was a nephew of Uvaisiy, a woman poet and the teacher of Nodira (b. 1792, Andijon; d. 1842, Kokand), who was a woman poet and was married to the khan of Kokand.[6] According to one account, Anbar Otin died of complications from fractured legs after a group of women, offended by her poetry, threw her down a staircase.[7] This chain of otins, reaching back to early nineteenth century Kokand, is known because the otins wrote poetry and because of their multiple relationships to noted political and literary figures. However, the identity of most otins remains obscure.

The lack of sources on otins does not indicate that they were few, but rather that their activities were unregulated. There were otins in most *mahallas* (traditional urban neighborhoods) and in many villages. The Tajik writer Sadriddin Ayni, born near G'ijduvon in the Bukharan Emirate in 1878, told of studying with an otin in his childhood village: "my father sent me, at six years of age, to the school connected with the mosque. Since I made no progress there, he sent me to a girls' school. This school was in the inner courtyard of the village khatib's home, and his wife ran it."[8] The fact that the otin taught in her home's inner courtyard, and not in a public space like a maktab, helps explain her absence from the public record. Although the traditional Islamic system of education did not have teacher training programs, a formal institution (the madrasa) trained the domla in religious knowledge; but the education of an otin was private. Maktabs, where boys studied, and madrasas, producing male scholars, were supported and regulated by the state and by religious foundations (waqfs), both in the khanate period and under Russian imperial rule. In Turkestan, school inspectors of the late nineteenth and early twentieth centuries had lists of domlas and maktabs. The otin, unlike the domla, was not a formal mosque employee and thus rarely appeared in school inspectors' records. An otin's education was tutorial; statistics about otins and their activities would probably have appeared only in the rare case when the otin taught at an official maktab connected with a mosque.

It was possible for girls to study at a maktab with a domla, but, unlike Sadriddin Ayni, most pupils studied in gender-segregated settings. Boys and girls began to study between ages six and eight. After studying for a few years with the domla or otin, boys might continue in higher education at a madrasa, but for girls there was no higher education. Occasionally a girl might continue to study with the otin beyond three years in order to become an otin.

According to my elderly informants who studied with otins, girls studied the same curriculum as boys. The maktab's curriculum was formed long before the modern state reached Central Asia and in a time when education's purposes differed from those of mass education sponsored by the nation-state. As Adeeb Khalid describes it, "If the transmission of knowledge (ta`lim) was one concern of the maktab, the other was the inculcation of proper modes of behavior and conduct (tarbiya)."[9] Both domla and otin taught children to perform prayers, recite the Quran, recite classical poetry, and behave according to accepted norms. The usual mode of instruction was oral repetition of a text until the pupil mastered its recitation.[10]

The curriculum began with the alphabet. Traditionally, letters were taught in order, repeated and recited. The system for teaching the alphabet changed in the early twentieth century, when educational reformers published the first new method primers for phonetic alphabet study. According to my interviewees, some otins adopted the new phonetic method, while others did not. Rahbar-oi, whose grandmother taught in Tashkent, reported studying an alphabet reader first. Malika-xon J. (b. 1912, Namangan) reported that she had no formal introduction to the alphabet in her old-style education, and thus she made no progress in learning to read. Her mother then sent her to a Jadid school, where she learned the alphabet quickly. Fotima Yo'ldoshbaeva wrote that in her two years of study with an otin near Kokand, she learned *abjad*, a traditional Islamic approach to the alphabet that emphasizes not phonetics and literacy, but numerical values for letters as a basis for chronograms and riddles.[11]

After the alphabet, children studied a text called *Haft-yak*, which was a collection of the briefer surahs from the Quran with all vowels and pronunciation marks included. Children memorized these surahs in Arabic, but there was no systematic study of the Arabic language, and the otin who understood Arabic was probably a rarity. Two of my informants were otins in the Soviet period. One, Latifot T., could provide an oral translation for an Arabic text into Uzbek. The other, Humoira H., said she did not know Arabic, but that her otin explained the meaning of Arabic and Persian texts in the curriculum.[12]

After *Haft-yak*, pupils studied *Chor-Kitob*, a Persian-language collection of instructions for religious faith and practice composed in rhyming couplets. After *Chor-Kitob* came more of the Quran and then poetry by Fuzuli and Bedil, in Persian, and Navoiy and Sufi Olloyor, in Uzbek. Most informants indicated that through their study with the otin, they learned to read their native language, and they remembered some of the poetry and could recite several surahs from the Quran and several prayers.[13]

Educating girls was not as common a practice as educating boys, but it was not rare either. In southern Turkestan, Bukhara and Khiva, maktabs were found in every village and every mahalla. Russian administration school inspectors recorded very low numbers of girls in maktabs, though girls attended maktabs in Tashkent much more frequently than in Kokand. The 1897 census revealed a wide variance in reported literacy rates for females: in rural Fargana Province, literacy for Turkic-speaking females age ten to nineteen averaged three in one thousand, while in Tashkent, 9 percent of that group were literate in their own language.[14] William Medlin, writing on education in Central Asia, regards the appearance of girls' maktabs as a new phenomenon in late nineteenth century Turkestan, one which "began to alter the traditionally exclusive nature of Muslim education in favor of the male sex."[15] Education was not exclusively male in Central Asia; there was indeed a tradition of women's education, literacy, and poetic composition. But Islamic education for both boys and girls may have increased in the late nineteenth century. The military governor of Fargana Province, Ivanov, drew a connection between rising wealth, a vast increase in Turkestani participation in the Hajj, and growing numbers of children receiving Islamic education.[16]

Domlas who taught boys collected tuition from pupils but were also paid by the mosque or waqf. Otins earned their income from "gifts" from pupils' parents in money or goods. Most informants who studied with an otin did not say they attended a maktab; they thought of a maktab as a public place. They referred to study with an otin simply as learning *eskicha*, old style, or *otincha*, otin style. Humoira, who became an otin, responded to my question, "Did you go to maktab?" by saying, "No, there was a buvotin on my street."[17] The informality of Islamic education for girls, and its remove from the public eye, are factors in its absence from the colonial record and in the Russian administration's impression that Sart girls were all illiterate.

Many Turkestani girls obtained Islamic education before the revolution. Most of the elderly Muslim women I interviewed who grew up in cities and were born before 1916 studied with an otin. This suggests the popularity of otin education in urban areas in the second decade of the twentieth century. However, even though the numbers of girls undertaking Islamic education with an otin may have been considerable, witnesses from the early twentieth century asserted that only a minority of those with traditional Islamic education attained literacy that could be transferred to new reading material, as opposed to knowing the texts they studied by rote.[18]

My informants confirmed that education with an otin was not available to all: those who reported coming from somewhat prosperous families were educated by otins, while those from poor families received no formal education before the Soviet government made education free and more widely available. But disposable income was not the sole factor determining whether a daughter would be educated. Several informants said that families with only one daughter would not send her to an otin because they needed her help in the household.[19] For boys, religious education opened several career opportunities. For girls, however, the value of religious education was intrinsic; in addition, knowing etiquette and Quran and prayer recitation brought respect. There was little possibility that a girl would gain income from religious education; rather, a family's main pragmatic concern in sending her to an otin would be to make her a more desirable candidate for marriage.

In the nineteenth century, reformers throughout the Islamic world began to reshape Islamic education. In the Russian empire, Tatar reformers introduced secular subjects, such as math, geography, and history, into the curriculum of Islamic schools. This *usul-i jadid*, or new method, education flourished in Tatar girls' schools around Kazan in the 1890s. One significant innovation was the establishment of teacher training courses for Tatar women as well as men. Tatar Jadids and Turkestani Muslims started opening Jadid schools in Turkestan in the 1890s, and by the early 1900s some were open to girls as well as boys.[20]

As Khalid observes, the Jadid movement, while promoting improved Islamic education, desacralized knowledge.[21] The kind of education that Jadids offered in the new maktab was consciously similar to that offered in Russian state schools and in Europe and was promoted as the only hope for strengthening the Turkestani nation. Jadids placed the highest value on literacy as a transferable skill, and the knowledge of particular religious texts was no longer education's primary goal. To teach literacy as a transferable skill demanded a new kind of teacher training, and the skills imparted at the madrasa lost value. This separation of education from the knowledge of the ulama, the Islamic scholars of the madrasa who traditionally dominated education, initiated a process that stripped the otin of her role as an educator.

The otin went unmentioned in Jadid proposals for the reform of girls' education, even though the Jadid vision for girls' education was an important element of their larger plans for the nation. Tohir Alimhanov wrote, "If we say we want our children to be like human children, it is wise to begin with educating mothers . . . No matter how well we educate boy children, if we do not educate girls who will become mothers as well, our people will remain in ignorance. If girls are uneducated, half the nation remains uneducated."[22] Nearly all contributors writing about women in the Central Asian Jadid press agreed that the national mother needed an education that only the reformed maktab, publicly supported and run by trained educators, could provide. The national mother would cease harmful practices such as putting her baby in a *beshik* (traditional cradle), and with her study of reading, sums, and geography would prepare her child from infancy for the world of modern education.[23]

Writers for the Central Asian press bewailed the utter lack of schools for girls, but their cry was an overstatement. There were many otins, and after 1910 there were Jadid schools in Turkestan devoted to girls' education or permitting coeducation. Writers who portrayed education for Turkestani girls in the bleakest terms were trying to gain support for more girls' schools. They frequently wrote that rather than waste money on celebrations the wealthy should open a girls' maktab and hire a mu'allima. Their terminology was specific: mu'allima was the name for teacher used in reformed Tatar schools, and none of the modernizers ever referred to the desired woman teacher as an otin.[24]

Jadid writers did not call for reforming the otin. Although some favored changing the maktab by creating training programs for domlas in the madrasas, there was no madrasa for girls in Turkestan. Otins had no associations and no madrasas; there was no institutional base for a curricular reform. In addition, some Jadids regarded otins as harmful. Zuhriddin Fathiddin-zade condemned otins for instructing girls in the use of amulets and recitations to Bibi Seshambe, while leaving them in the dark about how to raise children.[25]

Though unappreciated by the Jadids, otins continued to educate large numbers of Muslim girls in Turkestan. According to informants who studied with otins into the 1920s, the content of their curriculum did not change, except to emphasize learning the alphabet. Far from the modern, national ideal, otins concentrated on teaching girls religion and proper behavior, reading, and perhaps writing. Saodat Shamsieva (b. 1908) studied with an otin for three years (about 1916 to 1919). Her otin, a Tatar woman who taught in To'rtqo'l, a town near Khiva but under Russian rule, presented her girl students with the traditional course: *Haft-yak*, *Chor-Kitob*, and Navoiy. Perhaps more than in earlier times, literacy was emphasized. Saodat said that the Uzbek and Tatar girls learned to read "in Tatar, which is just like Uzbek," and to write. Saodat told of being punished by her mother for writing; evidently this was not a skill a girl was expected to develop under the tutelage of the otin. Bahriniso I. (b. 1910) studied in exactly the same way with an otin in the village of Sarai, near Andijon, in the early 1920s.[26]

As modern education spread, some parents seemingly came to believe that education with an otin ought to produce literacy. Malikaxon first studied for one year with an otin in Namangan, but when her illiterate mother, Hadija, asked Malika what she learned, she discovered her daughter did not know the alphabet. Hadija removed Malika and then, in 1918, placed her in a Jadid school, where she learned to read.[27]

## THE RUSSIAN-NATIVE SCHOOL

There was an alternative form of education for girls in Turkestan, one provided by the government. The Russian administration opened its first Russian-native schools in Turkestan in the 1870s. These were supposed to provide Turkestanis with education in Russian, in the curriculum of a Russian school, and with some lessons in their native language. The schools attracted very few Turkestani girls, and among those who did attend most were Kazakh. The sedentary communities continued to rely on their own domlas and otins. Bartol'd attributed the Russian-native schools' lack of success in attracting Turkestani children in part to these schools' inclusion of Christian religious instruction for Russian children and exclusion of Islamic religious instruction for Muslim children.[28] This may explain why parents infrequently chose to send sons to the Russian-native schools. Given the divide between native and Russian societies, with women as markers of native purity, it seems unlikely that parents would have considered sending daughters to these schools.

The Russian school system in Tashkent included the Women's Gymnasium, or Seminary, founded in 1879, providing higher education and some teacher training. With its entirely Russian curriculum, the Women's Seminary was even less successful at attracting Turkestani students than its male counterpart; in forty years only a handful of Central Asian girls attended.[29] However, the Women's Seminary did produce a few Muslim women teachers, including at least one who then taught in a Jadid school.[30] Several other Muslim graduates of the Tashkent Women's Seminary entered medical careers and later taught at the Tashkent Native Medic and Midwives School in the early 1920s.[31]

The Russian system graduated a handful of Turkestani women teachers, but the few families in Turkestan who wanted modern education for their daughters were more likely to choose a Jadid school than the Russian system, with its emphasis on Russian language and Orthodox Christianity. However, Jadid schools were rare and their existence precarious, and they had few means for producing the modern teachers they needed. For Jadids, the most significant divide between the otin and the mu'allima was the latter's formal training as a teacher. Graduates of Tatar women's reformed madrasas thus took up roles as mu'allimas for Turkestan.

When the Soviets established their government in Turkestan, with a slow beginning in Tashkent and gradual spreading of authority over more of Turkestan's territory, the Soviet Education Commissariat began opening schools in Turkestan. Like other government ministries, the Education Commissariat first took over existing resources and institutions, turning Russian state schools and private Jadid schools into Soviet schools. Between 1918 and 1922, the Soviet government seized waqfs and directed some of their wealth to the support of existing modern schools, now dubbed Soviet.[32] However, the Soviet state had limited reach and resources, and traditional maktabs and otin schools continued to attract more children than Soviet schools until 1927.

Madrasas and waqfs were supposed to have been shut down or confiscated just after the revolution, a plan that provoked most of the population's hostility. In fact, there was disarray in Turkestan's government from 1917 to 1920, followed by the disruptions of war between the Red Army and Basmachi groups. The Soviet government confiscated some properties, but either did not have sufficient control over Turkestan to close down the religious schools or lacked the will to try. In 1921, the Turkestan Communist Party decided not to interfere with waqfs that supported religious education, and in 1923 the government officially restored waqf properties that it had seized. The properties were returned with many strings attached, and the government increased its oversight of religious education. The move was a temporary retreat from radically antireligious policies and a strategic move to decrease anti-Soviet opinion and reduce popular support for Basmachis. Radical antireligious policies, including seizing waqfs, were put off until 1927.[33] In June 1923, the Education Commissariat counted 5,600 maktabs in Turkestan, with seventy thousand students.[34] The survey did not mention otins, whose numbers could not be ascertained, but they surely outnumbered the mu'allimas teaching in new-method and Soviet schools for girls.

Through the early 1920s, there was some confusion about which schools should be called Soviet and which should not. Many government and Party reports from the 1920s indicate that Islamic religious leaders were reorganizing their institutions and activities, including maktabs, in ways that would allow them to compete with the state educational institutions, though the reported rise in the numbers of students in religious schools in the mid-1920s cannot be documented, and reports came solely from opponents of this religious revival.[35] In some regions, the education budget supported "reformed" schools that taught modern subjects and religion and even schools that taught only religion. In official documents from the 1920s, all sorts of schools were denoted "Soviet," when those attending them would have regarded them as Jadid schools or traditional maktabs.[36]

Jadid schools for girls, and even some otin schools for girls, became Soviet schools for girls, generally without changing teachers and with a gradual change in curriculum. For example, the Mukai School for Muslim girls in Tashkent had been established in 1904, and it became part of the Soviet school system. A list of Soviet schools included the Nijat girls' school in Tashkent's Beshag'och neighborhood, which offered an otin's curriculum: "national language, ethics, and handwork." The curriculum at Umar al-Khayam girls' school in Tashkent was that of a Jadid school: national language, math, handcraft, ethics, singing, drawing, history, geography, science. It can be assumed that "ethics" meant religious education—Quran, prayers, and proper behavior. Both Nijat, an otin school, and Umar al-Khayam, a Jadid school, were supported by the state as Soviet schools. In 1919 there were forty-eight state-sponsored primary schools for Muslim children in old city Tashkent, and the number grew to sixty-six the next year.[37]

Although the Soviet Education Commissariat opportunistically made use of existing schools in forming its system, and Jadid schools, equally opportunistically, took advantage of state support, Soviet educational goals would not be satisfied by reformed Islamic schools. Education commissars made transforming the teacher the key to creating an education system that was Soviet in ethos. Teacher training courses and schools made possible the rapid expansion of primary education, as well as a thorough change in the content of education.

The first Turkestani women teachers with modern training graduated from the Xotin-Qizlar Bilim Yurti, or Women and Girls' House of Knowledge (hereafter Bilim Yurt). The Bilim Yurt's founding is somewhat obscure, but it grew out of a teachers' training course.[38] The teachers in this course were individuals who had been involved with education for Muslim girls for years. Zahida Burnasheva and Gavhar Alieva organized the course in Tashkent in 1919. Burnasheva was Uzbek, born in 1895; she had established a girls' school in a village near Qatta Qurg'on (Samarkand) before the revolution, and became a Communist Party member in 1918.[39] In its early years, the Bilim Yurt's teachers were mainly Tatar mu'allimas; there were also a few Uzbek Jadid men and women. The language of instruction depended on the teacher, so most classes and textbooks were in Tatar.[40]

In 1917, Tatar women in Muslim women's societies in Samarkand and Moscow proposed that Tatar mu'allimas should be recruited to teach in Turkestani girls' schools. Between 1917 and 1920 Tatar teachers took many teaching positions in newly opened schools in Tashkent. In 1923, of twelve teachers on the Bilim Yurt faculty, seven were Tatar women. In 1920 there were nineteen state-supported primary schools in Tashkent that enrolled Turkestani girls. Of the thirty-five women who taught at these schools, twenty-three were Tatar.[41]

In its first years, the Bilim Yurt attracted Muslim girls without preference by ethnic group, and the majority of students were Tatar, but by 1922 Uzbek girls were numerically dominant. The relationship between Tatars and Turkestanis, while often cooperative, had never been without tension. Some Turkestanis regarded Tatars as Russified and as agents of Russian domination, and some considered Tatars to be insensitive to Turkestani identity and cultural values. There was also jealousy: many educated Tatars who came to Turkestan found positions in journalism and education, and Turkestanis may have recognized that they would lose in competition for positions to Tatars who knew Russian.

By 1922, friction between Tatars and Turkestanis resonated in the Bilim Yurt, and the Education Commissariat proposed "to transfer all Tatars (f.) from the Uzbek Women's House of Enlightenment to a Tatar House of Enlightenment."[42] The proposal was not enacted; the number of Tatar students at the Bilim Yurt remained steady, and students from other ethnic groups—Kyrgyz, Uyghur, and Tajik—increased. But the school's name changed to the *Uzbek* Women and Girls' Bilim Yurt, and there was a proposal that non-Uzbeks be limited to 10 percent of the school's enrollment.[43]

Leadership of the school changed frequently in its first years, and so did the teaching staff. In 1922, Moscow cut off the financial subsidy for schools in Turkestan, and numerous teachers left their positions throughout the school system because salaries were not paid. Many schools closed, and the Bilim Yurt lost teachers and students, but recovered and began growing within two years.[44] Until the late 1920s, the Bilim Yurt's directors were strongly associated with the Jadid movement, and some later were arrested as Uzbek nationalists.[45]

Rahbar-oi, who studied at the Bilim Yurt, recalled that she began her education with her otin grandmother, and in about 1916 she enrolled in a Jadid school where boys and girls studied together. Some of the instructors at this school were Ottoman Turks, prisoners of war who were able to work outside their colony in Tashkent. She said, "The Bolsheviks came. They threw out all the Turks, and closed the Jadid school. In its place they made a Soviet school." When Rahbar-oi was twelve, and orphaned, her older brothers decided she should attend a girls' school. "At the girls' school, educated people gave lessons, educated women. The women's movement was very small, and so we brought in Tatars. There were many evacuees from Tataristan who were very educated, and they began to teach." Then a friend of Rahbar-oi's family, the Uzbek woman activist Bashorat Jalilova, came to the Tatar girls' school to recruit students for the Bilim Yurt. Rahbar-oi studied there for several years, withdrew, and returned after three years. The school had changed so much in her absence, about 1923 to 1926, that she did not recognize it as the same institution. The Bilim Yurt had moved to larger quarters, tripled in size, and had new leadership.[46]

In the first few years after the revolution, the republic-level Turkestan Education Commissariat's strategy for producing as many women teachers as quickly as possible was to establish three- to six-month training courses to turn women who could already read and write into literacy teachers. Zahida Burnasheva, who directed the Bilim Yurt in its first two years, described students in the first course there as "fifteen-year-old girls and forty-year-old women, including semiliterate and completely illiterate."[47] But the Bilim Yurt also attracted well-prepared students, like Tojixon Rustambekova. Tojixon's father, Rustambek Hojio'g'li, and her stepmother, Habiba Yusupova, after teaching boys in the new method, opened a Jadid school for girls in Tashkent. Yusupova's school became a state-supported Soviet school, and Tojixon was studying there when Gavhar Alieva, one of the Bilim Yurt's founders, recruited her for teacher training. While she was still a student, Tojixon taught math classes at the Bilim Yurt, and she was one of the first graduates, in 1923.[48]

The Bilim Yurt's purpose was to produce women teachers trained in modern subjects and teaching methods. It accepted girls who were teenagers and older who had several years of school—preferably, though not exclusively, new-method schooling—and trained them in a four-year course equivalent to middle school. The Bilim Yurt graduated its first group after only three years: "taking into consideration that presently the conditions of life do not permit Uzbek women to be in school for a long time—on the one hand there is early marriage, and on the other, family life—therefore, it is more sensible to abbreviate the school year and to give the majority of students the possibility of finishing the institute."[49] Numbers of students enrolled at the Bilim Yurt fluctuated, but were disproportionately high compared to the number that graduated and were certified to teach. In 1923, the school had a dormitory and 220 students, but when graduation took place in October only 7 women took degrees, "all that were left of 24 in the class."[50] With such a high dropout rate, the school's plan to speed graduation obviously addressed a concern that a longer course might never graduate any women. In 1925, the Bilim Yurt graduated 12, and in 1926 14 teachers, a tiny trickle when the school enrolled 600 students.[51]

The first group of graduates included some ambitious women who became leaders of the Uzbek intelligentsia. Tojixon Rustambekova, mentioned above, graduated in this group and went on to become an academic. She remembered that she and her companions wore their paranjis to graduation and were photographed thus for the newspapers. Her fellow graduates included Robiya Nosirova, who later directed the Bilim Yurt, and Manzura Sobir qizi, who became famous as a poet and playwrite under the pseudonym Oidin.[52]

While the number of graduates produced by the Bilim Yurt was small, not only graduates became teachers. The need for teachers in girls' primary schools and literacy courses was so great that students at the Bilim Yurt and at other schools were assigned teaching responsibilities. Bilim Yurt students helped to organize girls' schools in Tashkent, teaching in the morning and studying in the afternoon. When Rahbar-oi returned to the Bilim Yurt after marrying, she impressed the faculty with her entrance examination and was immediately assigned to teach at Bibi Xonum girls' school in the Beshag'och neighborhood in Tashkent. She studied at the Bilim Yurt in the afternoons. Similarly, Malika-xon, who entered the fifth level of Soviet school in Namangan after her primary years in a Jadid school, almost immediately began studying for a teacher's certificate in the afternoon while attending regular classes in the morning. She earned her teaching certificate before finishing middle school, and she taught in a primary class in the morning while studying in the upper grades at the same school in the afternoon. Chinnixon Ibrahimova (b. 1908), whose mother, Turaxon, placed her in a boarding school in Kokand in 1919, began teaching evening literacy classes for women when she was fifteen years old and in her fourth year of Soviet school.[53]

Brief teaching courses served to train literate women to teach in literacy courses and schools that offered the most basic primary education. Literacy was a cornerstone of the Communist Party's program for transforming society throughout the Soviet Union, and in 1920 the All-Russian Extraordinary Commission to Abolish Illiteracy began organizing literacy programs. The literacy commission in Turkestan, and then Uzbekistan, approached the task of producing literacy teachers with haste and practicality. It was far easier make literacy teachers out of already literate women and men who had studied with an otin or domla than it was to fully train a student in modern subjects and teaching methods. Girls who studied with otins were more numerous than those in state schools, and the brief literacy courses attracted young women like Bahriniso I., who had studied four or five years with her village otin. Bahriniso I. was married at age fifteen to a young man from a scholarly family, and he took her to Andijon where he was studying. In 1925, she enrolled in a three-month "End Illiteracy" course in Andijon and immediately became a teacher in literacy courses.[54] These three-month courses were one of the main services offered by the women's clubs that the Women's Division of the Communist Party organized, and women also attended literacy classes in workplaces and at neighborhood schools.

Brief teaching courses also allowed otins, as well as women who were teaching in state schools with only an otin-school background, to transform themselves into modern teachers. Habiba Yusupova began teaching girls in 1914 at a new-method school that she and her husband, Rustambek Hojio'g'li, founded. In 1918, she was one of three teachers in a state-supported school for girls in Tashkent. The school's other two teachers were Tatar women with "middle education," but Yusupova claimed only "lower education." In 1924–1925, the Bilim Yurt offered a six-month evening course for teacher training. Yusupova entered as a student and was taught by her former pupil and stepdaughter, Tojixon Rustambekova.[55]

## CLOSING THE DOOR

The Soviet system needed teachers, and otins and domlas apparently were admitted to the ranks with few questions in the early 1920s. Brief and repeated training courses began to transform the otin into a Soviet teacher. But by the mid-1920s, schools came under increased supervision, and after 1927 all religious subjects were excluded. The otin who would become a Soviet teacher had to abandon religious instruction (though not all did so).[56] In some places, teachers had to disavow religion formally. A set of personnel questionnaires for teachers in the Khiva region in 1928 included the questions, "What do you consider religion to be?" and "Since when have you been an atheist and among whom have you conducted anti-religious propaganda?" Most respondents gave answers that reflected a bit of atheistic education, explaining that religious traditions enslaved people or that religion served capitalist interests. Several commented that religion served no purpose in life, but answered "no" to the question concerning when they became irreligious.[57] Most religious teachers probably never went through the transformation into Soviet teachers. Instead, they took other work, and some continued their activities as religious teachers in private.[58]

By the late 1920s, the antireligious campaign was underway in Uzbekistan, as elsewhere in the Soviet Union. Pragmatically, the Party's need for tacit cooperation with and even tolerance of religious figures had diminished, and a wave of clergy arrests began.[59] In September 1927, the Uzbekistan Communist Party declared its intention to close down religious institutions, including schools:

12. As a result of the agitation and growth in influence of the so-called progressive part of the clergy, making full use of the apparatus of the Spiritual Directorate, in recent times we have obvious growth in old-method, reformed and clergy schools: qori-xona, madrasas, etc., and in some places the growth of this network of schools is taking place to the detriment of Soviet schools. Taking into consideration that one of the main reasons for the growth of the reformed schools is the inadequacy of our school network, which cannot absorb all children of school age, and its incorrect organization, before us stands a whole list of problems in the area of building our schools and improving their quality . . .

17. Considering the danger of reformed schools, in the future the reform of confessional schools should not be permitted under any circumstance, and in regard to already reformed schools, it is considered necessary to take all measures toward their closing, both by means of opening new Soviet schools in the same region (attract-

ing pupils in old-method schools to Soviet), and likewise forbidding the teaching of religious subjects in reformed schools, and in general, teaching by members of the clergy.[60]

Soviet schools could not compete successfully with reformed religious schools and disapproved of the muddling that went on with the retraining of religious teachers; the Party's Central Committee gave these as reasons for closing down all religious education. Although some otins joined the Soviet teaching ranks, Party members who worked with women tried to exclude otins from anything connected to the Women's Division. Women's Division workers were instructed to reduce the numbers of influential older native women in the new activities for women and to concentrate their efforts on attracting young women. In 1923, Serafima Liubimova, head of the Women's Division for the Central Asian Bureau of the Communist Party, reported that there was an internal argument over whether to "use the local intelligentsia" in cultural enlightenment work among women.[61] While in 1920 the Soviet educational system had to accept any literate person as a teacher, by the late 1920s Uzbek Soviet schools were beginning to graduate the first groups of girls from four-year elementary programs. These girls were hurried into courses to become literacy and primary teachers. Although numbers of Soviet teachers in Uzbekistan remained low into the 1930s, otins were no longer essential to the educational system, and antireligious pressure also forced many to cease teaching girls privately. Otins continued to fill religious roles, reciting for women during funerals and other life-cycle events, but they feared teaching young girls, whose parents equally feared sending their daughters to the otin. Otin education did not disappear entirely, but became a secretive matter, kept within the family.[62]

Manzura H.'s account of her upbringing illustrates this moment in the 1920s when repression of religious knowledge began to impinge directly on Uzbek daily life. Manzura's father, an Uzbek Communist, was away from the family for several months in 1927 or 1928, when Manzura was a child of six or seven. She lived in an extended family that shared a courtyard. In the mornings, Manzura would have tea with her uncle, just after he returned from morning prayer at the mosque. Her uncle would bring two friends home with him, both Islamic scholars, and the three would discuss the Quran. "I began learning a little," said Manzura, and "started saying the prayers a bit from this . . . but when my father found out, he forbade it. Forbade it. Because if a Communist's child is allowed to learn a surah of the Quran—I might go brag of it to other children. And then my father would get a letter, they'd throw my father out of the Party for this." Although Manzura was no longer allowed to visit her uncle for his morning tea and Quran sessions, her uncle continued to meet with his ulama friends until the three of them were arrested in 1931. Thus, although Manzura's father had a madrasa education and her mother and grandmother recited prayers, the transmission of religious knowledge ended with Manzura.[63]

While the Soviet state built on existing resources in constructing a modern school system in Uzbekistan, both the goals of education and the ideology imbuing education changed dramatically between 1917 and 1927. Before the revolution, Uzbek girls whose parents decided they should be schooled usually studied the curriculum of the maktab, with its emphasis on repetition and religious knowledge, under the tutelage of an otin. Jadid reformers in Turkestani society began to challenge the dominance of this form of education, calling instead for the creation of a modern school, where girls would be taught by a trained woman teacher, or mu'allima. The first Soviet schools for Uzbek girls were Jadid schools, and even some otin schools, that found state support. The challenge for the Soviet school system was to transform otins and mu'allimas, as well as their pupils, into Soviet educators. This entailed establishing a variety of courses, from brief training in literacy, to middle schools designed for teacher training. One of those institutions, the Uzbek Women and Girls' Bilim Yurt, became not only a base for producing women teachers, but also a center for shaping young Uzbek women to become activists and to enter the Communist Party. As the Soviet school became more secure, its leadership worked to shed the religious values that many of its teachers still held. Not content to shake off the influence of the otin and domla, the republic-level education ministry also discredited the whole Jadid approach to education and argued that the Soviet approach, free from religion and open to all children regardless of class, was superior.[64] A generation of young women who entered the Soviet system from otin schools formed the cadres who would expand literacy widely to women in the 1930s, but they also were left with an ambivalent heritage and an uncertainty about how to represent their own education. Denying the value of the otin was one way to assert the exclusive value of modern Soviet education.

# ❧ 5 ❧

# NEW WOMEN

A N ILLUSTRATED STORY ABOUT
a victim of superstition appeared in *Yangi Yo'l*, a magazine by and for
Uzbek women published by the Women's Division of the Communist
Party of Uzbekistan. The story itself represents one of the positions on
which Jadids and Communists in Uzbekistan found common ground.
As discussed in chapter 4, both were modernizers, and both saw many
of women's practices as backward and requiring eradication so that
women could become modern. The annual spring festival, referred to
as Sayil or Navruz, was an occasion when women gathered in each other's
courtyards for feasting and celebration. During the festival, women would
stay up all night cooking, singing, and dancing, and those who attended
the festivities would jump over the fire. The illustrated story indicates
that women associated beliefs with these rituals, viewing jumping over
the fire as a purification rite. For their own reasons, both Jadids and
Communists condemned these folk beliefs and practices, Jadids because
they represented superstition, meaning wrong belief, in the form of
accretions to or misunderstandings of Islam; and Communists, who also
viewed them as superstition, meaning the illogical, irrational beliefs and
practices of the uneducated.

The Uzbek women who were editors of *Yangi Yo'l* combined Jadid background with their own gradually formed understanding of Communism.

"Uzbek women and girls consider the month of Safar dangerous and bad; they try not to have weddings or new beginnings in this month."

*Top right:* "Did you all leap over the puppy? Yes, we leapt over. May all the evil spirits that roam in the month of Safar be buried with it."

*Top left:* "May all our woes and blessings be poured out with this libation."

*Bottom right:* "Children, you jump over [the fire] too, and all your sins will fall away."

*Bottom left:* "Oh no! Now what will I do? I tripped and fell because I was hurrying!" *Yangi Yo'l,* no. 10 (1926).

ﻮﺍﺑﻲ ﻗﻮﻟﻲ ﺑﺎﻟﺎﻡ ﻛﻮﻳﺐ ﻛﻴﺘﺪﻱ. ﺗﻴﺰﺭﺍﻕ —ﺱ؟ﺯ
ﺳﻮ ﻛﻠﺘﺮﺏ، ﺗﯚﺳﺘﻴﺪﻳﻦ ﺗﯚﻳﻜﻼﺭ.

— ﺗﺎﻧﺎﻓﻖ ﺗﻮﻟﺴﯚﻥ ﺑﺎﻟﻴﻢ، ﺗﺎﻧﺮﺍﻧﻴﻢ ﺑﺎﻟﻴﻢ.
ﻛﻴﻠﺪﻩﮔﻴﻦ ﺑﻠﺎﺩﻥ ﻗﻮﺗﻘﺎﺭﻣﺎﻗﻦ ﺗﻴﺐ، ﺳﻔﻘﺮ ﺑﻠﺎﺳﻴﻚ
ﺗﯚﺟﺮﻩﻣﺘﺪﻡ ﺑﺎﻟﻴﻢ...

ﺧﻮﺭﺍﻓﺎﺕ ﻗﯘﺭﺑﺎﻧﻲ ﮔﯚﺭﮔﻪ ﺗﺎﻟﺐ ﺑﺎﺭﺍﺩﻳﺮﻟﺎﺭ.

*Top right:* "Oh, no! My child is all aflame! Quick, bring water and pour it on her!"

*Top left:* "Oh, that your mother would die, my child! By trying to deter future tragedies, I brought on Safar's fate!"

*Bottom:* "The victim of superstition is carried to the tomb." *Yangi Yo'l,* no. 10 (1926).

They associated the Women's Division and its mission with their own transformation into "new women" who promoted modern education and public roles for women and condemned what they considered the ignorant and harmful lifestyles of other Uzbek women. In this melodramatic story, the girl who jumped the fire to be purified of her sins instead perished in the flames.[1] For educated Uzbek women who were committed to modernizing their own society, nothing could so clearly express the need for mass education and abandonment of superstition as this story. This chapter introduces five of these new Uzbek women, all editors and contributors to *Yangi Yo'l*. It then depicts some of the themes that the magazine explored, themes that would have been familiar to Jadid writers: education for women, reforming marriage, rights, and moral agency.

In the 1920s the number of Uzbek women who aligned themselves with the Communist vision for the future was tiny. In a population of 4.7 million, a few hundred Uzbek women joined the Communist Party. A few thousand went to work in factories, joined the Komsomol (Communist Youth League), or were educated in Soviet schools. The Communist Party's main instruments for establishing interaction with Uzbek women were its local branches of the Women's Division and the Women's Division journal, *Yangi Yo'l*, or *New Path*. Local Women's Divisions set up literacy courses, handcraft working groups (*artels*), and clubs; while few women became Communists, many thousands occasionally participated in these programs. Uzbek women who became activists in the Women's Division joined their own concerns to Communist Party visions for women, seeking to transform Turkestani women into their image of the new Uzbek woman. That these activists were few in number does not mean they were unimportant; in the Soviet state, the active minority that associated with the Communist Party was the only group that could shape state policies and practices. Uzbek women activists (not all of whom were Communists) had some success in enacting their vision of the New Woman, using the tools that the Communist Party made available.

The Communist Party centered in Russia had its own vision of the New Woman, presented to its Russian-language audience by the women's magazines *Rabotnitsa* (Woman Worker) and *Krest'ianka* (Woman Peasant). In the 1920s, these publications took what Lynn Attwood calls "a 'rationalist' rather than a 'romantic' approach" to female identity and roles. Women were to join the male public sphere, and the magazines portrayed them gaining education and skills, becoming politicized, and going to work. They suggested that the New Woman's domestic work could be met "by living in communes or joining cooperatives . . . to carry out domestic tasks collectively."[2] *Yangi Yo'l* drew on the models of these other Women's Division–sponsored publications, but its Uzbek editors emphasized a New Woman who had a distinctive sociocultural location. Unlike their Russian counterparts, they assumed the continuation of families, private houses, and women's primary roles as mothers; communes were far indeed from their experience and imagination.

## THE WOMEN'S DIVISION

The Women's Division of the Uzbekistan Communist Party (CPUz) fell under the leadership of the larger umbrella organization, the Women's Division of the Central Asian Bureau (CAB) of the Communist Party, which in turn was overseen by the central, Moscow-based All-Union Women's Division. The CAB placed in leadership "Russian" Communists—women who were appointed by the Central Committee in Moscow and sent to Tashkent for several-year assignments to oversee and coordinate Women's Division activities throughout Central Asia, to be the enforcers of Moscow's policies, and to act as the bridge of communication between the Party's center and the periphery.[3] By contrast, the CPUz Women's Division drew directors and leaders from the local population—Uzbek and Tatar women and Russians who were raised in Turkestan and knew the language.[4] Communication was a central problem for the Women's Division; Russians who came to Central Asia depended on translators, and Uzbeks who worked for the Women's Division knew about central policies of the Women's Division only when those were translated.[5] While other historians have examined Russian writings about Uzbeks, especially from the Russian-language journal of the All-Union Women's Division, *Kommunistka*, this chapter is concerned with what Uzbek women wrote about themselves, primarily in the journal *Yangi Yo'l*, and the ways they understood and promoted radical changes for other Uzbek women.[6]

Throughout the Soviet Union, both the Party and the people were wary of the Women's Division, which for most of its eleven-year existence struggled to justify its work. Many Party members thought that separate work among women would lead to feminism rather than to socialist equality. Much of the public, regardless of nationality, considered Women's Division programs insidious to family life and moral-ity.[7] The All-Union Women's Division promoted and publicized its tasks among women in Central Asia, using these to make a case for Party support. *Kommunistka* devoted a whole section in nearly every issue to articles about Central Asia, the Caucasus, and Siberia, featuring the backwardness of the eastern nationalities and the Women's Division's success in rescuing those oppressed women from abuse and ignorance.[8] Meanwhile, at least until 1928, the CAB Women's Division struggled to portray its work as humanitarian and relatively nonthreatening to social structures.[9] *Yangi Yo'l* consistently presented the CPUz Women's Division as a positive, progressive organization, and directed its criti-cisms toward other Party organizations for providing inadequate sup-port and toward all the enemies of progress for women.[10]

Early in 1924, a young Uzbek writer proposed establishing a society for women that would "accept all women without attention to whether they are Party or non-Party, poor or rich," and that would publish a jour-nal especially for Turkestani women. He wrote, "Someone who knows the Uzbek soul better should be made the leader of the Women's Divi-sion. Let them even be educated Uzbek women."[11] The main leader-ship roles in the CAB Women's Division continued to be filled by Russian women, Party members who did not know Uzbek. But in 1925, the CPUz Women's Division established *Yangi Yo'l*, a magazine for Uzbek women, edited by educated Uzbek and Tatar women who were mostly not mem-bers of the Party. In 1926, the CPUz named an Uzbek woman to head its Women's Division, which in its programs made little distinction about class or Party membership.

After the delimitation of the Central Asian republics, and with the creation of Uzbekistan, Uzbek women were no longer part of an undif-ferentiated mass of "eastern" women. Instead, they were the primary inter-est of the CPUz Women's Division. *Yangi Yo'l* was published only in Uzbek and was implicitly and explicitly for and about Uzbek women and girls. The journal defined Uzbek women and advocated for their interests. In the 1920s atmosphere of Uzbek nationalism, *Yangi Yo'l* inscribed wom-anhood with nationality, and nation-building with gender. Few of the writers for *Yangi Yo'l* had any experience with the Soviet Union outside Uzbekistan, and while they insisted that women of all nationalities were equal, they also made it clear that non-Uzbeks in Uzbekistan should accommodate to Uzbek ways by learning the language.[12]

# YANGI YO'L'S EDITORS

*Yangi Yo'l* had strong connections with the Uzbek Women and Girls' Bilim Yurt. In September 1924, when *Yangi Yo'l* was still a wall newspaper (posted on display boards as a means of distribution), Sobira Xoldarova, a young Uzbek woman and Bilim Yurt student, was appointed editor. Her fellow graduate, Manzura Sobir Qori qizi (Oidin), was on the editorial board. Robiya Nosirova, a 1923 Bilim Yurt graduate, became editor in 1926. Hosiyat Tillaxonova, another 1923 classmate, was a regular contributor and joined the editorial board in 1929. Tojixon Shodieva was the chief editor of *Yangi Yo'l* during the Hujum, but unlike her fellow editors she was not one of the Bilim Yurt's graduates. Like other daughters of urban Uzbek and Tajik families, these editors were given in marriage as teenagers. By the time they worked for *Yangi Yo'l* they were in their late teens and early twenties, most were mothers, and some were divorced. Of these five, only Xoldarova knew Russian well; Shodieva and Xoldarova were Party members. These women's own concerns and experiences shaped the images that they produced for other Uzbek women. Above all, they were dedicated to women's education. They were also ardent supporters of unveiling.[13]

*Yangi Yo'l*'s first editor, Sobira Xoldarova (b. 1907, Chust), was an ideologue. Unlike many of her Uzbek colleagues at the journal, she sought to communicate the Moscow-centered version of the Party's policies toward women. Xoldarova went to work as a housemaid in Kokand when she was thirteen years old. There she and her widowed mother came into contact with Party representatives who placed Xoldarova in a children's home. As a Bilim Yurt student from 1923 to 1925, Xoldarova edited the school's Komsomol newspaper, *Red Bell*, and also edited *Yangi Yo'l*. She greeted her acceptance to candidacy for Party membership in 1924 by unveiling publicly. She became a Party member while she was studying in Moscow in 1927. She studied Russian at the Bilim Yurt and may have known it well enough to use it in her work with Serafima Liubimova, the Russian head of the CAB Women's Division, when they were founding *Yangi Yo'l*. Her education in Moscow solidified her knowledge of Russian, as well as of Party doctrine. She contributed articles to the Uzbek press on Lenin, on women's liberation, and on the struggle against religion, as well as translating Nadezhda Krupskaia's writings into Uzbek.[14]

Xoldarova was married and had a son when she left for Moscow at

Sobira Xoldarova. Photo published
in *Yer Yuzi*, no. 18 (1929): 13.

age nineteen. In her memoir, she wrote of her arrival in Moscow in 1926
and her first meeting with Krupskaia, who expressed interest in Uzbek
women: "When she [Krupskaia] learned that I had abandoned my family and my little son to study, she was a little taken aback. 'You won't run
away from here, now?' she asked. Mixing my words with Uzbek, I said
vehemently that I would not leave Moscow without getting higher education. Nadezhda Konstantinova believed me, shook my hand and wished
me success."[15] From Moscow Xoldarova contributed to the Uzbek press
articles that reflected her increasing knowledge of Party policies. She
returned to Uzbekistan in 1929 and became the main editor of *Yangi
Yo'l* when it was transferred from the Women's Division to the Division
of Agitation and Propaganda. She also edited the journal *The Godless*
(*Xudosizlar*) and headed the Society of the Godless in Uzbekistan in 1930.

In the 1930s, Xoldarova advanced in the CPUz ranks to become a
regional first secretary. She married a second time, to a prominent Communist, and after her arrest in the 1937 purge, she raised a daughter
in prison and exile in Siberia. She returned to Uzbekistan in the 1950s
and resumed work in the press.[16]

Oidin (Manzura Sobir Qori qizi, b. 1906, Tashkent), like many of
her *Yangi Yo'l* colleagues, came from the *ziyolilar*, the traditional intelli-

Oidin (Manzura Sobir Qori qizi).
Photo published in *Ma'orif va O'qituvchi*, no. 2 (1929): 40.

gentsia of Central Asia. She was not an ideologue or a Communist Party member, and at the Bilim Yurt she worked on the literary newspaper, not the Komsomol newspaper. Oidin's father was a qori, a Quran reciter. She followed in the family intellectual tradition, becoming a poet, but she broke with her father in 1925 when her modernizing values clashed with his traditional values. In March 1925, her play, *A Step toward Modernity*, was published, and its heroine advocated unveiling. In the same month, *Yangi Yo'l* published an article featuring Oidin as a new poet, along with her photograph with unveiled face. Her father barred her from his home for this public display. Oidin fully abandoned veiling several years later, when she traveled to Moscow in 1927.

In her poetry and in her stories in *Yangi Yo'l* from 1926 to 1929, Oidin was an advocate of the New Life, meaning modern education for children and liberation for women. For her, the Party's importance lay in its support for modernization and women's rights. But she was not apolitical. From 1927 to 1929, she studied in Samarkand at the Pedagogical Academy, where she mixed with other young writers in the literature department. She became a member of the Writers Union of Uzbekistan and was its Responsible Secretary from 1932 to 1937. The Writers Union was a very politicized organization, and its members continually denounced each other for deviations from ideological norms. Somehow Oidin, who did not join the Party until 1943, avoided the arrest wave of 1937. She continued writing poetry until her death in 1953.[17]

Robiya Nosirova (b. 1900, Tashkent), who graduated from the Bilim Yurt with Oidin in 1923, served on *Yangi Yo'l*'s editorial board in 1926 and 1927 and contributed numerous articles on education. Like Oidin, she came from a *ziyoli* family. In a memoir from 1960, she described her early education as "old method," meaning the traditional program with the otin or domla. But her further description was in fact of "new method" education, with boys and girls in the same school, reading modern texts: "I found girlfriends of my age who attended the women's class with me, while my brothers attended the men's class and learned to read newspapers and books."[18] She participated in the 1916 demonstrations against conscription. She opened a girls' school in her home and was still teaching in 1919 when she had the opportunity to enter the newly opened Bilim Yurt and become a Soviet teacher.

Having studied and taught in Jadid schools before the revolution, Nosirova embodied a link to the Jadids, and hence in her writing she refused to give sole credit to the Party for all progress for women. Nosirova did not include in her own memoir that she was married, very young, to the Jadid Abdulhai Tojiev and that in her new family she was known for reading newspapers and books aloud to everyone.[19]

Nosirova abandoned veiling in 1924, and there are two stories about this event. In the 1961 collection *Awakened by Great October* (*Probuzhdennye velikim Oktiabrem*), where friendship of Uzbeks and Russians was an important political theme, Nosirova reported that she unveiled when she took a group of Uzbek girls to Moscow to study in a theater program for Uzbeks. However, according to L. Azizzoda's collection of biographies of Uzbek intellectuals, Nosirova participated in a locally organized unveiling meeting in 1924 in the Beshqairag'och mahalla in Tashkent, along with many other women from ziyoli families.[20]

In 1927, Nosirova became director of the Bilim Yurt. She embodied the ideal of modern, educated Uzbek womanhood and was featured in articles and photographs in numerous Uzbek publications. Apparently Nosirova did not join the Party during the 1920s.[21] She directed her activism to organizing non-Party women and promoting girls' education. These were the themes of her articles in *Yangi Yo'l* and *Qizil O'zbekiston*. In the 1930s, when others of her cohort were swept into political

Robiya Nosirova.
Photo published in many 1920s Uzbek periodicals;
this image reproduced from *Ma'orif va O'qituvchi*, no. 7 (1927): 13.

campaigns, worked for collectivization, and lost their careers in the
purges, Nosirova pursued a much less dangerous career in technical
education.

Hosiyat Tillaxonova (b. 1907, Tashkent), who wrote for *Yangi Yo'l* from
its inception and was appointed to the editorial board in 1929, attended
the Bilim Yurt from 1919 to 1923 with Nosirova and Oidin. She did not
graduate with them in 1923, perhaps because about that time she married and had a son. Like Nosirova and Oidin, Tillaxonova was from a
ziyoli family and had close ties to Jadids; in the 1920s she was also closely
linked to the "nationalist" Uzbeks. Tillaxonova was a modernist, an aspir-
ing intellectual, and an activist. In her Bilim Yurt days, she wrote for the
school's literary newspaper, *New Life*, and later her poetry appeared in
*Yangi Yo'l*. She was better known as a journalist and was published in the
most widely read Uzbek publications, *Qizil O'zbekiston* (the leading newspaper), *Ma'orif va O'qituvchi* (the teacher's journal), *Yer Yuzi* (a literary
journal), and *Mushtum* (a political satire journal).

In 1925, when Kalinin, the head of the Soviet state, gave a speech in
Tashkent, he prompted Tillaxonova to remove her veil. She was seated
onstage with him, and he was an elderly man to be regarded with respect;

Hosiyat Tillaxonova.
Photo published in *Ma'orif va O'qituvchi*, no. 11 (1927): 13.

when he asked her to unveil, she could not have refused. As a student at the Central Asian Communist University and a Komsomol member in 1925–1927, she organized unveiling meetings for wives of Komsomol members. In her writing and actions, she was an advocate of unveiling. She became a Party member in 1932.

Tillaxonova's elder brother, Salimxon, was a Jadid who directed the Bilim Yurt in 1922 or 1923. He was involved in Uzbek nationalist circles in the 1920s, was charged in a nationalist plot in 1929, and was executed.[22] Hosiyat Tillaxonova, as a Party member and editor of *Yangi Yo'l*, had plenty to worry about after her brother's arrest. In the 1930s, she stepped away from politically sensitive publications, and became editor of a textile industry paper. In 1937, during the wave of arrests, Tillaxonova died of natural causes.[23]

Tojixon Shodieva (b. 1905, Fargana[24]), chief editor of *Yangi Yo'l* in 1928–1929, had no connection with the Bilim Yurt. Unlike Oidin, Nosirova, and Tillaxonova, Shodieva was the abused woman rescued by the Communist Party. She was born into the family of a miner and was "sold" in marriage at age eleven or twelve to a man who already had several wives. Somehow, she learned to read and write. One biography says that she studied "privately," probably meaning with an otin. After the revolution, her husband joined the militia and then became a Communist Party member. When he went to Tashkent to study, he took

Shodieva with him. There she became a Komsomol member, studied at the Party school in 1921, and began to work for the Women's Division and the Komsomol organizations in 1922.

Shodieva gained a broad acquaintance with Uzbekistan through her Party work. Between 1922 and 1926, the Party sent her from Kokand to Khiva to work for the Women's Division. In 1925 she became a member of the newly organized CPUz, and she participated in its first congress. Her political career was much more important than her role as an editor. She quickly rose into leadership of the CPUz Women's Division. In 1926, when the Hujum was announced (see chapter 7), Shodieva was appointed to the seven-member committee to direct this campaign "attacking the old ways" in Uzbekistan, and she was also appointed to the Central Committee of the CPUz.

Shodieva was editor of *Yangi Yo'l* because she headed the CPUz Women's Division, not because she had a passion for journalism. However, she contributed articles, and *Yangi Yo'l*'s ardent support for unveiling in 1928 and its advocacy of a law banning the veil in 1929 certainly reflected Shodieva's position. There are several stories about Shodieva's own unveiling. According to one account, when she attended a Komsomol congress in Moscow in 1924, other delegates asked her to unveil and she did. However, another biographer adds that she re-veiled when she returned to Kokand and stopped wearing her paranji sometime between 1924 and 1926. She divorced her abusive husband around the same time and later married again. In the 1930s, she worked in a Fargana Valley Machine and Tractor Station, the division that was in charge of organizing and leading propaganda on collective farms. She became a regional first secretary and, along with much of the Uzbek Party leadership, she was arrested in 1937. Like Xoldarova, she spent eighteen years in Siberian prison and exile. When she returned to Uzbekistan in the 1950s she was readmitted to the Party, but worked as a collective farm director.[25]

Editors for *Yangi Yo'l*, like other Uzbek activists in the 1920s, came from two sources. There were new women from Jadid-influenced families, like Tillaxonova, Nosirova, and Oidin; and there were women like Xoldarova and Shodieva, who owed their transformation into new women to the Communist Party and its Women's Division. Both Jadids and Soviets were ideologically committed to the modern, and each rejected the past. Like Jadids, activists for the Soviet system sometimes advocated education for women and girls so that they would be good mothers, bringing children up in an enlightened way for the good of the nation, rather than emphasizing Communist doctrine on the social transformation of women.

In accounts from the 1920s through the 1960s, there was a conscious effort to boost Soviet accomplishments in education by portraying all that preceded the Soviet system as utterly ineffective.[26] This began with a Communist Party political attack on Jadidism in the mid-1920s; by the late 1920s, those associated with the government knew they were supposed to assess Jadidism as based in the bourgeois class and uninterested in educating the masses. By the 1930s, those who found success in Soviet structures, like Nosirova, shaped their autobiographies to project the required class background, and thus writers and politicians who came from ziyoli families presented fictional pasts of poverty and ignorance, narratives in which they owed all their success, and hence loyalty, to the Soviet system. But in the 1920s, this image was just being formed, and the editors of *Yangi Yo'l*, who came from diverse educational backgrounds, disagreed about how to represent Uzbek education for women. While Nosirova and other ziyolilar affirmed the connection between Jadid and Soviet goals for women's education, Xoldarova and others from the Communist side rejected any such assertion, insisting instead on the new Soviet anti-Jadid orthodoxy.[27]

Although the varied backgrounds of these women activists sometimes divided them, their goals for women, as far as can be known from their own writings, were fairly unified: they wanted women to know their rights, to unveil, to become educated, to enter public life through work or activism, and not to be forced into unwanted marriages. The new Uzbek woman, like the Jadids' modern woman, was radical by comparison with most Uzbeks, but these activists strove to make their vision of women's roles understandable and acceptable to Uzbek society.

A JOURNAL FOR UZBEK WOMEN

*Yangi Yo'l* was published for an audience whose literacy rate was quite low. In the 1920s perhaps 10 percent of urban Uzbek women could read, but in rural areas (where 85 percent of the population lived) the rate was 1 percent. The editors knew that many articles would be read aloud in Women's Division clubs, teahouses, factories, and at various gatherings.[28] Writers considered their audience, and those who wrote in high literary style in other publications—like Oidin, Tillaxonova, and

ЖУРНАЛ
Янги-Юл № 7-8.
На узбекском языке.

مدر بر خدتی ـ ساوادی بار خاتن ـ قزلارنك «يدنگی يول»
جورنالينی ئوقشلاری لازم·

"Every woman and girl who is literate should read *Yangi Yo'l*."
Back cover of *Yangi Yo'l*, no. 7–8 (1926).

Xoldarova—kept their prose simpler for *Yangi Yo'l*.[29] Stories, poems, and biographies presented scenes familiar to Uzbek women, with words chosen for emotional effect.

*Yangi Yo'l*'s lead article was usually a political piece, often a translation of an article or speech by a Russian Women's Division leader or an Uzbek politician's International Women's Day speech. Otherwise, the journal received solicited and unsolicited contributions of fiction, poetry, biography, and news from regional women's meetings. There were articles on science, medicine, health, women's education, child rearing, women in workplaces, and women in other countries. Most contributors were women; there were also occasional stories and poems from the young generation of male Uzbek writers, including

Elbek, Ramiz, Miyon Bo'zruk, and G'afur G'ulom.[30] The journal was similar in structure and layout to women's journals for other audiences in the Soviet Union, such as the magazine for Russia's women workers, *Rabotnitsa*.

*Yangi Yo'l* produced images of the modern Uzbek woman and her antithesis, the oppressed, backward Uzbek woman. Uzbek women in the magazine's pages were made into living, interpretable myths, inspiring the reader either by dying tragically at the hands of enemies or by overcoming oppression, defeating superstition, tradition, and men and entering the New Life. Uzbek women appeared in work situations, political and public life, and in education. Modern Uzbek women joined handcraft collectives, attended school, and fought oppressive men in court. Backward Uzbek women were at the mercy of malicious otins and fortune tellers and became victims of tradition.

## MODERNITY AND EDUCATION: INVENTING THE NEW WOMAN

*Yangi Yo'l* was a Communist Party organ whose authors steered away from ideology, trying instead to popularize their work among women. Rather than explain Communism in any complex way, the journal advocated modernity, the New Life. In the 1920s, young Uzbeks formed New Life societies where they tried to change gender-segregated patterns by holding family evenings that husbands and wives attended together. Much of the New Life that *Yangi Yo'l* promoted resembled Jadid modernity, in which everyone would become educated, read newspapers, and abandon superstitions. Mothers would take children to doctors. Girls would not marry before age sixteen, and marriage would be companionate. But Soviet modernity demanded even more social change than Jadid modernity. In the New Life, women and men had equal rights that needed to be made into reality and vigorously enforced. In the New Life, women could become economically independent through wage earning and landownership. In the New Life, Uzbek women would abandon the paranji and join in public life.

*Yangi Yo'l*'s images of the Uzbek woman, backward and modern, were images that Uzbek women produced to convince society to embrace modernity in a national, Uzbek form. A journal by and for Uzbek women could only have come about with the invention of Uzbekistan, and its service to the idea of shaping the modern Uzbek nation did not always fit well with the internationalist modernism of its Communist Party sponsors. The editors published contributions from hesitant modernizers as well as radicals. The journal sometimes asserted a vision of the New Life with the zeal of Russia's cultural revolutionaries, but often advocated gradualism, a modernity in dialogue with tradition and Islam. After 1918, all media except underground tracts and leaflets were government or Party owned, but points of view represented in the Uzbek press, including *Yangi Yo'l*, varied considerably until late 1929.

*Yangi Yo'l*'s authors and editors used fiction and true accounts to convince readers that they should embrace modernity. Since the journal belonged to the Women's Division, this often meant the story's heroine found help through one of the Women's Division's projects. But authors themselves knew that living the New Life took courage, because it meant breaking with dominant social attitudes. Women could not be forced into modernity. A 1925 story, "To Work," portrayed a woman who overcame her fear about the Women's Division and its modernizing agenda. Zulpixon, a widow with children, was the type of woman who could benefit most from the Women's Division's provision of medical services for children and its work collectives. The neighborhood rumor that the Women's Division forced women to remove their paranjis almost deterred Zulpixon from seeking aid, but her concern for her son's health proved more powerful than her fear. After the doctor at the women's club clinic successfully treated her son, Zulpixon's trust grew, and she joined the women's work collective. By working, she was able to provide for her children and free herself from depending on the charity of rich neighbors. Zulpixon learned that, contrary to rumor, "no one had been converted to a new religion, and no one's chachvon was removed by force."[31]

Many of the stories in *Yangi Yo'l* followed a pattern that might be called a salvation narrative, quite similar to stories found in missionary literature and in socialist realism. Somehow, the oppressed woman came into contact with the Women's Division or with some representative of Soviet government, and her life changed. She was released from oppression and entered the New Life, which meant education, employment, or unveiling.

In one story, "She Opened a Way for Herself," the heroine Salomat was saved from her husband's abuse, economic oppression, and backwardness by a new institution: the women's cooperative store. The government tried to encourage women to join work collectives, but the collective ventures that attracted the most Uzbek women were cooperative shops. At the women's cooperative store, women could shop without having to interact with men. The stores had "mother and child" corners where women could obtain child-care items and information about raising infants. Because most Uzbek women did not go to the bazaars to sell or buy unless they were deprived of male support, some Women's Division workers regarded the stores as a stroke of genius. The shops for women maintained gender segregation but brought women out of their homes and allowed them to make their own financial decisions.

The *Yangi Yo'l* story opened with Salomat being beaten by her husband and screaming for help. The neighbor women, hearing her cries, asked why her husband beat her. Salomat responded that he was upset she had spent money to buy cloth. A neighbor offered a solution: "You needed to get cloth, so why did you go to a private shop? . . . They are evil people who not resist taking the very last coin from poor people like us . . . We now have our own cooperative store that opened for women and girls. If you go and become a member of this shop, you will be able to buy everything, and it is cheaper and better than at any other store." Salomat joined the women's cooperative store and was pleased by its low prices. She gave a speech explaining how the store struggled against merchant oppressors, and she was elected to the cooperative commission. Fotima, the store's manager, wanted to make Salomat assistant manager, but Salomat needed education. She attended a course at the Women's Division club and learned to read in two months. She became assistant manager of the cooperative, but she told Fotima that she planned to continue studying and become a *vakila*, a women's representative. Her neighbor women commented on all the changes in Salomat's life that came about because she joined the cooperative store. She was very happy, she had become educated, and her husband no longer beat her.[32]

Salomat's story contained a crude presentation of Marxist economics, but depicted her oppression first as gender based. *Kommunistka* and *Rabotnitsa*, two Russian-language Party journals for women, fought against feminism as a bourgeois program that put gender solidarity before class solidarity, the vote before economic change, and served the interests of the exploiting classes. But a serious interest in class conflict came late to the pages of *Yangi Yo'l*, where women's enemies were men. The most serious enemies were mullahs, rich merchant men, and *bois* (large landowners). But male peasants and workers, who were supposed to take Uzbek women's side in the struggle, were recognized as oppressors as well, although their actions were often interpreted as the result of powerful men's manipulations.[33] Until late in 1929, magazine articles rarely divided women by class. Men belonged to classes, men and women belonged to national groupings, but women were most often divided by cultural markers, into Uzbek and other, urban and rural, literate and illiterate, veiled and unveiled.

The experience of the Uzbek women who wrote for *Yangi Yo'l* told them that modern education was liberating. They gave much more enthusiastic support to education than to women's participation in the labor force, both as an end in itself and as the means to achieve success and political consciousness. In the story of Salomat, and in many others, the workplace was a route to education, and the heroine's transformation included gaining education and entering political activism.

## LAND FOR WOMEN

*Yangi Yo'l* published stories to inform women of their rights and for a time emphasized women's right to own land. Uzbekistan began carrying out land reform in 1925, taking land from large landowners and redistributing it to the sharecroppers and landless farm workers; and dehqons (farmers) were told that women would have the same right as men to own land. Propagandists composed simple tracts contrasting enlightened Soviet land law with pre-Soviet land law. They cited the inequality in Islamic inheritance laws, in which a daughter's share is one-half that of a son, noting that Soviet law made daughters equal to sons. In Central Asia's Islamic court archives, there are documents showing that women did inherit land, but these are often accompanied by others showing that the land quickly wound up in the hands of male relatives. A widow might keep a portion of her husband's land if she had sons who were old enough to farm it.[34] Interestingly, Soviet law was also biased in Central Asia. In Russia, land reform declared that Russian peasant husbands and wives were equal owners of shares in communal farms.[35] Michurina's article on Soviet land law and women said that "the land laws codex made the dehqon woman the owner of a land plot. A dehqon woman who works equally with men is the owner of this land and all the property and stock on it."[36] But in Central Asia, where there were no communal farms, Soviet law declared that household heads owned land, and so women only had a right to newly divided properties if, as widows or divorcées, they were household heads and if they could work the land themselves. The purpose of land reform was not to advance women's equality, but to win support for the government from smaller farmers, to reduce the property and power of the rich landowners, and to increase cotton production.[37]

Stories in *Yangi Yo'l* about women obtaining land were realistic in that the protagonists were widows. The story "Land for Women, Too," told of Tursun-buvi, her daughter Robiya, and her granddaughter, who all lived on the lands of a rich man, Tojiboi. The government gave them an equal share when Tojiboi's lands were confiscated and divided, but they needed to find a way to work the land if they were to keep it. Fortunately, Robiya knew that she could turn to the government for help in obtaining a plough, and Tursun-buvi had a lifetime of experience in farming. Their first crop was a success, and they were happy to be able to keep their land. Tursun-buvi said to her granddaughter, "In these days, we women have entered the ranks of humanity. It seems we women too have a right to land and water."[38]

The number of women who were newly granted property in land reform was very small, not exceeding by much the number of women who owned land before reform. To keep women's land from falling into men's hands, Party strategists tried to unite women smallholders in collectives that would be able to work the land, hire services, and take loans together. But landownership would have made a widow a more attractive marriage prospect, and women-only agricultural collectives proved unworkable even before mass collectivization ended individual landowning.[39]

MARRIAGE: COMBATING TRADITION

Before the revolution, Jadids gave considerable attention to the question of appropriate marriage and the appropriate marriage age for girls. The Uzbek modernists of the 1920s were as strongly convinced as the Jadids had been that science, not Islamic law, should determine this issue. In a 1918 set of regulations for Samarkand province, judges—both qazis (Islamic judges) and People's Court judges—were instructed not to perform marriages for minors, but the regulations left establishing who was a minor up to the judge.[40] Turkestan's legal code was supposed to accord with the law codes of the Soviet Union, but until 1924 there was an ongoing project in the Turkestan Commissariat of Justice to codify Sharia and to make Sharia compatible "with the conditions of modern life" and with Soviet law. Its proposals included allowing Muslim men up to four wives and establishing twelve as the minimum marriage age for girls, fourteen for boys.[41] In 1923, the Turkestan Communist Party recommended setting the legal age of marriage at sixteen for girls and eighteen for boys.[42]

When Uzbekistan was established, new legal codes were constructed. There was no longer any pretense about agreement between Sharia and Soviet law, but there was a lag of several years in adopting a code that set the marriage age limit and a period of three years when both Islamic and Soviet courts operated. During this time, the Justice Ministry held discussions of the new code among citizen groups to increase public awareness of the new laws. Moderators also solicited opinions concerning the marriage age. In reports, most groups approved sixteen for girls, but a few requested that this be raised to seventeen.[43]

Before the new code was adopted in 1928, contributors to *Yangi Yo'l* lobbied for their own convictions about marriage age. A doctor, Izzedin Seifulmuluk, offered a scientific assessment of the proper marriage age for girls by contrasting the age of physical maturity of Uzbek girls with Arab girls. He believed that physical maturation and age of first menstruation were connected to climate. He asserted that while girls in Arabia showed signs of puberty by age ten, the records of doctors in Tashkent showed that Uzbek girls began menstruation at fifteen or sixteen. Without stating it directly, he appealed to the Islamic reformist idea that Islamic law (which would permit girls to marry at age nine) was in rational accord with the needs of everyday life. He let stand the dubious assertion that girls in Arabia menstruated by age ten, meaning that Sharia was rational in its original context. But such a law would obviously be inappropriate in a setting where girls first menstruated at age fifteen. Seifulmuluk added that girls should not be married until their bodies were fully developed for bearing children without significant hardship, and he placed this at eighteen to twenty-one for Uzbeks. "This law of nature" was "stronger than any law." He concluded that the science of preserving health demanded that Soviet law establish the age of marriage for girls at "not less than eighteen."[44] The law establishing the marriage age for girls at sixteen was finally ratified in October 1928 and was widely flouted in practice.[45]

There were numerous reports in *Yangi Yo'l* about girl minors being rescued from coerced marriage, but the magazine's fiction writers were most interested in imagining companionate marriage. They shared the assumption that everyone should and would marry. In a society that flouted the law and continued to practice polygyny, coerced marriage, the marriage of minors, and the payment of qalin, the generation of believers in the New Life tried to create a modern vision of marriage.

Z. Bashiri's story, "On Freedom's Path," incorporated didactic and romantic elements to create an image of companionship in marriage based on class comradeship and shared values. The protagonist, Oyimniso, was a young village woman who was committed to the New Life and to a new kind marriage. Her father wanted her to marry the son of a wealthy landowner: "rather than [consider] his daughter's spiritual happiness, [he] would prefer to make connections between himself and men who lived for their own pleasure." She refused and instead married a farm laborer for love. Unfortunately, her husband died after two years, and Oyimniso was left with a choice between providing for herself by remarrying or by working. She joined a women's farm labor collective, and met a Komsomol member, Eshimqo'l. They were "class comrades," but one day Eshimqo'l expressed his love for Oyimniso, who always sang as she worked, by saying, "If only I could have a nightingale that sang with such a beautiful voice in my cage." Oyimniso objected to the idea of a cage, and asked Eshimqo'l to explain his meaning. He explained that he wanted her to be his "life partner" because of her noble heart and her work-loving nature. Still, Oyimniso was more interested in obtaining an education than marrying, and so Eshimqo'l, in true comradeship, made arrangements for Oyimniso to study for a year to become a silk factory specialist.

The author introduced modern values through Oyimniso's conversations with Eshimqo'l and with her girlfriends. Eshimqo'l joked that Oyimniso's education would drive up the amount of qalin he would have to give for her and that he would have to improve his own education to be her equal. She responded, in an echo of a hadith attributed to the Prophet Muhammad, "Your knowledge, according to the New Life, will be the qalin of marriage."[46] One of Oyimniso's girlfriends who was Russian, but who spoke Uzbek, expressed to Oyimniso her own hesitation over marrying Ergash, an Uzbek, because of nationality differences. Oyimniso asserted that "honest comradeship" was more important than anything else in marriage, including nationality. The author was not radical enough to have Oyimniso marry a non-Muslim man; in Islamic societies, the acceptable international marriage, at least theoretically, had always been one between a Muslim man and a non-Muslim woman.

Oyimniso's freedom of choice in marriage was probably far removed even from the lives of the Komsomol girls and Bilim Yurt students who were *Yangi Yo'l*'s main readers and contributors. Rahbar-oi, one of my oral history informants, told a story that was more representative of her generation. Her elder brother, Ga'fur G'ulom, was a young writer and an enthusiastic supporter of the government of Uzbekistan. He and his brothers arranged a marriage for Rahbar-oi. *Sovchis*, family representatives in the marriage arrangement process, came to her house to look her over and to show her photos of prospective husbands. She rejected numerous options (something not every girl could do), until a sovchi came representing a local Komsomol leader, and Rahbar-oi consented. She imagined that this marriage might follow the New Life model; she had friends who were making their own wedding arrangements and who were having "new-style" weddings. But her brother went to the ZAGS (civil registry) and registered the marriage for her. She met her fiancé once before the wedding, to get his promise that after their wedding he would agree to her continuing her studies.[47]

Among my Uzbek informants, most were married by arrangement, without much attention to marriage laws or personal consent. Bahrin-iso I., whose parents arranged a marriage for her in 1925, when she was fifteen, and registered at the ZAGS (civil registry) for her, said that no one asked whether she agreed to the marriage. Habibi Sh.'s parents arranged a marriage for her in 1935 when she was fifteen; local authorities gave her a document that attested she was seventeen so that she could pass through the registry. Local authorities in Kokand did the same for Humoira H., who was below marriage age when her father arranged her marriage to a distant relative. Mafrat-xon M., whose mother was an activist and who was a Komsomol member herself, had an arranged marriage when she was fifteen. Muhobat H., a teacher, was given in marriage at age sixteen to a man who had seen her once; her parents did not ask for her consent. Shamsiyat B. had an arranged marriage when she was in her twenties, during World War II; at her wedding, she found out that her husband, whom she had never met before, already had one wife. Many of those informants justified their arranged marriages: several said that their parents wanted to give them to men who would support their education; one married her cousin so that they could raise the children of his deceased brother; and the one who became a second wife was poor, and "he had bread."[48]

Why was it so easy to break the marriage laws in Uzbekistan? Until 1932, very few Uzbeks had their births legally registered. Mullahs kept records of births and deaths in urban neighborhoods, but did not turn those records over to the Soviet government. Celebrating the anniversary of one's birthday was a custom adopted from Russians during the Soviet era. Most Uzbeks did not know the exact date of their birth, and many knew their age only according to the Central Asian twelve-year animal cycle. Uzbeks would go to their neighborhood committee to get a document attesting to their age. Parents could request a document and lie about their daughter's age; the local committee had more reason to agree to give the document, and thus maintain good neighborhood relations, than to insist on the letter of Soviet law. ZAGS offices accepted such documentation and usually permitted representatives to register a marriage on behalf of the marrying parties. After all, anyone could have an Islamic marriage instead of a state marriage, and the state wanted to encourage cooperation with registering. Strictly enforcing the law would only have discouraged registration. In 1932, when Soviet citizens age sixteen and older were issued internal passports, Uzbek ages became a matter of legal record, making it a bit more difficult, but not impossible, to flout marriage laws.

A few of my informants married entirely according to their own choice. Saodat Shamsieva ran away with a young man. Bahriniso Y., who studied at a workers' school in Moscow from 1923 to 1926, married an Uzbek soldier with whom she corresponded. Aisha B., an orphaned Tatar, married her classmate from the Tashkent Medical Technical School in 1927. Among my younger informants born in the 1920s, there were more who chose or influenced the choice of their marriage partner.[49]

While a few of Yangi Yo'l's writers wanted romance and free choice in marriage, most articles that touched on marriage concerned the new laws and problems with their enforcement. In the early 1920s, lawmakers in Turkestan considered qalin a Turkmen and Kazakh problem, because their qalin was oppressively large and constituted "sale of the bride." The 1921 marriage code made giving and receiving qalin payment a crime for Turkmens and "Kirgiz" but did not mention Uzbeks. The law forbidding qalin was applied to Uzbeks in 1924, in a general prohibition of the custom; and payment of qalin was punishable with one year of imprisonment.[50]

Women from towns across Uzbekistan wrote to report cases of forced marriage of minors and the sale of girls for qalin. G'afur G'ulom wrote of a seventeen-year-old girl from a poor family whose father essentially allowed a wealthy neighbor to rape her in partial payment for a loan. A letter to the editor told of a woman from Bukhara who arranged for a doctor to document that her eight-year-old daughter was eighteen, and then she sold her daughter in marriage. The matter was found out, the guilty parties were arrested, and the girl was placed in a children's home. In another letter, a local council charged a mullah from the Andijon region with selling his fifteen-year-old sister for 200 rubles, two sheep and a cow. Cases included a class element, since the wealthy were able to give more qalin than the poor. In one case, a landless peasant paid 270 rubles to a Party member for his fourteen-year-old daughter. However, the Party member, after taking the money, married his daughter to a qazi instead. The letter writer believed that both the Party member and the qazi should be punished, but not the landless peasant who had paid the qalin and been cheated. Party members whose involvement with qalin and the marriage of minors was discovered were subject to particular censure, removal from the Party, and imprisonment. Since giving qalin was entirely commonplace, involvement with qalin was a charge that could have been leveled at nearly any Central Asian, and the only defense was to say that what was given was a gift, not a purchase price.[51]

As the campaign to enforce the minimum marriage-age law and the law against qalin heated up early in 1929, *Yangi Yo'l*'s contributors tried to define what qalin was, why Uzbeks and others gave qalin, and what made qalin harmful. Mahbuba Rahim qizi asserted that "to sell a girl for wealth is to give her into slavery," and she encouraged *vakilas* and Komsomol members to be "the eyes and ears" that would prevent or uncover cases of qalin and underage marriage. Another author, X. Obid, charged that payment of qalin "is more widespread among Kazakhs, Kyrgyz, and Turkmens than Uzbeks," and reported on the large numbers of animals given as qalin by wealthy herders. Uzbek dehqons paid qalin "in animals, wheat, rice and clothing," and Uzbek merchants also paid money. "Qalin wealth prepares the ground for selling women and girls like property, giving them in marriage by coercion, bride stealing, and polygyny. All these things deprive women and girls of their human rights and put a great barrier in the way of their liberation." In a rationale that echoed prerevolutionary Jadid thought, authors argued that prohibiting qalin would prevent the selling of girls and would open marriage possibilities for poor men who could not compete with the qalin of the wealthy.[52]

These authors and other opponents of qalin were fighting an uphill battle. When Uzbeks gave qalin in rice, wheat, and clothing, most did not see that as buying a bride, but as "compensation for the dowry which was prepared for the girl . . . it gradually returns to the groom's home in the form of dowry, various presents, home furnishings, and so on."[53] It was easier to make the case that a girl had been sold when a substantial amount of money changed hands or when the girl was a minor and was being coerced into an inappropriate marriage. Among my informants, most regarded qalin as common practice, while one voiced Islamic opposition to qalin. Saodat A. recalled that the groom brought a sack of rice and some animals; and Bahriniso I. knew that at least five sheep were given for her marriage. Some did not know whether qalin was given, because they were young and their marriages were arranged by their parents. Those who made their own arrangements, especially Komsomol members like Havoxon A., had no qalin. Mag'ruba Q. noted that her father opposed qalin on the basis that "it is not in the Quran . . . in the book of hadith, it is written that taking qalin is bad." She came from an urban, xo'ja family of Quran reciters. She said that mahr was given: "[My husband's] uncle stood there and said, 'Daughter-in-law, for your mahr, there is nothing, just a cow, and this house, and food, and this porch—it is all yours.' It was just spoken, a formality." Enforcing the ban on qalin, as Douglas Northrop notes, became a defining issue in Communist Party purges, with Uzbek Communists marked as disloyal and criminal for continuing this social practice. While the ban came from the Communist Party, it put into reality a Jadid dream and apparently also promoted purity in Islamic religious practice that some Muslims agreed with.[54]

## UNVEILING, LAW, AND HONOR

Writers for *Yangi Yo'l* wanted women to embrace a new style of life, but within limits. They usually presented women adhering to Uzbek moral codes even as they became liberated politically and symbolically through unveiling. Uzbek society, like many Muslim societies, placed great emphasis on honor and shame, particularly as they related to women's bodies and sexual behavior. Many Central Asians, including Jadids and later modernizers, viewed Russian society as corrupt. In the 1920s, Central Asian concerns about the corrupting influence of Russians increased, drawing on rumors following the revolution that Communism meant women would become common property.[55] When the Party and the Women's Division began to support unveiling for Uzbek women, many Uzbeks saw this as a threat to male honor.

In the early twentieth century, traditionalist clergy sought to protect family honor by insisting that women should stay home, should veil, and should not have much education or learn to write; Jadids argued that educating women would enable them to become moral agents who could make good choices. Following the Jadid line of thought, a *Yangi Yo'l* story told of Mubarak, whose brother sent her to school and encouraged her to unveil. However, the brother was concerned that Mubarak, who had never spent time in the company of nonfamily males, would not know how to protect her honor in mixed-gender social settings that were a part of the New Life. He talked with her about these matters, and she was surprised: "Can it be that youths who love the New Life would also try to lead girls astray?" Adopting the new form of socializing, Mubarak and her friend Nodira went walking in the mountains with a group. They soon were laughing and joking with two young men, Sobir and Rahim. The youths asked Nodira and Mubarak to go walking again, and Nodira immediately agreed, but Mubarak was cautious. Mubarak told her friend, "There are all kinds of men, those who show the way and those who, on some pretense, lead one astray. So first you need to check them thoroughly, before you become involved." Nodira argued, "Do youths who are educated and who love the New Life want to ruin girls? One could expect that if they were the sons of *ishons* or merchants." The next week Nodira went with Sobir and Rahim. "Fooling her, claiming the New Life, Sobirjon, who led her into filth, tried to draw the corrupted girl to the worst extreme." Nodira was thrown out of school and her life ruined. Mubarak, whose brother's instructions had prepared her for moral agency in the New Life, avoided trouble and married a man with higher education.[56]

Unveiling posed the most obvious threat to the moral order. When the unveiling campaign began in 1927, villages and cities throughout Uzbekistan were awash with reports of men accusing all unveiled women of being prostitutes and with rumors about Women's Division workers prostituting young girls.[57] Writers for *Yangi Yo'l* looked for ways to ease social anxieties about women sharing public places with men. Q. Karlieva, in a report about Uzbek women factory workers, assured her readers that although women removed their paranjis while they worked, they did not feel ashamed or ill at ease. Men and women in the factory viewed each other as friends, and if any man was guilty of immoral relations, he was thrown out of work. "Uzbek women and girls only noticed these incidents when they first began to work in factories and plants. As for now, they are completely nonexistent."[58]

Writers wanted to persuade readers not only that women's appearance in public did not make them prostitutes, but that women had a right to go out, at least for significant reasons like school, work, or political activity. Oidin began one story with a scene in which a group of neighbor women were sewing and gossiping in the ichkari. They questioned their hostess, Nukra-xola, about why she allowed her teenage daughter, Karima, to continue going to school and asked why Nukra-xola's husband did not beat their daughter and force her to stay home. "At these words, Nukra-xola was very ashamed." She spoke to her husband, who went to Karima's meeting, dragged her home, beat her, and locked her in the ichkari. Karima wrote a note, concealed it in an apple, and put it on the courtyard wall, where her friend outside could reach it. Her friend took the note to the political secretary at school, who summoned the militia to Karima's home. When the militia inquired about her, Karima's father denied she was there, but Karima came out of the ichkari. She threw her paranji on the fire and made a complaint to the militia, who arrested her father.[59]

*Yangi Yo'l* presented the courts as defenders and avengers of honor. The journal carried articles called "reports from the court," which were both humorous and didactic. In one, Hafez qizi took her ex-husband to court, to force him to pay child support for their baby. Habibulla insisted that the child was not his. Until a year ago, he said, Hafez qizi had been a proper wife, but she unveiled and went to meetings that lasted until eleven o'clock at night. Habibulla's friend testified that he had been sitting in his shop and had seen another man walk Hafez qizi home after these meetings and kiss her. Several other witnesses attested that Hafez qizi was a good and proper wife. The judge determined that Habibulla's friend committed perjury; his shop would not have been open at eleven o'clock at night. The friend was sentenced to three months in prison for perjury, and Habibulla was ordered to pay child support. In this and other stories, Soviet law and courts were presented as punishing those who accused unveiled women of immorality.[60] The role of the courts in such cases was in fact quite unpredictable. While *Yangi Yo'l*'s writers put a hopeful face on Soviet law's defense of women, in reality murderers, rapists, and others who assaulted and insulted women were freed more often than convicted.

Even though women could not always rely on Soviet courts to defend them, the shift from the earlier, Islamic courts brought a significant change in power relations. In Soviet Uzbekistan, women had direct access to law and the courts on an equal basis with men. Unveiling, however, was not as simple as depicted in *Yangi Yo'l*. No degree of court protection could create an atmosphere conducive to such a dramatic social change, as will be seen in the next chapters.

The editors and writers for *Yangi Yo'l*, women like Xoldarova, Tillaxonova, Nosirova, Oidin, and Shodieva, did not always share a single vision for the modern Uzbek woman. Like their Jadid predecessors at the Tatar journal *Suyum Bike*, *Yangi Yo'l*'s writers were all certain that women needed literacy and enlightenment. However, some were strong advocates of the Party and its programs for women's transformation, while others promoted education as women's greatest need and as an end itself.

*Yangi Yo'l* created a body of literature and images of Uzbek women, for Uzbek women. It depicted and interpreted their lives in ways that both challenged and accommodated cultural values. In its pages, the new Uzbek woman could enter public life and participate fully in society with her honor secure and without necessarily abandoning gender segregation. *Yangi Yo'l*'s writers tried to present all of the social changes they aspired to as unthreatening to a good social order. They had little interest in battling against a cultural construct of honor and shame; rather they asserted that women's own agency, backed by the Soviet government, would protect honor. Their understanding of liberation for Uzbek women shared little with the visions of the more radical Russian members of the Women's Division.

## ❈ 6 ❈

# UNVEILING BEFORE
# THE HUJUM

$T$HIS CHAPTER EXAMINES THE
meanings of veiling in prerevolution Central Asia, why unveiling became
an issue, and why some Uzbek women chose to unveil long before the
Communist Party initiated its unveiling campaign. The chapter begins
with the transcript of an oral history interview with a woman who
unveiled before the Hujum. Saodat Shamsieva, an Uzbek who was born
in To'rtqo'l, Xorazm region, in 1908, became an activist and a women's
magazine editor. Her story ties together many of the themes raised in
previous chapters, as she exemplified the New Woman in Uzbekistan.[1]

SAODAT: [I was born in] the city of To'rtqo'l [in 1908], which
belongs to Karakalpak Xorazm. Beside it is a garrison town . . . Russian
soldiers lived there. My father baked bread for those soldiers . . . there
was a Russian fortress, Petroaleksanderskii . . . So the image of Europe
was close. We learned Russian from the children around the bakery.
There were Uzbeks, too, in that town, but Russians were the majority . . .
They said they were needed to protect Xorazm, which had been captured . . . I am one of eight children of my mother. Our mother had a
lot of children . . . Formerly there was no Uzbek school among us . . .
The Muslim school was a Tatar school. For Tatars—Tatars, Russians,
everyone lived in the same town. We first studied at that Tatar school . . .

Our teachers were Tatar . . . women. We read Quran, in the old style, we read the Quran and we read prayers . . . *Haft-yak* as well . . . Then in our custom, at age eleven or twelve one was shut up in a paranji . . . After age twelve, I didn't get to go out anymore. I was stuck at home . . . They didn't teach any languages. Just our Uzbek and Tatar.

KAMP: Can you read it, Tatar?

S: Tatar and Uzbek, because they are one. Just the same, they are Turkish. They didn't teach Russian in the school . . . Now, from my youth I was really astonished at this. These Tatar girls are Muslims, and we are Muslims too. Why do we have to be veiled, while they walk around uncovered? They would walk around with their heads completely uncovered. No paranji or anything of that kind . . . our Uzbek boys, they'd go around wearing wide pants and long robes and a turban wrapped up. The Russians all dressed in their own modern clothes, the Russians would put on good suits and walk around looking handsome, all of them. That amazed me. And there was a gymnasia [high school] in that little city . . . Russian-native. My older brother studied there. My older brother and all his pals dressed European style . . . My father was a smart man. He had no need to lower his face to anyone in this world. If we are Muslims, we should see to our work every day, and that's enough. If one knows God, that's enough, he said. That was his sort of view. Modern . . . He was not very literate, our own school, we are from Khiva. My father was from Khiva itself . . .

So, that was my life. One day my brother found me in a book. My brother had the book *One Thousand and One Nights* in the guest room, and I found it . . . I started reading it, and every day he would fight with me and scold me, so I read it in hiding, in the evenings. In it I saw how things should be, how one can be free, not afraid of anything. The girls in it weren't even afraid of death. I learned everything from that book. It was a very good book. Very good for young people. I was a thirteen or fourteen-year-old girl. So things went on like that, then matchmakers started to come, and my mother arranged for my older sister to marry. They were going to marry me off when I was younger than fourteen or fifteen. Every day, all kinds of people came . . . from our relatives, from our neighbors. But after *One Thousand and One Nights*, when they asked, I said, "I'm not getting married. I know that." . . . Finally, after things went on this way, they were going to give me to a man, a rich man. To be third wife to a sickly seventy-five-year-old man. My older brother was going to give me to him[2] . . . During this time, a young man came from

Fargana and stayed to set up a publishing house . . . 1923, I was four-teen or so, and it was the Soviet period. I don't remember the year now. But when he came, I saw him . . . Another of my older brothers had become this fellow's friend; . . . so he came to stay with us; my brother brought him to the guest room.[3] I was cooking for them; I see—this fel-low dresses so European, he is so free, but he is Uzbek!

So that's how it was, and one day on the table there was a letter, writ-ten to me. I could have picked it up. But I wasn't able to look at the let-ter or whatever it was. My older sister . . . what should she see but that these are all poems addressed to Saodat. Then my older brother came too, and they all questioned me, and my mother hit me and they all hit me. They said, "So you're going around us writing letters like this." What sort of letter had I written? I was even afraid to read this one. I cried and cried and got so sick, that I thought, if I didn't answer before, I'll answer now. If they kill me, OK. I was afraid to leave a letter; my mother would hit me. I got so sick that I thought, "[They say] you won't touch him, I'll touch him."[4] Enough already. A person only lives once, and doesn't need another life. Finally, I decided to do what I had not done. But I hadn't touched him up to then. Even if they killed me for it, I hadn't touched him. So he took me away. We ran away together . . . So, when we left a Russian woman helped us. She seemed to be a woman who helped women, and she defended me. So then we left. Then after I became a teacher . . .

VALIEV: Where did you move to?

S: To Fargana. He was from Kokand. When he came there he worked with establishing a publishing house . . . in Fargana, I entered and finished the technical school. He, my spouse, was called Zokirjon Shamseddin. There is that publishing house in the old city [of Tashkent], in Eski Juva . . . they made him the director of it, and they brought us here together . . . That's how it was that in 1924 we came to stay in Tashkent . . . then he gave me to study. My spouse was very good, a very good man.

K: Was he a Communist?

S: No. He wasn't a Communist, although later he became a Com-munist, it's true. He was the publishing-house director . . . Around the publishing house were all the writers and intelligentsia. There, I was unseen to people, so I went around not in a paranji, but in a scarf.

K: In 1924.

S: Yes, because no one knew me here, no one would keep forcing me to wear the paranji . . . The paranji still remained. They weren't collected. That's how it was, I wrapped up in a scarf and covered myself . . . then I studied. There was a teacher's institute [the Bilim Yurt], Hosiyatxon and all of us studied. The administration accepted me into the second year, I finished the third. Then I was sent to Xorazm and was made the director of a teacher's institute . . . I had never yet worked in my life. And I had a babe in arms too. My husband stayed here . . . they sent me for one year . . . after working there a year I ran away and came back. I was going to work by correspondence [she jokes] . . . When I quit work and came back here, I wanted to study again. We were moved to Samarkand . . . as a family. Then I went to study again at the pedagogical institute. But they didn't let us study at all, there were elections all the time, I was voted into Komsomol. There was no studying, no opportunity, because they said, "Work for the elections, work at the Party committee."

K: And you were in Komsomol. When did you enter?

S: That same year, 1925, when I came to the teachers' technical school. I was a very active Komsomol member . . . Then, my spouse became a drinker. Now, at the publishing house there was a lot of—all the intelligentsia there had a lot of money; our married life became impossible due to his drunkenness. After he started drinking, I was on the Komsomol Central Committee, and I worked as a representative to the Ministry of Education. I was to be sent to Moscow and all sorts of places for education . . . But at that time all of the leadership of our Ministry of Education were arrested, imprisoned, shot. All became enemies of the people. This was still 1929–1930 . . . In our ministry, the ministers Batu and Ramiz and all.[5] It happened with them. Then I didn't know what would become of me, and I sent myself off for education. Travel assignments came to me. I kept two travel passes to Moscow for myself. I found a place for my family, got permission, then went off to Moscow to study.

I went to the Journalism Institute . . . and studied three years . . . I read Russian. I knew some Russian. I had a hard time for two years, but then I got better at studies, I became rather Russian. Then someone came from the Party Organizational Committee there. "You worked at that ministry [the Uzbekistan Ministry of Education]; you have to take responsibility for it." I was scared. I had gotten the farthest away, it seems. After a while, I went to respond. "Why did you work there?" "I was Komsomol representative," I said, "I also did public work, and I worked for them, and I worked in the Komsomol."

After that, when I finished studying there was something called the political department, for collectivization. They sent me to Andijon . . . [19]33. I worked there three years. I went to be the editor for the political department newspaper . . . Then, in '35, the famine ended, yes, in '34–'35 it ended. Then, when I came to Tashkent, I got sick. When I came, they said they'd give me work at . . . *Red Uzbekistan*. Hosiyat-xon was also working there . . . Tillaxonova, with me.

After that, they called me into the Party Central Committee. By this time I was a Communist; I had entered the Party. Earlier, in Samarkand, I entered candidacy. I joined the Party in Moscow, because my candidate period ended. So then they call me in, they were giving me a job, they reviewed me, put the comments in the book: so, I had come from studying. Then I think, they want to take me and give me a job in the Central Committee. They'll call me and say, "Work." I'll say, "No I won't come there. My social situation is like this now, and offensive things will be said about me." They'll say, "Don't say, 'I won't come,'" but then they'll brand me a rich man's daughter.

K: A rich man's daughter?

S: My father had made a good life for himself. There was our house, our children, our land after all. My father . . . had his own private bakery . . . I was afraid they would write this on my record. No, they took me anyway. They made me deputy to the printing department, then director of the printing department. I worked one year, then in the second year they made me director of the department. Then matters came to 1937, and *Bright Life* began to be published. I look and see, *Yangi Yo'l* ended . . . two years earlier.[6] I said, make this like a literary *Rabotnitsa* [a Russian women's magazine] . . . I was prepared for Hosiyat-xon to be editor. But . . . they said, you be editor yourself. So I am both editor and director of a department. I got paid a lot from all this. Everyone got one salary, and at that time there was such a thing as a party maximum and a party minimum. It was quite a bit of money. Everyone called me rich; why was I getting a salary from two places? So I was made editor. And we started to publish it, *Bright Life*. How many issues were published—ten? Oidin Sobirova came.[7] I took her to be the assistant, Oidin, the writer. Then one or two other girls came to work, and we worked, but Hosiyat-xon didn't come to us. She became editor for a textile factory.

Then, I was made an enemy again. I was an enemy for the second time. They said I was a nationalist, as if I'm a nationalist . . . I fell under repression. I had risen to the skies, and now I fell to the ground. No place gave me work. I was fired from work; they did not even give me discharge papers. Thus I disappeared and did not come back anymore. Then, I had my mother, and my two children. I went with them to the NKVD [Soviet secret police], we wandered everywhere looking for help. I couldn't get work . . . My older brother took my mother as his guest . . . So, I went and worked on *kolkhozes* [collective farms] in Orjonikidze region, and I worked in a bread bakery, and all kinds of places . . . Being a worker, the days I saw were so bad, I couldn't find clothing to put on, and I really suffered. Things went on that way, and one day, thanks to God for Fotima Yo'ldoshbaeva.[8] One day this woman had seen me here, coming to Tashkent . . . I'd gotten thin . . . I was upset. Touching my arms she said, "Come, I'm taking you to Fotima." She forced me to go see Fotima, who was also an activist like me, and was now working at the Regional Party Committee . . . She said, "There are people who get killed and have their throats cut; what are you doing walking around?" She scolded me. We had been in Komsomol together, Fotima and I. She was the Party secretary for that area's regional committee. Then she said to me, "Now, you should go to such-and-such bakery. Fill your stomach, and take food for your children." I went to the bakery and became a worker there . . . What was it like? All the women were fighting like men, as if to slit each other's throats. But there was bread . . . "You go," she said.

Then the war [World War II] came, and things got a bit better for me. Then it wasn't good there, so we went to Parkent. There was a newspaper in Parkent that wanted to hire me . . . Fine, I said, and went. Then, before I had worked a year, someone else came from Angren. They needed to set up a newspaper there, for miners, in Uzbek. They said, "You go there and set it up." Now they had started coming to me like matchmakers . . . I went there and worked five or six years. And I was cleared; it was 1956.[9] They cleared everyone, and me too . . . I didn't have a house in Tashkent, so I said, whoever gives me a house, I come to them [to work]. Both *Women-Girls* and *Soviet Uzbekistan* called. [She returned to Tashkent and worked for *Uzbekistan Women-Girls*] . . . in 1960 I left on a pension . . .

Now, there is nothing else. Do you know, every night has a morning, and every morning has a night. Half poison, half honey, our life . . . and

in accordance with God's will, in my life there was good and bad . . .
Our times were that way. Time is at fault, isn't it so? . . .

K: After you were cleared, did you reenter the Party?

S: Yes, reinstatement was done there. Even before that they entered
me into the Party with the miners. I said, this isn't necessary, let them
give me my admittance. I was a Party member for fifty years. It was just
recently, two years or so I have been non-Party . . . [10]

K: I have a few other questions; for instance, was your mother literate?

S: No, she was not literate . . . At age fifteen they gave her in marriage to my father. He was forty-three.

K: He was forty-three at the time?

S: Forty-three is nothing! All the same, he wasn't seventy-five! . . .
No, my mother wasn't literate. At that time, you know, women weren't
literate. There were schools, but women and girls weren't sent. There
weren't many girls' schools in Xorazm . . .

K: What was your wedding like?

S: I left, but after I arrived at the other place, it seems they made a
mistake. The gossip went all over that Zokir brought back a Persian vizir's
daughter from Xorazm. He took a vizier's daughter and ran away here.
To straighten that out, I freely went out. But then they got together and
gave a very nice wedding . . . there was no one from my side, and I sat
there crying. No one from my side, everyone from his side. But they
gave a nice wedding.

K: How was the ceremony, old or new? [11]

S: Old style . . . If a domla had not come, I would have cried. In
To'rtqo'l it seems they had passed us through the ZAGS [civil registry]
in 1924.[12] I didn't understand. Then when we were going to formalize
the marriage here, I said that if there is no domla, this isn't going to
happen . . .

K: Generally, was your family religious or not?

S: Religious, all religious.

V: Religious, but compared with the present trend, they didn't make
such demands, everyone has to say prayers—

S: No, no, they were a little more . . . more atheistic, my father. Why
do I say this—every day he went to his ovens and stayed. Two ovens.
Filled them like this—how much bread he had to make! He never had
time. Hardworking. He'd go early in the morning, and on Fridays he'd
go to prayer, but not other days. He said, "No one who wraps his head

[wears a turban] has gone and come back, having seen . . . the next world. Don't be afraid." And he even gave my older brother to a Russian school. He wasn't afraid . . . He died in 1916, my father . . . we were left orphans.[13] My brothers worked, but in other trades. My older brother worked at a bank. Later it seems he worked at a Soviet ministry . . . he worked with Faizulla Xo'jaev. So he disappeared as an enemy of the people.

K: Did you participate in the Hujum, for instance, did you participate in the movement for unveiling in 1927?

S: I had not yet been able to finish my own education in 1927. It seemed to me everything was fine. I was going to school. I participated a little bit. If work was demanded of the cadres I would go . . . Then I worked for *Bright Life* and worked for women everywhere and in all ways. But during the years of the Hujum, that wasn't in my mind.[14] Because I was still young, and not that educated. So . . . I understand women's liberation very deeply. A person needs human rights.

[My father] left everything to my mother. She was young, age thirty-three or thirty-six. He left everything to my mother, then she kept giving to the children until it was all gone. In the end, then it came to me. After that we were declared Kulaks . . . They took away the horses . . . They took a lot of things . . .

V: Marianne, it is said that the condition of women in Xorazm was somewhat better . . . Women held men in their hands.

S: Because they were higher, really, women were powerful. Somehow independent . . . among us in Uzbekistan, Fargana is influenced by Kashgar. As for us [from Xorazm], there is Afghanistan's influence . . . When our grandfathers wandered and settled, our grandfather was an Afghan. He apparently was a slave who fled from Afghanistan. Then he married one of our Uzbeks, and had four sons, daughters too. One of the sons was my father . . . [so] then we are mestizo, and it seems after becoming mestizo, the blood gets purer. One gets more powerful . . . And young men of Xorazm were . . . the kind that like to wander [have affairs] . . . Because of this women have to look after them . . .

V: I could show you a lot of pictures . . . Those young women, at that time, were in the first ranks in the emancipation . . . [15] OK, so they were also Communists, they were forced to be Communist, but they took a progressive path in struggling to free women. They took a progressive road . . . If they hadn't been Communist, there would have been no opportunity at all. And even if they were forced to be Communist, they were taken up with the struggle to liberate women. My mother also threw off the—what's it called.

[Valiev and Saodat discuss current religiosity . . . Saodat is a believer but doesn't read or recite. Who has time?]

S: [Shows a book on Islam, and says in Russian] Look, this says there were 230 prophets before Muhammad, and he was the last. It says Adam was a prophet. Well, he was the only man, so to whom would he have been a prophet? You wind up with thousands of questions. [She shows us her copy of the Quran—an Arabic and Russian version.] The Quran is in Russian too. The language is hard to read. If you perform the ablutions, you use up half an hour. You need to do the ablutions five times a day. You have to be occupied with this all day. Of course, for us pensioners, there's really nothing else to do . . .

K: During the 1920s and 1930s, in order to be a Party member, was it necessary to deny God's existence?

S: It was necessary, in speech, but still God was not denied in my heart. Because you cannot deny God in your heart. You still have to recognize that someone created everything . . . And it is another matter when there are others; I had children to look after . . . although I was a member of the Party, nonetheless, God is. Recently Chinixon called and asked, "Why did you quit the Party?" I said, "I don't need the Party." Now Chinixon has left the Party.

V: Saodat-opa, in that Party, the Communist Party, there were also pure people. Most of them were innocent.

## STATES, UNVEILING, AND AUTHENTICITY

For reformers in Islamic societies in the early twentieth century, the veil in its many forms was the symbolic antithesis of modernity. Some radical reformers thought that women's liberation could be achieved only if the veil disappeared, while moderates believed that veiling would decrease as women gained modern education. Nationalist governments that embraced modernization programs, like Turkey and Afghanistan in the 1920s and Iran in the 1930s, gave state support to unveiling as a sign of national progress. In Egypt and India, where unveiling was not a state-supported initiative, feminists and modernizers viewed unveiling as an issue of women's equality, social advancement, and freedom

An Uzbek woman raises her chachvon. Front cover of *Yangi Yo'l*, no. 2 (1926).

to enter the public sphere. In all contexts, individual initiatives for unveiling blended with nationalist agendas and concepts of women's roles in the modern nation.

In Uzbekistan, where Uzbek women first unveiled individually, and then the Communist Party turned the unveiling movement into a mass campaign, the meaning of unveiling changed. The first Uzbeks who unveiled, and their society, understood their action as political. Unveiling was at first a public demonstration of women's embrace of the state's modernist promises of equality. But when the Communist Party made unveiling its own program, by launching the Hujum, removing the paranji became a marker of a woman's support for the Communist state itself.

When a state gives support to a social movement, that support may be regarded as co-optation or even force. Unveiling movements among Muslim women in Egypt and India, which were not subject to state support or opposition, are easily seen as expressions of women's agency. Feminist and nationalist groups promoted unveiling, and many women unveiled voluntarily. However, such unveilings, when interpreted as the outcome not of women's agency, but of a colonial situation and agitation by Europeans, may also be understood as the result of colonial domination. Women's own motivations for unveiling or remaining veiled are much harder to perceive when the state forced the issue, as in Soviet Central Asia, Iran, Turkey, and Afghanistan. Leila Ahmed argues that men of the ruling classes, "smarting under the humiliation of being described as uncivilized because 'their' women are veiled," enacted bans on veiling and agitated against the practice as "members of Muslim societies whose economic interests and cultural aspirations bound them to the colonizing West and who saw their own society partly through Western eyes."[16]

Ahmed's observations, while important, obscure two significant matters: women's own initiatives and the belief among modernizers in early twentieth-century Islamic societies that veiling and modernity were somehow incompatible. Instead of recognizing that some Turkish women had been arguing about veiling for fifty years, and that some had unveiled, attention instead is given solely to Mustafa Kemal Atatürk's 1926 pressure for women's unveiling. Reza Shah was the initiator of unveiling in Iran, and nothing that Iranian women thought really matters. Similarly, accounts of unveiling in Uzbekistan begin with the Communist Party and focus on the antagonism between the Party and the Uzbek population over unveiling. Ultimately, this writing of history renders unveiling inauthentic, the result solely of pressure from above, rather than of initiative from below or of broader social change. In Uzbekistan, the majority of women unveiled after the Communist Party launched its unveiling campaign and did so under duress; the Party pressured or forced them to do so. But before the Party's campaign, there was already an unveiling movement underway among Uzbekistan's modernizers.

Rather than approaching unveiling in Uzbekistan solely as a policy of coercion, this chapter discusses the meanings of veiling and unveiling before the Hujum, when unveiling was a topic of public argument and conflict. Unveiling had supporters and opponents from every social class and group within Uzbek society. There were women who unveiled in opposition to their families, and women who remained veiled in opposition to their families. Communists disagreed among themselves about unveiling, and supporters purged opponents from the Party. Neither did Communist supporters of unveiling agree on tactics. Some advocated a gradual approach, while others sought to ban the practice outright.

Focusing on this contestation permits a discussion of agency. Uzbek women, over a period of about twenty years, stopped wearing their traditional paranji and chachvon. Why did they do so, and what did unveiling mean to them? To address this, one must begin with what veiling meant among Uzbeks in the early twentieth century.

## VEILING PRACTICES AND DISCOURSES

Veiling among Muslims in the late twentieth century, the donning of *hijab*, was a public expression of piety and also a reflection of the internationalist character of Islamist movements that encouraged adopting a form of dress unrelated to local cultures and traditions. Wearing hijab was also, in many contexts, a political statement. Traditional veiling, however, is culturally specific. Central Asian tradition claims that the veiling of women among the sedentary, agricultural and urban population became common practice under Timur, who in anger over the allure of his favorite wife, Bibi Xonum, for an architect, ordered that her charms be hidden under a veil. Miniatures from fifteenth- to seventeenth-century Central Asia show women wearing paranji—robes with stylized, nonfunctional sleeves—as coverings draped from the head, with chachvon—a dark veil covering the front of the woman from the top of the head to the chest.[17]

In the early nineteenth century, the paranji was only one of many forms of outerwear in urban Central Asia, but by the late nineteenth century it was ubiquitous among urban Tajik and Uzbek women. Visitors to Russian Turkestan following the conquest were told that in Tashkent honest women needed to veil so they would not be taken for prostitutes.[18] If this were indeed the case, one might expect to find that veiling was not as widespread among sedentary peoples in Bukhara and Xorazm, where there was not as significant a presence of Russian soldiers with their camp followers, but the connection is not so clear. Urban

Bukharan women wore the paranji, but full seclusion of women was more pronounced in the city of Bukhara than in Russian Turkestan. In the 1890s, the British ethnographer Annette Meakin contrasted the abundant presence of veiled women in the streets of Tashkent and Samarkand with the lack of women on the streets in Bukhara: "I have roamed about Bokhara for days together without encountering one solitary female figure. In the towns that are completely under Russian sway one certainly sees more women about."[19] Veiling allowed women to enter the street and to move about in society with some measure of freedom; even though their identities and faces were hidden, veiling was a sign that a family did not observe the strictest possible seclusion of its female members.

The typical paranji was made of grey or white cotton with thin blue strips, so lacking in uniqueness as to render women anonymous in public. At home in her courtyard, a woman covered her head with a scarf, and if an unrelated man came into the courtyard, she would "veil" by pulling the scarf over her mouth. Among my interviewees who were young girls in the 1920s and 1930s, one came from a family in Kokand that observed strict seclusion; she reported that she did not veil in the paranji because she never left home at all after puberty.[20]

Women from nomadic groups—Kyrgyz, Kazakh, Turkmen, and Uzbek—did not cover their whole faces. Some would wear a robe draped from the head, or a turban with a half veil covering the mouth, but full veiling—that is, covering the whole face—was found only among the sedentary population. A sedentary woman who worked in the fields normally wore a *chopan*, a men's or child's robe, draped from her head in the style of the paranji, but did not normally wear the chachvon. She could pull the front edge of her chopan to cover her mouth in the presence of men. In the 1870s, the Russian ethnographer A. D. Grebenkin noted that town-dwelling Tajik women in the Zarafshan Valley wore the paranji when they went into crowded places and that the rural Uzbek woman "openly walks unveiled, and covers up only before Russians and the clergy." Some of my rural informants said that not all villagers could afford paranjis and that in the 1910s and 1920s only those women who did not work in the fields wore them.[21]

If indeed paranji wearing did increase after the Russian conquest of Central Asia, that may have been related to Turkestan's changing economic and political situation. Men may have felt a need to hide their wives from the eyes of outsiders, and Uzbek society associated unveiled women with prostitution. At the same time, a growth in Islamic institutions and learning in this period, with a rise in Hajj participation, may have produced greater adherence to Islamic norms, including veiling. Central Asia's growing wealth brought new, bourgeois values to Central Asians, and paranjis made of expensive materials became status symbols.[22]

Most of my informants who were born between 1901 and 1915 started wearing a paranji between ages twelve and sixteen. Several women from very religious families began veiling at ages nine and ten, and several Bukharan women told of veiling at seven. When a girl received her first paranji she also stopped playing with the mixed-gender group of children on the street and was kept at home.[23]

Visitors to Turkestan rarely asked why women veiled, and until the Jadid press began to discuss unveiling, records explaining or urging the practice are lacking. When Grebenkin asked Muslims in the Zarafshan Valley why women veiled, his male interlocutors told him that a woman "is lower than a man, and her presence among men is shameful for the latter. Therefore a woman should, upon coming across men, cover herself or hide."[24] One Russian government inspector cited early twentieth-century cases in which Sharia court judges had sentenced Turkestani women to imprisonment for appearing unveiled on the street. This suggests that the paranji had become religiously compulsory dress.[25]

Outsiders to Turkestan often recorded their distaste for the paranji, though they differed in their analysis of the practice. The Nalivkins described women in paranji as "reminding one, by their gray figures, more of mummies than of living human beings."[26] Decades later, Fannina Halle, a German activist, wanted to impress on her readers that the paranji was a more severe form of veiling than others they associated with Islamic lands: "A woman dressed in a *paranja* . . . looks like a ghost, a walking dark-room, whose formless, repulsive silhouette contrasts incomprehensibly and horribly with the brilliant, sun-drenched bazaars and squares of Samarqand, Tashkent, and Bukhara, and with the gay, coloured costumes of the men."[27]

Tatars in Central Asia were also impressed by the severity of the paranji, but understood it as related to the seclusion of women, the underlying practice that they saw as more harmful to women than covering when outside. Although Tatar women began discarding their own forms of veiling in the late nineteenth century, and most Tatar women in Central Asia did not veil, they disagreed over whether the veil itself was a serious hindrance to women. Their prerevolutionary analyses of veiling, seclusion, and their relative importance in women's inequality were repeated after the revolution in Uzbekistan.

Tatar conservatives and reformists argued publicly over veiling and even made unveiling a topic for the 1906 Muslim Congress. A conservative, `Abdulla ibn `Abdulla, criticized Jadids for establishing theaters where men and women mixed and women appeared without their veils. One of the founders of the Muslim Women's Association, Mu'allima Kamila bint `Azatulla Qasimova, urged women to veil, but objected to women's seclusion. She wanted women to participate in a gender-segregated public sphere where they could continue veiling while obtaining higher education and joining women's civic organizations. The editor of *Suyum Bike*, Jemaladdin Validov, also differentiated between veiling and seclusion: the former was pre-Islamic and harmless, but the latter was a "symbol of male dominance in the Eastern family" and contrary to the egalitarian essence of Islam.[28] Other religious scholars declared that veiling was not mandatory, and many Tatar women ceased covering their faces.[29]

By contrast, Central Asian Jadid writers had almost nothing to say about the veil before the revolution; they thought discussion of the veil was a diversion from more important issues. Hasanov, a Jadid teacher in Toqmaq, Turkestan (now Kyrgyzstan), wrote to *Alem-i Nisvan*: "The hijab question is being written about in all the newspapers and journals. Some say hijab is necessary, and others say it is not . . . the lack of new schools in Turkestan is more a hindrance to the progress in Turkestan than hijab . . . Kyrgyz and Kazakh women here do not wear hijab, but they too lack education."[30] After the revolution, the questions over veiling persisted among activists in Central Asia: was it required by Islamic law? Was veiling itself a cause of backwardness, or was veiling a way of breaking seclusion, which was the real source of inequality? Would education and modernization lead to veiling's demise?

Although to outsiders the paranji was an object of attention and some revulsion, for Turkestanis, it was a normal, accepted part of life and was not a subject of ideology or conscious promotion. Women and men assumed that the paranji was proper according to Islamic law and that for a woman to show her face to men outside the family was a sin. Why any Turkestanis began to consider getting rid of it is not entirely clear. Certainly prerevolutionary Tatar discourses about veils and unveiling raised the idea in Central Asia, and unveiled Tatar women could be seen in every Central Asian city. Of course Russian women in Turkestan's cities also were not veiled, but interviews with elderly Uzbek women suggest that Russian women were so different that most Uzbek women would not have thought of using them as examples; but Tatar women, otherwise culturally close and highly respected, could provide a challenge to Uzbek veiling. Saodat Shamsieva, for example, noted that Russians were plentiful in her town, but it was the fact that her fellow Muslims, Tatar girls, did not veil that made her question the paranji.[31]

Before the revolution, there were very few Uzbek women who unveiled, and they did so in limited contexts. Sattar Abdugafurov, a Turkestani who worked for the Russian colonial government in the late nineteenth century, had his wife unveil and mix socially with Russians. Oiposho Jalilova, who came from a Tashkent family of rather radical thinkers, attended Jadid schools, mixed with Russians, and spoke Russian, went out after a theater performance in 1917 without her paranji. Azizzoda writes, "She was the first unveiled Uzbek girl." Immediately after the revolution, Hamza Hakimzoda Niyoziy published a play in which the protagonist, a strong, intelligent Uzbek woman, unveiled. But unveiling was not yet an active controversy in Turkestan.[32]

In the first years following the revolution, there were scattered reports of Uzbek women unveiling and appearing in public. Until 1927, the Party took no formal position on veiling, and its members were divided about the usefulness of unveiling. To the extent that the Party promoted rights for women, it was more concerned with law than with symbols. Although the law made women men's equals in political rights, women were unaware of those rights. In 1924, O'ktam, an Uzbek Party member who had strong opinions about women's rights, wrote, "After the October transformation, men and women were made legally equal—so to say, externally equal. From the outside there is no evidence that women are socially and economically equal to men . . . They are still men's slaves." While searching for the route to factual equality, O'ktam revealed the ambivalence among Turkestan's progressives about unveiling:

A little dialogue:

"OK, how shall women be liberated?"
    "Only with throwing off their paranjis."
    "And with this, women will be free?"

"No, economic will remains in husbands' hands; that is, the reins are still in men's hands."

"If this freedom will come into women's hands as a result of unveiling, then do Kazakh, Kyrgyz, and other women of unveiled nations have their own freedom?"

"No, again, although they are uncovered, they are under the rule of husbands and fathers."

"It seems that being uncovered cannot be the cause of women's rights and liberation, so the paranji cannot prevent it."

(I am not a proponent of women and girls continuing to wrap up in the paranji, nor on the side of gradually banning it, as in the Ottoman reforms that lighten the paranji, as some are.) The issue of the paranji is a separate matter from the issue of women's rights. A foundation is laid for women to raise themselves from slavery to a husband, and when the necessity of it presses on them, they will have to remove the paranji themselves. But it is necessary to get rid of the religiosity and fanaticism that was taught to them and help to give them sense, knowledge, and education.[33]

O'ktam, echoing pre-1917 Tatar reformers, regarded the paranji as a symptom of Uzbek women's subordination to men, not a cause of her inequality. He believed the paranji would disappear as a result of women's education and liberation from "fanaticism." However, other Communists saw the paranji as one of the elements that maintained women's inequality. The Namuna Communist Party cell in Tashkent resolved that:

1. All Communists, education personnel, and Komsomol should have their wives and sisters study, should bring them to meetings without paranji, and otherwise set an example.

2. After noting that the issue of hijab is an obstacle to women's general improvement, we Communists find it necessary to do away with it summarily.[34]

This resolution, like many others before 1927, was entirely ineffective. Communists argued about unveiling, but women deciding to unveil were few. The prevailing atmosphere would have been enough to discourage all but the bravest. Azizzoda reported that Oiposho Jalilova and her sisters, whose family lived in the new city of Tashkent (the European side), began teaching in girls' schools in the old city of Tashkent in 1919 or so. Each day they would ride on a cart to the edge of the old city, unveiled, and then they would put on paranjis and *yashmaks* (half veils) to go the rest of the way to work. Even with this dress, they endured passersby throwing stones at them.[35] Yevdokia Tiukova, a Russian woman who grew up in Central Asia and worked in the Women's Division, reported that at Samarkand's International Women's Day celebration in 1922, about one thousand women gathered at the women's club and "did not cover their faces even when [men from the Party organization] appeared."[36] But this did not mean that those women then left the meeting and went unveiled on the streets; uncovering their faces for the meeting itself required daring.

Women's decisions to abandon veiling were significant, if not frequent. Some unveiled publicly, to set an example for others. After Women's Day in 1924, the newspaper *Turkiston* publicized one case:

On March 11, two Uzbek women took a step into the free world. Old city Tashkent residents G'azi Urtoq Yunus Muhammad O'g'li and Mir Mashriq Mir Yunus O'g'li came with their wives to the office of "Turkiston" with news that their wives came out of paranjis. They came with their children to share joy and to convince others. The women took a tour of the newspaper.[37]

For Women's Day, 1924, there were unveiling meetings in a number of Tashkent's neighborhoods. Rahbar-oi Olimova recalled in her memoir:

It was possible to see women with uncovered faces even in our own city. These were women and girls who were ahead of their time, who carried out agitation and propaganda among women: Hosiyat Tillaxonova, To'raxon aya Ibrohimova, Jahon Obidova, Sobira Xoldarova, Bashorat Jalilova, the poet Oidin opa Sobirova, and Bahri G'ulomova. But they comprised the minority in the conditions of the time.[38]

While unveiling was a public, political act for the wife of G'azi Yunus and for women activists, unveiling could also be a more personal matter. Saodat Shamsieva said that she stopped wearing her paranji when she and her husband moved to Tashkent. Although she was living in an Uzbek neighborhood where all of the women wore the paranji, she stopped wearing hers. "No one knew me here," she said. "No one could force me to wear the paranji." In her oral history, Saodat recalled unveiling as a personal choice, her own liberation from societal norms. Political influence and the example of others must also have played a role. Saodat was studying at the Bilim Yurt with other Uzbek women who had already unveiled, and she and her husband were friends of progressive young Uzbek writers who promoted unveiling and women's rights.

There are numerous accounts of women unveiling while abroad, especially when in Moscow on a delegation or for school. Some of these resumed veiling upon returning home, while others remained unveiled. One of the most publicized incidents took place in 1921, when the Women's Division planned an All-Russian Congress of Women of Oriental Peoples to meet in Moscow in June and invited delegates from throughout the Soviet "East." There was a planning meeting in Moscow in April, attended by workers among "oriental" women. Activists in Central Asia eagerly promoted the congress, inviting women to participate in the "Eastern women and girls' jihad."[39] The congress itself was delayed and ultimately canceled, but the Tashkent organizers, who had already invited women, and the women, who had already traveled to Tashkent from all over Turkestan and Bukhara, decided to make their journey to Moscow anyway. The seventy or so Central Asian women, accompanied by several Russian activists, spent a week in Moscow. They met with Women's Division leaders, went on excursions and visited factories, and most memorably, managed to waylay Lenin on his way to a meeting.[40]

At the Second International Conference of Communist Women, the Turkestan delegation removed their veils or uncovered their faces. One of the participants in the Comintern session described both the appearance of the Turkestan delegation at the session and the participants' response to the delegation:

A commotion took place. Black coverings, bright fabrics, headdresses sewn with silk and gold . . . the women of the Orient in a narrow line poured into the hall where there were representatives of women workers of the whole world.

Exactingly locked up in gray, stifled with heavy black fabric, the women of the East, mysteriously, came out in front of their western sisters. Their eyes glanced down shyly, unused to bright light; their weak shoulders stooped beneath the triple yoke of the prejudice of sex, patriarchal mores and the oppression of imperialism. Some of them with uncovered faces were so young and had such surprising eagerness in their whole appearance that they seemed, really, to have come out of another world . . .

We felt in them the incarnation of the *Tales of a Thousand and One Nights*, the melancholy of the harem, the magical tale of Perrault, and the fascinating stories of travels in Mongolia, the Caucasus, Bukhara and Persia. We met them as pioneers who were tearing themselves from their difficult, barbaric slavery. The chains still bound them: their veils were not yet thrown off.

The applause did not fall silent. No one could speak; everyone wept with joy. The West opened its embrace to the working women of the East . . . Would there be sufficient strength to tear away so many sacrifices of age-long oppression?

The veils began to rise, and one of the women in a small, embroidered cap with a haughty profile and blue-black hair braided in two plaits, stepped up to the tribunal. Without doubt, the gesture was purely symbolic. Out of millions of women sentenced to a life of total submission and unchanging labor, a few women had torn themselves away and come to us . . . But it is important that the movement has begun, and soon from one Muslim countryside to another news of this will be told . . . the veils were lifted and the women began to see.[41]

The florid exoticism of this account was not common to *Kommunistka* reports on Central Asian women, but Marie Vailliant-Couturier's representation of the event touches on the inherent contradictions in Women's Division efforts among Central Asian women: Muslim women took an action on their own behalf, such as traveling to Moscow and unveiling; the Women's Division recognized the action, took credit for it, and denied that the Muslim women themselves were acting in a meaningful way. Certainly Vaillant-Courturier underestimated the woman who removed her veil and went to the platform to greet the Comintern group on behalf of the Turkestan delegation. This was probably Shamsikamar G'oibjonova, who was managing director of the old city Women's Division in Tashkent. She was one of the first Uzbek women to join the Communist Party (in 1920), she spoke Russian, and she made a public greeting on behalf of the Turkestan delegation several days later at a parade on Red Square. The date when G'oibjonova gave up the paranji is not recorded, but a number of the women in this delegation abandoned veiling and did not put paranjis back on when they return to Turkestan. Similarly, "almost all of the delegates removed their chachvons and paranjis after returning from Moscow." One of the Russian organizers of the trip to Moscow, Tiukova, remembered that twenty women from Samarkand went on this delegation and that "when they returned home, all of them removed their paranjis." After the meeting, several of these unveiled women were assaulted. If they made a gesture of unveiling, it was more than symbolic.[42] These stories about Turkestani women going to Moscow and returning to unveil have much in common with those about Huda Sharawi, the Egyptian feminist. After attending a meeting of the International Woman Suffrage Alliance in Rome, she threw off her veil when she emerged from the train in Cairo as a public, political act.[43]

Women who left Turkestan often unveiled while they were away from home. Bahriniso Y., born in Kokand in 1907 or so, explained that in 1923 she was selected from a residential Uzbek girls school in Tashkent to study in Moscow. She lived in Moscow for three years, and upon returning to Uzbekistan she saw no need to start wearing the paranji. She may have been rather impervious to social opinion; she was orphaned and her older brother was a Communist Party member. To'raxon Ibrohimova, a Kokand women's organizer, began appearing at Turkestan Communist Party meetings in a paranji, but with her face unveiled. When she attended the All-Russian Conference of Soviets in Moscow in 1924, she lifted her chachvon to give a greeting, and Mikhail Kalinin, the president of the Supreme Soviet, asked her to remove her paranji. In her memoir, she recalled that she wavered, and Stalin, who was standing near, said to her, "Comrade Ibrohimova, since the delegates have requested it, then you must remove the paranji." She removed it, to applause.[44]

For women who were accustomed to being hidden from others' eyes, the paranji was not easily rejected. Manzura H.'s mother (b. 1898) lived in Moscow in the mid-1920s with her husband, an Uzbek Communist Party member. In Moscow, she did not veil, but when she arrived in Uzbekistan in 1927 she immediately put on her paranji, even though her husband did not want her to do so. She lived in a mahalla (traditional urban neighborhood), and she did not want to endure the sorts of insults and public harassment that unveiled women encountered daily.[45]

Harassment was not the only difficulty for unveiled women; some were attacked physically as well. In September 1926, the wife of a Tashkent tramway worker and Party member, Oxunjonov, decided to unveil. She went to a meeting of the Qoshchi Union, a union of poor peasants, and unveiled in front of union members and the public. The neighborhood committee condemned her and verbally attacked her. On October 1, according to different published accounts, members of the committee beat up either Oxunjonov or his wife. The worker's newspaper, *Ishchi Batraq Maktublari*, reported that the committee told Oxunjonova (the wife): "You've become corrupt! You've lost your religion! You've turned to idols!" and they beat her severely. *Yangi Yo'l* reported instead that the committee attacked and beat Oxunjonov (the husband) saying: "You've foolishly forgotten your religion! You've sold out to the Russians!" Both articles noted that an investigation followed, but the militia mishandled the case.[46]

THE COMMUNIST PARTY AND UNVEILING

After the national-territorial delimitation created Uzbekistan in 1924, the Party leadership did not issue any official calls for unveiling, even though individuals and small groups of women unveiled. The CPUz encouraged women's education and political organization through the Women's Division, women's clubs, and non-Party women delegate meetings. While some Communists wanted women to unveil, those who shaped policy in 1925 and 1926 may have believed, like O'ktam, that the paranji would disappear when young girls, educated in Soviet schools, would grow up and reject it, donning red scarves in the paranji's place.[47]

Women activists who wanted to encourage unveiling also needed to allay fears of this radical social change by stressing that no one would be forced to unveil. In her play, *A Step toward Modernity*, published in *Yangi Yo'l* in connection with the Uzbekistan Women's Day celebration of 1925, Oidin told of Mastura and her daughter Salima, who entered the New Life. The New Life, as in most *Yangi Yo'l* images, involved education, paid employment, adoption of some European-style house furnishings such as tables and chairs, and unveiling. In the play's first scene Salima and her neighbor gossiped about the degenerate Uzbek girls who unveiled and freely talked with boys on the street. Mastura expressed her repugnance at unveiling to a Women's Division delegate who visited her home to propose that Mastura learn to read and that she send Salima to school. The delegate told Mastura, "It has been three years since I entered the Women's Division. In that time, I have never thrown off my paranji. I carry on with my work wearing my paranji. Because of this, no one tries to coerce me. Everyone has her own wishes. Let those who wish to, throw it off. Let those who do not want to unveil go on veiling."

The delegate's insistence that women were free to choose whether they would unveil gave Mastura the assurance she needed to entrust her daughter to education in a Soviet school. In the play's final scene, three years later, Salima carried a book bag, wore European-style clothing, and went out to the theater without wearing a paranji. Her uncle, Mastura's brother, accused Mastura of corrupting her children: "What have you done by sending your daughter out without her paranji? I am dishonored by people in the street. You should make her cover up!" Mastura defended her daughter's choice to unveil, although she still wore her own paranji. The play ended with the militia arresting Mastura's brother for threatening the woman delegate with a knife.[48]

Between 1924 and 1926, Uzbek women activists, like the playwrite Oidin, promoted unveiling as a sign of women's commitment to modernity. In a few workplaces there were public unveiling meetings or ceremonies, and women who removed their chachvons were rewarded with official recognition. Mafrat-xon M.'s mother, Mahamat Sarimsoqova, a silk-factory worker, unveiled at a factory in Kokand in March 1926, but then became afraid and started wearing her paranji again.[49] Hadicha Kunasheva (b. 1888, Namangan) worked at a state-owned silk-cocoon factory in Namangan. Hadicha's daughter Malika wrote, "Hadicha-xon, responding to the government's call, became the first of the women who burned her paranji. In the archive file there is a certificate on which is written, 'To Hadicha Kunasheva, Number 1, March 1926' . . . The certificate which my mother received . . . proves that she was the first to throw off the paranji-chachvon and come out into freedom." Malika explained to me that her mother was an activist who organized women's clubs in villages around Kokand. She said that Hadicha had stopped wearing her paranji in 1924, but in 1926, at the factory meeting, she burned it.[50]

International Women's Day, March 8, became the main occasion in the Soviet calendar when the Party and the state promoted women's issues. Uzbek activists tried to use Women's Day celebrations to attract women from their homes and inform them about their rights and opportunities. For the 1926 Women's Day celebration in Tashkent, several thousand women gathered at the square in the old city, along with Komsomol members and members of the newly formed Uzbek national army. Bashorat Jalilova, who was director of the old city Women's Division, gave a speech calling for "an end to slavery" and threw off her paranji. Another woman from the Women's Division also unveiled, but Jalilova's attempt to spark mass unveiling went unanswered; the rest of the women remained as they were. A year later, when the Party launched its unveiling campaign on Women's Day, Jalilova reflected on her disappointment in 1926 and her excitement about the 1927 effort: " . . . after the revolution, some comrades unveiled their young wives and sisters, but the movement did not develop. Having a mass anti-paranji movement was considered a dream. Even a year ago in March [1926] no one would have thought of this . . . But the Communist Party laid the foundation for preparing women to unveil, under the slogan 'Hujum.'"[51]

This was simply untrue. The Party had not laid any foundation for preparing women to unveil. For about ten years, a handful of Uzbek progressives, both women and men, had tried to make unveiling possible and to popularize the practice, but they faced a society whose religious leaders preached that for a woman to show her face was a sin. The Party said little on the topic, concentrating instead on law-based approaches to women's emancipation.[52] However, by 1927 large numbers of Uzbek women had some point of contact with the interventionist state. Through voting, land reform, delegate meetings, attending state-sponsored schools, literacy courses, women's craft cooperatives, agricultural cooperatives, and consumer cooperatives, women interacted with a government that was trying to create mobilized, Soviet citizens in a land where citizenship and women's rights were both fairly new ideas. Women who themselves had no direct connection to the state could be pressured and influenced through their husbands' relationship to state enterprises, unions, workplaces, and organizations. Most of the Uzbek women who unveiled before the Hujum worked in state-owned workplaces, were students or teachers in state schools, or came from families where there were Party or Komsomol members or Jadids.

Veiling in the paranji until the time of the Hujum was not an action that revealed a woman's own decision; rather, it was simply the common practice imposed on young girls and reinforced by social pressure.

Image of men and unveiled women at a demonstration. *Insets, top-to-bottom, right:* probably Sobira Xoldarova; Yo'ldosh Oxunboboev; unidentified woman; Nadezhda Krupskaia; *bottom center:* Ene Kulieva; *bottom left:* unidentified man. Front cover of *Yangi Yo'l*, no. 10 (1926).

Unveiling before 1927 was a demonstration of a woman's own decision making and flew in the face of common practice, and perhaps common sense as well. An Uzbek woman who unveiled voluntarily knew that she would be the object of scorn and harassment. But while unveiling was clearly related to women's agency, in a way that veiling was not, unveiling also was a result of social and ideological change. The women who chose to unveil individually often belonged to families where such ideas had male support. According to *Yangi Yo'l*, Oxunjonova, the wife of the Tashkent tramway worker who unveiled and was beaten up, had talked with her husband about unveiling, and he, a Party candidate, agreed with her that she could and should unveil. Hosiyat Tillaxonova was the first student to unveil at the Tashkent Women's Bilim Yurt, where radical ideas were discussed and where her brother, a Jadid, was the director. Marhamat Sarimsaqova and Hadicha Kunasheva were workers in the silk industry, and both were involved with the Communist Party's Women's Division. Oiposha and Bashorat Jalilova came from Jadid families that supported unveiling. Shamsikamar G'oibjonova and To'raxon Ibrohimova were self-supporting poor women who were workers and activists even before the revolution; their lack of dependence on males meant they were not under family pressure to remain veiled, and it is possible that their appreciation of the Communist government made them willing to undertake radical actions, defying social conventions. Saodat Shamsieva said that she stopped veiling when no one in her family could force her to veil anymore.

To unveil before the Party initiated the Hujum was to defy society, but it was also to assent to an ideology, transmitted by some Communists and Jadids through schools, media, and state institutions, that declared the paranji was a hindrance to modern life. With substantial social or familial support, and ideological prompting, a few Uzbek women decided to unveil.

Gregory Massell notes, concerning what he was able to learn about the "first generation of native Central Asian female cadres emerging under the tutelage of the new arrivals [i.e., Women's Division activists from Russia]," that "they tended to be orphans, runaway child-brides, young widows, or divorcees."[53] There is both more and less here than meets the eye. Russian activists for the Women's Division believed, with justification, that they would have more success in attracting women by offering services to those in need—orphans, abused wives, divorcées—than by offering the same services to women whose families provided for them. Uzbek women often turned to the Women's Division out of desperation. But at the same time, many Uzbek women who became activists, and who unveiled, were shaped by families where at least one member—a brother, a husband, or a father—was a Jadid or a Communist.

Saodat's 1993 interview with me contrasted with her own earlier interpretation of her life. In an account that she wrote in 1960, she followed an orthodox narrative line for Communist autobiography: she portrayed her family as entirely backward and repressive, she attributed her escape from that family and into Soviet education to the miraculous effects of the "revolution," and she made no mention of her own unveiling, but instead focused the anti-paranji section of her story on a speech she made in 1929. In an account of her life to a journalist in 1988, she erased the negative portrayal of her family and included an explanation of her escape from an unwanted marriage to an elderly man—that she eloped with a young man who came to stay with the family. In 1988 she did not mention her own unveiling, but again focused on a public unveiling demonstration in the late 1920s. In the story that she told me, she emphasized that unveiling was a choice she made in 1924 or 1925, and she presented images of her early years that contributed to her motivation for unveiling: her comparisons of Uzbek with Tatar and Russian dress, her reading of *One Thousand and One Nights* and determination to reject marriage, her exposure to the Soviet press, her elopement with Zokir, and her enrollment in Soviet education.

At the end of 1926, when the Party leadership suddenly decided that cultural revolution in Uzbekistan would have unveiling as its symbol, unveiling was already a topic of debate among Uzbeks. A few hundred Uzbek women had unveiled, had written about unveiling, and had held unveiling meetings. To unveil was to take a daring step that flew in the face of convention and that attracted immense criticism and some abuse. When unveiling changed from a small progressive movement to a Communist Party campaign, widespread violence erupted.

## ❧ 7 ❧

# THE HUJUM

I**N** 1926, **THE COMMUNIST**
Party leadership in Moscow, with strong input from the Women's Division and from Central Asia Bureau members, decided to launch a campaign that would radically change women's lives. The Hujum, or "attack," was supposed to be a sort of cultural "Great Leap Forward," designed to bring women from the "backward" nationality groups, especially Muslims of Central Asia and the Caucasus, into modern Soviet life. The Hujum as originally envisioned focused on enforcing laws that gave women equality, creating literacy programs and bringing women into the labor force. Communists in Central Asia and the Caucasus were supposed to attack every obstacle to women's equality. In Uzbekistan, this meant expanding a concern for women's rights beyond a narrow circle of urban supporters and convincing Communist Party members and government workers that they should take action in their own communities. The Party relied primarily on its own members, on Komsomol members, and on Women's Division leaders to fulfill plans for what they called women's liberation.

The Hujum put activists into direct confrontation with the Islamic clergy. Until the revolution, family law had been left to religious leaders. The gradually introduced Soviet laws contradicting Sharia, such as the law banning polygyny, had been widely ignored; most people were

The unveiling ceremony of Tursun Otajonova, an activist in the Hujum. Kokand Museum photo. A copy of this photo appeared in *Yangi Yo'l*, no. 6 (1927): 13, identifying it as a March 8 unveiling in Kokand.

unaware of new laws, and even when they became aware of them there was no enforcement. But when the Uzbekistan Communist Party leadership made unveiling the major symbol of the Hujum, a showdown began, one that pitted not only Communists and modernists against clergy, but Communists against other Communists.

This chapter examines the Party's approach to unveiling and the ways that some women responded to the Party's Hujum campaign. It explores what Uzbek supporters of unveiling thought they would accomplish and why the Party defined unveiling as an antireligious action. This chapter also compares Uzbekistan's unveiling campaign with government-led unveiling programs in other countries, raising questions about why outcomes in Uzbekistan were so different than in Turkey or Iran.

An oral history interview provides a glimpse into the first days of the Hujum and insight into one woman's motivations for unveiling. Rahbar-oi Olimova was born in Tashkent in 1908, and unveiled on International Women's Day, March 8, 1927.[1]

RAHBAR-OI: All of our paternal forebears were from Tashkent . . . My mother was also from Tashkent. Her father had a store selling *atlas*[2]. . . My father's father was a *ming-boshi* in Tashkent.[3] His name was Mirza Orip. Generally they were people with a good lineage. They did not come from the common folk. For generations they were literate . . . My father's father lived on the border as an ambassador. And he was a ming-boshi for a long time. Then he was an ambassador for a while and lived on the Afghan border and the Iranian border . . . At that time, we did not have passportization among Uzbeks. But my grandfather and my father both had passports. Because in order to turn gold like that over to the bank, they needed passports[4] . . . My father was a very educated man . . . He attained the degrees of *ulama* and *fuzalo*.[5] . . . Over in the old city there is a madrasa connected to the Ministry of Religion. My grandfathers studied at that madrasa, and my father too, and [my older brother] G'afur G'ulom also studied there for a little while.[6] Then he, G'afur G'ulom, studied at a Russian-native school. And then at Soviet schools. He also studied with a domla, for the primary years.

My mother was the only daughter . . . She was a *bek*'s daughter.[7] There is no such thing as an illiterate bek's daughter. She had a bit of literacy. My father's house, it was a place superior to a madrasa. My grandmother, that is my father's mother, gathered the boys and girls from the neighborhood and gave them lessons.

KAMP: At home. Was she an otin?

R: Well, yes. A simple otin, the kind who recites? Not that kind. She did not like them. But she was an educated otin, one who educated the people . . . Our grandmother first taught us all to read. Then we went to Soviet school, all of us . . . My grandmother, the otin, taught the children by herself, and my mother helped her as a *mudarris*. She was very bright.

Before they taught children the *Haft-yak*, they taught them the alphabet. Then they had them read *Haft-yak*, and then they passed on to the Quran. Then, by reading Navoiy, Fuzulli, Bedil, the classical books, they became literate, and then the girls left to get married. They were taught writing . . . in the Arabic alphabet . . . All our classical books, our literature, is in the Arabic alphabet. Now it cannot be used by the Uzbek people. This was a wrong done by the Bolsheviks.

I went to a Jadid school . . . There were Uzbeks, Ishon Xo'ja Xoni, and Xon Xo'ja Xoni, who were very educated. At that time, during the tsarist regime, they gathered all the rich men's children. Before that, they had given their own daughters higher education. Then they told the wealthy men: "Come, be our guest," and they would call forth one girl. He would say, "Go up to the blackboard." The school was furnished European-style, school desks, chairs, tables, good accommodations, a rich man's room. So, as I heard, the rich men would sit there, and the girl would immediately write whatever they requested, everything. They would prove themselves in doing sums. At this the rich men would all say, "Hmm, all right, it seems girls can be taught! If they stay at home, they could read. But they could also go out and work in trade and other things. But the paranji protects them . . . Covered. Her face is covered in the paranji," they would say, and then Ishon Xo'ja Xoni and Xon Xo'ja Xoni would say, "Give some money" . . . And then the rich men would say, "Ha, ha, ha," and they gave money and kept on giving money, and the school kept growing. Before that, my father had already died . . . and my grandmother and mother survived him. They . . . put us all in school there, G'afur G'ulom, myself, and my little sister. After finishing at my grandmother's school, I went directly into the Jadid school . . . [Ishon Xo'ja Xoni] strokes our heads, speaking softly, sympathizing, "You've been orphaned, orphaned."[8] Our father died at age forty-five, in 1912 . . . Then my older brother fell in love with studies, and we all really liked learning. It was something new for us. Formerly, lessons meant [reciting something in Arabic]. That was how we read—word by word. But at this school, the textbooks went into mathematics, Uzbek language, literature, history, geography . . . And I earned honors . . .

Then my mother died suddenly, when I was ten. Pneumonia. She died suddenly at age thirty-eight, and we five children were left orphans . . . We were really sad—first our father died, and now our mother. My older brothers were now looking after us, the twenty-three-year-old and G'afur G'ulom, at age fifteen, had two orphaned little sisters in their household.[9]

I want to tell you a few things about the Jadid school. There were some very good Turks—during the First World War . . . Turkish officials [officers] came to Tashkent during the war[10] . . . Xon Xo'ja Xoni . . . took one of them into the school. He became the assistant director, the organizer . . . Then some Uzbeks started going to Turkey for education.

A little bit of time passed, and suddenly the Bolsheviks came. They drove away all the Turks. They closed the Jadid school. In its place they made a Soviet school, and with that, girls and boys were separate. In our Jadid school we were mixed . . . My little sister went to the Soviet school. She could go to a mixed school because she was little, not yet wearing a paranji.

All my relatives got together and came to me—if you do not have a father and mother, fathers and mothers become plentiful! My aunts came and said, "G'afur, look. Your younger sister has grown up. Now she has to cover up with a paranji." I was twelve. They covered me in a veil. "I can't walk, I can't walk," I said at first. For days it seemed so dark to my eyes that I couldn't walk. After this they sent me to a girls' school . . . [where] educated women were giving lessons. The women's movement was so small, so Tatars [were teaching] . . . But the lessons were not satisfying to me, because I already finished all of this, at the good Jadid school . . . this was repetition. And then there was a certain ishon's daughter, . . . One day she came for the two brightest of us . . . She was Bashorat Xonim, from the old city.[11] She came from a family that had known my parents . . . She took us to a place in Shaixontaur, the home of a very rich man, Valah Xo'ja Boi—it was his house, and the Bolsheviks had appropriated it, driven him out, and opened a school there. But this was not just a school, it was the Dar al-Mu'allimot. This is an Arabic name—for preparing women teachers . . . I entered there to study. The director was a very educated man named Salim-xon. Hosiyat Tillaxonova, who threw off the paranji, was also studying there then. All of us watched . . . It was about 1923 or 1924 . . . In 1925/6 I got married. I had to leave that school. She [Tillaxonova] was the first, the first. She would go about alone, walking, wearing a hat. I'll show you her picture. She was a beauty.

We would go to the teacher's school in our paranjis and then take off our paranjis and sit at our desks. There were educated Tatars there as well. Tatars, Uzbeks, Russians—but Russians who knew the language. Men also gave lessons. We did not flee from the men. Oh, how happily I studied there at that place, because I could read all the very newest things. It was satisfying. I came happily home, I would cook, I would look after my older brother and iron his clothing. So that's how I went about, in my paranji. But then one day my aunts came to our house, my maternal and paternal aunts came. They all said, "G'afur, your little sister has grown up. She has no mother or father, and you don't know when she comes and goes because you are at work. You need to keep and protect her at home for a while, until she is given in marriage. We are afraid [for her], because those who go walking around on foot—rumors spread. They say that all those [girls] who go to study are bad, they are all morally corrupt, bad, corrupt."

K: Was it true? These rumors?

R: No, there were one or two [who were corrupt], not all. We all kept studying because we loved studying, and especially me . . . But they insisted: "Starting today, Rahbar is not going to school. When she gets married, she will study, she can continue." Then my brother said, "Sister, we are forced to do this. I have to fulfill society's decisions. Temporarily, you will stay home and cook for us. I will find and give you such a man that he will have you study, he will have you continue. That is the man I'll give you to. Now, don't be upset, don't cry." I cried and cried. Then I wrote a poem . . . :

When one says "school," fires burn in my heart.
When one says "school," lightning flashes before my eyes.
My dearest older brother, send me to my school!

My older brother and I did not talk with each other as Russians do: "blah, blah, blah." We have our own Eastern approach . . . Between my brother and me there is a curtain that Uzbeks call modesty. This modesty cannot be destroyed . . . So instead I wrote this, and then I gave him the paper. Reading it, he laughed and said, "All right, little sister. I've given you my word. If you say so, I'll give you to a man who will have you study. But for the time being, you won't study." This did not calm me either; I cried. I stayed at home reading books. My father had left a great many books. I read the classics and consoled myself.

I hadn't started Russian at all. My brother had begun studying Russian; he studied at the Russian-native school I mentioned. We just started, my younger sister and I, with my brother's books. They were interesting for us. Looking at the Russian clothes: "Oh my, any interesting thing imaginable actually exists!" They amazed us, even though we could not read, and we gradually learned to read, word by word in Russian. We read books in Uzbek, in the Arabic script. Then the books we read were in Persian, Arabic, and Uzbek, but we didn't understand Persian or Arabic . . .

When we were children . . . we would all sit together in the evenings, and we would bring out all sorts of books, like these: Xo'ja Hafiz, and then others, Sufi Ollohyor . . . and little brochures with stories like those . . . My uncle's wives, my uncles, many of them, and my grandmother would all sit together. They would give us grades . . .

Among us, marriage is arranged through a sovchi. I don't marry by making my own plans . . . So then, every day, sovchis would come. Women would come, and would look me over. One woman—it seems an educated man's wife had died. When my brother showed me the picture of this older man, I didn't like him. "Hey, I'm not going to marry an old man." "The sovchi sent this—he is a very educated man!" He was a fuzalo, my brother's teacher. When a woman would come, I would go straight to the kitchen . . . Even though I fled, one woman found me . . . I had a lot of long hair, and my hair was thick. She grabbed my hair, like this, and started to inspect it. As if to say, "I don't like this price, so I won't buy the goods." As if I were not a bride, but they were shopping, as if I were a thing. "I won't marry, not for anything!" We refused them all. They kept coming and asking. Then a sovchi came representing a leader of the Komsomol. His father had been rich . . . They showed me his picture. I took to thinking, "He's a Komsomol, in the leadership. Let's call him, we could meet, I could see him!" My friends were already marrying at their own initiative, in my neighborhood. The changes had begun—they were marrying according to their own plans. If father and mother objected, they ran away and were married. A very rich man's daughter ran away and married one of my teachers. They were already having new-style weddings . . . They even rejected Uzbek music and had a brass band play! . . .[12] So, that photo . . . I was lying in bed, asleep in the morning. A woman came, talked and talked with my brother, and she brought the picture. "Please give me the girl's picture too," she said. Then my brother came in laughing. "Rahbar, I have a gift for you. Here take it!" and he threw it at me. "What kind of gift is this?" I stooped to pick it up. "It's your fiancé's photo!" "I don't need that kind of gift," I barked. We laughed for a little while, then stopped. He was acceptable. I thought that now he'll call on me . . . and we'll talk a bit . . . No, no, no. He went to the ZAGS and registered the marriage himself. I was really surprised about that. So then, the first time we met, I made my request to him: "I need to study. Give me permission to study. Let me continue my studies at the place where I was studying" . . . "Fine," he said . . . So then I got married.

K: How, modern-style?

R: Modern.

K: Did you go to the ZAGS yourself, or did your brother?

R: My brother went.

K: He signed for you?

R: People had only just started going to the ZAGS.

K: Did you have an Islamic ceremony at home?

R: There was an Islamic ceremony, in Arabic. The mullah came. There was music playing, and I slowly took a look at my groom through the window. I lifted up the curtain a bit and kept on putting on powder and perfume. [She laughs] You've found a person who gives a real interview, eh? I was waiting there, and it came time to recite the wedding ceremony, with my groom and the domla. I stood looking—he was husky . . . He was good-looking. So we entered our married life. We had a good marriage . . . He was a real what-do-you-call-it, a Bolshevik. A Communist, a member of the Party, leader of the Komsomol . . . He was twenty-three. I was seventeen . . . . He established the Komsomol in the Old City . . . A little while passed, while I served my mother-in-law, and did household tasks. Then after that, every day, studies, studies . . .

They called it the Xotin-Qizlar Bilim Yurti [Women and Girls' House of Knowledge] . . . When I went, I was almost ready to graduate, having studied at the Dar al-Mu'allimot. They accepted me immediately and had me go up to the board. They told me, "Write all of this," and I wrote and wrote and fulfilled all they required. The teachers, men, were our own Uzbeks. One of them was surprised. Then they immediately assigned me to a school . . . number twenty-two, Bibi Xonum Maktab . . . The new style of teaching came in . . . From morning until twelve or one o'clock I taught, and then I headed in the other direction, where I studied, in the Old City. It was great. I was happy. Before this, my husband prepared his family. None of them had studied, none had thrown off the paranji . . . I dressed European-style. None of them dressed European-style. So they called me "Russian bride." They didn't know any different. They had seen Russians . . . I was bringing the new ways to them, European culture, my husband and I . . . And then my mother-in-law cried: "I'm ashamed. I've died. Now what will I do? If my daughter-in-law goes out to study, everyone will gossip." I went in my paranji, to study and to teach.

In 1927 we wrote a letter to the government—Komsomol members, women teachers, students—saying: "Give us a decree calling for unveiling!" The government refused: "Unveil yourselves voluntarily. We will not issue a decree." They said that it should be voluntary. Some of the progressive women were the first to unveil. The progressive women unveiled on the eighth of March, 1927. First of all we saw to preparations. Our teachers told us, "You will be out in front." Tashkenters in all of the organizations gathered their families; they sewed dresses and made jackets. "Oh, we'll have such a party tomorrow, we'll throw off our paranjis! We'll throw off our paranjis!"

But before this, there was a revolution in the family. My husband prepared my mother-in-law and his younger sisters. All of them were opposed. They cried and wailed: "Oh, no, our daughter-in-law will go out of the house without her paranji!" I was happy, but I didn't show them that. My husband told me not to: "You wait, and don't say anything." After that, my mother-in-law gave me her approval. I went to the teacher's school, the Komsomol members gathered, and we stood in rows, like soldiers. We all were wearing our paranjis, and were singing revolutionary songs. We went to—do you know the statue of Kalinin in the Old City? There. There were so many people, the trams couldn't move . . . All the important people came: Oxunboboev, Akmal Ikromov, Faizulla Xo'jaev. Then they said, "You aren't being forced at all. No one is scaring you. Let the people know that you really are unveiling according to your own desire." At that, all of us, putting up our hands inside our paranjis, like this [to raise it from the face], spoke, and my turn came to speak. "Comrades! No one has scared us or forced us. According to our own desires—we know that the paranji is harmful. It is difficult for us to benefit from the sun, we can't get fresh air, we can't work in the factories with the paranji. We cannot live a free life. Learning of these harmful effects, we choose to throw off the paranji." Saying, "An end to slavery, an end to the paranji, long live freedom!" I immediately threw it off. I added a new paranji for the fire. It could be a gift to Oxuboboev.

Other women threw off their old paranjis. There was a bonfire . . . paranjis were burned up on it. At first this battle was very difficult for us. Everyone watched. Oh, my, my, it was difficult. We were young. We didn't have children yet. I had just turned eighteen—nineteen . . .

NODIRA: Grandmother, were there terrorists?

R: They cut throats, the Basmachis, they attacked Uzbek women and cut them, knifed them. I ran away to my older brother's place. I hid there. After that I got my Communist education.

K: During the unveiling, I've heard that women were harassed on the streets, gossiped about, and some were killed. Did you know any-one who was killed?

R: Yes, there is a region called Yangi Yul. There, a woman's husband killed her with a knife . . . And there was that actress. She was Halima's understudy. Her husband bit off her nose, just like that . . . Those were [my] acquaintances I was talking about. Their exact names don't come to mind anymore. The actress Tursun-oi was killed.

DILAROM: Marianne wants to ask whether this was a mass thing, or here and there?

R: One by one. The Communists did not let it become a mass action.

D: Two and a half thousand women were killed.

R: In all of Uzbekistan. I can't say, exactly. But the Communists defended us, or everyone could have been killed. There was a special show at the theater. Halima Nasirova was playing. [At the theater] a girl's father killed her. She was divorced from her husband. Many fathers had their daughters divorced from Communist husbands. Lots of them. Even if they loved each other. They would say, "This man is not a Muslim. He is an infidel. He is a Russian." And then they would cause a divorce. There were many instances of this. Some women started wearing the paranji again . . . everyone unveiled eventually . . . It continued for a long time, for ten years. After that being unveiled was widespread.

And just now they are starting to wear it again, religious people . . . I don't agree with them. Back then, I fought for my belief, against veil-ing, and I still have the same opinion. In the whole world, there is no paranji. In Muslim countries, in Arab countries, there is no paranji. We had it here in Asia, in Uzbekistan and Tajikistan . . .

Women from the intelligentsia, women from the leading class, we gave our request to the government for a decree against the paranji . . . all the Komsomol members gathered, the leading women who had thrown off the paranji, and those who were wearing the paranji, went out with songs, happily . . . I said that we went out wearing European-style clothing. Putting on a skirt and a jacket . . . I faked tears in front of my mother-in-law: "They're making me into a Russian, what can I do about it?" . . . My paranji was new, the one about which I said, "Com-rade Olimova gives this as a gift to Oxuboboev." They said, "She's giv-ing a gift!" and they took the paranji. My mother-in-law had made that paranji and chachvon, and it was expensive. They took it to the *raikom* [local Party] office and left it there, the paranji and chachvon. The next day I went out, and my mother-in-law made a huge fuss: "You give me my paranji!" . . . She shouted at me. My husband said to me, "You aren't getting a second paranji to replace that one. You are unveiled, and you won't see the paranji anymore." And he did not return it to me. Because if he had returned it, it would have been put on again. It was really difficult . . . Even though photographs came out in the paper, announcing widespread unveiling, everyone put the paranji back on the next day . . . but my paranji had been taken away, and I couldn't put it back on.

K: Were you involved with the Women's Division?

R: No. Even on the day of preparing for unveiling in the Old City, I sneaked away without working for the whole day. It was like a judge's court, the Women's Division. [A certain woman] was beaten, blood flowed from her, she was bruised . . . The Women's Division takes a doctor and goes. The doctor examines the wounds as a witness. They took it to court and had a trial. Matters turned out very badly. When I saw that, I thought, no, this work is not for me. I didn't even work there a whole day, though I was there one day. They became very litigious among Uzbeks, the Women's Division.

K: Who were most of the Women's Division participants, Russian women?

R: Uzbek women. Russians were there too, at their side. Red Kerchiefs, the Russians. Oh, those Marusas got more and more common.[13] . . . Their numbers grew, and they were illiterate women. They liked to say "hooray, hooray!" They knew very little of the Uzbek language. They would go out into the fields and agitate. They would tell the women, "Go on into the mahalla. It's OK if you don't wear the paranji, nothing will happen." The next day, the women would go without the paranji, just like that. [And then men would say] "So what is happening to our people? Women seem to want to show everything to everyone, how can I put up with this? I'll cut off her head!" I saw this with my own eyes, I heard it with my own ears. Then there were really bad things, some of them were driven away, they called them *delegatkas* [representatives] . . . [they were] the illiterate who had joined the Russians. And then there were some Uzbek women who were really terrified. They tried to scare them. When they were in secluded places, they would be attacked. I can tell you about one of them; she was in the liberation movement in Yangi Yul, and her husband bit off her nose. Now she'll wear her paranji! There was a court case, and he was sent off to prison and died. [My husband] went and set up a commission . . . He bit it off! . . .

Communist woman with banner leading Central Asian women dressed in various
traditional styles. Front cover of *Yangi Yoʼl*, no. 3 (1926).

There was also Chinixon, and there was Tursun-oi. She was really a leader, an actress who acted before Halima. She was killed too, by her husband, who stabbed her. He stabbed her face, saying, "Let her be ugly." It didn't stop with ugliness, she died of it. OK, you say I must have been a hero too. In the mahalla, I was the only one [who unveiled then] . . . I used to do this with a newspaper [she demonstrates walking with a newspaper in front of her face]. I didn't tell you about that. Everyone was staring at me. At the little bazaar I would get on the tram. There was a tea-seller there . . . They [the men at the teahouse] watched. There was one who stared really badly. He'd look at everyone and say, "Look at that!" They'd say, right in front of me, "Must be some Russian's wife, unveiled like that." So then, poor me, I walked with a newspaper . . . That's how I would go about, before changing trams at the next stop.

## THE HUJUM: THE PARTY'S UNVEILING CAMPAIGN

Rahbar-oi Olimova unveiled at the behest of the Party, on March 8, 1927. However, like the women who unveiled individually, she came from a background that provided support for unveiling. She was strongly influenced by the Jadid movement, her older brother was a Communist intellectual, and her husband was a Komsomol activist. Rahbar-oi's first struggle was against seclusion: going out to school each day was her joy, even after she started wearing the paranji; but her relatives insisted she withdraw and stay home until she was married. She negotiated with her husband for permission to study, but nonetheless had to overcome her mother-in-law's objections before she could resume schooling and begin teaching. The Hujum provided Rahbar-oi with an opportunity, but even for her it was not easy to unveil. She faced criticism within her husband's family and tension and abuse on the streets. Unlike most women who unveiled at the Party's demand, Rahbar-oi did not re-veil, though she did consider it. Rahbar-oi's story of unveiling at a public demonstration was typical, but her enthusiasm for unveiling, her stolidity in the face of counterattack, and her refusal to veil again were unusual.

Why did the Party decide, in 1926, to promote unveiling? At a conference of Women's Division organizers in October 1926, I. A. Zelenskii, the Russian head of the Party's Central Asia Bureau, gave a speech declaring that the time was ripe for a drive for cultural transformation: greater enforcement of laws against "backward" traditions, more effort

ایا دمجی مارت والدرغا جلاری

بوخارا نزكروكى خانلار بولساك كالدیا كالندا ﺧﺎﻥ بولوب نعزالاری

"The swallows of March: members of an 'uncovered' club at the Bukhara district Women's Division." Sometimes publications identified unveiled women as swallows, birds that herald spring or new beginnings. Published in *Ma'orif va O'qituvchi*, no. 3 (1928): 11.

for education and health care, and mass opportunities for Central Asian women to leave seclusion and enter workplaces and political life. He focused on the activities of Party members, calling on them to make certain that laws were carried out and criticizing those who thought this work was the task of the Women's Division alone.

Party workers had come to the same conclusion that prerevolution Tatar activists drew: women's seclusion had to end if the government was to succeed at transforming Central Asia. Some Russian Women's

Division enthusiasts tried to convince the Party that the Hujum would turn Central Asian women into a substitute proletariat, the force that would provide the Party with necessary grass-roots support for building socialism.[14] But Uzbek women activists tended instead to promote the Hujum as an extension of Jadid ideals, especially breaking women's seclusion and providing them with new public roles.

In his speech at the conference, Zelenskii called for a struggle against seclusion but did not mention veiling or unveiling. Zelenskii spoke in Russian and named the campaign with a term suited to the Party's militarized vocabulary: *nastuplenie*, meaning "attack" (as in a battle). Communists "attacked" social problems and presented themselves as soldiers on social and economic battlefronts. The translation of Zelenskii's speech into Uzbek in the leading newspaper, *Qizil O'zbekiston*, was unfortunate. The translator rendered "attack" as *tajovuz*, which is often used in a phrase meaning sexual assault, an unfelicitous beginning for a campaign to improve women's lives. By December 1926, Uzbek publications changed the slogan to *hujum*, meaning "attack" or "assault," but not sexual assault. However, hujum connoted aggression, and the campaign was indeed seen as aggression against Uzbek ways of life.[15]

Women's Division members first discussed plans for the Hujum in Moscow in May 1926, and the plans included attention to unveiling, but this was not supposed to be the main focus of the campaign. Serafima Liubimova, who as head of the Women's Division for Central Asia had considerable influence, argued against agitation for unveiling that year in her advice to women organizers, saying it might "play into the hands of basmachis."[16] Robiya Nosirova attended the meeting in Uzbekistan where Zelenskii announced the Hujum, as well as follow-up meetings, and she noted that there was disagreement about unveiling within the Women's Division. At the Uzbekistan Communist Party Central Committee meeting, some Party members voiced "strong support for freeing women and girls from the slavery of [the] paranji and chachvon," but in regional meetings Communists supported a more subtle unveiling movement, with unveiling meetings only for wives of "responsible workers."[17]

In Uzbekistan, a high-level Hujum Commission implemented the Party's plans for the attack. The commission included the leading figures of Uzbek politics, Yo'ldosh Oxunboboev, president of the Uzbek Soviet government, Akmal Ikromov, first secretary of the CPUz, and Faizulla Xo'jaev, chairman of the Council of People's Commissars of Uzbekistan. Two women sat on the commission: Zinaida Prishchep-chik, who had come from Moscow in 1926 to head the CPUz Women's Division, and Tojixon Shodieva (introduced in chapter 5), who was appointed to the CPUz Central Committee and was made deputy direc-tor of the Hujum Commission. While plans for the Hujum came from Moscow, CPUz members made decisions concerning what the Hujum would mean in Uzbekistan.[18]

Although it is unclear who decided that the Hujum would empha-size unveiling, it is certain that Uzbek political leaders on the Hujum Commission strongly supported the idea. Between December 1926 and February 1927, the commission made its strategy known: mass, public unveilings would be the Party's instrument for breaking down seclusion and drawing Uzbek women into public life. In the internal Party argu-ment over whether the paranji was a symptom or an instrument of women's subordination, the latter explanation had won: for women to be free and equal, the paranji had to disappear. The need to unveil was emphasized in Party and government circles, where members were told that the women in their families would be called on to unveil on Inter-national Women's Day, March 8, 1927.

In February, *Yangi Yo'l* published a large announcement, the first sign of its support for mass unveiling: "Comrade women and girls! You have freedom and the right to throw off your paranji and chachvon! Since the paranji has been the chain of enslavement, no woman or girl can set herself free from slavery while she is under the paranji!" *Yangi Yo'l* repeated the message in its March issue: "Throw off your paranji and chachvon, the legacy of custom and religion, which stands between you and work, you and civilization."[19] This presented the CPUz official inter-pretation of unveiling; such action would strike a blow at religious tra-dition and would bring women into the public and the work force.

Unveiling agitation increased in February, in prelude to the March Women's Day celebrations. In the CPUz newspaper, *Qizil O'zbekiston*, there was a flurry of attention to women's liberation. Debate about unveiling was heated. One reporter, A'zam, wrote excitedly, "It used to be that we had no social thought . . . but now it will be clear to anyone who goes out among the people . . . the movement for throwing off the paranji has demonstrated that social thought has been born and exists." He reported on arguments among workers about unveiling, and con-cluded that "we have an invitation" for those men who think women need to veil: "Cover yourself up in a paranji."[20] *Qizil O'zbekiston* started publishing frequent reports of public unveilings, noting that 112 women unveiled in Chust, the city of Fargana, and Kokand and that student activists and wives at the Central Asian State University held an unveiling meeting, as did members of the Party and the army, with their wives. "They made speeches that they would not re-veil and that they would convince others to unveil."[21] At meetings in schools and among activists, participants were directed to organize processions and join in public ceremonies on March 8.

Aisha B., a sixteen-year-old Tatar girl, was studying at the Medical Technical School in Tashkent when the Hujum was announced. She was a Komsomol member. Komsomol girls who could speak Uzbek were told to go to Tashkent's mahallas, call on women, and invite them to the March 8 demonstration in the heart of the old city. Aisha paid calls on Uzbek women with an Uzbek classmate, Salomat Nazarova. On March 8, she and Salomat went to Uzbek homes and led the women by the hand to the square. Uzbek Party leaders gave speeches urging women to unveil. As women unveiled, Aisha helped to collect the paranjis and chachvons, throwing them on a fire. She said that at the time, she participated mainly because she was told to, and it was interesting. She was not really aware of activism among Uzbek women. She did not regard burning paranjis as a serious matter and said that only later did she understand the degree of opposition and violence that some unveiled Uzbek women faced.[22]

Rahbar-oi remembered the presence of the major Uzbek political leaders at the Women's Day unveiling demonstration in Tashkent. In 1927, Russians were a small minority of Uzbekistan's population, but they outnumbered Uzbeks in the Party. But the public unveiling meetings were singularly Uzbek events. They were not instances of Russians forcing Uzbeks to Russify or Uzbeks mechanically carrying out Russian plans. They were occasions when an active minority of Uzbek progressives who were Party members called on other Uzbeks to change a particular tradition of dress and behavior. Xo'jaev, Ikromov, and especially Oxunboboev were national leaders, well known and authoritative among Uzbeks, and they repeatedly argued on behalf of unveiling, even though this was not a popular position among Uzbek Communists. Unveiling meetings in other cities and for the next several years were led by prominent Uzbek Party members; several other women informants remembered Oxunboboev's presence at their unveiling meeting. These demonstrations seem unique as public expressions of Uzbek identity and as occasions instrumental in forming that identity through the performance of a public ritual.

The language of these unveiling meetings was specific to Uzbek culture: "Throw off your paranji!" While accounts in Russian described the Hujum as a campaign against "veils" (*pokrival*) or "chadras," the word used in the Uzbek context was always "paranji." If other Muslim women wore other veils, this was not the concern of the Uzbek Hujum, and if Uzbek women chose to don other head coverings after burning the paranji, most did not consider that a violation of the spirit of the campaign.

In major cities there were large unveiling meetings, and newspapers triumphantly proclaimed that hundreds or thousands of women unveiled. There were also many small meetings in villages and neighborhoods, where activists tried to convince neighbors to unveil. Bahrin-iso I. told of receiving a letter telling her that, as the village school teacher, she needed to hold an unveiling meeting in March 1927. She unveiled, and so did seventeen village women.[23]

O'lmas-oi H. was a sixteen-year-old school girl in Kokand in 1927 and the sister of a Party member. She recalled,

> I covered up [veiled] for one year—no, three months. We studied at Kamol-qazi school. There were rich men's daughters studying there too. They came wearing the paranji. I was tall by that time, and they laughed at me: "O'lmas-oi comes to school without a paranji!" I cried over the injustice of it. I said, "I won't go to school. They'll make fun of me again, saying, 'She isn't wearing a paranji!'" My older brother [a Communist] immediately . . . went and got a paranji at the bazaar. Then, after I had worn that paranji three months, we had women's liberation, carried out by my older brother, and then the paranji was put aside. My older brother became a Party member in 1918 . . . in 1927, in our home, he taught women's liberation . . . my older brother . . . invited them [neighborhood women], they came, then, there was an invitation, then the women took their paranjis off. They threw them off. My brother was the first to start this.[24]

O'lmas-oi, who came from a family that did not put her in a paranji at age twelve, veiled because of social pressure and then unveiled at her brother's urging. When the Hujum Commission could appeal to male

Kokand unveiling ceremony, 1927. Kokand Museum photo.

supporters, like Rahbar-oi's husband or O'lmas-oi's brother, the Party's strategy often worked.

Party and family influence was not always effective. Mafrat-xon M. (b. 1914, Kokand) was the daughter of an activist, Marhamat S., who had herself unveiled in 1924. Mafrat-xon, like O'lmas-oi, wore the paranji only briefly, but she began wearing it in 1929, at age fifteen, well after the Hujum was underway and against the example of her unveiled mother, whom she had accompanied to unveiling meetings. Mafrat-xon said that the women of the mahalla scorned her mother, calling her an infidel and saying, "You have no shame, going around with no paranji." Perhaps because of this social pressure, Mafrat-xon began wearing a paranji, but then she removed it, also in 1929, at an unveiling meeting. She said that she was not afraid, even though people on the streets tried to scare her. She remembered that when she unveiled "we had a domla, an Uzbek man with a big turban. He followed us and said, 'Kill them.' But gradually things became more peaceful." Mafrat-xon did not have religious education as a child and said about the clergy, "We knew they were the enemies of freedom." Mafrat-xon not only stopped veiling; as a Komsomol member, she became an activist for unveiling and gave lectures. She said, "We made women stop wearing paranjis. There were fines for making a paranji. Old-fashioned men, domlas, told their wives, 'You stay home, don't go out. You'll become corrupt.' But I became liberated. We were happy." Mafrat-xon worked with the Women's Division, going to homes, visiting women in the ichkari, giving them "a chance to become free," checking up on polygyny and underage marriage, and getting involved with elections for women's representatives. She saw the Hujum as more than just unveiling. "After a woman got a job, she was fine. If she did not work, she would not be liberated. So we tried to send women to work in the fields. They learned to work and earn money."[25]

Milli-xon Ibrohimova (b. 1911, Kokand region) began wearing a paranji at age fourteen and unveiled after joining the Komsomol at age seventeen. By this time she had already been married and divorced and was back in school, on her way to becoming a teacher. Unveiling was not easy for her: "My older brother said, 'You will throw it off!' My grandmother said, 'You will NOT throw it off!'" The Komsomol insisted, and in 1929 she unveiled at a meeting. She then went to school unveiled, and her mother became angry, refusing to let Milli-xon attend school, or even eat, and speaking harshly to her. In 1931, Milli-xon's brothers forced her mother to unveil. Milli-xon, like others, was uncomfortable walking the streets unveiled, and so she covered up with scarves. Ultimately, as a Party member and government official, Milli-xon led another campaign against the paranji in Namangan after World War II. During the war, many women appeared on the streets in paranjis, and Milli-xon said that in 1946 "eight thousand paranjis were removed. We did away with it!"[26]

Most women who unveiled were uncomfortable appearing in public, and many re-veiled. Women who were not used to being seen in public were self-conscious, and women who thought that showing their faces in public was sinful were ashamed. But discomfort was not only internal, religious, and psychological: it was produced externally by rumors and threats. The association between unveiling and prostitution was strengthened by rumor, so that any unveiled Uzbek, regardless her character, was likely to be called a whore on the street, and false rumors about her actions would spread rapidly through the neighborhood. In addition, threats of death were not empty; verbal attacks turned into physical attacks, rape, and murder, as will be discussed in the next chapter. Many women's reluctance to unveil, and motivation for re-veiling, came from real fear of possible social and personal consequences.

## THE PARTY'S LEVERAGE

The Party announced that all women should unveil, but it worked through families where there was Party or government influence. Party members and government workers were not simply told that they should unveil women in their families; they were threatened with expulsion if they did not fulfill this directive. However, threats and coercion aimed at male Party members did not always work; women had to balance many needs and pressures. With all of the pressure against the veil, pressure to conform to the tradition of veiling was even stronger. No matter how many unveiling meetings were held, and no matter how many women threw off the veil for a day or a week, in the late 1920s, during the height of the Hujum, the vast majority of Uzbek women remained veiled or returned to veiling.

Some veiled contextually, wearing the paranji when social pressure was most severe and doffing it when conditions made doing so easy. In 1927, having returned from Moscow where she had not veiled at all, Manzura H.'s mother, the wife of a Tashkent Communist, was attending a school where most of the women were unveiled. In Tashkent, she would leave her home wearing the paranji, stop at a relative's home en route to school, leave the paranji there, and attend school unveiled. On the way home she would stop and don her paranji. After several years of this, her husband came under severe pressure from the Party to make his wife stop veiling, and he insisted that she attend an unveiling meeting. She went, taking her nine-year-old daughter, Manzura. When Manzura saw her mother go on stage and throw her paranji onto a pile, she slipped up to the stage, retrieved the paranji from the pile, and took it outdoors. When her mother exited the theater, having been added to the list of unveiled women, Manzura handed her mother the paranji and she put it back on. Manzura said that her mother stopped wearing the paranji completely in the early 1930s, by which time unveiled women were at least a comfortable minority in Tashkent.[27]

Manzura's mother's retention of the veil should not be understood as a form of religious resistance to the state, but as an accommodation to the pressures of her community. When Manzura's mother lived in Moscow, she did not veil. Clearly, then, she did not see veiling as either necessary or as some desirable symbol of her Uzbek identity or religious piety, or she would not have abandoned it so easily. When she returned to Uzbekistan, she wore it because her neighbors wore it, and she abandoned it when unveiling had passed its "early adopters" stage. Pressured by the Party, her husband, and her community, she made her own decisions about veiling and unveiling.

## PERSUADING WOMEN

In the Women's Division's ideal, women would unveil as a conscious sign of their understanding of their rights and equality with men. This ideal shaped Soviet accounts of the Hujum, but evidence of such consciously political unveiling was not frequently met. Rahbar-oi, perhaps, fulfilled that ideal. She used an opportunity that the state and Party provided through the mass-unveiling campaign to get rid of her hated paranji, acting according to her own wish and her husband's wish and contrary to the rest of his family. She was glad to unveil and gave her testimony at the unveiling ritual with prompting, but without coercion. Many other women also saw these meetings as an opportunity to take an action that they might not have been brave enough to take alone. However, others who attended these public rituals, led there by girls like Aisha and prompted by national leaders, were forced to unveil. The government's internal police agency reported from all over Uzbekistan unveiling meetings where most of the women did not want to unveil, but where they were threatened by political leaders, and sometimes Party and Komsomol members at the meetings pulled chachvons and paranjis off women.[28]

Some women activists tried to encourage a more limited form of veiling, rather than persuading women to burn paranjis on ritual bonfires. Some called for women to "uncover," that is, to remove the chachvon from their faces, rather than "throw off the paranji." Local branches of the Women's Division offered literacy courses and other benefits to "uncovered" women, including those who were willing to lift their chachvons but not to remove their paranjis. Similarly, as Camron Amin notes, even in Qasim Amin's late nineteenth-century writings about unveiling, what was meant was uncovering the face, not the head, and in Turkey and Iran's unveilings, uncovering the face was the usual understanding of unveiling; going about with uncovered hair was a radical second step.[29] Most Uzbek women who threw off their paranjis adopted some other form of head covering. Young activist women often wore *do'ppis* (embroidered caps), but older and married women were more likely to wear a large scarf that could be used to cover the face if the unveiled woman felt uncomfortable in the public eye. Even Jahon Obidova, one of the leading activists in the Party and a true Communist, frequently wore a scarf to cover her head and hair.[30]

Both the veiled and the unveiled feared they would be harassed—the unveiled by traditionalists, and the veiled by Communists. Rahbaroi was so uncomfortable without her paranji, with the stares and jeers, that she would carry a newspaper with her when she went out, holding it in front of her face when she walked. On the first day after the mass unveiling, she would have re-veiled if possible—not because she liked veiling, but because of her discomfort in being one of very few unveiled women in public places. At the unveiling ceremonies some paranjis were burned, partly for the symbolism of the gesture, but partly so that the unveiled could not re-veil. However, urban women often owned more than one paranji, or they borrowed paranjis from other family members or bought new ones. Discussions in *Yangi Yo'l* from 1927 to 1929 recognized that women who unveiled often re-veiled, and the journal proposed strategies to counter this trend through persuasion and incentives.[31]

Sobira Xoldarova and many of *Yangi Yo'l*'s writers called upon daughters to bring their mothers to unveiling meetings. Oidin's play, *A Step toward Modernity*, was performed for the March 8 holiday at women's clubs, and the anti-veiling film *Chachvon* played in theaters in 1927. Fiction writers attempted to allay women's fears and counter widespread rumors and threats that deterred unveiling. The heroine of one such story was torn between her Communist husband's wish for her to unveil and the instructions of local religious practitioners who told her that her son's illness was God's punishment for her unveiling. Ultimately,

Communism and modernity triumphed when Ana-bibi's husband called a doctor who successfully treated her son.[32]

Rahbar-oi reflected another piece of anti-paranji propaganda in her speech at the March 8 unveiling ceremony, as she remembered it decades later. She accused the paranji of harming women's health. During the late 1920s, various doctors, no doubt with government instruction, carried out research to demonstrate that the paranji contributed to diseases of the eyes, eclampsia, and the slowing of child development.[33] Anti-paranji propaganda used nearly every available device for persuasion, from scientific and religious arguments, to fiction and personal testimony, to threats.

*Yangi Yo'l* published several histories of the paranji that sought to discredit it as foreign. Miyon Bo'zruk, a scholar who was strongly influenced by Turkish modernism, wrote a history of veiling, tracing it to pre-Islamic customs, to the Prophet's teachings, and to Arab and Persian culture. In Central Asia, where urban Muslims adopted the paranji but nomads did not, "it made an already corrupt life even worse. It strengthened men's already great authority . . . and it made women's sentence more severe." Bo'zruk linked unveiling to improved motherhood:

It is wrong to express ideas such as, "Since today's mothers do not want to lift the paranji, let us start with the younger generation, putting them on the path to new life." It is in the younger generation's interest to remove the paranji from today's mothers. Because the paranji is the companion of custom and legend. It is the relative of old logic and thinking. A child brought up by a mother who cannot separate herself from old customs and beliefs is one who is brought up badly . . . A child brought into the world from a stupid, thick-headed, and spineless fount like a piece of meat—how will that child become intelligent, clear thinking, strong willed?[34]

By contrast, the Jadid-turned-Communist G'azi Yunus, whose wife unveiled in 1924, sought to dissociate the widespread use of the paranji from Islam. He insisted that the paranji should be abandoned because it was a distortion of the Prophet's teachings. The Prophet's instructions about dress were intended kindly, to force slave owners to provide slaves with clothing, but misguided ulama had misused those teachings for their own economic benefit. G'azi Yunus noted that the Jadids had often raised the "hijab issue": "Raising [the hijab issue] has extended the division that existed before the October Revolution between some of the proponents of modernity and Jadids, and the ulama who were on the side of tradition." He viewed the Hujum in 1927 as a continuation of the earlier debate. He also drew parallels with other countries, saying that much of the Islamic world had freed itself from the veil and that a similar contest was taking place in Turkey, Iran, and Egypt. While Miyon Bo'zruk appealed to Turkish and nationalist arguments for unveiling, G'azi Yunus argued as a Jadid, trying to reassure believers that they could unveil without abandoning religion.[35]

Soviet accounts of the Hujum stressed the campaign's antireligious aspects. Women were assumed to be acting out a conscious rejection of Islam when they unveiled. However, Uzbeks who wrote articles and stories for an Uzbek reading public did not use strongly antireligious arguments in trying to persuade their audience to abandon veiling. Their critiques of religion tended to continue Jadid criticisms, arguing against "superstition," abuses by religious leaders, and wrong understandings of Islam, rather than against religion as a whole. Overtly antireligious arguments for unveiling, while they played an important role in the Russian-language All-Union Women's Division journal *Kommunistka*, and thus shaped historians' understandings of the discourses used in the 1920s, were often deemphasized by Uzbek advocates of unveiling. However, poet and playwright Hamza Hakimzoda Niyoziy tied the paranji to the corrupt wealthy, to degenerate mullahs, and to foreign cultures and influences. Hamza, a former Jadid, was a fighter for Communism and he wrote words designed to provoke and divide:

*Today is March 8*
Oh, you foreign thing called paranji, your hand is filthy; don't come
    near Uzbek women and girls, get yourself out of here! . . .

Oh Rich Man!
All lubricating oil inside!
Face a drum, nose a surnai [oboe].
Today a hand-caddy of mud is more valuable than you.
Deflowering brides, selling maidens,
Holding slave girls and servants . . .

Don't stay; go into exile, cursing.
Today it will be hard for you, bad for your condition . . .

Do you see there? Women announced freedom, throwing off
   paranjis.
Don't cast your evil eye on them . . .

Oh Domla!
Bite your fingers in amazement, twist your beard until it looks like
   rice straw. When you've tightened your turban, hang your head
   a bit. If you're upset, saying, "Why are women throwing off their
   paranjis?" look to yourself in tears . . .

Oh fanatic vermin!
Smoke your opium sitting by the grate!
Take pleasure, sip green tea,
And bind your belt for a journey to the Day of Judgment!
But I have some advice for you:
Take the paranji and chimmat [chachvon], which you brought,
   away with you and go to your grave with it!
Paranji and Chimmat!
Go back quickly whence you came,
Make your Hajj to Mecca,
Find your place in Hell!

While G'azi Yunus, another Jadid turned Communist, wanted some
accommodation with Islamic ideas and leadership to encourage unveiling, Hamza linked unveiling to overthrowing the influence and authority of both the wealthy and the clergy.[36]

My informants included Uzbek women who were in their teens and
twenties during the 1920s: six of them never wore paranjis, at least fourteen unveiled in the 1920s, and two did not unveil but lived in seclusion until much later. The secluded women's lives differed greatly from
both the veiled and the unveiled. Humoira H. (b. 1913) was the daughter of a scholar who taught at a Kokand madrasa. She studied with an
otin in childhood, but never attended Soviet school. When her father's
madrasa was closed, he continued teaching religious students privately
at home and found work that allowed him to stay outside the Soviet system. He arranged his daughter's marriage to one of his students, who
was a merchant. Both before and after marriage, Humoira stayed inside

the courtyard constantly. She said she did not wear a paranji because she did not go outside. After her father was arrested, and her husband disappeared in World War II, she could no longer maintain a life of seclusion, and she went out, unveiled, to work.

Another informant, Sottiba-xon M. (b. 1920, Namangan) was the daughter of a farmer who raised flowers. He sent her brothers to school, but did not allow her to leave home or attend school. During collectivization, he managed to retain his land as an individual owner. Because he made his living outside the state system, his family life did not come under state scrutiny. Although Sottiba-xon was taken to a demonstration once to unveil, she lived entirely in seclusion until 1953, when her brother arranged a marriage for her to a man who encouraged her to interact in the public.

These two cases suggest that families that managed to make a living without entering the state-run economy were able to preserve a separation of family life from the intrusive, modernizing state. Neither Humoira's nor Sottiba-xon's father was faced with all of the state's force to unveil women. Continued seclusion meant that these two girls, unlike other urban girls, did not obtain any modern Soviet education. Their experience contrasts with that of Muattar S., who lived in seclusion until her husband died in the 1920s, but afterwards unveiled under duress, attended a literacy course, and taught a primary class in Bukhara.[37]

The Party's call, "Throw off your paranji!" was often interpreted as an order from an increasingly powerful government. While there was no law against the paranji, many local authorities acted as though a law existed. Saodat A., born in 1906 in a village in northern Tajikistan, did not recall exactly when she stopped wearing the paranji, but said everyone in her village was required to throw it off. She reported that "the government would not let [women] wear the paranji . . . There were lots of representatives of the government, so no women went out with the paranji—they would snatch it off . . . There were meetings. There were fines for wearing the paranji." After throwing off the paranji, women in her village wore chopans (men's robes) on their heads. Other informants mention that paranji wearers or sellers were fined.[38]

Most women unveiled because of coercion. Either government representatives told them to unveil, or their husbands, under government pressure, told them to unveil. Bahriniso I. said that most women did not agree to unveil; rather, "their husbands were forced to make them unveil . . . Their husbands were working! At work, what should a man say when he is told to 'make your wife unveil'? . . . If he says to her, 'Don't unveil,' the husband of the woman who does not unveil will be put out of work." Mahtab-oi A., from Bukhara, said that she unveiled because her husband urged her to; he was working for a government store, where he came under pressure to conform to political directives.[39] Havo-xon Ataqulova said that her mother, a nursery-school teacher, was coming home on a train from some travel, and there was a meeting at the railway station where women were all told they must unveil. So her mother unveiled.[40] Aziza-xon I., who wore a paranji from age nine, unveiled when she was told to do so, as a student at the Fargana Teacher's Training School in 1928. She said that she, like others in her family, thought showing her face was a sin, but she did as she was told. The conviction that only the paranji fulfilled religious requirements may have faded. When I asked Aziza-xon whether she had unveiled, she snapped, "Well, you don't see me wearing it now, do you?"[41]

Muattar S. said that "Soviet power" told women in Bukhara to attend a meeting and burn their paranjis. Most reports from Bukhara, both accounts from 1928 and from informants in the 1990s, said that unveiling there was quick and thorough. Halima M., as a small child, went with her mother to an unveiling meeting and watched the paranjis burn. Her mother never wore a paranji again; as she said, "the government would not allow it."[42] Informants said that in Bukhara, women might cover their faces with scarves, but the paranji was not seen on the streets much after 1928. However, one informant, Ho'shvaqt I., from a village near Bukhara, suggested another explanation. She said that her older sister unveiled at a meeting at a teahouse, where paranjis were burned, but that afterwards girls did not go out into the streets much at all. She said that a veiled woman on the street would be abused.[43] Reinforced seclusion of women was one response to the Hujum.

Local activists used numerous strategies for getting women to unveil. In Samarkand, rumors spread that the husbands of women who did not unveil would be shot. Local committee members wrote lists of women's names, gathered them at a meeting, and refused to let them go home in paranji. In one mahalla, a reporter wrote that at an unveiling meeting, eighty women unveiled, twenty-five because they wanted to and the rest under duress. An activist who was the daughter of a local Islamic religious leader pulled paranjis from women's heads at the meeting. The militia gathered some women and told them that unveiling was the law, while others were told they would pay a tax for veiling. Around Andijon, there were unveiling meetings where local authorities told men to bring their wives or pay a fine.[44]

Activists for unveiling, in particular the higher levels of Women's Division leadership, wanted to believe that unveiling would be the result of a change in consciousness.[45] Women, upon learning of their rights under Soviet law and the opportunities of modern life, would voluntarily unveil and then enroll in literacy classes or look for work outside the home. Some of my informants proved them right. Rahbar-oi Olimova, O'lmas-oi H., Mafrat-xon M., Saodat Shamsieva, and Milli-xon Ibrohimova. remembered unveiling as personally significant, a moment when they and other Uzbek women took a conscious step toward liberation and education. But more women unveiled because of coercion than conviction. Unveiling rarely changed their beliefs, practices, family structures, or lifestyles, and it was easily reversed. One woman from Bukhara, responding to my question about why women unveiled, answered, "It was written on their foreheads."[46] In Central Asian Islamic belief, God writes one's destiny on one's forehead; unveiling must have been willed by God.

Even if the campaign against the paranji did not instill political awareness in all Uzbek women, it did begin to erode the practice of paranji wearing. Many informants recalled that their mothers continued to wear the paranji until death, but few who were born after 1916 wore a paranji. Most were brought up to wear some sort of head covering. They were told as children, even daughters of Communists, that it was shameful for a woman to go around with a bare head. The most common forms of clothing for all but a few Uzbek women continued to fulfill Central Asian norms of modest dress.

## COMPARISONS: TURKEY, AFGHANISTAN, AND IRAN

State-sponsored unveiling campaigns were a part of broader modernization schemes not only in the Soviet Union, but also in Turkey, Afghanistan, and Iran. The historian Dilarom Alimova writes,

A study of materials in Uzbek convinces one that the idea of women's emancipation was carried forward by the example of Turkey. In Central Asia at that time the reforms of the bourgeois governments of Turkey and Afghanistan had great resonance, specifically the publishing of laws outlawing the wearing of the chadra, attempts at economic innovation, encouraging women to work in production . . . the possibility of ending the paranji by decree attracted wide attention . . . A. Ikromov and S. Liubimova were adherents of this point of view.[47]

Central Asians who read publications like *Qizil O'zbekiston, Yangi Yo'l,* and *Yer Yuzi* learned about reform efforts in other countries, and Turkey attracted considerable attention in Uzbekistan. There was no law against veiling in Turkey, but even Uzbek political leaders had the impression that Turkish women's unveiling was accomplished by decree and apparently, because of the press coverage, they also believed that Turkish women's unveiling was widespread.[48] Uzbeks were presented with photos of unveiled Turkish women, and advocates of unveiling could point to these in order to persuade their fellow Uzbeks.

Kemalists in Turkey and Communists in Uzbekistan supported the modernizing regimes and were the most likely, and were under the most state pressure, to promote new norms, such as educating their daughters in modern schools and bringing women into public spaces unveiled.[49] In both Turkey and Uzbekistan, the unveiled woman was a symbol of the regime's modernizing program. In neither Turkey nor Uzbekistan was veiling outlawed by the central government, but the state in both places made clear that the veil was an obstacle to modernization.

Turkey was heir to a state, the Ottoman Empire, that had regulated men's and women's dress through law. Mustafa Kemal ridiculed the traditional dress of both men and women in Turkey and promoted a "Europeanization" of the dress of both. In 1925 and again in 1934, the government passed laws to Europeanize men's dress. First the "hat law" banned the fez and decreed that men wear European-style brimmed hats. Then the state banned religious garb, such as turbans and robes, outside houses of worship.[50] These measures, later imitated by Reza Shah in Iran, asserted the state's control over the bodies of its male subjects. Camron Amin notes that the hat law for Iranian men was "an invasive and annoying display of state authority, and there are records of people resisting the change."[51] In both Turkey and Iran, this state assertion of control over men's bodies and men's dress preceded its appropriation of authority over women's bodies.

Women's veils, Mustafa Kemal said, made Turkey's enemies think that Turkish women "are kept away, by Turkish men, from life, world, humanity, and business gains." To change this false image, women were told to abandon the veil and adopt modern European clothing—as long as that dress was modest. Mustafa Kemal promoted women's unveiling largely through propaganda and by example, presenting his unveiled adopted daughters in public and urging others to unveil. Some local bans on veiling appeared, and a national decree against veiling was proposed in 1935 but was defeated.[52] Unveiling proceeded "voluntarily," or through social and state pressure, with those attending modern schools and families associated with Kemalist politics leading the effort. For a woman, to be modern and Kemalist meant not only uncovering one's head, but also wearing European dress, appearing in public, and mixing socially with men.[53] Western dress was the symbol of Mustafa Kemal Atatürk's modern republic for both men and women.

By contrast, the unveiling campaign in Uzbekistan focused only on women's dress and was mainly concerned with the veil as a symbol of patriarchal oppression and women's seclusion.[54] Some women activists wanted to make women's dress modern and European, but this was a peripheral matter. The veil, in Uzbek Communist ideology, was what kept women locked away, enslaved to men, uneducated, unequal, unable to participate in the building of socialism. Unveiling would free women to enter the public realm, to become educated, and to work. An actual decree against the paranji and chachvon was proposed and defeated in 1929 in Uzbekistan. While the Uzbek state did not use law to force change in dress, the Communist Party had more tools at hand for promoting and coercing unveiling than did Turkey's Kemalists: in addition to propaganda and mass unveiling demonstrations, there were rewards for unveiled women, pressure on Communist men to unveil wives or be removed from the Party, and pressure on non-Party men to unveil their wives or lose their jobs. For a time in the late 1920s, as the state stepped up punishments for hindering women's unveiling, the Party seemed to see proof of its own effectiveness and legitimacy in women's unveiling.[55]

King Amanullah's unveiling campaign in Afghanistan does not appear to have been an inspiration for Uzbekistan, but the Hujum may have inspired Amanullah's policy. Amanullah, formerly an opponent of unveiling, launched his attack on the veil in 1928, well after the Uzbek Hujum was underway, and it failed miserably. In Uzbekistan, the news from Afghanistan in this period focused on that country as a haven for Basmachis; *Qizil O'zbekiston* presented Afghanistan not as a model of successful modernization, but as a channel for the British military threat.[56] Amanullah decreed unveiling, but there is little indication that Uzbek activists saw that decree as successful; Amanullah abdicated his throne in January 1929.

Iran's unveiling campaign began much later, in 1936. Unveiling in Iran, as in Uzbekistan, was a part of a broader project to transform women's lives, with similar emphases on bringing women into society, into mixed social gatherings, and into education and the workplace. The Shah's effort at modernizing women faced serious social and religious opposition and also suffered from the internal contradiction that modern did not mean equal. Women in Iran were to be modern in the sense that they would participate in the public realm, but they would not be equal under the law nor have the full rights of citizens. While Reza Shah's regime was avowedly anti-Communist, and scholarship on women in Iran in the 1920s and 1930s offers only Turkey and the West as inspirations for the Iranian "Women's Awakening" campaign, it would be surprising if the Iranian left, at least, was not fully aware of the Soviet Hujum.[57]

In Turkey, if there were violent responses specifically to the state's equalizing policies for women, or to the state's promotion of unveiling, researchers have not discussed them. There were, of course, broader instances of violent resistance to the Turkish state's modernizing policies, including revolts in the late 1920s aroused by the state's suppression of religious orders. In Iran's later unveiling campaign, the only reports of violence against women for unveiling were made in the 1940s, while there were many reports of violence against the veiled, at least in the form of ripping off veils in public. In Uzbekistan, violent opposition to state policies and violence against women merged. Women who unveiled, as well as women activists who took on new roles in local Soviet government, became murder victims at alarmingly high rates.[58]

## A COMMUNIST UNVEILING

The Communist Party, while promoting the Hujum, was also engaged in a struggle against the Islamic clergy. The madrasa-educated clergy who were employed in the higher levels of the religious structures in Central Asia were divided: some supported many of the Party's programs, including land reform and unveiling, while others strongly opposed both. Village clergy, who were often not attuned to urban trends in Islam, tended to oppose both unveiling and land reform, in word and in deed. As discussed in the next chapter, many clergy actively propagandized against unveiling and even advocated attacking and punishing unveiled women. However, there were also mullahs who declared that the paranji had no support in Sharia and who encouraged women to unveil.

The Communist Party opposed attempts to subvert the meaning it assigned to unveiling. The progressive mullah who proclaimed that the Quran did not require the paranji ultimately was deemed an insidious enemy of the Party. This put activists and would-be unveilers in a quandary. Even if they could have found social support for unveiling from Islamic clergy members, they were supposed to reject that aid as a poison pill, one that would empty unveiling of its significance for creating a new Communist society. The historian Bibi Pal'vanova describes attempts by ishons (clergy) to support unveiling as a subversive form of opposition:

> In the face of the massive striving by women to throw off the paranji, the provocations of the bois [the wealthy] and ishons suffered failure. The ishons with more foresight understood this and therefore set out on different stratagems. Unable to counteract the movement, they, in some places, attempted to capture it in their own hands. Several ishons unveiled their own wives, attempted to spread their influence to unveiled women . . .
>
> In Fergana oblast, the clergy made public a legal opinion (which they really wanted to publish in the press and requested permission) which says that in the Quran there is no directive for veiling women.[59]

Another historian, Roza Karryeva, following interpretations of mullahs' actions that can be found in government reports from the late 1920s, argues that those who unveiled their wives sought to deceive: "In this way, they were able to confuse a portion of the illiterate dehqons [farmers] who had backward ideas. And even individual Soviet women workers were not able to understand what was happening. These actions—teaching women literacy, removing paranjis— were seen as indications of common interest."[60] According to Pal'vanova and Karriyeva, the progressive mullahs were responding to mass unveiling. These mullahs declared that veiling was not necessary because they saw women unveiling and feared it indicated their own influence was waning. Obviously, the same charge could be laid at the feet of the Communist Party, which did not support unveiling until 1927; before that, Communists saw women deciding to unveil, and perhaps their own declaration of the Hujum was an attempt to gain control of a movement.

As plans of the Hujum campaign were underway, *Qizil O'zbekiston* published a discussion about requesting a fatwa (a religious decision) from the progressive clergy to support unveiling. One of those arguing for a fatwa thought it might reduce the potential that unveiling would drive men to divorce unveiled wives.[61] A *Yangi Yo'l* article that appeared after the Hujum began indicated some of the arguments that Uzbek women were hearing, pitting the Party's unveiling against unveiling as proposed by Jadids and progressive mullahs:

During the Jadid period, when the native-national press was carrying on an interesting discussion of the "hijab issue"—from its fruit may even one thing prosper—nothing was put into action . . . The Bolsheviks addressed the issue of women's liberation with different methods and approaches. They took a completely different way; [not] dry, aimless agitation, or forced removal of the paranji as in Turkey . . . In its agitational campaign, the Hujum is not only against the paranji but against the whole old way of life . . .

In the Jadid period the "hijab issue" did not go beyond the standards of the Shariat . . . In fact, it remains clear that Islam, like other religions, separates men from women, and Muslims from other religious people, viewing the first as higher and discriminating against the second. Since that is the way the matter stands, nothing other than idiocy will come of addressing the "hijab issue" with reexaminations of the Shariat. Since the issue of the Hujum has been raised, it is evident that these ideas have not yet ended . . . Getting a "fatwa" from the "ulama and fuzalo" over the paranji issue is unnecessary . . . What do we need their fatwa for? Let's liberate ourselves from following the umma [the Islamic community]! Since the umma has acknowledged the Soviet government as its own government and has recognized well the two-faced spiritual leaders who have been fooling them for centuries, is there still a need for their fatwa? Certainly not; from now on the people will not follow them . . .

Some individuals who came out at the front of the Hujum say the Hujum campaign should be seen as an opening exercise. Some of them say, "Let the Central Executive Committee take a decision for a universal casting off of the paranji." However, the Bolshevik Party, bearing in mind the triviality of such measures, began to carry out the Hujum campaign in the right way, and it is evident that in this matter the Party's hopes are coming true and prospering. Today paranji-removing celebrations will begin all over Uzbekistan.[62]

In 1927, Jadid ideas were still attractive to Uzbek intellectuals, and in analyses of the OGPU (Soviet secret police) even Uzbek Party leaders sometimes saw the Party's antireligious measures as a continuation of Jadid efforts to reform Islam rather an effort to crush religious activity. Hadicha, in the excerpted *Yangi Yo'l* article, tried to discredit Jadids by pointing out that at their peak of influence their hijab discussions did not result in mass unveiling. She assumed her readers were impressed by Turkey's unveiling, and she tried to discredit that as well, as coerced, while arguing that the Uzbek campaign was superior because it was based on voluntary responses to propaganda. She argued that the people knew mullahs to be deceptive and did not need a fatwa from them. However, according to Uzbek Communist Party records from June 1927, the progressive clergy had become the dominant element among religious teachers and prayer leaders. The progressives, who according to the Party were closely tied to the merchant class, were increasing in organizational strength, setting up schools, and initiating women's activities.[63] The Uzbek historian R. Kh. Aminova notes that "the women who unveiled on March 8 [1928 in Tashkent] turned out to include 80 wives of the city's mullahs and rich men, though no emancipation propaganda was carried out among them."[64] In a revision of earlier Soviet assessments of the potential for progressive-clergy support for unveiling, Dilorom Alimova describes the relationship of the Party and the clergy thus:

Alongside [the conservatives] existed the so-called progressive clergy, striving to hold the wide masses of women under their influence, and therefore relating positively to liberation. Several workers of the Women's Divisions suggested establishing contact with the progressive clergy with the goal of using it in the process of the "Hujum" for neutralizing the activities of the reactionary representatives of Islam. That was a constructive suggestion. However, in those years any contact with the clergy by the Party or Soviet workers was inconceivable.[65]

If the Party had allowed the progressive mullahs to issue a fatwa in the Party-censored press, if it had appeared to cooperate with them, the course of unveiling might have eased considerably. But unveiling in itself was not the Party's goal; the Party's goal was to transform society by diminishing traditional authority and consolidating its own authority. If unveiling had been sponsored by the progressive clergy as well as the Party, then it would have had multiple meanings. In the Hujum, removing the paranji was to symbolize women's liberation from the oppression of religious tradition, not her participation in modernizing Islamic values. It was also meant to demonstrate her support of the Soviet state.

## ❧ 8 ❧

# THE COUNTER-HUJUM
## Terror and Veiling

IN A SIX-MONTH PERIOD IN 1927 and 1928, at least 235 Uzbek women were murdered for unveiling. During the three main years of the Hujum campaign, from 1927 to 1929, some 2,000 were murdered in connection with unveiling.[1] During the Soviet period, historians either minimized these murders as a distraction from the Party's overall success in transforming women, or emphasized them as evidence of Uzbek society's dire need for the Party's helping hand in establishing equality for women.[2] More recent opinions on this gruesome episode have leaned instead toward blaming the Party for prematurely or inappropriately initiating the Hujum, thus stimulating a wave of violence against women who had no protection.[3] Shirin Akiner writes, "For Central Asians, [the Hujum] was a defeat and a brutal rape; the honor and dignity of the community was suddenly and monstrously violated. No other measure of Soviet policy . . . provoked such violent and outspoken resistance . . . More than a thousand unveiled women were murdered."[4]

These recent interpretations take blame away from the perpetrators of the murders and place it instead on the state—as if those who murdered women for unveiling were destined to do so. The assumed understanding of Central Asian society naturalizes violence against women and does not question why men's response to state intrusion into family life would be to harm women. In exploring this three-year burst of violence against women in Uzbekistan, from 1927–1930, this chapter emphasizes three points.

First, this burst of violence against women was an anomaly, not an expansion of a norm, and its context is exceedingly important in explaining it. The context was not simply the Party's Hujum campaign, but rather a terrific social upheaval and low-scale war situation that had begun with the 1916 uprising. Soviet policies since 1918 had sought to disrupt community structures and to remove traditional authority figures from their positions. Violence pervaded Central Asia, with resistance groups—the Basmachi—bringing armed conflict to villages in their struggle against the Red Army and Soviet government. The 1920s were not a peaceable time in Uzbekistan, and the wave of murders of women emerged in the midst of a broad social and political conflict that had been going on for ten years.[5]

Second, murders of women for unveiling were not spontaneous crimes of passion. They were premeditated, incited, and often involved groups of people. They were not usually responses to particular moments of unveiling. That is, while the Party did force women to hold Hujum meetings and to unveil at meetings, these incidents were not followed immediately by murders of women; offense at the state for forcing unveiling, or at women themselves for unveiling, does not seem to have translated directly into murders of women. The murderers instead acted with malice and planning and expressed hostility to the individual victim and her actions—unveiling, going to school, getting involved with the state's programs. They also expressed coordinated opposition to the state and the Communist Party, demonstrating that the local community, not the state, had authority over women's actions.

Third, murders of women were intended to terrorize other women. They were a demonstration—often deliberately gruesome, involving cutting, dismemberment, and the disposal of the body with symbolic dishonor. If this wave of violence can be compared to another, perhaps racist lynching in U.S. history would be an appropriate comparison.

In the turbulent and unsettled political, social, and economic context of 1920s Uzbekistan, violence was widespread. The state arrested and shot its enemies, political conflicts within villages often led to murder, and Basmachis and Red Army units attacked each other as well as uncooperative or unsupportive villagers. However, there is a difference between coercion and violence. While the state coerced women to unveil by every means available, the coercion to reveal one's face in public cannot be made the moral equivalent of murder, or even rape, as Akiner suggests. The state did not murder women for refusing to unveil. Uzbek men who opposed unveiling murdered women for showing their faces in public. In this chapter, state actions to force unveiling are noted as coercive; violence is reserved to describe the brutal physical attacks that some men carried out against women who unveiled.

Carroll Smith-Rosenberg, discussing gender tensions in another context, observes that:

> Hierarchical societies, concerned with the rigid maintenance of order, will act out these concerns upon the physical body . . . They will insist upon rigid dress codes and rules of physical decorum. Alternatively, societies or specific social groups that are in the throes of rapid change—in movement toward either less structure or a new and untried structure—will experience physical and sexual disorder as particularly threatening . . . Those who are perceived as outside and marginal to society, outside its regulations or between social categories, will be treated as simultaneously sexually dangerous and physically polluting. Stern efforts will be made to control them.[6]

Smith-Rosenberg connects times of rapid change to society's efforts at controlling perceived disorder, either by regulating those deemed most threatening to order—or perhaps by regulating those who are most easily controlled. In Uzbekistan's rural and urban sedentary communities, society was firmly patriarchal and Uzbek women's bodies were bounded by the paranji. But the rapid and forced social changes in Uzbekistan included a state attack on men's authority over women, and on Uzbek separateness from Russians and others, as well as an attack on nearly all socially prominent actors, namely the wealthy landowners, the merchants, and the clergy. In this context, women's unveiling was magnified as threatening and socially polluting. Murders of unveiled women were physical attempts to reassert one social boundary, to enforce at least one aspect of a social order that was under a full-scale Hujum.

The Hujum was not the only or even the most prominent of the Party's dramatic plans for change in Central Asia. In the sphere of culture, 1927 also brought a direct attack on religion, including the closing of maktabs and madrasas. The cultural revolution in Uzbekistan was similar to the Kemalist cultural revolution in Turkey: in both countries in 1926 and 1927, the veil, the Arabic alphabet, and the institutions of religion came under state attack. Uzbek leaders were conscious of Kemal's programs, and the Uzbek media published photos and articles on unveiled Turkish women and the new Turkish alphabet even as Uzbekistan launched its own new alphabet and anti-veiling campaign. But in Uzbekistan, sweeping economic changes were already underway when the cultural revolution started, and the most disruptive of these was land reform.

In 1920, after the fall of the Bukharan emir and his flight to Afghanistan, the Soviet government arrested hundreds of bois, members of the old elite and owners of large estates. After this, the remaining large landowners were left alone until after national delimitation in 1924. At that point the Party became more serious about class warfare in Central Asia. In 1925, the Uzbekistan Soviet government embarked on land reform, sending survey teams to every reachable village, assessing land use, and dispossessing large landowners. Their lands were redistributed to others, in theory to the poor and the landless. If they gave up their land to their tenants without a struggle, these landowners might be left in the village, but many were arrested or encouraged to leave. Some former large landowners retained enough social capital to get themselves elected to the local soviet (council). However, many others were dispossessed and exiled from their lands, leaving a leadership vacuum in many rural areas. Dehqons who were not so wealthy joined the Party so that they would be favored for local government, and here and there women were elected to village councils. This was a dramatic change in the rural social order. While old elites lost their sources of capital and social power, new, pro-Soviet classes took control, and the countryside lost any ability to unite or rally against Soviet power. In many places, though, bois and their supporters fought back; there were regular reports of the murders of people who had been elected to local councils and of government representatives who entered villages where there was Basmachi influence.[7]

Land reform had two goals: to take underutilized land from large landowners and put it into the hands of peasants who would be interested in fully exploiting the land; and to break village patronage relationships, freeing the poor and landless from their dependency on the wealthy. Politically, ideologues saw land reform as a means to initiate class warfare in the Uzbek countryside and to gain mass support for the Communist government.

In the cities, between 1924 and 1927, the Soviet government aimed to take control of the economy. Merchants with licenses for wholesale trade came under ever heavier taxation and scrutiny, and the government deliberately strove to undercut their social influence. The government gradually captured various sectors of the economy by taking control of banking and moneylending and of factories. By 1927, the government had extended control over cotton-collection points in the countryside and could thus set prices and sell the raw cotton exclusively to state factories, to the detriment of private and artisan producers, producing resentment. In 1926, Basmachis (which by now meant anyone who carried out violent and criminal acts in the countryside) attacked a cotton-collection point in Tashkent region and killed the workers there.[8] By 1929, when the state effectively controlled cotton production through its monopoly on credit and promised cotton-growing peasants an adequate supply of grain in exchange, there were numerous rural uprisings over grain shortages.[9] Similarly, the government took control of distributing silkworms on contract and collecting silk cocoons. H. Tillaxonova wrote an article criticizing the government for taking all of the silk produced in Uzbekistan, shipping it to Moscow factories, and leaving none for Uzbek artisan production.[10]

Until 1927, the government took a gradualist policy toward suppressing Islamic institutions, working at competing with them by undermining waqf revenues and directing them toward state schools. But in 1927, the government's anti-Islamic policy hardened. The government decreed the closing of all religious schools, as well as Islamic courts, putting the large clerical establishment out of work. At the same time, government propaganda discrediting the Islamic clergy increased rapidly.[11] When the state launched its major attack on Islamic clergy, common people may not have agreed with the state's view of mullahs as parasites, but did not defend them either. One of my informants, Bahriniso I., recalled that the mullah in her village was arrested in 1929 and that although people did not believe he was their enemy, "they stayed silent out of fear. [At first] none of them had been killed, none of them arrested. But after they were arrested, what could be done? People were afraid to their very souls."[12] There was resistance, including scattered demonstrations and uprisings, but the state's efforts to crush the wealthy landowners, merchants, and clergy deprived most villages of leadership that could have organized opposition.

This broad attack on the pillars of Uzbek society severely undermined the structure of Uzbek community, whose hierarchies had ossified in the Russian imperial period. Uzbek community boundaries were established through religious ritual, through rhetoric and proper behavior, and through the practice of separation from Russians. Those boundaries were already threatened by social changes before the revolution, but starting in 1925 the Soviet government set out to rid Uzbek society of the structures that maintained community boundaries. Many of those who found their status and their lifeways threatened fought back by joining Basmachi groups to oppose Soviet government actively, by emigrating, or by subverting government plans and programs, and by attacking local government and Party representatives.

This context for the Hujum is important for explaining its violent results. Many in Uzbek society understood the Hujum as one piece in a larger drive for social upheaval. A police report from the village of Bobkent showed ordinary farmers making this connection. A dehqon told his neighbors: "Soviet government carried out land reform and now carries out reform on the woman question, taking second wives from those who have them and giving them to the landless peasants. Removing the paranji is one of the means of the Soviet government to carry out this reform."[13]

Gregory Massell, seeking an explanation for the Hujum, emphasizes the ideology that its Moscow leaders articulated and argues that the Party sought to turn women into a "surrogate proletariat," that is, a group that would fulfill the revolutionary role of the working class in overthrowing the power of the wealthy. But a broader reading of the publications of the 1920s shows that the Party relied primarily on poor farmers and landless farm workers to become its revolutionary arm in Uzbekistan. Poor farmers were happy to receive land taken from the rich and played active roles in dekulakization (dispossession and sometimes arrest and exile of the wealthier farmers). Although Party rhetoric emphasized women's lost labor potential as a reason for women's liberation, efforts to bring women into the labor force or more generally into public life were small compared with land reform's redistribution of wealth to the

Paranji-burning ceremony at the Number 2 Cotton Factory, Kokand, 1934.
Kokand Museum photo.

poor male farmer and the resulting shift in power relationships in the
countryside.

Revolutionizing women was a consistent but much smaller emphasis for the Party, and the results of the two campaigns—the Hujum and
land reform—are telling. The Hujum did not turn Uzbek women into
a surrogate proletariat, but a few years of effort in the countryside did
break the ties between rich and the poor farmers and laid a foundation
for radical collectivization, which began in November 1929. Party planners started the Hujum in 1927 in only a limited number of regions,
those where land reform had already begun—namely the Fargana Valley and Tashkent and Samarkand regions. Bukhara, Xorazm, Qashqa

Daryo, and Surxon Daryo did not see much land reform until 1928, and that was also when the Hujum began in those regions. In general, the Communist Party of Uzbekistan was cautious about launching radical initiatives until 1930. The leadership was reluctant to push for change without at least a minimal number of local Party members and sympathizers; however, it turned out that even Party members were not reliable supporters of the Hujum.

## VIOLENCE AND UNVEILING

Until 1927, although there were Uzbek women who unveiled individually, women were not being killed for unveiling. There was, of course, violence against women in Uzbek society, including murders of women, but there is no evidence that Uzbek men ordinarily used the threat of murder to control women's actions. Some observers in the Women's Division portrayed violence among Uzbeks as unusually severe. In 1922, a Russian Women's Division worker characterized Uzbeks in the pages of *Kommunistka*: "The Uzbek woman-chadra-wearer, dim, sightless slave, whose husband beats her with 'blows of death' is trying to liberate herself from economic dependence and become independent."[14] Russian-language publications from the Women's Division drew on a body of records from local branches in Central Asia, branches that often handled cases of women who were fleeing abusive husbands. To some extent the Women's Division functioned as a battered women's shelter, but that distorted record does not indicate that Uzbek society treated women any more, or less, violently than any other society. While the Women's Division portrait must be seen as skewed, it did provide many examples of violence against women, violence that was both family-based and political. Several activist women were murdered, including one, Shermatova, who had divorced her husband when he took a second wife. Late in 1926, her ex-husband stabbed her to death; he was sentenced to death in March 1927.[15] The case attracted attention because Shermatova was an activist, but her husband's reason for murdering her seemed linked to the divorce more than to her activism.

Before the Hujum began, some Uzbek women had unveiled and they faced harassment and opposition, but there are no stories of women being murdered for unveiling until unveiling became a clear-cut Communist Party project. As soon as the Hujum began, popular stories associating unveiling with prostitution and sexual misconduct became rampant, reports of the rape of unveiled women became widespread, and many clergy members not only took a stand against unveiling but actively encouraged men in their communities to "punish" unveiled women. Reports of Hujum-related murders began to appear in the Uzbek press only days after the International Women's Day in 1927.

The Hujum Commission relied on Party members to unveil their wives and to support unveiling in their communities. This meant they leaned on people, mainly men, whose motives for joining the Communist Party varied widely, whose knowledge of Communism was usually limited, who were mainly illiterate, and who were generally savvy enough not to burn bridges in their own communities for the sake of a Party principle. Uzbek Party membership increased rapidly in the 1920s, as the Party sought supporters by opening membership while exercising little scrutiny and carrying out minimal training or oversight of members.[16] While a few Communists were idealists who genuinely supported Party programs, many more were apparently quite upset that the Party charged them with enforcing the unpopular Hujum. Some refused, and others undermined the Hujum in ways that actively harmed women. As violence exploded in Uzbekistan, the OGPU (Soviet secret police) investigated and reported on those incidents, records that I use here to examine the connection between incitement and murder.[17]

In Kassansoi, a Komsomol meeting in the spring of 1927 presented the Party's Hujum campaign, and eight women unveiled. After the meeting, the Komsomol secretary went to a teahouse and told the other men there that unveiled women were prostitutes.[18] In Shahrixon, near Andijon, the Women's Division director Hadija-xon G'oibjon qizi convinced a number of women to unveil on March 8, 1927; one week later she was murdered and so was her husband. Party members in Shahrixon, when asked about women who unveiled, said that unveiled women were all prostitutes and that respectable women would not unveil. As a result, according to *Qizil O'zbekiston* "all eighteen women who unveiled have now re-veiled."[19]

As soon as the Hujum began, clergy members in Andijon "spread propaganda . . . starting a very active movement" against unveiling. They preached that in other countries syphilis had emerged after women unveiled and told men not to give their wives permission to unveil because it was forbidden by the Quran.[20] In Bukhara, police reported that some members of the clergy said, upon seeing unveiled women wearing headscarves, "Look at how Muslim women have debased themselves.

It is not enough that men do this before the Russians, and look like monkeys, but women do too." One of them, Nurallaev, said, "They want the whole people to become infidels. Muslim women are throwing away their religion and turning to another." Some preached that neighboring states would attack the Soviet government for the unveiling campaign. In a provocative move, a group of sixty unveiled Bukharan women rode in an automobile caravan to an open-air meeting, passing a mosque on the way. Sixty men who were there for prayer became upset and began cursing them and propagandizing that unveiled women would become prostitutes.[21]

OGPU records contain reports from towns throughout Uzbekistan, noting that government workers, village council chairmen, and Party members all were among unveiled women's worst enemies, along with the clergy. Bahriniso I., a teacher who led a group of women to unveil in her Fargana Valley village, was the daughter of a rather wealthy landowner who had become a member of the village council. After unveiling, she avoided her father for several months, fearing his reaction.[22] In other Fargana Valley villages, within a few months of the beginning of the unveiling campaign council workers made indecent proposals to unveiled women, scorned them, and called them prostitutes. In Tuda-Maidon, an ishon collected false evidence about the wife of a village council representative, a woman who unveiled on March 8, trying to demonstrate that she was a prostitute. Under this pressure, she re-veiled. A student at the Tashkent Medical Technical School, Pulatova, committed suicide because her classmates insulted her, calling her a prostitute for unveiling.[23] Family members of unveiled women also had to endure these aspersions. Some of the murders of women were undoubtedly responses to public, social stigma, and shame; that is, they were attempts to restore family honor by killing women who were blamed for bringing shame on themselves and their relatives. Inability to cope with the public stigma of unveiling affected men as well as women. Some men divorced unveiled wives, and in Bukhara a shoemaker committed suicide because his wife unveiled.[24]

Men in public roles often preyed on the unveiled, and especially on those who turned to the government for help. There were many reports similar to this one: in Chirchik region, near Tashkent, an unveiled woman, Fazileva, was thrown out by her husband. She turned for aid to the president of the poor peasant committee, who kidnapped and raped her. About twenty of her relatives came to his home and demanded he be brought to court. Ultimately, Fazileva went to the president of the village council, who convinced her to return to her husband. Thus, apparently, the situation was resolved without serious concern for Fazileva's well-being and without any prosecution for the rapist.[25] In Shahrisabz, an official raped a woman who came to him with a request for help with a divorce. Elsewhere, four public officials, including village council members, the librarian, and a regional commissioner, together raped the director of the women's club.[26] Public officials took the same attitude toward unveiled women that other men in their communities did, but because women in crisis turned to them for help, they had more opportunity than others to act out their hostilities.

Anti-unveiling violence carried a threatening message. In Tashkent, one day after unveiling, a woman named Qumri-xon was sexually assaulted by two young men while on her way home from a meeting.[27] In Qashqa Daryo, an ishon physically attacked a woman teacher for her activism among women. In Kemandi, four men raped an unveiled woman and then killed her. Two men went to a farmer's home, raped his daughter, and then told him, "In these times you can do anything you want to a woman, and there will be no investigation." In Kassansoi, Party members demanded that a certain unveiled woman appear before them. They forced alcohol on her, raped her, and dropped her off at her home. The police noted, "Thus, the people say that the Party wants to unveil women so they can rape them." In Mahram, after Party members raped an unveiled woman, 100 out of 170 unveiled women put their paranjis back on. They understood the message.[28]

In many villages, social leaders carried out the same kind of agitation during the Hujum that they had in the 1916 uprising, calling on the population to oppose this new, unwanted government intrusion by attacking everyone involved. In Oq Yer, near Rishtan in the Fargana Valley, the village council members initiated one of the experiments of the Hujum, calling for a "family evening," where families would mix socially, men with unveiled women, and listen to lectures. Family evenings were a radical attempt to break down gender segregation, and they met violent opposition. The village council in Oq Yer tried to force attendance, threatening to fine members who did not appear. There was a religious celebration on the day before the designated family evening, and the clergy leaders decided they would prevent the meeting. They attacked and almost killed a member of the village council, and they disrupted the event. Reports from clergy meetings said they made plans to form an Islamic council and kill Soviet workers, and they called for expanding religious schools and ending the attempts to unveil women.[29]

In Andijon, dehqons were told that if they had been given land in land reform, their wives needed to attend the family evenings. Some wrote to say they would give up their land instead. A police reporter noted that the dehqons used the same language of opposition to unveiling that the rich and the clergy used. They said, "God forbids it," "I forbid it," and "She'll become a prostitute." In Qashqa Daryo, a rich man, Krimjon o'g'li, declared: "The government demands unveiling women ever more strongly. We will kill them if they uncover, both our wives, and those who put them up to it. And then, finally, we will tell the government not to mess with our lives."[30] This language, advocating killing unveiled women and their supporters, was extremely widespread and may have normalized this crime in the minds of some. Remembering the Hujum, activist Saodat Shamsieva remarked, "The father, husband, or older brother of every woman or girl who threw off the paranji in the mahalla [traditional urban neighborhood] or village would, having killed her, come to us saying, 'I killed her because I did not want her to uncover and to cause me shame.'"[31]

In Bukhara, the OGPU reported that Adolat Burkhanova, age eighteen, was murdered by her husband on the street four days after Bukhara's first mass unveiling, on March 8, 1928. Her husband, a Party candidate, forbade her to enter school, but she tried to enroll anyway and he killed her.[32] The OGPU collected a long list of murders that took place between January and August 1928. Usually women were stabbed or beaten to death. Two women activists were murdered. One man murdered his unveiled wife and cut her to pieces. Another body of a woman was found with teeth broken and knife wounds in the mouth. An activist was shot. A man beat his wife for going to work and she died. A man shot his sister who had unveiled and become an activist. A Party candidate beat and killed his wife for unveiling. A man divorced his wife for unveiling and then killed her. Two men smothered a woman for unveiling. A man smothered his married daughter for unveiling. A man, with help from three "bandits" killed his wife and sister because they planned to unveil. A militia man shot his wife and killed her because she went to meetings for the unveiled. In Bukhara, a woman was poisoned by her mother-in-law for unveiling. In Qashqa Daryo, a man slit his wife's throat and threw her in a well for unveiling. In Samarkand, a man beat his wife for unveiling and going to a family evening. When investigated, he told the police that even if he killed his wife, that was none of their business. In Sarak Tepe, an unveiled woman, Jurabaeva, was murdered by her brother, under the influence of a local rich man. In Tashkent region, an activist was murdered by her husband and four Party members. Another man slit his wife's throat. She had gone to work in the women's cooperative store. The murderer went to the police and told them the reason that he murdered her was jealousy.[33]

A police report from Xorazm counted twelve women killed there in two or three months. The author noted that murderers often claimed that unveiling was not the reason:

It is characteristic in cases of the murder of women that the physical murderer (husband or brother) presents as his reasons for murder purely family reasons ( jealousy, dishonoring the family), rejecting a political element to the murder. But the conditions accompanying the murder (in most cases the victim was planning to unveil or was unveiled) give reason to suspect that not only family and daily life relations played a role in the murder. These murders without a doubt, objectively reflect "that work" that is being carried out by groups who are our enemies, against the liberation of women, and is a direct result of their "work."[34]

When the Hujum was launched, the OGPU, the Women's Division, and the Hujum Committee clearly did not anticipate that women who unveiled would be murdered, and they certainly did not foresee the swift rise in murders. They attributed this rise to active provocation by the clergy and the wealthy. Women whom I interviewed, from those who supported unveiling like Rahbar-oi Olimova and Mafrat-xon M., to those who reported unveiling under duress like Aziza-xon I., remembered hearing clergy members declaring that unveiled women should be killed. The OGPU included in one report notice of a letter, signed by eighty people, declaring they would kill the unveiled and their helpers.[35] As the wave of murders continued, laws making penalties for violence against women were strengthened when that violence was connected to "women's liberation," and so investigators tried to ascertain whether murderers killed women for unveiling and activism, or killed them for reasons that were not political.

Many women were murdered for unveiling during 1927, in the first year of the Hujum, and the numbers of murders and the panic they generated, both in the government and among women, increased throughout 1928. The Women's Division leadership became increasingly concerned about this violence, but throughout 1927 the CPUz Women's Division seemed hesitant to raise public panic about the murders. Activists who were encouraging unveiling did not want to increase women's fear of unveiling by drawing attention to anti-veiling violence.

In 1927, although *Qizil O'zbekiston* began reporting murders of unveiling activists as soon as the Hujum began, the journal *Yangi Yo'l* avoided direct mention of such murders until December. The journal had previously reported on the murders of women activists in the land reform campaign, but coverage of the Hujum in 1927 was upbeat, describing regional unveiling meetings and calling for measures to strengthen the effort for unveiling and for the Hujum's other social objectives. Stories appeared in which women were threatened, but these were given promising endings, showing the militia and the courts protecting women who wanted to unveil.[36] The leadership was aware, however, that legal organs were not doing their job: in April 1927, the Second Congress of Soviets of Uzbekistan declared its commitment to women's unveiling, calling on the courts and judges to defend women after they unveiled.[37]

Although it was slow to discuss the matter in public, the Women's Division was aware of stabbings and other violence against the unveiled from the very first demonstrations on March 8. Rahbar-oi mentioned that she was assigned to work at one of the Tashkent Women's Division offices after the unveiling celebration that day and that she fled from working there in part because bloodied women were showing up. In general, Rahbar-oi had a negative impression of the Women's Division as an organization that spent all its time in court cases; she characterized it as "litigious." Shimko, director of CPUz Women's Division in 1927, reported that threats against women and charges that unveiled women were prostitutes were being sounded in mosques and that mullahs were calling for attacks on women. After telling of a mullah attacking a newly unveiled woman with a knife, Shimko noted, "Many sacrifices have been made, and many cases have piled up at court over this; every day new petitions are coming in."[38] By September, Hosiyat Tillaxonova was alarmed by women's reasons for re-veiling. She called on the Party to bring to open trial "those who slander, and those who have shed blood on paranjis, and those who have committed hindrance and oppression against the unveiled."[39]

At the end of 1927, *Yangi Yo'l* published its first full article on an unveiling murder, and the topic would receive regular and substantial coverage for the next two years as Women's Division workers tried to pressure the courts and militia to provide protection and justice. The account concerned a young women named Adolat, who joined in the May 1 unveiling celebration over her husband's objections and then attended an evening theater performance with other women. That night her husband stabbed and killed her in her bed and attacked her sister as well. Her husband, Mahmud the butcher, was tried and sentenced to be shot.[40] This was not a typical outcome for an unveiling murder case, many of which were never satisfactorily investigated, let alone tried, but the journal's editors apparently wanted to reassure readers that the state was serious in its pursuit of justice.

Over the next two years, accounts of murders and the numbers of murders of unveiled women and activists were published in nearly every issue of *Yangi Yo'l*. Reports of mass unveilings also increased, featuring speeches by women who proclaimed that murders would not deter them from unveiling. *Yangi Yo'l* drew direct connections between murder and women's public activities. Stories featured village women like Ulug'-oi, murdered by her husband and a gang of accomplices after she unveiled and left him to study in the city.[41] Readers were told of Zainab Qurbon qizi, who, as a member of a land reform committee, was directly involved in dispossessing wealthy men and who denounced local political leaders as former Basmachis. A group of men, including village political leaders and militia, shot her and mutilated her body.[42]

Women who were working for the Women's Division in Uzbekistan, and who wrote for *Yangi Yo'l*, understood murders of unveiled wives by their families and murders of women activists by political opponents equally as political crimes. They reported on ties between murderous husbands and "alien classes," namely the wealthy, the Islamic religious authorities, and the merchants. This produced some tortured explanations: when poor men, who were supposed to be revolutionary, murdered women relatives for unveiling, it was ideologically necessary to find that they were under the influence of the rich or the clergy. OGPU reports gave substantiation to these explanations, pointing to the anti-unveiling propaganda that religious leaders and village elites carried out.

Why did so many men murder women for unveiling during the Hujum? The historian W. Fitzhugh Brundage describes Jacquelyn Dowd Hall's argument regarding lynching in the United States, writing that lynching "was a drama that helped to cement the entire southern social order. The dramatic spectacle of each lynching taught all southerners, male and female, black and white, precisely where in the social hierarchy they stood."[43] Anti-unveiling murders in the Hujum served the same purpose. Murdered women had first transgressed the fixed and patriarchal social order, simply by breaking seclusion, unveiling, and showing their faces in public or more actively by becoming participants in public and political activities that threatened local hierarchies. Murders were planned and incited and were calculated in some cases to "restore honor" as well as to teach other women a lesson: that they should not unveil and should not join forces with the Soviet state.

Prior to the Hujum, Uzbek society clearly placed men in authority over women and strictly regulated women's behavior, movements, and dress. Many assumed that women who unveiled became impure. The society's understanding of sexual relations held women responsible for sexual impropriety; as elsewhere in the Islamic world, women were associated with *fitna* (chaos).[44] To murder women who unveiled was to attempt to restore a rapidly eroding social order by terrorizing other women into submission. However, perpetrators often had to be convinced to carry out their acts. Others in the community, often powerful men whose social positions were threatened by the government's struggle against religion and against private property, met with male family members and told them unveiling was a sin and that unveiled women lost their religion, became Russians, were prostitutes—in effect, had thoroughly betrayed their Central Asian community—and extracted promises and oaths that someone in the family would murder the transgressing woman.[45] Even in cultures where "honor killings" seem to be a deeply ingrained practice of social control, murders are incited, killers are put under social pressure to avenge honor, and there is planning and calculation.[46] In Uzbekistan, where there is no evidence that honor killings were prominent in the social control of women before the Hujum, incitement to murder was important in normalizing the idea that it was appropriate to kill women who unveiled.[47]

Murdering women did terrorize others very effectively. Thousands upon thousands of women who had unveiled, whether by choice or under duress, re-veiled out of fear for their personal safety. After the murder wave began, unveiling activists fought an uphill battle to convince women to risk not only their reputations, but possibly also their lives for the sake of going into public places without the paranji. Without family approval, without reliable police and courts, and without even the support of local Party members and government actors, the unveiled were undefended. Throughout the Hujum, women activists constantly called for stronger legal protection for the unveiled, but this depended on judges, police, and local administrators, none of whom were reliably pro-Hujum.

In trying to explain the widespread re-veilings of 1928 and the general persistence of veiling into the 1930s, Douglas Northrop argues that Uzbeks became more insistent on veiling because it became an element in anticolonial resistance: "conflict over the hujum became an arena of national struggle, especially but not exclusively between Russians and Uzbeks."[48] The brutality of widespread murders and rapes in response to unveiling, carried out by Uzbeks against other Uzbeks, and almost never involving Russians in any way, suggests to me quite a different interpretation. Just as lynchings were horrifically effective at reestablishing the racial hierarchy of the American South in the late nineteenth and early twentieth centuries, femicide in the form of murders of Uzbek women who had the temerity to unveil taught the rest a strong lesson: better to accept veiling and seclusion, and even preach in favor of veiling, than to risk one's life for the prospect of "liberation."

## CORRUPTION IN THE WOMEN'S DIVISION: KALIANOVA

Party leaders who initiated the Hujum placed unfounded trust in Uzbek Party members to support women's unveiling. Worse still, even Women's Division workers did not always support the Hujum. Early Hujum reports were full of rumors that Women's Division workers were contributing to corruption in various ways, such as brokering prostitutes and thus harming the reputations of the unveiled.[49] The Women's Division leadership probably tended to dismiss charges that Women's Division activists were drunks or agents for prostitutes. Mutual denunciations among Communists grew during the purges of 1928 and 1929–1930, when, as Northrop discusses, Party members' actions or reputation for supporting the Hujum became one of the tests of Party loyalty. In villages, charges that Party members had not unveiled their wives could mean not only expulsion from the Party, but sudden exposure as a "class enemy" followed by dekulakization or exile.[50] The Women's Division, with its stacks of reports about real cases of male Party members who not only did not support the Hujum, but themselves murdered unveiled women, were understandably skeptical about accusations from male Party members against Women's Division activists. But in 1929, a case arose in Besh Arik region, near Kokand, that had to be taken seriously.

In the village of Saur Tepe, a young woman, Adil-bibi, was murdered. She was pregnant at the time, and her body was found with the hands chopped off. The Uzbekistan Communist Party and the Central Asian Bureau sent numerous investigators to examine the case, because it involved a conflict between the local Women's Division director, Kalianova, the local Communist Party leader, Saifutdinnov, and a group of poor peasants, led by Zakir Xo'ja. Saifutdinnov accused Kalianova of murdering Adil-bibi, her daughter-in-law, while Kalianova accused Zakir Xo'ja and a group of nine landless peasants. By 1929, when the murder and investigations took place, a sweeping Party purge was underway, and Kalianova and Saifutdinnov were both suspect for their class backgrounds. The CAB Women's Division director, Muratova, was unwilling to believe the accusations against Kalianova and kept sending out more investigators, hoping to discover that someone else was responsible for the murder.[51]

The investigators did not want to give credence to Saifutdinnov's charges against Kalianova. His name had come up in a previous anti-Soviet murder case, and he was associated with the nationalist intelligentsia, the target of purges in 1929–1930. The OGPU reporters declared that the nationalist intelligentsia opposed women's liberation and "is trying to drive a wedge between the Party and the dehqon," using this characterization to depict Saifutdinnov as a likely suspect in the murder.

However, the investigators found that Kalianova also had credibility problems. She had been a soothsayer, came from a xo'ja family, and maintained close connections to the village wealthy.[52] Her husband, Muzafar, falsely presented himself as a landless peasant in 1924 and gained entry to the Party. He then arranged for his wife to work among women, but she used her Women's Division position to legalize the marriage of minors. She would send grown women, under paranji, to the ZAGS to register in place of underage girls. A Komsomol girl, Nishanbuva Mamedova, made an open accusation about Kalianova's actions, and Kalianova used her influence to have Mamedova thrown out of the

Komsomol. Mamedova became the Women's Division director in a neighboring village. According to the report, Kalianova forced Adil-bibi to marry her son, and she seized the property of Adil-bibi's father. When he protested this land confiscation, she accused him of not supporting women's liberation.

Kalianova had substantial power in her village, and she used it to shape the economic changes that were underway. She was involved in land reform, and made sure that lands confiscated from waqfs were divided and given to her friends, "to bois and alien elements." In 1926, she became involved in the cotton cooperative and misused its property. She gave co-op-owned grain to her rich friends and directed credit to those who already had money. Egamberdieva, a Party activist in a neighboring village, tried to obtain credit from the cooperative for an irrigation project, but Kalianova refused and would not let Egamberdieva see the cooperative's accounts. When Egamberdieva challenged her, Kalianova claimed connections to Yo'ldosh Oxunboboev, president of the Soviets of Uzbekistan. Kalianova had poor peasants thrown out of the Party and deprived her enemies of their voting rights.

Zakir Xo'ja, a local landless peasant, wrote a complaint about Kalianova. She in turn accused him of raping Adil-bibi. However, when the rape was investigated, Adil-bibi said that no such thing had happened. Zakir Xo'ja then organized a group of landless peasants to struggle against Kalianova's influence. Then, Adil-bibi was murdered. Kalianova accused Zakir Xo'ja and had him and nine accomplices arrested. But Saifutdinnov spread rumors that Kalianova herself ordered the murder, and eventually investigators arrested her son, Murtaza, and one accomplice, Juraboi Pazilov.

The two competing versions of the murder attracted attention from the central government, which sent a commission. Muratova, the CAB Women's Division head, sent her own commission, launching a full investigation of the whole Party organization in Besh Arik region. Muratova and her supporters argued that the accusation against Kalianova was just an attempt to slander and undermine the Women's Division and to divert attention from the rightful targets of the local Party purge, Saifutdinnov and his rich associates. But the central government's report declared that Muratova had been misled by Sher-Muhammedov, an important Party member who sided with the Kalianova faction, before she ever began looking into the matter.

The CPUz Central Committee held a hearing on the matter; the matter's importance to the Party was indicated by the presence of Akmal Ikromov (who headed the CPUz) and I. A. Zelenskii (head of the CAB). The committee condemned nearly everyone involved, including Saifutdinnov for his factionalism and for being a national chauvinist who tried to divide Uzbeks from Tajiks and Russians, and Sher-Muhammedov for misleading Muratova. But the committee determined that Kalianova, whose case had been sent to the high court, had indeed been the instigator of Adil-bibi's murder. They determined that she had hired her son to carry it out because she wanted to silence Adil-bibi, who knew of Kalianova's misuse of power in land reform and credit, in women's affairs, and in driving poor peasants out of the Party.[53]

Violence against women was important, but was overshadowed by other intra-Party issues. Adil-bibi's brutal murder and dismemberment became one element in the Kasimovshchina, a sweeping series of trials wherein one Party group eliminated another influential group, made up of judges and their relatives accused of being in league with the wealthy to undermine land reform and women's liberation, in part by giving light sentences or no sentences to murderers of women activists.[54] The Kasimovshchina trials, which began with charges of corruption against the presiding judge of the Uzbekistan High Court, dominated the news of court cases in 1930, while stories of murders of women no longer attracted high-level Party attention.[55]

### STRENGTHEN THE LAW, BAN THE PARANJI

Most of my informants remembered at least one of the most notorious murders from the Hujum period: Nurxon and Tursun-oi, Uzbek actresses. In her memoir, Uzbek activist Fotima Yo'ldoshbaeva related the case of Nurxon Yo'ldoshxo'jaeva, a teenager from the Fargana Valley who ran away from home and joined a traveling theater troupe in Samarkand.[56] Very few Uzbek women were actresses in 1927; if showing one's face in public was disgraceful, going on stage would have been far more so. When Nurxon's troupe performed near her home village, her aunt invited Nurxon and her friends to her home, and some of Nurxon's male relatives appeared. Salixo'ja, her brother, drew Nurxon into a separate room, ostensibly to talk privately:

> Her brother closed the door tightly and immediately, in a mad rage, stabbed his sister again and again with a knife . . .

Nurxon Yo'ldoshxo'jaeva, actress, murdered in 1929.
Kokand Museum photo.


As was later shown, the murder of Nurxon was planned in advance. Participants included the ming-boshi, the mullah Kamal G'iasov, and the girls' father Yo'ldoshxo'ja Salimxo'jaev. It was they who forced Salixo'ja to swear on the Quran that he would kill his sister, who had disobeyed her father's will. In court, Salixo'ja admitted that he committed murder at the order of his father.

The case was tried publicly and attracted much media coverage, which helps explain why my informants remembered Nurxon's murder more than six decades later. Ultimately, Nurxon's father and brother were sentenced to death by shooting, and the ming-boshi and mullah "were sentenced to five years' exile from Fargana region" according to Yo'l-doshbaeva. While prosecution for murder of ordinary women for unveiling was weak, the murders of several actresses allowed the state to conduct show trials, to levy severe sentences, and thus to demonstrate some support to unveiled women.

Women's Division workers repeatedly called for strengthening penalties for murder and for providing stronger protection for unveiled women. Local law enforcement remained inadequate for preventing crimes, but laws defending victims of unveiling-related violence were strengthened in 1928, and again in 1929. In August 1928, section 274b of Uzbekistan's criminal code was amended to declare that "killing a woman or severely wounding her on the basis of religious and daily life crimes connected with her liberation carries a sentence of not less than eight years severe isolation. Carrying out lesser attacks on a woman brings not less than two years severe isolation. Insulting a woman in connection with unveiling carries a sentence of three years."[57]

The strengthened laws were designed to help local authorities defend women, as well as to punish not only murderers and rapists but even those who harassed and insulted unveiled women. Unveiled women also wanted other measures in addition to stronger legal protection. In Tashkent region, women demanded that the government recognize that Communists were not unveiling their wives and that the unveiled were being murdered. Women also advocated that the government take "cruel measures against the adversaries of unveiling." In February 1928, a group of unveiled women teachers in Samarkand wrote a complaint to the government that it was not adequately promoting unveiling. They argued that the government should boycott women in paranjis by giving them no government services, or else should not be surprised if the group of teachers all decided to re-veil.[58]

In addition to changing laws punishing unveiling-related crimes, the Party raised and then abandoned the idea that veiling might simply be made illegal. A ban was proposed as early as 1924 by some Uzbek Communists. In 1928, when the Hujum had gone through several waves of enthusiasm and several periods of backlash and re-veiling, Women's Division workers throughout the Soviet East opened public discussion of a possible anti-veiling decree. Serafima Liubimova, formerly head of the CAB Women's Division and now head of the All-Union Women's Division's Eastern Group, supported the idea.

Based on her encounters with women in Uzbekistan, Liubimova asserted that such a decree would make unveiling significantly easier for women who might want to unveil. These women would then have an argument to convince their husbands, who wanted them to maintain social standards, and Islamic clergy, who claimed that women would go to hell for unveiling. Liubimova referred to women who would unveil for the "reason of respect."[59] This exact phrase does not occur in Uzbek accounts of unveiling, but was Liubimova's astute observation of Uzbek women's etiquette. In many activists' memoirs, there are accounts of women unveiling in response to a direct request from a person in authority.[60] Liubimova told of an Uzbek woman who came to the Women's Division office in Tashkent and said, "I want to remove the *parandzha* but my husband will not permit it. Tomorrow at such-and-such a time, I will be at such-and-such a shop at the bazaar. Come up to me and force me to remove it. Then I'll be content, and my husband won't say anything."[61] Liubimova believed a decree would have the same effect as complying with a person in authority. She also argued that a decree would firm unveiled women's resolve not to re-veil: "The decree is needed, so that along with the issue of removing coverings—to say something about the protection of unveiled women, about placing them in an atmosphere of support and sympathy. A decree is needed, so as to reveal as enemies of the workers all who oppose the massive movement for removing the parandzha."[62] However, other Women's Division workers argued that a decree was untimely, could not yet receive adequate support from the government, and would have an effect opposite to the desired one, forcing women to stay home rather than to come out into public life.[63]

Oxunboboev spoke out strongly and repeatedly in favor of a decree against the veil. In 1928, at the All-Union Congress of Workers among Women of the East, he stated that in Uzbekistan the Soviets intended to carry out propaganda for an unveiling decree during the upcoming local council elections, and "if at the end of this reelection campaign the masses themselves demand a decree about the veil, we should go to meet them and satisfy that demand." His opponent at the congress was Zhukova, a Russian Women's Division worker based in Bukhara, who insisted that any decree would be premature and that "the issue of the decree is being pushed by the petty bourgeoisie and the intelligentsia." She continued her insinuations that Oxunboboev and other Uzbek leaders' class backgrounds were questionable: "We need to have manly revolutionaries, in order to oppose [alien] elements and to oppose that sort of Communist who demands that [a decree] be published, wishing to protect himself with that decree."[64] Political leaders in Uzbekistan, including Oxunboboev, went forward with agitation for a decree, perhaps thinking that they could pass such a law in Uzbekistan much as Uzbekistan had passed its own marriage laws that were not strictly in accordance with Soviet law.

Massell writes that "by January, 1929, it was clear that all proposals for outlawing the veil were to be shelved indefinitely," but in fact agitation for a decree grew in Uzbekistan until April 1929. In January 1929,

*Yangi Yo'l* published the following in the CPUz Women's Division agenda: "The Women's Division and all activist women will need to work very hard in order to explain the necessity of issuing a general decree ending the paranji, and making it agreeable to the public." The Women's Division and the Komsomol collected signatures on petitions for a decree, and the movement culminated in a demonstration and speeches demanding a decree at the All-Uzbekistan Congress of Soviets in April. Many women expected that such a decree would be made on May 1, 1929.[65]

Throughout the first months of 1929, meetings for activists, council election campaigns, and union meetings all involved discussions of a ban on veiling. At the Central Asian Communist University in Tashkent, women activists circulated petitions in favor of an anti-veiling decree; Rahbar-oi remembered signing one. *Yangi Yo'l*'s editors were avid supporters of a decree; the journal published many accounts of meetings and demonstrations favoring the anti-veiling law and tried to make this campaign seem widely popular. Their coverage was so one-sided that they did not even address anti-decree arguments or acknowledge widespread anti-unveiling attitudes. *Qizil O'zbekiston* articles recalled the large numbers of women activists murdered in 1928, and demanded that a law against veiling be enacted in their memory. When the Third Congress of Soviets of Uzbekistan opened in April 1929, Saodat Shamsieva, a Komsomol member, marched down the main avenue in Samarkand with a column of women who were carrying signs and banners for an unveiling decree. As a Komsomol representative, she gave a speech to the congress, asking for a decree.[66]

In mid-April 1929, the congress indirectly rejected the proposed unveiling decree. The congress's published statement accused those agitating for a decree of losing perspective on women's liberation and ignoring class consciousness; certain comrades were acting as though women's liberation would happen only after unveiling and were ignoring more important matters such as attracting women to work. The statement declared that Uzbekistan now had two groups of districts: in Bukhara, Qashqa Daryo, Surxon Daryo, and Xorazm, activists were carrying out women's liberation in the right way, concentrating on the working class; while in Tashkent, Samarkand, and the Fargana Valley, activists were ignoring class and class enemies.[67]

This criticism reflected broader trends in Party politics both across the Soviet Union and in Uzbekistan. The Party was purging from its ranks members who had "wrong" class backgrounds. In Uzbekistan in 1929–1930, the purge of Party membership swept away a group of Uzbek intellectuals and Jadids; the leader of the group, Munavvar Qori, and other members were accused of enacting an Uzbek nationalist agenda within various government ministries. The accusations that decree advocates and activists for unveiling in three of Uzbekistan's regions (including Tashkent and Samarkand, home to most *Yangi Yo'l* writers) were insufficiently class-conscious revealed another site of battle within the Communist Party, as well as an interesting shift: those previously accused of associating with alien classes and charged with insufficient Party loyalty for not sufficiently supporting the Hujum turned the tables and accused the too-enthusiastic Hujum supporters of being in league with alien classes instead.[68]

In June 1929, the editors of *Yangi Yo'l* tried to explain to their disappointed readership why, after all the agitation and demonstrations, the government had not enacted an anti-veiling decree. The article explained the Third Congress of Soviets' contention that women might unveil, but could still be dominated by and financially dependent on husbands. "The problem is not in the decree; at some point, a decree will be needed," the article claimed. But in the meantime, increasing the number of girls' schools and bringing women into the workplace were higher priorities:

In this matter, we can take the good example of other Eastern countries, Turkey, Iran, and Afghanistan. The comrades who understood this, and thought, "The greatest effort is to put forth a decree on the paranji," should know this. Turkey's petty bourgeois national government put forth a law forbidding the wearing of the chadra! But how much did the lives of Turkey's women improve with this? They have remained in the same economic enslavement as before. What does this demonstrate? It shows that freedom does not come with a decree, but will take place with methodical work.[69]

Obviously, *Yangi Yo'l*'s editors still had not given up all hope for a decree. Why were they so convinced that a decree was necessary? Saodat Shamsieva and others who demonstrated in 1929 saw voluntary unveiling in a rather different light than did Zhukova or Krupskaia

(Lenin's widow), who both insisted that unveiling should be voluntary and conscious, otherwise it would serve no purpose in the larger scheme of revolution. Saodat understood that unveiling in Uzbekistan was a matter of rejecting family and community authority and challenging norms of honor. She and other activists believed that if unveiling were not a matter of individual choice, but were required by the government, then women would happily unveil, and men would cease to hold women individually responsible for defying their authority and bringing them dishonor.[70] In addition, if all women were forced to unveil, then the early unveilers would cease to be an unusual and harassed minority on Uzbekistan's streets; life for the modernizers would become a bit easier. She and other decree advocates had come to their own conclusion in the debate that simmered among Jadids and modernizers over the veil: they viewed the veil as a cause, not a symptom, of women's subordination.

Uzbek women activists wanted to use unveiling to create modern Uzbek women, assuming that action, not consciousness, would break seclusion and lead to modern education and roles in the public realm. However, the Party's goal in promoting unveiling, at least as the All-Union Women's Division in Moscow saw matters, was to induce social and cultural revolution. When the struggle over unveiling became a distraction from the Party's more pressing goals of rapid economic transformation, the Party decreased its attention to the Hujum. In the controversy over the decree, the difference between Uzbek activist women's goals and Communist Party goals was clear.

While the Uzbekistan Soviets, under the guidance of the Communist Party, did not ban veiling, in 1929 the Soviet government made punishments for opposing unveiling more severe. After April 1929, murdering a woman for unveiling, or for activism, could be considered an act of terrorism. This meant that Statute 64, which allowed death sentences for acts of anti-Soviet terror, could be applied when men murdered their unveiled wives. The statute had been used to prosecute murderers of activists since 1927, but after 1929 the law could be more broadly applied.[71] In 1930, the Soviet government strengthened this law, declaring that the murder of women in the course of liberation was a counterrevolutionary crime and could be prosecuted under Article 8 of the criminal code.[72] In addition, a new law permitted anonymous accusation so that victims were not required to accuse their attackers in person in court; legal scholars believe this law encouraged women to report crimes.[73] Rather than backing down from its campaign against the veil, the Party rendered local law and order authorities more effective and deterred unveiling murders with harsh punishment. The government came to define these murders as acts of defiance against the state, not as family crimes or as "crimes of everyday life," as it had classified them in at the peak of the Hujum.

The Soviet state's increasingly harsh treatment of its opponents in the late 1920s, its attack on the wealthy in the collectivization campaign, and the rise of the powers of the OGPU to accuse and arrest combined to extend state authority to the Uzbek countryside; and with that authority came state ability to combat the murder wave. But the shift in state policy, especially toward rapid collectivization, gave state opponents new targets: by 1930, murders of activists and council officials involved in forcing collectivization on Uzbek peasants rose, while murders of women for unveiling decreased, even though agitation for unveiling increased.[74]

UNVEILING AND AGENCY

Soviet historians' accounts of the Hujum describe unveiling as the result of the Communist Party's success in explaining rights to women. Unveiling was a conscious symbol of a woman's liberation from the restrictions of religious tradition, and was the initial step in her new role as citizen and worker in the socialist state. A new consciousness may have explained some women's unveiling, but for the majority of women, veiling, unveiling, and re-veiling were probably a response to social and political pressure.

In 1928, the OGPU tried to assess women's own attitudes toward unveiling. One agent wrote that women could be divided into three groups. One "small" group not only rejected unveiling, but consciously opposed it. For example, in the village of Kara-Palvan, Muria-bibi Oxunboeva was invited to recite at a funeral. There were one hundred women present, and she used the occasion to agitate against unveiling. The second group, the majority, viewed unveiling as their husbands did—they were for veiling if their husbands were for it, opposed to unveiling if their husbands were. So, "to speak of their own individual, direct expression or opinion about the question of unveiling on the part of this group is inappropriate." The third group, mainly poor, were not only for unveiling, but also became village activists.[75] While activists in the

Women's Division needed to portray their own propaganda as effective, a more careful and realistic view would admit that the organization did not persuade the majority of women.

In Soviet histories in general, the negative results of Party policies are explained as "excesses," "administrative measures," or "bureaucratic measures." In other words, problems resulted not from bad policy but from incorrectly applied policy. Accounts of unveiling were designed to explain the Party's role in liberating Uzbek women, and they treat the massive reports of forced unveilings without much interest. By contrast, some anti-Soviet and post-Soviet accounts have so emphasized the role of force that unveiling becomes interpreted as the mindless action of Soviet dupes, while retaining the veil is interpreted as conscious and deliberate resistance to Soviet state intrusion. Neither side asks seriously whether women made their own decisions, and under what conditions.

While the women whose stories were told in chapters 5, 6, and 7 clearly were making decisions about veiling, based in part on their own experiences and thoughts as well as on family and neighborhood influences, most women were constrained from making their own decisions either to veil or to unveil. Uzbek women who unveiled in the face of threats of violence, and did so in order to challenge the patriarchal order, were exercising resistance to patriarchy, even as they were conforming to the Party's desires. The above-mentioned religious teacher, Muria-bibi Oxunboeva, consciously and deliberately retained the veil and preached its retention in opposition to the Soviet state. In actively agitating on behalf of the veil, women like Oxunboeva exercised resistance to the Party, even as they conformed to the dictates of a patriarchal society. But when other women found their lives and reputations threatened for unveiling, their continued veiling or re-veiling should be seen as pragmatic self-preservation rather than as political or religious opposition to Soviet policies. When the Party pressured men to make wives unveil, and when family and community members threatened the unveiled with death, women's decision making was a matter of negotiating between two counterposed negative pressures—the coercion of the state and the violence of society.

The shift in the direction of violence in Uzbekistan—from large numbers of murders of women during the Hujum (mainly 1927–1930) to large numbers of murders of activists for collectivization during the collectivization campaign (1929–1934)—highlights the political nature of these murder waves as expressions of widespread social opposition to state interventions. The wave of anti-unveiling murders also reveals a society trying to reinforce gender hierarchy. Unveiled women had stepped out of socially regulated categories and represented a threat to the boundaries of communities that were undergoing the strains of rapid economic change and heightened government intrusion. Members of Uzbek communities (mostly men), incited by opponents of these changes, murdered unveiled women and thus made what Smith-Rosenberg calls a "stern effort to control" all women. The violence effectively deterred women from mass unveiling, but was not effective at changing the state's policies toward women, nor did it preserve women's seclusion in the long run. This murder wave subsided with the even greater social upheaval of collectivization, which thoroughly undermined village social structures and enabled the state to crush its opponents, including those who incited murders of women for unveiling.

### ❦ 9 ❦

# CONTINUITY AND
# CHANGE IN UZBEK
# WOMEN'S LIVES

T HE HUJUM DID NOT CHANGE
common attitudes about women's roles in the family, but it did initiate
changes to women's material conditions and their roles in the public
realm. The Hujum was not just about unveiling; it was a multifaceted
campaign to increase the numbers of girls in school and women in End
Illiteracy courses, to enforce laws against polygyny and the marriage of
minors, to bring women into workplaces and promote them in the Party
and government, to end qalin, and to explain to women their rights.
In the three decades that followed this initial Party commitment to transforming women, each of these areas saw dramatic change, even though
the ideals of many Women's Division activists remained far from fulfilled.[1] Soviet economic transformation and modernization do not
account for all of the changes; the Party and government's ongoing political attention to women's issues directed efforts and funds. Between the
1930s and 1950s, the rise in girls education for girls and in numbers of
women in paid employment were the most significant changes; these
broke the dynamic of women's seclusion and their exclusion from the
public arena. Many Uzbeks' concepts of women's abilities were transformed, but there was no attempt by the government, and no movement from below, to challenge gender ideals and roles. And although
sexual revolution accompanied women's movements elsewhere, includ-

Uzbek woman as mother, teacher, farm worker, weaver, and factory worker.
Front cover of *Yangi Yo'l*, no. 11–12 (1926).

ing in Russia (before Stalinist conservatism set in), in Uzbekistan the
idea that women should have control over their own sexuality never
spread.

The Women's Division, under attack by some in the Party from the
time of its foundation as a potentially feminist organization whose inter-

ests might not align with those of the Party, met its demise in 1930. The end of the Women's Division was not, however, the end of official interest in women's participation in the Party or the Soviet state. Although the structure that had supported the Hujum disappeared, state efforts to make a new Uzbek woman continued. The Party's stated reason for dissolving its Women's Division was that women had been successfully liberated and made equal with men. Statistics on Party membership, labor, and education certainly did not bear this out, not in the European regions of the Soviet Union and far less in Uzbekistan, but legal equality was established and was to some extent enforced. In its final years, the Women's Division leaders—Communist women who were strong backers of the Party's whole program—were persuaded to emphasize class conflict in their own work and to attract only women of the worker and peasant class to their programs. The Women's Division in Uzbekistan followed suit, at least in its rhetoric of 1929. This course made Women's Division activities more acceptable to the Party leadership, but if the Women's Division emphasized class over gender this strengthened the Party argument that the Women's Division was unnecessary.

The Hujum itself may have tarnished the Women's Division's image. Concerted efforts to unveil women met a violent backlash, and the Women's Division leadership had difficulty explaining why this radical program should continue to merit Party support. They did not even agree among themselves on the best response to the violence.[2] But the Hujum did not cause the Party to decide on the Women's Division's dissolution; the policy was consistent with the Party's broader tendency to distrust and finally eliminate branches of the Party that had potential to promote factional interests.[3] Interestingly, Turkey's policy again paralleled Soviet policy: Turkish women were fully enfranchised in 1934, and in 1935 the new president of the Women's Federation dissolved the organization, saying that "since women had been given all the rights that they had organised to demand, there was no need for the Women's Federation."[4]

In 1930, the Women's Division's central apparatus ceased to exist. Local branches of the Women's Division were designated "Women's Sections" of local Party organizations. The Women's Sections continued to function in Uzbekistan, organizing activities and promoting women for entrance into the Komsomol and the Party, but their coherent voice was lost. The journal *Yangi Yo'l* was turned over to the Division of Agitation and Propaganda and was no longer primarily concerned with women's issues. Workers from the Women's Division were reassigned, many to Machine and Tractor Stations, which were in charge of Party propaganda and oversight in Uzbekistan's rural areas. Activists like Saodat Shamsieva and Sobira Xoldarova were sent to rural posts, where if their local contacts were strong they might be able to report crimes against women, but where their work focused on strengthening collectivization rather than representing women. In 1937, some of the leading Uzbek women activists were purged and exiled, along with much of the leadership of the Uzbekistan Communist Party.[5] In 1936, the CPUz decided to re-create a journal for women, but not until the 1960s would the Party again emphasize women's organizations. With the Hujum's pressure diminished, but not entirely extinguished, the Party and the police exercised inconsistent oversight on issues that concerned the lives of women and girls.[6]

## COLLECTIVIZATION AND UNVEILING

The Hujum began in 1927 in many of Uzbekistan's cities and larger towns, but efforts to transform and unveil rural women generally accompanied or followed collectivization (1929–1934) in many regions. Collectivization in Uzbekistan was rapid and forced, but like the Hujum, it did have some supporters among rural Uzbeks. In the first years of collective farms (kolkhozes), living standards plummeted for most rural people; those who were even moderately well-off lost their land and livestock to the collective farms, and many farms were not allowed to raise necessary food crops, but instead had to plant cotton. In the early 1930s, more than thirty-one thousand households were dispossessed and their members exiled, either through forced resettlement in Uzbekistan or to labor colonies elsewhere in the Soviet Union. This reorganization of the countryside greatly expanded the state's ability to control and intervene in the everyday life of most Uzbeks.[7]

In my interviews with elderly collective farmers throughout Uzbekistan, most men and women reported that at a time not long after the collective farm was organized, a public meeting was held and women were told to unveil. Archival materials show that rural women were occasionally murdered by their families for unveiling or activism in 1930 and 1931, during mass collectivization, but the numbers were lower than in 1928. At the same time, murders of men who were linked to collectivization rose.[8]

These interviews also revealed striking differences in Hujum policies and actions from village to village. In various districts of Tashkent province, women in some farming communities did not ever wear the paranji, and thus never were pressured to remove it. In villages around Parkent, some communities had mass unveilings along with organizational meetings for collective farms. In others, women unveiled more gradually, during the 1930s, as they faced increasing pressure to go out and work in the fields, and several farmers remembered that women on their collective farms unveiled after World War II. In the small city of Parkent, by contrast, many women were still wearing paranjis in the 1950s. During one interview with an elderly collective farm woman there, women guests at her feast talked about unveiling in the 1950s. One such guest, who had been a teenager and a Komsomol member, told me that in the 1950s her parents made her start wearing the paranji when they withdrew her from school at age sixteen to arrange a marriage for her. She wore her paranji for one year following her marriage, because her husband wanted her to, but then government officials held a public unveiling meeting and she stopped wearing her paranji.[9]

Responses in Bukhara province were just as varied. F. S. attended the demonstration where his mother unveiled before collectivization. The women were forced to attend, he said, and "paranjis were pulled off by force, and there were also those who unveiled willingly." R. Sh. explained that some women in his village, including his mother, unveiled before collectivization in response to a Hujum speech about women's equality; the rest unveiled soon after collectivization. N. B., from Bukhara province, said that on his collective farm there was opposition to unveiling and that the women gradually unveiled, fearfully, after they were certain "that they wouldn't be killed." Raj. Sh. told of how women on his collective farm were fooled into unveiling in the mid-1930s; they were told that their paranjis would go to make clothing for children. N. J. watched her mother unveil after collectivization; born in 1921, she never wore the paranji. U. M. remembered that in his village women unveiled well after collectivization, in 1938 or so, after there had been quite a lot of propaganda on the kolkhoz urging women to go out to work and families to send daughters to school. A. J. reported that in his village, even the poor upheld seclusion: "They wouldn't reveal their wives to many people, and even during collectivization, in 1932–33, they wouldn't even say the name of their wife to anyone. It was a matter of honor." That the Soviet government even wanted husbands to declare their wives' names was shocking, let alone that on the kolkhoz men and women were supposed to work together.[10]

One woman, O. X., born in 1903 in a Xorazm village, said, "The year we entered the kolkhoz was when they had us take off the paranji . . . They say, 'Men and women are equal. So then, why wear the paranji? Throw it off!' A couple of women spoke. They said, 'We'll throw off our paranjis,' and they threw them on the fire, and then everyone else did the same." In many villages in Xorazm and Qashqa Daryo provinces, women wore either a *jelak*, which was a short robe draped from the head without a chachvon, or they wore scarves. The Hujum did not address *jelak* wearers, who gradually stopped wearing this form of head covering. E. S. said that in his village, wearing the paranji "was not the fashion. It was worn only for celebrations and at weddings."[11]

L. U., from a very religious family in Shahrisabz, said that unveiling agitation took place there in 1928, but that his mother continued wearing the paranji until her death, and until 1960 a number of other women did as well. In his kolkhoz, "based on the view of Islam," men and women remained separate. Men worked outdoors, while women formed a silkworm and embroidery *artel*. O. B. said that women were still wearing the paranji during World War II in his village and that the village head told them to unveil in 1954. B. Sh. said that even though eight women unveiled in 1928 at a Hujum meeting, the rest all continued wearing the veil until after World War II: "They would go out covered; they would not go out naked!"[12]

Party attention to veiling and unveiling was inconsistent in the 1930s, with continuing pressure to unveil in some communities and little or none in others. Nonetheless, as the kolkhoz became the most widespread organizing factor for rural communities, and as kolkhozes demanded women's labor, women on most collective farms gradually went to work and also ceased veiling in the paranji.[13] Kolkhozes built schools, the local Party and government pressured families to send daughters to school, and rural values changed, so that parents saw benefit in sending their children to school. Girls could not veil at school, and this contributed to the paranji's gradual demise. Though there was an urban revival in paranji wearing during World War II, which some authors have associated with the increase in religious freedom that Stalin granted during the war, the paranji had become a heavily discouraged choice adopted by few women.

Milli-xon Ibrohimova was a Party member who became mayor of

Namangan in the 1940s. She said that in Namangan in the late 1940s and early 1950s families were still giving young girls in marriage, men were taking several wives, and many women were still wearing the paranji. In 1946, there were eight thousand women in paranji; many had started wearing it again during the war. "We did away with it!" she said. Ibrohimova and others in the city government held a public unveiling meeting to convince women to get rid of even their expensive paranjis. Paranji wearing in Namangan was sufficiently entrenched that repeated unveiling ceremonies in the 1920s, 1930s, 1940s, and even 1950s did not succeed fully. Hojiraxon Kirgizbaeva, who began to work as Namangan's city prosecutor in 1963, said that in the 1960s, "most" women in Namangan still wore the paranji, and she, like Ibrohimova, held public demonstrations for unveiling. Party and government officials like Kirgizbaeva and Ibrohimova used the same methods and forms of propaganda to get women to unveil as those that were used in the 1920s.[14]

Douglas Northrop uses reports from the 1930s to conclude that "by the 1930s . . . [the paranji] had spread more widely among poor and rural women, and by 1941 had come to be accepted—even by those who did not wear them—as a basic component of Uzbek Muslim identity." He notes that it is impossible to assess how many women were veiled or unveiled, but on the basis of widespread reports in the 1930s of veiled women, concludes that the Hujum spread and solidified veiling because Uzbeks endowed it with political, anticolonial meaning.[15] The evidence he poses is problematic. Activists and the OGPU were encouraged to report on places where unveiling was not succeeding, and they did so. But reporting was not at all systematic, and places that were not seen as trouble spots got far less attention and coverage than those where activists wanted support for change. By definition police archives feature crimes, not their absence. While veiling remained tenacious in some villages, in many places collectivization led to unveiling rather than to increased seclusion. Northrop's explanation of the increased veiling phenomenon, that it was anticolonial, is linked to his explanation for why paranji wearing did ultimately decrease. He puts the decline in the 1950s and identifies the causes as increased intercultural contact—due to the flood of outsiders who began moving to Uzbekistan in World War II—and changes in Uzbek identity arising from participation in the war. Paranji wearing went away because Uzbeks became Soviet.[16]

Relying on different evidence, and because I view the contest over the veil as more significantly an inter-Uzbek dispute over identity and modernity than an Uzbek-Russian conflict over colonialism, I draw different conclusions. Most evidence suggests that veiling decreased in a serious way by the late 1930s with collectivization and the increase in availability of both rural and urban schools. During World War II, most able-bodied Uzbek men were mobilized in the army, and most Uzbek women, urban and rural, were compelled to work for pay outside their homes, unveiled. When Uzbek soldiers returned, they had been exposed to the Soviet Union in a broad way, they had learned some Russian, and they flooded into the Party. The World War II experience transformed Uzbek society, and the disappearance of veiling is linked to this transformation as well as to the economic and social changes that began in the 1930s. Uzbeks unveiled in part because they became Soviet, but becoming Soviet meant fulfilling a dream that Uzbek reformers themselves had promoted before Stalin did: creating the New Woman.

## DEVELOPMENT MARKERS:
## EDUCATION, EMPLOYMENT, HEALTH

In 1939, official statistics put the literacy rate at 73 percent for females in Uzbekistan between ages nine and fifty, and at 83 percent for men under age fifty. Twenty years later, the state claimed literacy rates between 97 and 99 percent for its age nine-to-fifty population.[17] Statistics on rates of schooling do not support such high literacy figures. According to the 1959 census, in the whole population above age ten about 575 people out of every 1,000 had attended school. Rates were substantially higher among younger cohorts than older ones, but even so, in rural communities 737 boys out of every 1,000 between the ages of ten and nineteen had some schooling, while 672 girls out of every 1,000 in the same cohort had some schooling. In cities, rates of schooling for boys and girls were relatively equal, both about 760 of 1,000. Thus, if literacy correlates largely to schooling, then literacy rates among youth in Uzbekistan were 70 to 75 percent. Statistics on school attendance do not reflect the mass effect of the End Illiteracy campaign of the 1930s, in which several million adults learned to read through evening classes. If the 1939 statistic for women's literacy is to be believed, the dramatic rise from the 1920s (when Uzbek women's literacy was 5 to 10 percent in cities and 1 percent in rural areas) was largely due to the End Illiteracy program.[18]

The availability of education increased both in cities and in rural communities between the late 1920s and 1959. Collectivization of agriculture in the 1930s was usually accompanied by the building of a primary school and the introduction of Soviet education. Nonetheless, statistics show that as in the 1950s, in rural areas one-quarter of boys and one-third of girls did not go to school. Remote rural families could only educate their children if they were willing to send them away to boarding schools, and the difference between the number of rural boys and rural girls in schools reflected some continuing bias against educating daughters. While literacy and schooling rates were lower than in European regions of the Soviet Union, it is also worthwhile noting that they were far higher than in any other countries in Uzbekistan's region, such as Iran, Afghanistan, Pakistan, or China.[19]

Formal employment for women rose rapidly in the 1930s, though not necessarily because women wanted to work. Rather, following collectivization rural women were enrolled as collective farm members, and many were forced to work in the fields. While most rural women provided some farm labor before collectivization, after collectivization many women became full-time farm laborers, and by the late 1950s women outnumbered men as active members of the collective farm labor force in Uzbekistan. In the cities, economic need—due to the famine of the early 1930s and the absence of working-age males during World War II—sent many women into the labor force. In 1939, 36.9 percent of all women were employed, as were 54.7 percent of men; rural women's employment was considerably higher than that of urban women.[20]

Uzbek girls who obtained middle and higher education were encouraged to enter certain careers, in particular education, health care, communications, and bookkeeping, though by 1959 women's representation in chemistry and engineering was also rather high in Uzbekistan, reflecting a trend throughout the Soviet Union. Women workers also dominated textile production, though as in other areas of economy women usually did not fill positions that demanded the highest skills and paid the best.[21]

While Soviet provision of health care was often rudimentary in rural communities, nonetheless most collective farms eventually constructed clinics, and visits to the doctor became relatively commonplace. In 1958, Uzbekistan's minister of women's affairs, Z. R. Rahimboboeva, cited statistics on Uzbekistan's falling rate of infant mortality: "If in 1913, out of every 1,000 children born, 273 died before the age of one year, in 1940 it was 184 children per 1,000; in 1956, 47 per 1,000; and in 1957, 45 per 1,000."[22] Even though the Soviet Union softened its infant mortality statistics, there was a major decrease in both infant and maternal mortality. The gender imbalance seen in the 1926 census, when in many age cohorts there were 8.8 women per 10 men, disappeared in 1959 census figures. Stalin's pro-natalist policies, which encouraged mothers to give birth to as many children as possible by providing substantial monetary rewards and public recognition, may have curtailed the effects of Central Asian son preference on the survival of female children.

Development indictors, such as increasing numbers of schools, hospitals, and factories, rose dramatically in Uzbekistan between the 1930s and 1960s, and women's lives changed with them. A woman would typically study in school for at least a few years; work for pay outside her home for at least a few years, gaining credit toward a state retirement pension; and by the 1950s it was not unusual for even rural women to give birth in hospitals, rather than at home. All of these changes resulted from the Soviet Union's relentless, top-down modernization drive. The Party's values included guaranteeing and requiring free public education for all, promoting labor participation in state-owned enterprises as necessary for economic growth and essential for the development of socialist values in individuals, and supporting basic health care as a right and to enhance labor-force health.

However, while modernization's effects are clear—education was available, literacy rose, and health care improved—the Soviet economy put little investment into modernizing Uzbekistan's agricultural sector until the mid-1950s. Until then, large numbers of collective farms had no mechanization at all and no infrastructure improvements either. Most farm labor was done by hand, roads were unpaved, electricity was rarely available, and only with the rise in wealth in the 1950s were farmers able to invest in glass windows and corrugated steel roofs for their houses. The sector that employed the vast majority of Uzbek women, agriculture, employed most of them in nonspecialized work. This meant that from the founding of collective farms in the 1930s Uzbek women expended most of their farm labor time planting cotton, hoeing cotton, weeding cotton, pruning cotton, and picking cotton. Raising silk cocoons also remained unmechanized, highly labor-intensive work, performed mostly by women.

In cities, many women preferred moving from traditional homes into modern apartment blocks simply because the latter provided some amenities that were entirely lacking in the mahallas: running water, flush toilets, heat, and electricity. Unlike European regions of the Soviet Union, communal apartments were unusual in Uzbekistan; instead, multigenerational families shared both traditional homes and apartments. Amenities like electricity and running water began to reach a few rural villages in the 1950s, but are still lacking in some homes in twenty-first century Uzbekistan. The burdens of housework, cooking, cleaning, and laundry, remained arduous for women in cities and in the countryside.

Politically, although many Uzbek women participated in Women's Division activities and in delegate meetings in the 1920s, few joined the Communist Party in the years when women's membership was strongly promoted; and, of course, under Soviet dictatorship there were no alternative possibilities for political participation. The Hujum did not lead to a strong rise in numbers of Uzbek Communist women. In 1927, Uzbek women were a mere 2.5 percent of all Party members and candidates in Uzbekistan, while women of all nationalities in Uzbekistan comprised 13 percent of the Party. Through the late 1920s and early 1930s, the Party kept up its extremely rapid expansion in Uzbekistan, reaching 54,500 in 1931 and 81,600 in 1933, and women continued to comprise between 9 and 14 percent of the Party.[23] After this, the Party began purging its members, and the numbers dropped by more than half. Women's membership fell from a high of 11,000 in 1933 to 4,500 in 1936, but they were still 15 percent of Party members.[24] After the 1930s purges, numbers in the Party rose more steadily, and women made up 18 or 19 percent of membership in the 1960s and 1970s. In the one-party state, membership in the Party became a vehicle for career advancement; women who joined were those with career aspirations for which membership would be an asset.

## AFTER THE PARANJI

The paranji became an ever rarer form of dress, as elderly women who adhered to it passed on and few younger women wore it; but Uzbek concepts of proper clothing for women continued to emphasize modesty. Although some reformers of the 1920s and 1930s wanted Uzbek women to adopt European dress, this received very little emphasis in the Hujum. European-style clothing spread in the 1930s, when collective-farm stores were provided with supplies of ready-made clothing from the Soviet Union's European factories, but photographs and images in magazines continued to present Uzbeks with distinctive forms of dress. In the 1930s, the do'ppi, the embroidered skull cap, was stylish for both men and young women. Photographs show mature women wearing large, loose scarves as head coverings. Multicolored silk fabric (*atlas*) remained the prized textile for women's clothing until the 1990s. The usual fashion for Uzbek women's dress until the 1990s was a *kuylak*, a loose dress that covered arms to the wrists (or nearly) and fell below the knees, with *lozim* (necessaries), loose pants that covered the legs to the ankles. University students from rural villages near Namangan told me in 1991 that everyone in their village expected them to dress this way, and if they wore shorter sleeves they might be considered *bo'zuq*, or morally spoiled.

Both rural and urban married women wore colorful headscarves, tied at the back of the neck. Many older women would add a second scarf, a large one that draped from the head and fell loose at the front; the end could be used to cover the face. In the early 1990s, I frequently saw women with the scarf clamped in their teeth. By contrast, women from families that were careful adherents of Soviet values and culture often symbolized that identification by leaving heads uncovered and by wearing the same kinds of clothing that could be seen anywhere in the Soviet Union.

The Hujum had placed so much emphasis on the paranji that in later years it was only remembered as "the time when we threw off the paranji," and not for any of its other emphases, such as ending seclusion and bringing women into schools, workplaces, and public life. The Hujum had been a radical movement, one that promoted the legal equality of men and women, but by the standards of the All-Union Women's Division, most of the Hujum activists in Uzbekistan had rather modest goals. The Russian founders of the Women's Division, Aleksandra Kollontai and Inessa Armand, had dreamed of a world where women's opportunities would be the same as men's, where women and men would share the burdens of family maintenance, and where many household tasks would be turned over to the socialist state. It would have been hard to find any Uzbek activist who even considered the possibility of that version of gender equality. At their most radical, they were working to end the marriage of minors and polygyny, dreaming of choice and companionship in marriage, and arguing that women, too, could get an education, join the Party, and leave their homes to participate in society. As had been the case with Jadid reformers, for Communist Uzbeks gender roles remained fixed: girls would marry (young), become mothers, continue to cook, clean, make clothing, and so on, and men would continue to be the primary providers for their families.[25]

Uzbek activists had not really thought outside these parameters in the radical years of the 1920s; it is hardly surprising, then, that they did not recast gender relations after Stalinist conservatism in family matters was established in the late 1930s elsewhere in the Soviet Union. Between the 1930s and 1960s, as the Soviet social welfare system developed and encouraged population growth through payments to mothers of many children, the majority of women in Central Asia were rewarded for bearing and raising children. Both Soviet economic policies and Uzbek social values provided continuing support for the status quo in gender roles.

Donald Carlisle argues that "Stalinist strategy was to accept the continued co-existence of traditional and modern society for the long term."[26] He describes a divide in Uzbekistan between urban Europeans and traditional Uzbeks, though many in Uzbekistan would argue that there were Europeanized and traditional Uzbeks. But in life histories that women told me, elements collide and combine. Uzbeks who embraced certain aspects of Soviet modernization, especially education, labor, ending seclusion, and modern health care, also reproduced fixed attitudes toward gender roles and carried on practices like arranged marriage that perpetuated extended family hierarchies and lifestyles seemingly antithetical to Soviet visions of the modern family.

Soviet scholars and activists who have written about the Hujum and about women in Uzbekistan often portray a rosy situation where women were liberated and, except for a few "relics of the past," were fulfilling the promises of modernity and living in equality with men. Later Soviet scholars, such as Sergei Poliakov, who published their findings during perestroika, attack these exaggerated images and strongly emphasize the failings of Soviet promises.[27] During the Soviet period, scholars from the West and expatriate Turkestanis launched bitter attacks on the Soviet system, arguing that it had failed Central Asians and simply perpetuated empire.[28] In a late-perestroika judgment, Martha Olcott reviews many of the issues confronting Central Asian women, based on perestroika-period reporting of problems; she notes a rise in the infant mortality rate, perpetuation of arranged marriage, the phenomenon of women's suicide by self-immolation, lack of employment opportunities, and a rise in Islamic observance—this last factor being the only one she regards as potentially positive for women. She concludes that changes that were underway in the late 1980s "may make the lives of contemporary Central Asian women easier. It is hard to imagine that it can make their lives harder."[29]

Because I interviewed elderly Uzbeks only after independence, between 1992 and 2004, the stories that they told me usually compared pre- and postindependence life. Elderly Uzbeks, both women and men, often expressed happiness about the demise of the Soviet Union: having an independent state and being able to practice Islam were frequently mentioned as positive changes. But most also remembered that in the late-Soviet period, from the 1960s to 1980s, their living standards increased. They built better houses, with glass windows and corrugated steel roofs, with electricity and running water (at least into the courtyard). More importantly, wages and pensions were paid in full and on time, and meat was inexpensive. Those who were "middle class" had occasionally traveled and vacationed at Soviet resorts.

The life stories that elderly Uzbek women told me in the early 1990s were often framed by a narrative of progress; they were never framed in a narrative of unmitigated decline and disaster. They reported on hardships in their lives, largely connected with the famine of the 1930s and the overall disruption of World War II, but viewed their own lives as having improved. They talked about sending daughters, as well as sons, to school. They compared the high infant mortality in their natal families with their own greater success in bringing children to adulthood. They spoke with pride about their working careers and status as pensioners. And while many of them had unveiled because they were forced to do so, none expressed any regret at the paranji's disappearance or any desire that it should again be worn. One of my informants, Latifot, an otin, wore a paranji when going to the mosque to recite for others, but did not wear it in her ordinary activities.[30] They had not lived their lives making conscious comparisons between themselves and women elsewhere, whether in the European parts of the Soviet Union, or in Western Europe, or in the Middle East. Rather, they assessed how their lives had changed through comparison between their earlier and later years. They would have been quite surprised at Olcott's declaration that their lives in the late-Soviet period could scarcely have been harder; they knew how difficult their lives had been (especially in the 1930s and 1940s) and how much they had improved.

# ❧ 10 ❧
# CONCLUSIONS

$I$N PREREVOLUTIONARY TURKE-
stan, a few Jadids began to write about reforming women, breaking the
Central Asian tradition of female seclusion, giving girls a new-method
education, and turning them into companion wives for men who
wanted to change their whole society. Their recommendations met direct
opposition from conservative clergy and influenced only a few hundred
families in major cities. A few Uzbeks sent their daughters to new-method
schools or gave their daughters access to new ideas. Most Turkestanis
did not welcome the Bolshevik revolution, and the Jadid movement
divided between those who saw in the new state the possibility for enacting their modernizing ideas, and those who found Bolshevism too radical and the new government too much a continuation of Russian
domination. This book has focused on Uzbek women whose own understanding of progress was shaped by Jadidism and who became partners
in the Soviet project to transform women. I have argued that they developed their own synthesis between Soviet goals and the modernizing goals
of Jadidism, making the Bolsheviks' program for women's equality
accommodate their own concept of the New Woman. Far from radical
in most of their expectations for change, they primarily embraced education as the key to ending women's seclusion and inequality. But they

came to see veiling as incompatible with modernity and eventually supported making the paranji illegal.

Uzbek proponents of women's rights and of unveiling were not numerous, but they were the people who communicated these ideas to other Uzbeks. Russians, although they were heavily overrepresented in the Uzbekistan Communist Party and numerous in the Women's Division, almost never spoke Uzbek; they depended on translators to communicate their understanding of the Party's programs to the Uzbek masses. Uzbeks in the Party and in the Women's Division communicated directly with Uzbeks, and they presented ideas about the reform of women that were their own. Central Asian society was not at all unified; among the many political divisions, the Jadid versus traditionalist conflict reappeared in new forms after the establishment of Uzbekistan, with Jadids turned Communists still trying to promote their modernizing programs and still meeting the same sort of opposition as before the revolution. The difference was that with the backing of the Soviet state and Communist Party, modernizing ideas gained new power. Communists in Moscow looked at Central Asia and saw a need, among other things, to liberate women. Jadids turned Communists looked at their own society and saw a similar need to reform women. Their ideas merged in the Hujum. I understand the Hujum and the counter-Hujum as an expression of continued cultural conflict among Uzbeks, not as a project dictated by Moscow and resisted by anticolonial Uzbeks.

I have argued that the Soviet state did not succeed in transforming Uzbek gender ideals, nor did the state even try; but it did make huge changes to the way Uzbek women lived their lives economically and socially, and some of these changes—ending seclusion, providing universal education, making room for women in public, and providing basic health care—should be recognized as positive. Although activists from the Moscow-based All-Union Women's Division articulated some proposals for entirely new and equal gender relations, Uzbek activists' own goals were much more limited: they strongly upheld difference in gender roles, traditional concepts of women's sexual honor, and views of marriage that stressed companionship more than equality.

When the Communist Party began promoting women's unveiling in 1927, some women eagerly unveiled, some zealous Party members forced unwilling women to unveil, and many Uzbeks responded with violence against unveiled women. While scholars like Shirin Akiner have understood the Hujum as a form of violence against Uzbeks—forcing unwanted change and shaming Uzbek women by uncovering their faces, thus triggering a wave of murders—I question this understanding of the murder wave. I argue that it is important to note that the victims of violence and murder were ordinary Uzbek women who unveiled; they were not the powerful Communist elite or the colonialist Russians. Rather than assume that murdering women was a normal part of Uzbek life (that is, adopting the Party's mid-1920s position that murder was a "crime of everyday life" along with common practices like polygyny), I examine the context of this unexpected and ferocious murder wave. The state was working to undermine many forms of social power in the 1920s, by putting wealthy merchants and clergy out of work and taking land away from wealthy landowners. I see these murders of unveiled women as male efforts to reestablish the one aspect of social hierarchy that they had not yet lost—patriarchy—by frightening resisting women, or women who might decide to resist, back into subordination. Murder was a way of dealing with uppity Uzbek women; it was not an effective strategy for changing anything at all about the Soviet state.

In a work examining Egyptian women's responses to welfare institutions, Iman Bibars differentiates between opposition, meaning "coping with constraints," and resistance, meaning "challenging oppressive structures."[1] She argues against James Scott's expansive meaning of the term resistance, popular among feminist scholars (and among historians of the Soviet Union as well) that understands everything from disguise to "hidden transcripts" as forms of resistance. Bibars instead classifies these as opposition, in that they do express dissent from the system in question, but in ways that reinforce the system rather than ways that threaten overthrow. She remarks, "The currently popular discourse of women's resistance distracts attention from the pain of subordination. It lets oppressors off the hook because if women can resist, the oppression must not be so absolute or tyrannical." She takes issue with scholarship that asserts women's choice to veil is a form of resistance or social protest: "what they have actually done is play by the rules of the dominant group; they have not tried to change the situation."[2] This analysis informs my own feminist reading of Uzbek women's agency in the Hujum.

Uzbek women who struggled to end seclusion engaged in a life-threatening form of resistance against their subordination to men. However, unlike women's struggles elsewhere, this one took place in a context of competing hegemonies, one where, unusually, the state acted in opposition to patriarchy. One hegemonic force—Uzbek patriarchal culture—trained most women to comply with the norms of veiling and seclusion in return for provision and protection (what Deniz Kandiyoti terms the "patriarchal bargain"[3]). The hegemonic Soviet state and Communist Party, on the other hand, shut down any forum for political dissent and turned every program for change into an assault on its enemies. Women who decided to resist seclusion were successful in the long run not because they alone managed to convince Uzbek society to adopt new norms of equality, but because they found support from a state that intervened harshly. However, because so many women were forced to unveil, it is impossible to understand all or even most of the unveiled as consciously trying to overthrow an oppressive structure; the resisters of patriarchy were a minority. But when unveiled women were able to mobilize government support, the relations of power changed: in place of women's subordination to men, the state made men and women subordinate to itself.

What then of the others—the men who reinforced seclusion using violence, and the women who never unveiled, and the women who re-veiled? Men who incited violence against the unveiled were opposing the Soviet state and its programs and were drawing on concepts and ideas (usually claiming they were upholding Islam) from dramatically different sources than the state's. Their actions were not aimed at overthrowing the state's overall authority. Most of their actions were not addressed to officials who could have changed the direction of government policies; instead they attacked and murdered women who had resisted male authority. In this I find a similarity to racist lynchings in U.S. history, hostile actions that showed opposition to government policies of race equality and were effective at reinforcing racial subordination in action, but were not aimed at overthrowing the government's laws on legal equality. Rather, they sought to subvert those laws.

In considering the actions of women who remained veiled and those who re-veiled, violence against the unveiled has to be seen as a significant factor. In recognizing this, I do not assume that all women really wanted to unveil or to break seclusion; many did not. But in a context of competing hegemonies, women at least had the possibility of agency, of considering whether they would actively choose the system they had been brought up with or the alternative of Soviet life. In reality, most were entirely constrained. Even if male heads of household were not fully convinced by the anti-unveiling propaganda telling them that unveiled women were prostitutes and would burn in hell, even if they were open to the possibility of ending seclusion, simple concern about women in their families after the wave of murders started would have convinced many to keep women veiled and secluded, and thus protected from insult and attack. A veiled woman had every reason to think that the incentives and support for unveiling that the state could offer were rather small compensation for the risks she would take by unveiling. Veiling was not resisting; it did not challenge the Soviet system. Instead, it was compliance with patriarchy, compliance informed by a very rational bargain.

As the balance of power in Uzbekistan shifted away from patriarchal dominance to state dominance, the terms of the bargain women made also changed. I argue that the extension of Soviet state power in collectivization meant that the state could, at last, enforce at least some of its laws concerning women in most parts of Uzbekistan. While the state was never able to eradicate all of the practices that it outlawed, Soviet modernization did change material conditions in Central Asia. Combined with the state's ideology of women's equality, this led to changes not only in material conditions for women, but in Uzbek norms as well: sending a daughter to school became possible, and eventually normal, and so did the ideas that women did not belong in seclusion and did have a right to a place in public. I attribute these cultural and material changes to Soviet modernization and its uniquely Uzbek interpretation, in part expressed through the Hujum.

## EPILOGUE: PERESTROIKA, INDEPENDENCE, AND VEILING

In the late 1980s, one of the hallmarks of Soviet General Secretary Mikhail Gorbachev's policy of perestroika (restructuring) was liberalization of the Soviet Union's treatment of religions. In 1988, the state recognized the one thousandth anniversary of Russian Orthodoxy, a celebration accompanied by the removal of many restrictions on Christian practice and education. This was followed by open practice of Islam in Central Asia, with communities reopening mosques or building new mosques. By 1991, there were ad hoc Quran schools, with domlas and otins instructing adults and children in prayer and Quran recitation. In Tashkent in 1991 to 1993, I frequently saw girls and young women who were wearing international-style hijab, borrowing norms from Muslims elsewhere. The new hijab was distinctive, looking nothing like either the paranji or standard Uzbek women's dress, with its colorful headscarf. In those years, I occasionally saw women in paranji, but their numbers could not compare to the new hijab wearers.[4] The new hijab (*yopinchik*, in Uzbek) involved a white, light blue or green, or black headscarf, drawn close to the face and under the chin, allowing no possibility that any hair would show. In rare cases, a woman would pin a flap of the scarf to cover her nose and mouth, leaving only her eyes uncovered. The headscarf wearers usually also had on a single-colored loose robe that covered their bodies from shoulder to toe.

In the early 1990s, Uzbeks often expressed respect for people who were studying Islam, who prayed five times a day, and who fasted throughout Ramadan. International-style hijab was identified with this more rigorous practice of Islam. However, among my elderly informants, many expressed some surprise or chagrin over the new veiling. Several exclaimed that they had fought to end the paranji, while more generally elderly women said they did not understand why the new veilers wanted to cover up.

In the home of my host in Kokand, I had a long conversation with a woman, a very young grandmother, who had begun wearing the new hijab. Her husband had recently invested his time in studying Islam and they made an '*umra* pilgrimage to Mecca, where they visited with Uzbeks from the exile community. When they returned home, he told her she should quit her job at the local ZAGS office and stay home. She adopted the headscarf and reluctantly resigned her position. Her headscarf was a demonstration of her piety and of her identification with Islam as practiced by Muslims throughout the world.[5]

The new hijab was as distinctive a marker for Uzbek women as a beard and a white skullcap were for Uzbek men (who rarely wear beards and often wear a black and white or green and white embroidered do'ppi). Although the modesty goals of hijab could easily be fulfilled with typical Uzbek women's dress, the new hijab wearers were expressing a different identity. Their identification with international trends in Islam, symbolized and made public through their choice of dress, drew respect from the public, but by the mid-1990s attracted suspicion from the government of independent Uzbekistan.

Following independence, the Republic of Uzbekistan, under the leadership of President Karimov, first welcomed interaction with many Middle Eastern and South Asian states. Turkey created a TV network to reach Central Asia and began investing in business there. From Turkey and other countries came Muslim educators eager to open up lycées, incorporating religious instruction, where Uzbek students could study. Uzbekistan sent college students abroad to study, especially to Turkey, where they were exposed to such new Islamist movements as that led by Fethullah Gülen. As Karimov consolidated his power (changing the Constitution to extend his term of office several times), he removed potential rivals; and by 1994 he seemed concerned about the potential power of Islam as an independent organizing force. In the late 1990s, his government cracked down on and arrested individual mosque leaders, closed down the foreign schools, brought back students from Turkey, and arrested members of groups that were commonly referred to as Wahhabi. In this context, "Symbols of religious piety, including beards and headscarves, became signs of political partisanship."[6]

The government of Uzbekistan worried that so-called Wahhabis had ties to the Islamic Renaissance Party in Tajikistan, where there was civil war from 1991 until 1996, and to groups in Afghanistan and Chechnya. In 1997, when a dissident group murdered four policemen in Namangan, the government started a campaign to arrest Wahhabis and initiated heavy propaganda against international or foreign forms of Islam and in support of "Uzbek tradition." That is, the campaign juxtaposed the two, defining what was "Uzbek" as acceptable and what was "foreign" as unacceptable.[7]

For the government of Uzbekistan, convincing those who had taken up wearing the new hijab or beards to renounce those symbols was a way to combat a threat. The state again interpreted the veil as an instrument, one that could be used to manipulate the whole structure underlying it. In 1997 and 1998 at various institutions of higher education, students who wished to perform prayers were no longer allotted any space to do so, and the bearded and headscarved were told they should change their appearance or they would be expelled. Interestingly, the discourse used to support these new measures attacked these practices for their foreignness as well as for their apparent connection with political Islam. Young women who wore hijab were told that if they replaced their headcovering with the Uzbek style of headscarf they would not be expelled. Some students conceded to demands, shaving or abandoning hijab, while others asserted their right to dress as they chose and brought legal cases against institutions. All of those cases lost, and expulsions were upheld. In 1998, the government passed a law against wearing "ritual dress" in public places, and universities have used this law in subsequent years to deny education to veiled women.[8]

In February 1999, several car bombers struck central Tashkent, and in the aftermath the government cracked down against people reputedly connected with two groups, the Islamic Movement of Uzbekistan (IMU) and Hizb ut-Tahrir (HT). Sweeping arrests put thousands in jail, and a public show trial of defendants in the 1999 bombings resulted in a number of death sentences. Many public expressions of piety were repressed, and the numbers of women veiled in obviously foreign hijab decreased markedly. In 2003, I saw a only a few young women wearing rather obviously Islamic forms of headscarves, but in colorful fabrics designed to create very stylish, elegant, modest dress.

Independent Uzbekistan's fierce campaign against veiling and beards obviously has roots in Soviet policies of state-enforced secularism, but also breaks with earlier concerns by paying attention to men's appearance as well as women's. The Hujum established that the state could take an interest in the ways that Uzbeks dressed, and the state and Party asserted control over women's bodies by demanding unveiling and calling on women to present themselves in public. However, the Hujum was carried out in a context of opposite social pressures, where families and religious leaders insisted on their own control of women's bodies and threatened women with physical harm if they unveiled. In the 1920s, women's socially determined default was to veil; they did not veil by choice. The state used many strategies to persuade women to unveil.

In the 1990s anti-veiling campaign, the context was one of official secularism and almost uncontested state hegemony. Those who veiled found support from networks of friends, but they faced sustained social pressure to unveil (meaning to cease wearing international hijab, even if they replaced it with Uzbek-style headscarves). Human Rights Watch found that many veiled women reported that their families strongly urged or pressured them to unveil. Regardless of their individual beliefs about dress, parents did not want to see their daughters sacrifice their opportunities for education and argued that they should conform to the state's demands. Veiling in Uzbekistan in 2000 required as much individual fortitude as unveiling did in 1927.

Arguments against veiling in independent Uzbekistan are vastly different from arguments against the paranji. The Hujum's rhetoric focused on establishing equality for women and named the paranji the enemy of women's education, opportunity to work, and opportunity to participate in social life. It attacked Islam as well, though inconsistently. The paranji was not seen as a symbol of the wearer's individual piety or political commitment; it was assumed that women wore it because everyone did, not because of ideological conviction. The government of Uzbekistan's anti-hijab efforts are predicated on the idea that international hijab indicates a political identity and thus symbolizes a threat. That the style is similar to that worn by Islamists throughout the Middle East heightens the perception of a threat of foreign meddling. Just as before the revolution conservative clergy members condemned Uzbek men who adopted European shirts and hairstyles, and as traditionalists in the 1920s accused unveiled women of becoming Russian, selling out to their conquerors and opening the door for corruption, the Uzbek government now condemns hijab wearers as representatives of foreign values that will undermine both the state and the culture.

In France and Turkey, where state secularism also has placed controversial limits on Muslim women's dress choices by insisting that they unveil in schools and other public institutions, those who want to veil have substantial social movements on their side, movements that contest government policies. In Uzbekistan, those who have chosen veiling as yet have only their principles to defend them, and no large body of sympathizers to help them make a case to the government for their freedom to dress as their conscience (or their social movement) dictates.

# NOTES

## INTRODUCTION

1. Gregory Massell, *The Surrogate Proletariat: Moslem Women and Revolutionary Strategies in Soviet Central Asia, 1919–1929* (Princeton, NJ: Princeton University Press, 1974); Douglas Northrop, *Veiled Empire: Gender and Power in Stalinist Central Asia* (Ithaca, NY: Cornell University Press, 2004).

2. Western historians include the above mentioned Massell and Northrop. Defining Soviet works include Rakhima Aminova, *The October Revolution and Women's Liberation in Uzbekistan*, trans. B. M. Meerovich (Moscow: Nauka, 1977); Dilarom Alimova, *Zhenskii vopros v srednei Azii: Istoriia izucheniia i sovremennye problemy* (Tashkent: Fan, 1991).

3. Massell, xxxii–xxxiii. This admission by Massell was perhaps what most strongly provoked my interest in this topic.

4. Northrop, *Veiled Empire*, 347.

5. Marfua Tokhtakhodjaeva [To'xtaxo'jaeva], *Between the Slogans of Communism and the Laws of Islam*, trans. from Russian by Sufian Aslam (Lahore, Pakistan: Shirkat Gah Women's Resource Centre, 1992), 17.

6. Tsentral'noe Statisticheskoe Upravlenie, *Itogi vsesoiuznoi perepisi naselenii 1959: Uzbekskaia SSSR* (Moskva: Gosizdat, 1962), 41, table 25. This was clearly an exaggeration, but did reflect that by the 1940s the majority of Uzbek girls attended public schools.

7. United Nations, *Demographic Yearbook*, 1960, table 11, and 1979, tables 33 and 35 (New York: Statistical Office, United Nations).

8. Stephen Kotkin, "Modern Times: The Soviet Union and the Interwar Conjuncture," in *Kritika: Explorations in Russian and Eurasian History* 2, no. 1 (2001): 111–64. See also David Hoffman and Yanni Kotsonis, eds., *Russian Modernity: Politics, Knowledge, Practices* (New York: St. Martin's Press, 2000); and David Hoffman, *Stalinist Values: The Cultural Norms of Soviet Modernity (1917–1941)* (Ithaca, NY: Cornell University Press, 2003).

9. Laura Engelstein, "Culture, Culture Everywhere: Interpretations of Modern Russia, across the 1991 Divide," *Kritika: Explorations in Russian and Eurasian History* 2, no. 2 (2001): 363–93.

10. Works stressing the continuity of Russian and Soviet colonialism include Edward Allworth, *Central Asia: 120 Years of Russian Rule* (Durham, NC: Duke University Press, 1989); Hélène Carrère d'Encausse, *Islam and the Russian Empire: Reform and Revolution in Central Asia* (Berkeley: University of California Press, 1988); Northrop, *Veiled Empire*; and Paula Michaels, *Curative Powers: Medicine and Empire in Stalin's Central Asia* (Pittsburgh: Pittsburgh University Press, 2003). Works stressing the lack of continuity between Russian colonialism and Soviet policy include Francine Hirsch, "Toward an Empire of Nations: Border-Making and the Formation of Soviet National Identities," *Russian Review* 59 (April 2000): 201–26; and Terry Martin, *The Affirmative Action Empire: Nations and Nationalism in the Soviet Union, 1923–1939* (Ithaca, NY: Cornell University Press, 2001).

11. Kotkin, "Modern Times"; Theda Skocpol, *Protecting Soldiers and Mothers: The Political Origins of Social Policy in the United States* (Cambridge, MA: Harvard University Press, 1992); Seth Koven and Sonya Michaels, eds., *Mothers of a New World: Maternalist Politics and the Origins of Welfare States* (New York: Routledge, 1993).

12. Ellen L. Fleishmann, "The Other 'Awakening': The Emergence of Women's Movements in the Modern Middle East, 1900–1940," in *Social History of Women and Gender in the Modern Middle East*, ed. Margaret L. Meriwether and Judith E. Tucker (Boulder, CO: Westview, 1999), 99.

13. Adeeb Khalid, *The Politics of Muslim Cultural Reform: Jadidism in Central Asia*, (Berkeley: University of California Press, 1998), 80–113.

14. Works discussing the Soviet Union's policies on women in the 1920s and 1930s, largely concerning Russia, include Wendy Z. Goldman, *Women, the State and Revolution: Soviet Family Policy and Social Life, 1917–1936* (Cambridge: Cambridge University Press, 1993); Elizabeth Wood, *The Baba and the Comrade: Gender and Politics in Revolutionary Russia* (Bloomington: Indiana University Press, 1997); and Barbara Evans Clements, *Bolshevik Women* (Cambridge: Cambridge University Press, 1997).

15. For recent comparisons, see Marnia Lazreg, ed., "Making the Transition Work for Women in Europe and Central Asia," Europe and Central Asia Gender and Development Series, Discussion Paper No. 411 (Washington, D.C.: The World Bank, 2000).

16. Aminova, *October Revolution*; Massell, *Surrogate Proletariat*; Shoshana Keller,

"Trapped Between State and Society: Women's Liberation and Islam in Soviet Uzbekistan," *Journal of Women's History* 10, no. 1 (1998): 20–44; Douglas Northrop, "Nationalizing Backwardness: Gender, Empire, and Uzbek Identity," in *A State of Nations: Empire and Nation-Making in the Age of Lenin and Stalin*, ed. Ronald Suny and Terry Martin (Oxford: Oxford University Press, 2001), 191–220.

17. Lata Mani, "Contentious Traditions: The Debate on SATI in Colonial India," *Cultural Critique*, no. 7 (1987): 130, 152.

18. Margot Badran, *Feminists, Islam, and Nation: Gender and the Making of Modern Egypt* (Princeton, NJ: Princeton University Press 1995), 3.

19. Joan Scott, "The Evidence of Experience," *Critical Inquiry*, no. 17 (1991): 793.

20. Sherry Ortner, "Theory in Anthropology since the Sixties," *Comparative Studies in Society and History* 26, no. 1 (Jan. 1984): 157.

21. Keller, "Trapped between State and Society."

22. Michael David-Fox, Peter Holquist, and Marshall Poe, eds., *The Resistance Debate in Russian and Soviet History*, Kritika Historical Studies 1 (Bloomington, IN: Slavica Publishers, 2003).

23. Rosalind O'Hanlon, "Issues of Widowhood: Gender and Resistance in Colonial Western India," in *Contesting Power: Resistance and Everyday Social Relations in South Asia*, ed. Douglas Haynes and Gyan Prakash (Berkeley: University of California Press, 1992), 62. See also Veena Talwar Oldenburg, "Lifestyle as Resistance: The Case of the Courtesans of Lucknow," in ibid., 23–62. In the seminal subaltern studies work on "resistance," O'Hanlon and Oldenburg emphasize that women's resistance may be defined by their opposition to patriarchal family structures rather than to the state. Because in many cases the state reinforces patriarchal family structures, resistance to one may be connected with the other. Soviet Uzbekistan is a rare case where the state did not reinforce patriarchal family structures, so women's resistance to the family differed from resistance to the state.

24. Deniz Kandiyoti, "Bargaining with Patriarchy," *Gender and Society* 2, no. 3 (1988): 280.

25. Jerry Garcia, "The Measure of a Cock: Mexican Cockfighting, Culture and Masculinity," in *I am Aztlán: The Personal Essay in Chicano Studies*, ed. Chon Noriega and Wendy Belcher (Los Angeles: UCLA Chicano Studies Research Press, 2004), 120.

26. There were plenty of indigenous people in Uzbekistan who did not fit the definition; Kazakh, Kyrgyz, Turkmen, and Tajik, as well as myriad smaller group designations, were told that they had their own autonomous republic or union republic homelands; many Tajiks moved to Tajikistan rather than remain as a minority in Uzbekistan, where the rewards of the new national identity were directed to Uzbeks only.

27. Clements, *Bolshevik Women*, chapters 3 and 4.

28. While in much of the empire imperial subjects were treated equally, regardless of nationality (with the exception of discrimination against Jews), Central Asians were granted citizenship and a passport only if they attained special

standing by association with the colonial government. Unlike other of the tsar's subjects, Central Asian men did not serve in the army and were not subject to conscription, except the Turkmens who formed a special brigade.

29. Russian-language documents of the period commonly use the description "backward, Eastern"; see, for example, Serafima Liubimova, *Rabota Partii sredi truzhenits vostoka* (Moskva: Gos. Izdat, 1928), 3.

30. Northrop, in his study of the Hujum, argues that in the struggle for unveiling the veil itself became the defining feature of Uzbekness, a national symbol worn by women. Northrop, *Veiled Empire*, 31. I think this is too narrow a reading of Uzbek identity, one formed by the limitations of using only Party archives and Russian-language publications for the 1920s, a period when questions of Uzbek identity were being articulated far more broadly and fully in the Uzbek press.

31. My 1992–1993 research was supported by a long-term grant from IREX. Subsequent research for this book was supported by Whitman College and the University of Wyoming.

32. I conducted these interviews along with Eylor Karimov, Russell Zanca, and researchers from the Yo'sh Olimlar Jamiyati of Tashkent, Uzbekistan, for a project entitled "Collectivization in Uzbekistan: Oral Histories," with sponsorship from NCEEER, from the University of Wyoming, and from Northeastern Illinois University. Elderly farmers, men and women, were interviewed in the provinces of Tashkent, Xorazm, Bukhara, Qashqa Daryo, Fargana, Namangan, and Nurota, Uzbekistan.

33. Kamp, "Three Lives of Saodat: Communist, Uzbek, Survivor," *Oral History Review* 28, no. 2 (2001): 21–58.

34. Jochen Hellbeck argues that the revolution created a particular Soviet subjectivity in which the self was consciously woven into the collective; I do not find this to be a prominent feature of Uzbek presentations of the self written in the 1920s. Hellbeck, "Working, Struggling, Becoming: Stalin-Era Autobiographical Texts," *The Russian Review* 60, no. 3 (2001): 358–59. Anna Krylova argues that the "triumph of the resisting human spirit" is a "structuring fantasy of the American historical profession," one that has prompted American historians of the Soviet Union to search for the "liberal subject" in the Stalinist era. Krylova, "The Tenacious Liberal Subject in Soviet Studies," in David-Fox, Holquist, and Poe, *Resistance Debate*, 199. Because my research is more concerned with continuities that bridge 1917 than with defining Stalinism, it does not directly engage these issues.

35. Trevor Lummis, *Listening to History: The Authenticity of Oral Evidence* (Totowa, NJ: Barnes and Noble, 1988), 123, 126.

36. Kamp, "Three Lives of Saodat"; Kamp, "Remembering the Hujum: Uzbek Women's Words," *Central Asia Monitor* 1 (2001): 1–13.

37. While *korenizatsiia* (nativization) policies stated that Russian Party members should learn and use the language of majority populations in the national republics, the policy was never successfully carried out. Martin, *Affirmative Action Empire*, 75.

38. In oral history research for a forthcoming volume on collectivization of

agriculture in Uzbekistan, I have found that most rural Uzbek men, born 1900 to the 1920s from all regions of Uzbekistan, reported they only began to learn Russian when they were called up for military service in World War II. Before that they had neither opportunity nor reason to learn Russian.

39. The 1926 census included Tajikistan's population in Uzbekistan because Tajikistan was an autonomous republic within Uzbekistan; its population was about 10 percent of the total figure. Russians and other nonindigenous peoples overwhelmingly lived in cities; only about forty-five thousand lived in rural communities, which explains why rural Uzbeks had so little contact with them. *Vsesoiuznaia perepis' naseleniia: Okanchatel'nye itogi*, vol. 15, *Population, UzSSR* (Moskva: Tsentral'naia Upravleniia Statistiki, 1926); N. X. Xaidarova, ed., *Sovet O'zbekistoni kitobi/kniga Sovetskogo Uzbekistana, 1917–1927: Bibliografik ko'rsatkich* (Toshkent: O'zbekiston SSR Davlat Kitob Palatasi, 1976).

40. Uzbekistan State Archive (hereafter Uz. St. Arch.), R-34, op. 1, d. 1881, l. 89–115, anketi, or personal information forms from Xorazm, 1928. Russian teachers read *Pravda Vostoka*, a Russian newpaper published by the Party's Central Asian Bureau in Tashkent, and *Uchitel'skaia Gazeta* (Teacher's Newspaper), published in Russia. Uzbeks and Tatars read the Uzbek-language *Qizil O'zbekiston* (Red Uzbekistan), a newspaper of the Uzbekistan Communist Party; *Inqilob Quyoshi* (Dawn of the Revolution); *Yer Yuzi* (Face of the Earth), a literary and social journal; and *Ma'orif va O'qituvchi* (Education and the Teacher), an education and general-interest journal.

## 1. RUSSIAN COLONIALISM IN TURKESTAN AND BUKHARA

1. Interview with Muattar S. (b. 1899, Bukhara). Central Asians did not usually record birth dates; respondents from this period often knew their birth year according to the Central Asian twelve-year animal cycle. Central Asians first received internal passports in 1932 and had to make official declaration then of their year of birth.

2. The emirate ended in 1920 with revolution. The last emirs were Abd al-Ahad (r. 1885–1910) and Alimxon (r. 1910–1920). Islamic education for girls is discussed in chapter 4.

3. Jadidism is discussed at length later in this chapter and in chapter 2.

4. Numerous works discuss the topic of defining nationalities in Central Asia, but perhaps the most complex treatment is found in John Schoeberlein-Engel's "Identity in Central Asia: Construction and Contention in the Conceptions of 'Özbek,' 'Tâjik,' 'Muslim,' 'Samarqandi' and Other Groups" (Ph.D. diss., Harvard University, 1994). See also Adeeb Khalid, "Nationalizing the Revolution in Central Asia: The Transformation of Jadidism, 1917–1920," in *A State of Nations: Empire and Nation-Making in the Age of Lenin and Stalin*, ed. Ron Suny and Terry Martin (Oxford: Oxford University Press, 2001), 156–59.

5. Seymour Becker, *Russia's Protectorates in Central Asia: Bukhara and Khiva, 1865–1924* (Cambridge, MA: Harvard University Press, 1968). See also, for exam-

ple, N. P. Ignatiev, *Khivinskaia ekspeditsiia, 1839–1840* (Sanktpeterburg: Tip-a Obshchestvennaia Pol'za, 1873).

6. Robert Geraci, *Window on the East: National and Imperial Identities in Late Tsarist Russia* (Ithaca, NY: Cornell University Press, 2001), introduction; Daniel Brower, *Turkestan and the Fate of the Russian Empire* (New York: Routledge/Curzon, 2003), chapter 1.

7. In this chapter, "Turkestan" usually refers only to Fargana, southern Syr Darya, and Samarkand provinces, the parts of Turkestan where the population was predominantly sedentary, agriculturalist or urban and ultimately became identified as Uzbek. The northern sections of Russian Turkestan, now forming southern Kazakhstan and Kyrgyzstan, were conquered earlier and had a largely nomadic population and very different development, including a large influx of Russian settlers.

8. Ron Suny, "The Empire Strikes Out: Imperial Russia, 'National Identity,' and Theories of Empire," in Suny and Martin, *A State of Nations*, 41; Andreas Kappeler, "Czarist Policy toward the Muslims of the Russian Empire," in *Muslim Communities Reemerge: Historical Perspectives on Nationality, Politics, and Opposition in the Former Soviet Union and Yugoslavia*, Central Asian Book Series, ed. Kappeler, Gerhard Simon, Georg Brunner, and Edward Allworth (Durham, NC: Duke University Press 1994), 141–56; Jeffrey Sahadeo, "Creating a Russian Colonial Community: City, Nation, and Empire in Tashkent, 1865–1923," (Ph.D. diss., University of Illinois, 2000).

9. Richard Pierce, *Russian Central Asia: a Study in Colonial Rule, 1865–1917* (Berkeley: University of California Press, 1960), 77. Urban and agriculturalist Turkestanis, mainly Uzbeks and Tajiks, followed Islamic law and were judged by a *qazi*, a Sharia court judge, while nomads, mainly Kazakh, Kyrgyz, and Turkmen referred to a government appointed *bii*, or judge in a court that followed "custom." On the latter, see Virginia Martin, *Law and Custom in the Steppe: The Kazakhs of the Middle Horde and Russian Colonialism in the Nineteenth Century* (Richmond, Surrey: Curzon Press, 2001).

10. On land law in Turkestan, see Pierce, *Russian Central Asia*, 141–52. Eugene Schuyler discusses the early 1870s discussion of introducing Russian communal forms to Central Asian land ownership. Schuyler, *Turkistan: Notes of a Journey in Russian Turkistan, Kokand, Bukhara, and Kuldja*, vol. 1 (New York: Scribner, Armstrong and Co., 1877), 297–303. Regarding land law in Bukhara, see Carrère d'Encausse, *Islam and the Russian Empire*; and N. A. Kisliakov, *Patriarkhal'no-feodal'nye otnosheniia sredi osedlogo sel'skogo naseleniia Bukharskogo Khanstva v kontse XIX-nachale XX v* (Moskva: Izd-vo Ak. Nauk SSSR, 1962). Landholding in southern Turkestan did not follow the dominant Russian pattern of large estates with peasant labor. Instead, both Turkestanis and immigrant settlers were smallholders, with the exception of some large experimental Russian-owned cotton estates.

11. N. S. Lykoshin, *Pol' zhizni v Turkestane: Ocherki byta tuzemnago naseleniia,* (Petrograd: Sklad T-va "V. A. Berezovskii," 1916), 52–54; Andreas Kappeler, *The Russian Empire: A Multiethnic History,* trans. Alfred Clayton (New York: Longman, 2001).

12. However, Muslims had much easier access to divorce than Christians, whose family status was ruled by Russian Orthodox church laws.

13. Validimir Petrovich Nalivkin and M. Nalivkina, *Ocherk byta zhenshchiny osedlago tuzemnago naseleniia Fergany* (Kazan': Tipografiia Imperatorskago Universiteta, 1886), 229. The Nalivkins' source for commentary on Islamic legal practice is not clear. If the conditions that they described were based on actual practice, then practice in Central Asia varied from the Hanafi school, which dominated legal teaching in Central Asia. Leila Ahmed notes that that Maliki school, but not other schools, allowed women to petition for divorce on the basis of "desertion, failure to maintain her, cruelty, and her husband's being afflicted with a chronic or incurable disease detrimental to her." Ahmed, *Women and Gender in Islam: Historical Roots of a Modern Debate* (New Haven, CT: Yale University Press, 1992), 91. In Islamic law, a groom presents two-thirds of mahr to his wife upon marriage, and that sum becomes her personal property, while one-third is held back against the possibility that he divorce her. Qalin was a Central Asian tradition not subject to Islamic law; it was money or wealth given by the groom to the bride's parents as part of a series of property exchanges with the arrangement of a marriage.

14. Arminius Vambery recorded one case of stoning in Khiva. Vambery, *Travels in Central Asia* (New York: Harper Brothers, 1865), 170. Stoning as a penalty for adultery is one of numerous possible Sharia judgments; pratice varied with regional culture and school of Islamic law. Evidence that this form of execution for adultery was practiced elsewhere in Turkestan is lacking. Pierce writes that the death penalty was altogether abolished and that hard labor and Siberian exile were sentences handed down by Russian courts for serious crimes. Pierce, *Russian Central Asia*, 77. However, the death penalty was not permanently abolished; in fact, Turkestan was under extraordinary military law for most of the colonial period, and Turkestani rebels were sentenced to death after uprisings.

15. *Turkiston Viloyatining Gazetasi*, Mar. 5, 1874, 4. This newspaper was published in Turki (literary Central Asian Turkic) by the Russian government of Turkestan for a very limited readership. Issues from this period contain numerous accounts of attacks on women.

16. Nalivkin and Nalivkina, *Ocherk byta zhenshchiny*, 216–18.

17. Numerous mid- and late nineteenth-century accounts discuss slavery, including N. P. Ignatiev, *Mission of N. P. Ignat'ev to Khiva and Bukhara in 1858*, trans. John Evans, (Newtonville, MA: Oriental Research Partners, 1984); Vambery, *Travels in Central Asia*; Nalivkin and Nalivkina, *Ocherk byta zhenshchiny*; and Schuyler, *Turkistan*. A scholarly account of Bukharan slavery is found in T. Faiziev, *Buxoro feodal jamiyatida qullardan foydalanishga doir hujjatlar (XIX asr)* (Toshkent: O'zbekiston SSR "Fan" Nashriyoti, 1990). There were some Russian slaves in Central Asia, but in much smaller numbers than Persians or Dungans.

18. Nalivkin and Nalivkina, *Ocherk byta zhenshchiny*, 111. Both major groups of slaves, Persians and Dungans, were Muslim. Sunni Turkmens and the Bukharan and Khivan rulers justified enslaving the Shia Persians on the basis that they were not true Muslims. Dungans, or Chinese-speaking Muslims, were sometimes cap-

tured and enslaved by "Taranchis," one of the groups that are now regarded as Uighurs, during the conflicts that plagued Eastern Turkestan in the nineteenth century. Andrew Forbes, *Warlords and Muslims in Chinese Central Asia* (Cambridge: Cambridge University Press, 1986); Schuyler, *Turkistan*.

19. Suny, "The Empire Strikes Out," 23–66.

20. Stuart Thompstone, "Russian Imperialism and the Commercialization of the Central Asian Cotton Trade," *Textile History* 26 (1995): 238, 251. Thomas Skallerup notes that the Central Asians increased their own investment in shops producing cotton and silk cloth for the local market, in spite of an influx of machine-manufactured cotton textiles coming into Central Asia from Russia. Most of these shops had a few weavers working with handlooms, but several invested in mechanical looms. Skallerup, "Artisans between Guilds and Cooperatives: A History of Social and Economic Change in Russian Turkestan and Soviet Central Asia" (Ph.D. diss., Indiana University, 1990).

21. Edward Sokol, *The Revolt of 1916 in Russian Central Asia* (Baltimore: Johns Hopkins, 1953), 27. Sokol shows a rise from 873,000 puds of cotton exported from Turkestan to Russia in 1888, to 10,700,000 puds in 1907.

22. *Dehqon* meant both a farmer who owned and farmed his own land and a peasant who worked on land owned by a large landowner or a waqf. I translate *dehqon* as "farmer" in order to emphasize the element of landownership; dehqons in Turkestan were not equivalent to Russia's peasants, and Russian documents obscure this difference.

23. Pierce, *Russian Central Asia*, 162–71; Richard Lorenz, "The Economic Bases of the Basmachi Movement in the Farghana Valley," in Kappeler, *Muslim Communities Reemerge*, 280–84; Stuart Thompstone, "Russian Imperialism and the Commercialization of the Central Asian Cotton Trade," *Textile History* 26 (1995): 233–58.

24. A. D. Grebenkin, "Uzbeki," in *Russkii Turkestan: Sbornik izdannyi po povodu politekhnicheskoi vystavki*, vol. 2, ed. N. A. Maev (Moskva: Universitetskaia Tipografiia, 1872), 60; Nalivkin and Nalivkina, *Ocherk byta zhenshchiny*, 118.

25. *Pervaia vseobshchaia perepis' naseleniia Rossiiskoi Imperii, 1897 g.* Vol. 89, *Ferganskaia oblast'* (St. Peterburg: Izd. Tsentral'nago Statisticheskago Komiteta Ministerstva Vnutrennikh Del, 1897), table 22, 120–23.

26. Grebenkin, "Uzbeki," 60; Nalivkin, *Ocherk byta zhenshchiny*, 95, 112, 119–20.

27. There are two major groups of Tatars, from the Volga and from Crimea. They are an ethnically and linguistically Turkic Muslim minority in Russia. The initiation of Jadid thought, calling for modernization of Islamic education and activism in political life, is generally attributed to a Crimean Tatar, Ismail Bey Gasparali (Gasprinski) in the 1870s. The movement spread among Tatars. Central Asians encountered Jadidism both by traveling to Russia and because Tatars immigrated from Russia to Central Asia following the Russian conquest. See Azade-Ayşe Rorlich, *The Volga Tatars: A Profile in National Resistance* (Stanford, CA: : Hoover Institution Press, Stanford University, 1986).

28. Khalid, *Politics of Muslim Cultural Reform*, 157–60.

29. M. Virskii, ed., *Spravochnaia knizhka Samarkandskoi oblasti na 1895 g.*, vypusk' 3, (Samarkand: Tipografiia Shtaba Voisk, 1895), 40.

30. I refer to the combination of robe and face veil simply as the paranji. It appears as *parandzha* in Russian publications; I use the Uzbek form, paranji, except in quotations.

31. Veiling in the paranji and its history is discussed extensively in chapter 6.

32. Kokand, Samarkand, Andijan, and Tashkent all grew in the Russian colonial period, with both colonizing populations and Central Asians moving to the "new city" districts. The Russian adminstration established Skobelev (now Fargana) as an administrative city separate from Marg'ilon, Kagan separate from Bukhara, and various other administrative and military towns, such as Petroaleksandrovsk, on the border of Khiva.

33. These Uzbek delineations parallel Persian ones: *birun* and *andarun* for the outer and inner spaces of the house.

34. Nalivkin and Navilkina, *Ocherk byta zhenshchiny*, 74–82, contains a lengthy description of houses and uses of household space around Namangan, c. 1880. Other descriptions are found in A. N. Voronina, *Narodnye traditsii arkhitektury Uzbekistana* (Moskva: Gos. Izd-vo Arkhitektury i Gradostroitel'stv, 1951); E. E. Nerazik and A. N. Zhilina, eds. *Zhilishche narodov srednei Azii i Kazakhstana* (Moskva: Izd-vo Nauka, 1982); Kisliakov, *Patriarkhal'no-feodal'nye otnosheniia*; O. A. Sukhareva, *Bukhara XIX-nachalo XX v.* (Moskva: Nauka, 1962); K. Sh. Shaniiazov, *Etnograficheskie ocherki material'noi kul'tury Uzbekov konets XIX-nachalo XX v.* (Tashkent: Fan, 1981).

35. O. A. Sukhareva, *Istoriia sredneaziatskogo kostiuma, Samarkand, 2-ia polovina XIX-nachalo XX vek* (Moskva: Izd-vo Nauka, 1982), 91.

36. O. A. Sukhareva, *Islam v Uzbekistane* (Tashkent: Izd-vo Akademii Nauk Uzbekskoi SSR, 1960), 40–41; Nalivkin and Nalivkina, *Ocherk byta zhenshchiny*, 151–53, 190–92. Devotion in the form of saying five daily prayers varied considerably in Turkestan; men attended the mosque where government officials enforced this behavior, as in Bukhara, but elsewhere men seem to have made choices based on family and local social norms. Women did not attend prayer in the mosque.

37. Some poor families sent adolescent daughters to be servants, while others married adolescent daughters as third or fourth wives to wealthy men, in whose homes they lived and worked like servants. There may have been little difference between the treatment of a teenaged servant girl and a teenaged second wife, except that as a wife she had legal status and brought more material benefit to her parents than as a servant. I. Finkel'shtein, ed., *Probuzhdennye velikim Oktiabrem* (Tashkent: Gos. Izdat. Uzbekskoi SSR, 1961), 110, 140–41, 162, 212, 219, 244.

## 2. JADIDS AND THE REFORM OF WOMEN

1. Both Massell and Northrop emphasize the point of view of the Communist Party Women's Division's Russian leadership, that through the Hujum (the unveiling campaign of 1927), Uzbek and other Central Asian women would become a "surrogate proletariat," playing the revolutionary role that their societies other-

wise lacked. I do not see the "surrogate proletariat" argument as a particularly important one among Uzbek Party activists of the late 1920s; Massell and Northrop's emphasis relies on Russian points of view and neglects the voices and ideas of the Uzbek political actors who shaped the Hujum.

2. Khalid, "Nationalizing the Revolution in Central Asia," 149.

3. Khalid, *Politics of Muslim Cultural Reform*, 110.

4. Partha Chatterjee, *The Nation and its Fragments: Colonial and Post-Colonial Histories* (Princeton, NJ: Princeton University Press, 1993).

5. Khalid includes a valuable chapter delineating the complexity of the idea of nation and other forms of identity in Turkestan. Khalid, *Politics of Muslim Cultural Reform*, 184–215. Schoeberlein-Engel also addresses this topic in "Identity in Central Asia."

6. Beth Baron, *The Women's Awakening in Egypt: Culture, Society, and the Press* (New Haven, CT: Yale University Press, 1994), 13–14, 111.

7. *Alem-i Nisvan* (The World of Women) was published by Shafiqa Hanum, the daughter of the founder of the Jadid movement in the Russian empire, the Crimean Tatar Ismail Bey Gasparali (Gasprinski). Published for one year in Bahchesarai, Crimea, *Alem-i Nisvan* featured news about Muslim women in Russia, *hadith* concerning women, biographies of Muslim women, and fiction. A fuller description of the publication is found in Şengül Hablemitoğlu and Necip Hablemitoğlu, *Şefika Gaspıralı ve Rusya'da Türk Kadın Hareketi (1893–1920)* (Ankara: Ajans-Türk Matbaacılık Sanayii, 1998).

8. Sartiya (or more commonly, Sart) women would be women from nonnomadic and nontribal Central Asian ethnic groups. By the second decade of the twentieth century, some urbanites preferred the more inclusive "Turkestani," while by the 1920s many who had earlier referred to themselves as "Sart" began to call themselves "Uzbek." The use of Sart was contested: both Central Asians and Russian administrators wrote articles discussing whether the term was simply perjorative or was the group self-name of particular Central Asians—urban speakers of Turkic and Tajik who did not have tribal affiliations. If the 1897 census reflects the ways that Central Asians identified themselves, Uzbek was a more popular self-designation in Kokand, with 54,673 Uzbek residents, while 20,907 were Sarts. In other cities such as Tashkent, Namangan, and Andijon, the ethnonym Uzbek ranks second or third to Sart and Turko-Tatar. *Pervaia vseobshchiia perepis'*, vol. 89, 2–3. N. S. Lykoshin notes that the census takers were native Turkestanis. Lykoshin, *Pol'zhizni*, 17–23. Khalid discusses the debate over "Sart" in *Politics of Muslim Cultural Reform*, 199–208.

9. Tajie was refering to Crimean and Volga Tatar women.

10. "Noghai" refers to Turkic speakers from Crimea. By the early twentieth century Noghai was consciously dropped and replaced with the broader ethnonym Tatar. Tajie alluded to Muslim women teachers who came from Russia to Turkestan to open new-style girls schools.

11. Xo'qandli Ashraf ul-Banat Tajie, letter to the editor, *Alem-i Nisvan* 35 (1906):

572–74. The nickname Tajie chose to write under, Ashraf al-Banat, or the Glory of Women, suggests she may have come from an *ulama* family. Hablemitoğlu and Hablemitoğlu provide a nearly complete transcription of Tajie's letter and include Shafiqa's answer. Shafiqa responded that with such a noble thinker in their midst as Tajie, the women of Kokand should indeed soon wake up, and she encouraged Tajie to write again for publication in *Alem-i Nisvan*. Hablemitoğlu and Hablemitoğlu, *Şefika Gaspıralı*, 43–44, 45.

12. The literature on this topic is abundant: Badran, *Feminists, Islam and Nation*; Margot Badran and Miriam Cooke, eds., *Opening the Gates: A Century of Arab Feminist Writing* (Bloomington: Indiana University Press, 1990); Lila abu-Lughod, ed., *Remaking Women: Feminism and Modernity in the Middle East* (Princeton, NJ: Princeton University Press, 1998); Gail Minault, *Secluded Scholars: Women's Education and Muslim Social Reform in Colonial India* (Oxford: Oxford University Press, 1998); Fleischmann, "The Other 'Awakening.'"

13. Neither Orthodox missionaries nor Russian feminist organizations made Central Asian women their project, with one exception. Nikolai Petrovich Ostroumov noted that an "eccentric Russian Feminist, O. S. Lebedeva," presented a brochure entitled "On the Emancipation of Muslim Women," to the governor-general of Turkestan in 1900. Lebedeva was familiar with the Egyptian Qasim Amin's writing on unveiling. I have not been able to find this brochure. Ostroumov, *K 50ti letiu Tashkenta: Tashkentskie Sarty pod Russkim upravleniem* (1915), 63–65.

14. *Pervaia vseobshchaia perepis'*, vol. 86, 84–97, and vol. 89, 94–95, statistics on women's literacy in Andijon, Tashkent, and Kokand.

15. Kokand's population grew from 34,000 to 120,000 between 1880 and 1915. M. A. Akhunova, Kh. Z. Ziiaev, and G. R. Rashidov, *Istoriia Kokanda* (Tashkent: Fan, 1984), 12. In the early twentieth century, the term "Noghai" was used in Turkestan to refer to Muslims who came from Russia (that is, Tatars), as in a letter from Tashkent to *Terjuman* 23 (1906): 4. At this point, Muslims in Russia were debating their own identity and names; *Terjuman* in 1906 featured a series of articles entitled "Are We Tatars, or Not?" By the year 1912, "Tatar" had displaced "Noghai" in most Central Asian publications.

16. In Akhunova et. al, *Istoriia Kokanda*, 16–19, 25–27. The authors note that there were twelve new-method schools in Kokand in 1908; Lorenz, "Economic Bases," 282–83.

17. Fotima Yo'ldoshbaeva (b. 1910, near Kokand) wrote that when she was very young, her father abandoned her mother, Nuriniso Muminova, with two small daughters, leaving them without provision for two years while he wandered about and traveled to Mecca. Nuriniso was fortunate that her father-in-law provided for her. Fotima Yo'ldoshbacva [Fatima Iuldashbaeva], *Moia sud'ba* (Tashkent: Yosh Gvardiia, 1972), 10–12.

18. For 1897, five hundred native prostitutes registered their occupation, but later statistics are lacking. *Pervaia vseobshaia perepis'*, vol. 83, 100–101, vol. 84, 144–45, vol. 89, 122–23.

19. For a discussion of state regulation of prostitution in the Russian empire, see Laurie Bernstein, *Sonia's Daughters: Prostitutes and Their Regulation in Imperial Russia* (Berkeley: University of California Press, 1995).

20. Nalivkin and Nalivkina, *Ocherk byta zhenshchiny*, 236, 240. The Nalivkins noted these wives were usually widows or divorcées, as parents would not knowingly put a virgin daughter into such a marriage.

21. Nalivkin and Nalivkina include a chapter on prostitution, *Ocherk byta zhenshchiny*, 235–44. Such works, characterizing Muslim women as full of sexual desire and hampered by the constrictions of harem life, are common among French and British colonial accounts, as were depictions of "normal" sexuality—between women and men in any form, contrasted with the "perversion" of dancing boys and homosexual forms of sexual activity. While no Russian account compares with Flaubert's travels in Egypt for sheer lasciviousness, several sections of the Nalivkins' work, ostensibly authored by husband and wife together, present a male, colonial point of view, describing veiled "Sart" women as trying to seduce the male writer, as well as other men. Scholarship on nineteenth-century women raises the question of prostitute as agent or victim in a variety of contexts: see Bernstein, *Sonia's Daughters*; Antoinnette Burton, *Burdens of History: British Feminists, Indian Women, and Imperial Culture, 1865–1915* (Durham: University of North Carolina Press, 1994); and Christine Stansell, *City of Women: Sex and Class in New York, 1789–1860* (Urbana: University of Illinois Press, 1982).

22. For example, S. Mufti Zade, "Bir jama badalida fahshg'a rivoj," *Turkiston Viloyatining Gazetasi*, Jan. 12, 1916, 2; and Yusufxon Mirza, "Iz Kokanda," *Turkiston Viloyatining Gazetasi*, Jan. 11, 1915, 1–2.

23. M. M. Khairullaev, et. al., eds., *Islam i zhenshchiny vostoka: Istoriia i sovremennost'* (Tashkent: Fan, 1990), 43–44.

24. For an account of a gap used as a forum for Jadid discussion, see Tahir Alimhon, "Yana to'i masalasi," *Sado-i Farg'ona*, no. 28 (June 18, 1914): 2, and Khalid, *Politics of Muslim Cultural Reform*, 96, 132. Theodore Levin describes a modern gap in *The One Hundred Thousand Fools of God: Musical Travels in Central Asia* (Bloomington: Indiana University Press, 1996), 34–37.

25. Khalid, *Politics of Muslim Cultural Reform*, 80, 136–154. On such movements elsewhere in the Islamic world, there is a wealth of literature, but a classic treatment is Albert Hourani's *Arabic Thought in the Liberal Age, 1798–1939* (Cambridge: Cambridge University Press, 1983).

26. Edward Allworth, *The Modern Uzbeks: From the Fourteenth Century to the Present; A Cultural History* (Stanford, CA: Hoover Institution Press, Stanford University, 1990), 136.

27. Abdurauf Fitrat, *Oila, yoki oila boshqarish tartiblari* (1916), repr. edited by Dilarom Alimova (Toshkent: Manaviyat, 1998), 96. Fitrat wrote his tract on the family in 1914; it was first published in 1915, with another edition in 1916. Fitrat, a Bukharan Jadid about whom much has been written elsewhere, presents his argument for girls' education as an argument against Bukhara's conservatives.

28. Fitrat, *Oila*, 97. Fitrat repeatedly contrasted *jahillik*, which can be interpreted

as both ignorance and darkness, with `ilm, the word he used for knowledge and science. *Jahillik* takes its root from Arabic; Islamic religious language refers to the time before Islam as *jahiliya*—darkness and ignorance.

29. Fitrat, *Oila*, 97.

30. Fitrat, *Oila*, 98.

31. Mahmud Xo'ja Behbudi [Selected by M.], "Erkak ila ayol na tashrihan farqi?" *Oina*, no. 10 (1915): 256–58.

32. Qasim Amin, *The Liberation of Women; and The New Woman: Two Documents in the History of Egyptian Feminism* (1898, 1899), trans. Samiha Sidhom Peterson (Cairo: American University in Cairo Press, 2000). Amin's second work, *The New Woman*, was published in 1899 and was translated into Russian (*Novaia zhenshchina*) by I. Iu. Krachkovskii as a supplement to the journal *Mir Islama* in 1912. In *The New Woman*, Amin contends that Egyptian women should unveil. The two works caused a considerable stir in the Islamic world and provoked numerous responses. While I have not found direct reference to Amin in the works on women by Russia's Muslims, some may have been acquainted with his writing through the Arabic version, from travels in the Middle East's literary centers, or through the 1912 Russian edition.

33. Sara Muzafiriya, "Aib o'zimizda," *Sado-i Turkiston*, Aug. 14, 1914, 1. Elizabeth Frierson points to a book published in Leipzig by Dr. Paul Möbius as triggering a similar debate in the Ottoman press. Frierson, "Unimagined Communities: State, Press, and Gender in the Hamidian Era" (Ph.D. diss., Princeton University, 1996), 130–31.

34. Hanifa Khanim bint Ismatulla, *Targhib mu`allimalarga maktab ravshanda yazilmishdir* (Kazan: Dombrovskii, 1898). Many of the arguments Tatar women made were similar to those found in the Ottoman women's press (see Frierson, "Unimagined Communities"), to which many Muslims in Russia had access.

35. Rizauddin Fakhriddin, *Aila* (1905), Uzbek repr., Rizouddin ibn Fakhriddin, *Oila* (Toshkent: Meros, 1991), 21, 23. The original date and publisher are unknown to me, but the booklet went through a number of editions between 1905 and 1910.

36. Ziyad, "Taraqqiiparvar fida`i yaki `anqa shimali," *Din va Ma`ishat*, no. 4 (1909): 83–84.

37. Turkistonlik Noghai Mullah, "Yangi fikrchi, eski fikrchi," *Turkiston Viloyatining Gazetasi*, Jan. 7, 1910, 2.

38. Fakhriddin, *Aila*, 8, 12.

39. Afsaneh Najmabadi explores this limitation in greater depth in the context of early twentieth-century Iran in "Crafting an Educated Housewife in Iran," in Abu Lughod, *Remaking Women*, 91–125.

40. Mahmud Xo'ja Behbudi, "Hifz-i sihat-i oila," *Oina*, no. 47 (1914): 1126–28; Abdurauf Fitrat, *Rahbar-i najat*, Tajik reprint, "Rohbari najot," ed. Muhabbat Jalilova, *Sadoi Sharq*, no. 9 (1992): 40; Fitrat, *Oila*, 17.

41. *Pervaia vseobshchaia perepis'*, vol. 89, 18, and vol. 83, 14. The reliability of these statistics is questionable. The striking imbalance between men and women

varies so widely within age cohorts that it would be difficult to attribute it to higher female mortality alone; it probably reflects some falsification, or lack of knowledge, of ages.

42. Behbudi elaborated on men's sexual needs in multiple sections of "Hifz-i sihat-i oila," arguing for males marrying in their late teens or early twenties; while Fitrat, in *Oila*, used men's sexual needs as an argument for polygyny.

43. Fitrat, *Rahbar-i najat*, 40.

44. Khalid mentions implied criticism of arranged marriage in plays and novels by Haji Muin and Hamza Hakimzoda Niyoziy. Khalid, *Politics of Muslim Cultural Reform*, 144–45, 225.

45. Fitrat, *Oila*, 20–23.

46. Zaynab Aqchurina and thirty-three other signatories, "Musulman khatun-qizlarinda harakat," *Suyum Bike*, no. 14 (1914): 17–18.

47. Fakhr ul-Banat Sibghatulla qizi, *Aila sabaqlari* (1913), Uzbek repr., *Oila sabo-qalri*, ed. Teshaboi Ziyoyev (Toshkent: Yozuvchi, 1992), 58–62. Fakhr ul-Banat, a *mu' allima* (teacher) and `alima` (religious scholar), authored other tracts and translated *Ta' limi Banat*, the work of Ottoman author Alii Nazima, into Tatar as *Qizlar Tarbiasi.*

48. Fitrat, *Rahbar-i najat*, 41–42. Fitrat reiterated a common Islamic teaching about marriage. For example, one piece of eleventh-century Turkic didactic literature condemned selecting a wife for wealth, nobility, or beauty; only her piety was a good basis for choice. Khass-Hajib Yusuf, *Wisdom of Royal Glory (Kutadgu Bilig): A Turko-Islamic Mirror for Princes*, trans. Robert Dankoff (Chicago: University of Chicago Press, 1983), 186.

49. Fakhriddin, *Aila*, 9, 27–28.

50. Fakhriddin, *Aila*, 30, 45; Fitrat, *Rahbar-i Najat*, 40–41; Fitrat, *Oila*. Similar critiques appeared in Turkestani newspapers under headlines about *tois* (wedding feasts).

51. Mahr and qalin documents remain from late nineteenth-century Sharia courts in Khiva and Bukhara. A. K. Jalilov, "Vasiqalar namunalari haqidagi qo'l-yozma (XIX asr)," *Obshchestvennye nauki v Uzbekistane*, no. 1 (1991): 48–54; Khair-ullaev, *Islam i zhenshchiny vostoka*, 62–66.

52. Fitrat, *Oila*, 28–33. All of Fitrat's suggestions on family reform were framed in the interests of men; he did not consider women's interests. While high mahr could delay marriage for men, delayed mahr could serve as a deterrant to men divorcing their wives: a man who divorced his wife at least had to pay her something.

53. The most thorough description of this process came from an oral history interview with Manzura H. (b. 1921, Tashkent). Her description and those in other oral histories contended that qalin was usually a sum of money given by the groom's family to the bride's parents, who would then use it for costs of feasting and gifts. The Nalivkins discussed qalin extensively and examined attitudes about "selling" a daughter in *Ocherk byta zhenshchiny*, 200–205. Kisliakov offers a comprehensive review of Russian and Soviet ethnographic description of qalin in *Sem'ia i brak u*

*Tadzhikov*, Trudy Instituta Etnografii: New Series, vol. 44 (Moskva: Ak. Nauk SSSR, 1959), 145–54. F. E. Liushkevich critiques ethnographers' presentation of qalin in "Traditsii mezhsemeinykh sviazei Uzbeksko-Tadzhikskogo naseleniia srednei Azii (k probleme bytovaniia *kalyma* i drugikh patriarkhal'nykh obychaev," *Sovetskaia Etnografiia*, no. 4 (1989): 58–68.

54. *Pervaia vseobshchaia perepis'*, vol. 89, 18, and vol. 83, 14.

55. Turkistonlik Noghai Mullah, "Yangi fikrchi, eski fikrchi"; Fakhriddin, *Aila*, 30; Sibghatulla qizi, *Aila Sabaqlari*, 59.

56. Behbudi, "Hifz-i sihat-i oila," *Oina*, no. 48 (1914): 1148–52.

57. Behbudi, "Hifz-i sihat-i oila," *Oina*, no. 48 (1914): 1148–52, and vol. 49 (1914): 1171–74. Behbudi's assumptions about the relationship of two factors here are interesting: that delay in or lack of marriage somehow produced criminality and insanity, rather than that those conditions might deter the possibility of marriage. There was also a strong suggestion that Europeans had these problems because they had the wrong attitude to marriage; Behbudi did not discuss criminality or insanity among Turkestanis.

58. *Al-Qur'an: A Contemporary Translation*, rev. ed., trans. Ahmed Ali (Princeton, NJ: Princeton University Press, 1988), 4:3.

59. Muhammad Abduh and Qasim Amin were strong proponents of this interpretation, and Abduh tried to bring legal limits to polygyny so that a man wishing to marry an additional wife would have to demonstrate in court that he could support both equally. Hourani, *Arabic Thought*, 166; Badran, *Feminists, Islam, and Nation*, 129.

60. Sibghatulla qizi, *Aila Sabaqlari*, 58.

61. Fakhriddin, *Aila*, 40.

62. Fitrat, *Oila*, 15–19. It should be stressed that the Quran says no such thing. In *Rahbar-i Najat*, Fitrat stressed only the oppressive aspect of polygynous marriage and did not defend the practice (89).

63. Having first read Fitrat's *Rahbar-i Najat*, I was surprised by the exclusive androcentrism of Fitrat's arguments about women and family in *Oila*. However, men's arguments for the reform of women in texts from elsewhere in the Islamic world, texts that Fitrat probably read, also display this tendency. In *Women and Gender in Islam*, Ahmed reads Qasim Amin's famous tract, *The Liberation of Women*, critically, pointing out the misogynist aspects of his arguments. Her analysis, that Amin was not wholeheartedly concerned with women's interests in promoting their unveiling and education, informs my own reading of Central Asian Jadid writings.

64. Qaramiqef [*sic*], "Maktublar," *Suyum Bike*, no. 11 (1915): 20.

65. The congress was organized to prepare for Russia's first postrevolution elections, March 5, 1917. "Musliman khatunlarining tavushlari," *Suyum Bike*, no. 9 (1917): 142.

66. I. Hilali, "Maskav muslimalari kamiteti tarafindan khitabname," *Suyum Bike*, no. 11 (1917): 165–74. One of the participants, Zahida Burnasheva, may have been the same person as the founder of several girls' schools in Central Asia (see chapter 4).

67. "Birdan artuq khatun aluv haqinda," *Suyum Bike*, no. 18 (1917): 280.

68. In the other two cases the husbands probably took advantage of inept bureaucracy, or of moving to a new city, and their own social position to register the second marriages. Interviews with Sottiba-xon M. (b. 1920, Namangan); Latifot T. (b. 1931, Bukhara region); Shamsiyat B. (b. 1918, Bukhara).

69. Richard Stites, *The Women's Liberation Movement in Russia: Feminism, Nihilism, and Bolshevism, 1860–1917*, 2nd ed. (Princeton, NJ: Princeton University Press, 1990). Tatar women reported on Russian women's activism in *Suyum Bike*, but organized themselves separately.

70. Najie, "Khatunlar tarafindan musulman Duma a'zalarina," *Alem-i Nisvan*, no. 7 (1907): 1–2, reprinted from the Tatar periodical *Vaqt*.

71. Kamila Muzafiriya, "Aidingiz birga!" *Suyum Bike*, no. 2 (1914): 11.

72. A. Gh., "Khatunlar," in *Khanumlar Islahi*, ed. Mu'allima Kamila bint `Azatulla Qasimova (Kazan: Beraderan Karimilar, 1908), 47–49.

73. For example, Zakir al-Qadiri, who referred to Muhammad Abduh in *Qizlar Dunyasi*, (Kazan: Yefremov, 1911), 11.

74. Fitrat, *Rahbar-i Najat*, 43. Most of Fitrat's statements were typical of Islamic modernist writing; exactly the same contention, with the reliance on "equality in difference," is found in the early twenty-first century on many Islamic Web sites.

75. A *hadith* is an account of the Prophet Muhammad's words or deeds, which serves as a source for Sharia.

76. Al-Qadiri, *Qizlar Dunyasi*, 17–24. Al-Qadiri based his assertions on the Shaf'i school of Islamic law, but most Tatar and Turkestani religious scholars followed the Hanafi school.

77. Sibghatulla qizi, *Aila Sabaqlari*, 63, 72.

78. A. Ismeti, "Shariat qashunda khatun qizlar," *Suyum Bike*, no. 1 (1913): 4.


3. THE REVOLUTION AND RIGHTS FOR UZBEK WOMEN

1. These were the Russian Federated Soviet Socialist Republic and the Soviet Socialist Republics of Ukraine, Uzbekistan, Turkmenistan, Transcaucasus, and Belorus. In Central Asia, Tajikistan was an autonomous republic within the framework of Uzbekistan until 1929. Kazakhstan and Kyrgyzstan were autonomous republics within the Russian Federated Republic until 1936.

2. Dov Yaroshevskii points to Imperial Decree 44424a of 1867, forbidding giving military ranks or awards to "'Bashkirs, the Kirgiz, Kalmyks and other inorodtsy tribes.'" He suggests that leaders of *inorodtsy* (foreign-born, alien) groups also negotiated exclusion from conscription. Yaroshevskii, "Empire and Citizenship," in *Russia's Orient: Imperial Borderlands and Peoples, 1700–1917*, ed. Daniel Brower and Edward Lazzerini (Bloomington: Indiana University Press, 1997), 69.

3. For greater depth on the uprising, see Sokol, *Revolt of 1916 in Central Asia*.

4. Even though Russian authorities looked for evidence of "pan-Turkism" in the uprising—that is, evidence that it was connected with a pro-Ottoman stance— in point of fact anti-Russianism in Central Asia emerged from colonial experience.

Turkestanis rose up against an immediate grievance, not in the name of a larger Turkic cause. The uprising was longer and more sweeping and violent among Kazakhs, who siezed lands that the Russian government had recently appropriated and given to a massive wave of Russian settlers. The 1916 uprising has undergone numerous interpretations, as pan-Turkist, as proto-Communist and class-based, and as a movement of national liberation. Angry statements from demonstrators indicated that they wanted to throw the Russians out and would not send Turkestani boys to fight, but the causes and intentions of this uprising were not indicative of some grand political program.

5. Kh. Z. Ziiaev, "Natsional'no-osvoboditel'noe vosstanie 1916 goda v Turkestane," *Obshchestvennye nauki v Uzbekistane*, no. 7 (1991): 27–36; D. Ismoilova, "Farg'ona Viloyatida 1916 yil halq qo'zg'oloni," *Obshchestvennye nauki v Uzbekistane*, no. 8 (1991): 26–33.

6. A. V. Piakovskii, ed., *Vosstanie 1916 goda v srednei Azii i Kazakhstane: Sbornik dokumentov*, doc. 108 (Moskva: Akademiia Nauk, 1960), 185.

7. Piakovskii, *Vosstanie 1916 goda*, doc. 157, 250–52. Nizhnii Asht was located in Namangan district. Ismoilova refers to this case in "Farg'ona Viloyatida 1916 yil halq qo'zg'oloni."

8. Roza Karryeva, *Ot bespraviia k ravenstvu* (Tashkent: Uzbekistan, 1989), 22–23.

9. Tikhotskii's report is in P. G. Gazulo, *Vosstanie 1916 goda v srednei Azii: Sbornik dokumentov* (Tashkent: Gosizdat UzSSR, 1932), 15; Ziiaev, "Natsional'no-osvoboditel'noe vosstanie," 33.

10. Gazulo, *Vosstanie 1916 goda*, 33–34.

11. Rabiia Nasyrova [Robiya Nosirova], in Finkel'shtein, *Probuzhdennye velikim Oktiabrem*, 150. Nosirova's account reflected the official interpretation of the event from a 1960 perspective. She noted that the male participants were "poor," supporting the thesis that this was a class-based uprising. This is also the thesis in the introductory article to Piakovskii's 1960 document collection, even though a document from that collection pointed out that two of Tashkent's wealthiest and most influential Uzbeks fully supported the uprising. Piakovskii, *Vosstanie 1916 goda*, 269–70. However, she deviated from the official intepretation and upheld the more common Uzbek narrative in saying that the demonstration was against "tsarist colonizers," while the official version repeatedly argued that Turkestanis were not opposed to colonizers in general, just to the administration. Piakovskii, *Vosstanie 1916 goda*, 5–22.

12. Ziiaev, "Natsional'no-osvoboditel'noe vosstanie," 34.

13. Gazulo, *Vosstanie 1916 goda*, 15, 34.

14. Ziiaev, "Natsional'no-osvoboditel'noe vosstanie," 33.

15. Gazulo, *Vosstanie 1916 goda*, 67.

16. Laziz Azizzoda, *Yangi hayot kurashchilari* (Toshkent: Fan, 1977), 117.

17. Karryeva, *Ot bespraviia*, 9–22.

18. Sahadeo, "Creating a Russian Colonial Community," 302–12.

19. Women demonstrated in the 1906 Iranian revolution and fought in the

1911 defense of Tabriz; Egyptian women made a similar, surprising, demonstration in the 1919 Egyptian revolution. Janat Afary, *The Iranian Constitutional Revolution, 1906–1911: Grassroots Democracy, Social Democracy, and the Origins of Feminism* (New York: Columbia University Press, 1996), 77–208; Badran, *Feminists, Islam, and Nation*, 75–78. V. Kasparova made comparisons among some of these moments in a 1922 article. Kasparova and Ye. Ralli, "Probuzhdennye trudiashchiisia zhenshchiny vostoka," *Novyi Vostok*, no. 2 (1922): 400–420.

20. Saidakbar A'zamxo'jaev, *Turkiston Muxtoriyati: Milliy-demokratik davlatchilik qurulishi tajribasi* (Toshkent: Manaviyat, 2000), 97–98.

21. Works in English on this period include Alexander Park, *Bolshevism in Turkestan, 1917–1927* (New York: Columbia University Press, 1957); selections by Carrère d'Encausse in Allworth, *Central Asia*, 189–265; and Adeeb Khalid, "Tashkent 1917: Muslim Politics in Revolutionary Turkestan," *Slavic Review* 55, no. 2 (1996): 270–96.

22. A'zamxo'jaev, *Turkiston Muxtoriyati*, 112–27.

23. The approved version of Uzbekistan's history in 2000 devotes many pages to the anti-Soviet leaders and the war between Soviet and anti-Soviet forces. M. Jo'raev, ed., *O'zbekistonning yangi tarixi*, vol. 2, *O'zbekiston Soviet mustamlakachiligri davrida* (Toshkent: Sharq, 2000). Almost half of the 685-page volume on the Soviet period (1917–1991) is devoted to the turbulent years 1917–1924. Biographies of Kurbashi leaders appear in abundance. I use "Basmachi," rather than "Kurbashi" or "Istiqlol Haraqatchilar" for these forces, because most sources refer to them as Basmachi, and among my oral history interviewees all who ever encountered them called them Basmachis.

24. Marco Buttino, "Study of the Economic Crisis and Depopulation in Turkestan, 1917–1920," *Central Asian Survey* 9, no. 4 (1990): 59–74; Tsentral'noe Statisticheskoe Upravlenie Turkestanskoi Respubliki, *Materialy Vserossiiskikh sel'skokhoziaistvennykh perepisei*, vol 1, *Samarkandskoi oblasti* (Tashkent: Izdaniie TEU Turkrespubliki, 1924), and vol. 3, *Syrdariinskoi oblasti* (Samarkand: Ts.S.U, UzSSR, 1925).

25. On Enver Pasha and the Basmachis, see Glenda Fraser, "Enver Pasha's Bid for Turkestan," *Canadian Journal of History* 23, no. 2 (1988): 197–213; Masayuki Yamauchi, *The Green Crescent under the Red Star: Enver Pasha in Soviet Russia, 1919–1922* (Tokyo: Institute for Study of Languages and Cultures of Asia and Africa, 1991); and H. B. Paksoy, "The Basmachi from Within: an Account of Zeki Velidi Togan," *Nationalities Papers* 23, no. 2 (1995): 373–99. Both Alexander Park, *Bolshevism in Turkestan, 1917–1927* (New York: Columbia University Press, 1957), and Shoshana Keller, *To Moscow, Not Mecca: The Soviet Campaign against Islam in Central Asia, 1917–1941* (Westport, CT: Praeger, 2001) discuss the Bolshevik retreat from these radical policies.

26. This national delimitation drew up new "nationally" based republics on the lands that had been the Steppe Governate, Turkestan Territory, Transcaspia, the Khivan Khanate, and the Bukharan Emirate. The Soviet Nationalities Commissariat designed, in their place, the Soviet Socialist Republics of Uzbekistan and Turkmenistan, the Autonomous Republic of Tajikistan, and the Autonomous Republics

of Kazakhstan and Kyrgyzstan. Boundaries among these republics underwent a number of changes until the 1960s.

27. R. Viadyanath, *Formation of the Soviet Central Asia Republics: A Study in Soviet Nationalities Policy, 1917–1936* (New Delhi, India: People's Publishing House, 1967), 165. See also Hirsch, "Toward an Empire of Nations."

28. Alexandre Bennigsen and S. Enders Wimbush assert that Muslim National Communists "rejected on principle Soviet plans for creating small, modern nations in the different ethnic regions of the Muslim borderlands. In 1924 they opposed the division of Central Asia into five national republics." Bennigsen and Wimbush, *Muslim National Communism in the Soviet Union: A Revolutionary Strategy for the Colonial World* (Chicago: University of Chicago Press, 1979), 67. However, while it is true that certain Turkestan Muslim Communists and nationalists like Mustafa Chokaev clung to the vision of unity, others such as Faizulla Xo'jaev seem to have adopted the new division of national states in Central Asia with enthusiasm. In Viadyanath's volume, which is based on a fairly thorough examination of the Russian-language public record from 1924 and later scholarship, it seems clear that while some of the Turkestan Communist Party's members advocated a single Central Asian republic, others advocated division into several republics, and most argumentation concerned which of the new "nations" would claim the most desirable territories. Viadyanath, *Formation of the Soviet Central Asian Republics*, 166–83.

29. Hirsch shows that petitioners who questioned the borders were primarily concerned with being separated from the republic that represented their ethnic group, such as Kazakhs living in the new Uzbekistan, or Uzbeks in Kyrgyzstan. Hirsch, "Toward an Empire of Nations," 215–20.

30. Viadyanath, *Formation of the Soviet Central Asian Republics*, 151–52, describes the disagreement between Soviet and anti-Soviet scholarship (or polemics) regarding the delimitation of national borders.

31. Martin, *Affirmative Action Empire.*

32. Roger Kangas, "Faizulla Khodzhaev: National Communism in Bukhara and Uzbekistan, 1896–1938" (Ph.D. diss., Indiana University, 1992), 12–24.

33. Before the new republican borders were made public, the Communist Parties of Turkestan, Bukhara, and Khiva dissolved and reformed as the Communist Parties of Uzbekistan, Turkmenistan, and so on. *Kommunisticheskaia Partiia Uzbekistana v rezoliutsiiakh s'ezdov i plenumov*, vol. 1, *1925–1937* (Tashkent: Uzbekistan, 1987), 14. Xo'jaev's home language was Tajik, and many Tajik-speaking Bukharans viewed him as a traitor for identifying with the larger, stronger, Uzbek republic, rather than defending a Tajik nationalism.

34. *Kommunisticheskaia Partiia Uzbekistana v rezoliutsiiakh*, 17–18, 54. The decision to create republican Red Army divisions was made in Moscow; the Uzbekistan Communist Party only formalized it. For an example of such a Xo'jaev speech, see S. I., "Eski Toshkentda Ta'rixi Majlis," *Qizil O'zbekiston*, Mar. 5, 1926, 1. Military service was voluntary, and Park notes that by 1927 the Uzbek national army divisions were having difficulty attracting Uzbeks, who formed 37 percent of the officers and only 5 percent of the troops. Park, *Bolshevism in Turkestan*, 177.

35. In this, Uzbek-language newspapers in the 1920s differed sharply from the Russian-language paper belonging to the Party's Central Asian Bureau, *Pravda Vostoka*. If one reads *Pravda Vostoka*, one comes away with a strong impression of Moscow's continued colonialism in Central Asia; Central Asians are strangers, the others in a dialectic with the normal Russian face of the Soviet Union. But very few Uzbeks read *Pravda Vostoka*. Instead, they read and wrote for the Uzbek press, according to which Uzbeks ran their own affairs, and Moscow was far away.

36. Benedict Anderson, *Imagined Communities: Reflections on the Origin and Spread of Nationalism*, rev. ed. (London: Verso, 1991), 121.

37. Anderson, *Imagined Communities*, 57.

38. Nilüfer Göle, *The Forbidden Modern: Civilization and Veiling*. Critical Perspectives on Women and Gender (Ann Arbor: University of Michigan Press, 1996).

39. Deniz Kandiyoti, "Emancipated but Unliberated? Reflections on the Turkish Case," *Feminist Studies* 13, no. 2 (1987): 323.

40. Variants of this interpretation for Turkey are found in Kandiyoti, "Emancipated but Unliberated"; Zehra Arat, "Turkish Women and the Republican Reconstruction of Tradition," in *Reconstructing Gender in the Middle East: Tradition, Identity, and Power*, ed. Fatma Müge Göçek and Shiva Balaghi (New York: Columbia University Press, 1994), 57–78; Zehra Arat, "Kemalism and Turkish Women," *Women and Politics*, 14, no. 4 (1994): 57–80; Canan Aslan, "The Legacy of a European-Oriented Transformation: Gender Relations in Contemporary Turkey," *European Legacy* 1, no. 3 (1996): 981–87; and in Aysegul Baykan, "The Turkish Woman: An Adventure in Feminist Historiography," *Gender and History* 6, no.1 (1994): 101–16. In literature on Uzbekistan, Massell emphasizes the instrumental reasons for the Party's "liberation" of Muslim women in *Surrogate Proletariat*.

41. Ahmet Icduygu, Yilmaz Colak, and Nalan Soyarik, "What is the Matter with Citizenship? A Turkish Debate," in *Seventy-five Years of the Turkish Republic*, ed. Sylvia Kedourie (London: Frank Cass, 2000), 194–95.

42. Both Massell and Northrop begin with the Soviet state, as do Aminova and most Uzbek scholars.

43. Massell, *Surrogate Proletariat*; Northrop, *Veiled Empire*.

44. Recent scholarship on women in Turkey includes Kandiyoti, "Emancipated but Unliberated?"; Yeşim Arat, "From Emancipation to Liberation," *Journal of International Affairs* 54, no. 1 (2000): 107–24; and Z. Arat, "Turkish Women and the Republican Reconstruction of Tradition." Historical studies for Turkey, however, are limited and are based only on published sources.

45. Göle, *Forbidden Modern*, 76.

46. In noting this, I am not advocating that law should be made according to the preference of the majority; indeed, I believe that laws that protect human rights and that try to bring about human equality often do not have majority preference, but nonetheless should be made and enforced.

47. Z. A. Astapovich, ed., *Velikii Oktiabr' i raskreposhcheniie zhenshchin srednei Azii i Kazakhstana (1917–1936 gg): Sbornik dokumentov i materialov* (Moskva: Mysl', 1971),

26. "Dekret o grazhdanskom brake, o detiakh i o vedenii knig aktov sostoianiia," Uz. St. Arch., F. 38, op. 2, d. 28, l. 9.

48. Uz. St. Arch., F. R-38, op. 285, d. 2, l. 122; Kh. S. Sulaimanova, *Istoriia Sovetskogo gosudarstva i prava Uzbekistana*, vol. 1, *1917–1924* (Tashkent: Izd. Ak. Nauk Uzbekskoi SSR, 1960), 263.

49. Massell, *Surrogate Proletariat*, 250.

50. In Russia and other parts of the Soviet Union, divorce could be obtained by one party filing a document, without court involvement.

51. By contrast, the Soviet Legal Code of 1918 established a six-month term of alimony in cases where one spouse was unemployed, and unlimited term alimony for a disabled spouse. In 1927, the latter changed to one year. Goldman, *Women, the State, and Revolution*, 52, 300.

52. Kh. S. Sulaimanova, *Istoriia Sovetskogo gosudarstva i prava Uzbekistana*, vol. 2, *1924–1937* (Tashkent: Izd-vo Ak. Nauk Uzbekskoi SSR, 1963), 221–28.

53. Gaye Patek-Salom and Pina Hukum, "Women's Emancipation after the Ataturk Period," in *Women of the Mediterranean*, ed. Monique Gadant (London: Zed, 1986), 95.

54. Aslan, "The Legacy of a European-Oriented Transformation," 982.

55. Göle, *Forbidden Modern*, 74–76.

56. Z. Arat, "Kemalism and Turkish Women," 64.

57. Nermin Abadan-Unat, "The Modernization of Turkish Women," *Middle East Journal* 32, no. 3 (1978): 291–306.

58. Z. Arat, "Kemalism and Turkish Women," 64.

59. Records of these discussions are in Uz. St. Arch., F. R-86, op. 1, d. 4932, ll. 2–50.

60. The *vakila* or *delegatka* was elected at a meeting of women in her town or urban quarter, and she attended a Women's Division–sponsored conference; she was encouraged to volunteer for some public-service position when she returned home.

61. Douglas Northrop, "Subaltern Dialogues: Subversion and Resistance in Soviet Uzbek Family Law," *Slavic Review* 60, no. 1 (2001): 126–29. Local soviets regularly gave out documents that asserted a false age for an underage girl.

62. Abadan-Unat, "Modernization of Turkish Women," 295.

63. Stanford Shaw and Ezel Kural Shaw, *History of the Ottoman Empire and Modern Turkey*, vol. 2. (Cambridge: Cambridge University Press, 1977), 385.

64. Nükhet Sirman, "Feminism in Turkey: A Short History," *New Perspectives on Turkey* 3, no. 1 (Fall 1989): 3–10; Patek-Salom and Hukum, "Women's Emancipation," 94–95.

65. Baykan, "The Turkish Woman," 108–9; Mete Tuncay, "Kadinlar halk firkasi," *Tarih ve Toplum* 9, no. 51 (1989): 158.

66. Şirin Tekeli, "Introduction: Women in Turkey in the 1980s," in *Women in Modern Turkish Society*, ed. Şirin Tekeli (London: Zed, 1995), 1–21.

67. For example, Fotima, "Holida Adiba Xonum ma'orif naziri," *Turkiston*, Mar. 9, 1924, 3.

68. Nermin Abadan-Unat, "Social Change and Turkish Women," in *Women in Turkish Society*, ed. Nermin Abadan-Unat (Leiden, Netherlands: Brill, 1981), 13.

69. Marfua Tokhtakhodjaeva [To'xtaxo'jaeva], "Women and Law in Uzbekistan," in *Assertions of Self: The Nascent Women's Movement in Central Asia* (Lahore, Pakistan: Shirkat Gah, 1995), 5–22.

70. Massell drew his *Surrogate Proletariat* title from articles by Aleksandra Artiukhina, who headed the Moscow-based All-Union Women's Division in the late 1920s. Artiukhina argued for Central Party support for the Hujum by proposing that the campaign would politicize women, bring them into public action, and make them into Central Asia's most revolutionary element. Clements, *Bolshevik Women*, 272. Massell subsumed all of the Party's efforts in Central Asia under the surrogate proletariat notion, leading readers to assume that creating a revolutionary element was indeed the Party's goal in trying to change the status of women there. However, the argument for making women a surrogate proletariate was just that, an argument, and one pitched by a Women's Division head who was seeking more money and support from the the Party's Central Committee; it was not the underlying reason for pursuing the Hujum in Central Asia, which had its base not in a specialized understanding of Central Asian women, but in a general Communist policy of women's equality that was pursued everywhere in the Soviet Union. Had the Party decided to exclude women in Central Asia from its modernizing agenda, and to focus only on men, that would have constituted a unique approach to Central Asia.

71. Kotkin, "Modern Times."

## 4. THE OTIN AND THE SOVIET SCHOOL

1. Interview with Rahbar-oi Olimova (b. 1908, Tashkent). Much of the information about otins and traditional education comes from my research in Uzbekistan in 1992–1993. Among my informants, two (Humoira H., b. 1913, Kokand, and Latifot T., b. 1931, Bukhara region) were otins, and about half had been educated by otins.

2. Annette Krämer, *Geistliche Autorität und islamische Gessellschaft im Wandel: Studien über Frauenälteste (otin und xalfa) im unabhängigen Usbekistan*, Islamkundliche Untersuchungen, Band 246 (Berlin: Klaus Schwarz Verlag, 2002). Krämer discusses the various names for women in this role: *buvotin, oi-mulla, otin bibi*, and so on (48–56). There were similar women religious teachers in Afghanistan, Turkey, and Iran, but little has been written about them.

3. A man who studied in the madrasa, upon mastering certain fields, could be recognized as an *olim* (scholar); the female equivalent would be *olima*. In the Soviet period, Olima became popular as a given name for Uzbek girls, perhaps expressing their parents' hopes for their educational achievements.

4. Levin describes a session with a *baxshi*, a woman healer, and discusses possible shamanic-Islamic syncretism. Levin, *Hundred Thousand Fools of God*, 242–59. A recording of such a session can be seen in the video series *Where the Eagles Fly:*

*Habiba, a Sufi Saint from Uzbekistan,* produced by Constanzo Allione (New York: Mystic Fire Video, 1997. Krämer discusses the distinctions between Islamic and shamanic roles in *Geistliche Autorität und islamische Gessellschaft,* 97–102.

5. "Dilshod Otin," in *O'zbek Soviet entsiklopediyasi,* vol. 4 (Toshkent: O'zbek Soviet Entsiklopediyasi Bo'sh Redaktsiyasi, 1973), 39 . Dilshod composed a brief autobiography.

6. Nodira was the wife of Khan Umar (1810–1822); she is the best known of women poets in the Uzbek (or Chagatay) classical poetic tradition.

7. "Anbar Otin," in *O'zbek Soviet entsiklodepiyasi,* vol. 1, 343–44; Khairullaev, *Islam i zhenshchiny vostoka,* 43.

8. Sadriddin Ayni, *Yoddoshtho,* vol. 1 (Dushanbe: Adib, 1990), 80. A *khatib* was a preacher in the village mosque.

9. Khalid, *Politics of Muslim Cultural Reform,* 21.

10. Khalid describes the standard curriculum and educational approach of the Central Asian maktab in *Politics of Muslim Cultural Reform,* 20–28.

11. The new method of teaching reading, *usul-i jadid,* gave its name to the larger movement for cultural reform; see Allworth, *Modern Uzbeks,* 130–43. One example of the phonetic alphabet primer is Said Rasul Xo'ja Domla Daid Aziz Xo'ja Mahdum Mufti O'g'li, *Ustod-i avval,* repr. of a 1909 lithograph (Toshkent: Meros, 1990). Several informants mentioned "Alifbo" as their first text; interviews with Rahbar-oi Olimova (b. 1908, Tashkent), Malika-xon J. (b. 1912, Namangan). Yo'l-doshbaeva, *Moia sud'ba,* 15–18.

12. Latifot T. (b. 1931, Bukhara region) was Irani. She learned religious knowledge from her grandmother, an otin, and her grandfather, a *qori,* or Quran reciter. She demonstrated her knowledge of Arabic by orally translating prayers, written in her notebook in Arabic, into Uzbek for me. I do not know Arabic, but I do not have reason to doubt her translation was genuine. Humoira H. (b. 1913, Kokand) was Uzbek. Her father was a *mudarris,* a teacher in a madrasa. While he, like Latifot's grandfather, the qori, probably knew Arabic, he did not pass this knowledge on to his daughter.

13. Krämer describes the standard works that appeared in the otin's curriculum. Krämer, *Geistliche Autorität und islamische Gessellschaft,* 130–45.

14. *Pervaia vseobshchaia perepis',* vol. 89, 78–99, and vol. 86, 92–99, 144–45. Girls in this cohort had the highest literacy rates; older cohorts had lower rates.

15. William K. Medlin, William M. Cave, and Finley Carpenter, *Education and Development in Central Asia: A Case Study on Social Change in Uzbekistan* (Leiden, Netherlands: Brill, 1971), 32.

16. Ivanov, "Doklad Ferganskogo voennogo gubernatora Ivanov, Dekiabr' 1916 g," in Gazulo, *Vostaniia 1916 goda,* 69–70. Similarly, in Khiva there was growth in the building of madrasas in this period, as becomes obvious when one goes on an architectural tour.

17. Humoira H. (b. 1913, Kokand).

18. Annette M. B. Meakin, a scholar from Britain, visited an otin in Tashkent in 1892 and asked for evidence of her literacy; in this case, the otin was fully lit-

erate, able to read and write. Meakin, *In Russian Turkestan: A Garden of Asia and its People* (New York: Charles Scribner's Sons, 1915), 87–92. Some of my informants said they learned to read and write; others remembered that they only mastered recitiation of several prayers.

19. Latifot T. (b. 1931, Bukhara region) reported this about her mother, as did Rahbar-oi Olimova (b. 1908, Tashkent) about her mother.

20. Rorlich, *Volga Tatars*, 99–101. These changes also affected Russian Azerbaijan. Arguably, the first name in modernization of Islamic education and society was Akhundzade of Tiflis, whose writings had influence in Russia and Iran in the 1860s. Some of the reformers in Turkestan, and some of the teachers of the early 1920s in Turkestan, may have come from Azerbaijan, but because they were called Tatars they are rarely differentiated from Volga and Crimean Tatars in sources from that period.

21. Khalid, *Politics of Muslim Cultural Reform*, 126–27.

22. Alimhanov, "Yana to'i masalasi," 3.

23. The beshik is designed so that the infant lies on his back and is tied down; a hole below his behind allows waste to be drained away. The baby is unable to move much, and can be fed and cared for without being picked up. Jadids and Russians criticized the beshik as harmful to infant development. Mahmud Xo'ja [Behbudi], "Beshiklarimiz miyamizni uyaldur," *Oina*, no. 8 (1915): 181–83. On mothers' importance in rearing and educating children, see Zuhriddin Fathiddin-zade, "Huquq-i nisvan," *Sado-i Turkiston*, no. 47 (1914): 3, and part 2, no. 51 (1914): 2–3; also, Mulla Abd al-Salam al-Azimi, "Ta'lim va tarbiya," *Oina*, no. 13 (1915): 346–49. Behbudi responded to al-Azimi's call for women's education by arguing that the women of Turkestan already had too much work in the household and did not have time for additional responsibilities in rearing children.

24. When Jadid schools first appeared in Turkestan is disputed. V. V. Bartol'd, "Istoriia kul'turnaia zhizn' Turkestana VII: Shkoly," in *Sochineniia*, vol. 2, part 1 (Moskva: Izd-vo Nauka, 1964), 297–318; Allworth, *Modern Uzbeks*, 130–31; Akhunova, *Istoriia Kokanda*, 27. There are reports in the Jadid press of mixed maktabs for boys and girls in Bukhara and Samarkand. Zaineb Dinikaeva, "Bukharada uyg'atuv asr-lari," *Suyum Bike*, no. 12 (1914): 9–10; Muzafiriya, "Aidingiz birga!" Calls for mu'al-limas are found in Toshkentlik bir Mu'allima, "Turkiston mu'allimalari tarafindan bir sado," *Sado-i Turkiston*, no. 11 (1914): 1–2; and Tufagan Xojim, "Hamshiralar tilindan," *Sado-i Turkiston*, no. 53 (1914): 3.

25. Fathiddin-zade, "Huquq-i nisvan," no. 51, 2. Bibi Seshanbe was one of several women "saints" to whom women turned for release from troubles. Krämer explains recitations concerning Bibi Seshanbe and Bibi Mushkil-i Koshad in *Geistliche Autorität und islamische Gessellschaft*.

26. Interview with Saodat Shamsieva (b. 1908, To'rtqo'l); Saodat's interview is featured in chapter 6. Interview with Bahriniso I. (b. 1910, Namangan region).

27. Malika-xon J. (b. 1912, Namangan).

28. Chernisheva, "O'zbekistonda xotinlar ma'orifi," *Yangi Yo'l*, no. 6 (1928): 3–5; Bartol'd, *Sochineniia*, 301–2.

29. In 1883 the Women's Seminary had 333 students, 10 of whom were Turkestani; in 1896 there were 8 Turkestani students. Chernisheva, "O'zbekistonda xotinlar ma'orifi." Chernisheva used the same statistical source as Bartol'd, *Sochineniia*, 300.

30. Valida Kuchukova (b. 1883, Tashkent). She was the daughter of a Bashkord interpreter for the Syr Darya provincial court. She finished the gymnasium in 1901, and in 1909 she taught in a "private Russian-Tatar school associated with a Muslim women's school, where there were up to 45 Tatar and Uzbek girls." Namangan Filial, Uz. St. Arch., No. 66, dated 30.12.1925.

31. Gulosum Aserichbiieva (surname partially illegible), Kazakh, born 1880 in Chimkent, graduated from the Women's Seminary and then studied at the Peterburg Women's Medical Institute. She became a doctor in 1908, working in Turkestan. She was director of the Tashkent Native Medic and Midwives School in 1923. Zulfia Nishtsova, Sart, though from her surname probably married to a non-Muslim, graduated the seminary in 1915, attended the Peterburg Women's Medical Institute until 1918, and studied in a medic course and in the newly organized Central Asian Communist University's medical department from 1920 to 1922 before teaching at the midwives' school. Maryam Yakubova, a Tashkent-born Tatar, also graduated from the seminary, went to medical school in Peterburg, and practiced medicine in Turkestan hospitals before teaching at the midwives' school. Uz. St. Arch., F. 34, op. 1, d. 1333, ll. 250, 254, 255. Another 1914 Turkestani graduate of the seminary, Oisha-hanum Urazaeva, was a teacher in Skoblev (Fargana) Middle School number 1 in 1924. Yo'ldoshbaeva, *Moia sud'ba*, 24.

32. Keller, *To Moscow, Not Mecca*, 36–37.

33. Park, *Bolshevism in Turkestan*, 217–18, 242–43; Keller, *To Moscow not Mecca*, 40–42.

34. Uz. St. Arch., F. 32, op. 1, d. 2314, l. 2. Park reports that in 1923 there were "773,000 native children of school age" in Turkestan, in *Bolshevism in Turkestan*, 362. This would mean a little less than 10 percent were studying in Quran schools, probably mostly boys, and mostly from the sedentary population.

35. Aminova, *October Revolution*, 188.

36. Malika-xon J. (b. 1912, Namangan) referred to the school she attended in the early 1920s as a Soviet school in her written memoir for the archive, and as a Jadid school in her oral interview with me. In her interview, Bahriniso Y. (b. 1909, Kokand) referred to her postrevolution school in Kokand as a Jadid school. In her memoir, Muharram Arifxanova described her school in Kokand as "new method" (i.e., Jadid) in one sentence, and "new soviet" in another, in Finkel'shtein, *Probuzhdennye velikim Oktiabrem*, 130–34.

37. For Tashkent schools in 1919, see Georgii Safarov, *Koloniial'nia Revoliutsiia (Opyt Turkestana)* (Moskva: Gos. Izd-vo., 1921), 149; schools in old city Tashkent in 1920, Uz. St. Arch., F. 34, op. 1, d. 703, ll. 143–93. Many of the boys' schools listed religion or "ethics" in their curriculum.

38. Informants who attended the Bilim Yurt between 1922 and 1927 referred to the institution with a number of names, including Dar al-Mu'allimot, a name

used until about 1924, Inpros (Institut Prosveshcheniia), Internat (the students who boarded at the school called it "the boarding school"), and documents from the period also refer to it as Kraevoi zhenskii Uzbekskii institut. Uz. St. Arch., F. 34, op. 1, d. 1014, l. 42. In the Uzbek-language press, Bilim Yurt was the most common name, but Azizzoda, a Tashkent intellectual, called the Bilim Yurt "Zebiniso." This seems to be a mistake; Zebiniso was a neighborhood primary school, part of the state network, that attracted girls from Tashkent's ziyoli (intelligentsia) families. Azizzoda, Yangi hayot kurashchilari, 115–19. The Bilim Yurt was reorganized, moved, and expanded in the mid-1920s.

39. Jahon Obidova (Dzhakhan Abidova), a leading Uzbek Communist Party member in the 1920s, recalled that Burnasheva organized the course in 1918; Obidova was one of the students. Finkel'shtein, Probuzhdennye velikim Oktiabrem, 110–11, and n. 257. Burnasheva may have been involved in the prerevolution Muslim Women's Association. Hosiyat Rahim, "Xotin-qizlar Bilim Yurtiga ta'rixi bir qarash," Yangi Yo'l, no. 5 (1927): 5–8. Gavhar Alieva was Tatar, from Ufa. Azizzoda, Yangi hayot kurashchilari, 141–43. Uz. St. Arch., F. 34, op. 1, d. 1014, l. 1 has a list of teachers for 1921–1922.

40. [Robiya] Nosirova, "Xotin-qizlar Bilim Yurtining o'n yiligi," Yangi Yo'l, no. 5 (1929): 4–5.

41. Uz. St. Arch., F. 34, op. 1, d. 1333, ll. 153, 251, 690b, 81–82, 152. The other teachers at the Bilim Yurt in 1923 included two Uzbek men, one Tatar man, one Russian man (who knew the "Sart" language) and one Russian woman. There were no Uzbek women on the faculty in 1923, although several had founded the school, and three were on the faculty in 1922. Uz. St. Arch., F. 34, op. 1, d. 1014, l. 1. Among women teachers in Tashkent primary schools in 1923, nationality was indicated for 35 of them: 23 Tatar, 3 Uzbek, 9 "Turk" (this could have numerous meanings), 1 not indicated. Among male teachers, Turk was the most common identification. Uz. St. Arch., F. 34, op. 1, d. 703, ll. 143–93. The presence of Tatar women in Turkestan's schools is noted by Azizzoda, Yangi hayot kurashchilari, 141–43, and was a theme that arose in several Tatar women's oral histories as well.

42. Uz. St. Arch., F. 34, op. 1, d. 1014, l. 42, Dec. 10, 1922. On the tension between Tatars and Turkestanis in the early 1920s, see Allworth, Modern Uzbeks, 190–91.

43. Uz. St. Arch., F. 34, op. 1, d. 1014, l. 3.

44. On the financial situation in Turkestan in 1922, see Park, Bolshevism in Turkestan, 242, 361; also "O'lka O'zbek xotin-qizlar bilim yurtining xozirgi holda," Qizil Bairoq, Dec. 17, 1921, 1.

45. Bashorat Jalilova, an Uzbek woman from Tashkent, and one of the Bilim Yurt's early organizers, was an activist in the Communist Party Women's Division who had been involved with Jadid education for girls before the revolution. Azizzoda, Yangi hayot kurashchilari. Robiya Nosirova, director in the late 1920s, had run her own Jadid school before the revolution. See chapter 5. Directors of the Bilim Yurt in the early 1920s were Jadid men who were associated with Turkestani nationalism: Salimxon Tillaxon, Shahirjon Rahimi, and Mannon Ramiz or Ramzi. Uz. St. Arch., F. 34, op. 1, d. 1014, l. 1; F. 34, op. 1, d. 1333, ll. 20b, 152. On Tillaxon's

nationalist connections, see chapter 5, n. 22. Mannon Ramiz, after heading the Bilim Yurt, was in the leadership of the republic-level Education Commissariat in 1930 when he and most of the staff were arrested and charged with nationalism. Allworth, *Modern Uzbeks*, 190, 192; Saodat Shamsieva (b.1908, To'rtqo'l), partially transcribed in chapter 6.

46. Rahbar-oi Olimova (b. 1908, Tashkent). Rahbar-oi grew up in the Tashkent neighborhood of Beshag'och, where there were three girls' schools, with several Tatar teachers. Uz. St. Arch., F. 34, op. 1, d. 703, l. 189.

47. Burnasheva in Finkel'shtein, *Probuzhdennye velikim Oktiabrem*, 45.

48. Rustambekova in Finkel'shtein, *Probuzhdennye velikim Oktiabrem*, 174; Uz. St. Arch. F. 34, op. 1, d. 1014, l. 1; Azizzoda, *Yangi hayot kurashchilari*, 123–26, 127–29. Habiba Yusupova's school appeared in the list of Soviet schools as number 47, established in 1918, with 110 Uzbek girl students in 1920. Uz. St. Arch., F. 34, op. 1, d. 703, l. 184.

49. Uz. St. Arch., F. 34, op. 1, d. 1014, ll. 3, 42.

50. Rahim, "Xotin-qizlar Bilim Yurtiga"; Bibi Pal'vanova, *Emantsipatsiia musul'-manki: Opyt raskreposhcheniia zhenshchiny sovetskogo vostoka* (Moskva: Idz-vo Nauka, 1982), 60.

51. Rahim, "Xotin-qizlar Bilim Yurtiga"; Burnasheva in Finkel'shtein, *Probuzhdennye velikim Oktiabrem*, 47.

52. Rustambekova in Finkel'shtein, *Probuzhdennye velikim Oktiabrem*, 175, 191. Finkel'shtein lists the 1923 graduates as Tojixon Rustambekova, Manzura Sobirova (Oidin), Manzura Yangulatova, Nazmi Maxsumova, Hamida Tojieva, Robiya Nosirova, and Hosiyat Ziyaxonova (Tillaxonova).

53. Finkel'shtein, *Probuzhdennye velikim Oktiabrem*, 46; Rahbar-oi Olimova (b. 1908, Tashkent); Malika-xon J. (b. 1912, Namangan); Chinnixon Ibrahimova [Chin-nikhan Ibragimova] in Finkel'shtein, *Probuzhdennye velikim Oktiabrem*, 146. Chin-nixon's mother was an early Party member and labor organizer.

54. Bahriniso I. (b. 1910, Namangan region). Russians called these courses Lik-bez, for "liquidate illiteracy," but the Uzbek name was less violent: Savodsizlik Bitsin, or "end illiteracy."

55. Finkel'shtein, *Probuzhdennye velikim Oktiabrem*, 174, 175; Azizzoda, *Yangi hayot kurashchilari*, 127–29; Uz. St. Arch., F. 34, op. 1, d. 703, l. 193. "Lower education" had no strict definition, but documents suggest that for Turkestanis "lower" meant traditional Islamic religious education in the maktab.

56. The mother of one informant, Saodat X. (b. c. 1958, Namangan region), studied in a girls' school in the early 1930s and came out with a substantial knowl-edge of prayers and religious texts.

57. The term *dinsiz* translates more precisely as "without religion" or "without faith." Uz. St. Arch., F. 34, op. 1, d. 1881, ll. 89–120, questions 25–26.

58. Several of the women I interviewed had fathers who were involved in reli-gious teaching. Humoira H.'s (b. 1913, Kokand) father, a *mudarris* (instructor at a madrasa), made his living as a guard after the Soviets closed his madrasa, and he taught students in his home until his arrest in 1937. Mag'ruba Q.'s father was a

qori, a Quran reciter; after the revolution he worked as a gardener and in a movie theater and confined his religious activities to his home. Interview with Mag'ruba Q. (b. 1929, Tashkent). Aisha B. recalled that her husband had studied with a certain domla in Kokand. Many years later, in 1961, they saw him when he had become mufti of the Muslims of Russia in Ufa. From the 1920s to the 1940s, this religious teacher worked as a bookkeeper. Interview with Aisha B. (b. 1909, Ufa). Sheila Fitzpatrick points out that religious figures were designated as "socially alien" from the first year of the revolution and that changing professions was one strategy that priests and others identified as "class enemies" employed in the late 1920s to try to escape stigmatization and disenfranchisement. Fitzpatrick, "Ascribing Class: The Construction of Social Identity in Soviet Russia," *Journal of Modern History* 65, no. 4 (Dec. 1993): 745–70.

59. See Keller, *To Moscow, Not Mecca.*

60. VI Plenum Ts. K. KP(b) Uzbekistana, Samarkand, 13–15 Iunia 1927 g., in *Kommunisticheskaia Partiia Uzbekistana v rezoliutsiiakh*, 303–4.

61. Serafima Liubimova, "K itogi soveshchaniia po rabote sredi zhenshchin vostochnykh narodnostei," *Kommunistka*, no. 5 (1923): 11–12. The Central Asian Bureau of the Communist Party united and oversaw Central Asian Communist Party activities on Moscow's behalf.

62. Latifot T. (b. 1931, Bukhara region).

63. Manzura H. (b. 1921, Tashkent). Manzura's father was arrested in 1938 and did not return.

64. This state effort to discredit Jadidism is discussed in chapter 5. In fact, Soviet schools in Uzbekistan did not admit all children regardless of class. By the late 1920s, when dekulakization (dispossession of wealthy farmers) and the suppression of private trade were underway, children of the "exploiting" classes did not have a right to free education in Soviet schools.

## 5. NEW WOMEN

1. There is nothing in Islam that associates fire with cleansing. The ritual of jumping over a fire on Navruz (March 21, the Iranian pre-Islamic new year) also appears in Afghanistan and Iran, and is clearly linked to this pre-Islamic holiday. The folk belief that fire cleanses appears in these Irano-Turkic societies, unfortunately, as a factor shaping suicide by self-immolation. Waves of suicide by self-immolation, almost always by women, have plagued Central Asia, northwest Iran, and Afghanistan in recent decades.

2. Lynne Attwood, *Creating the New Soviet Woman: Women's Magazines as Engineers of Female Identity, 1922–53*, Studies in Russian and East European History and Society (New York: St. Martin's Press, 1999), 168.

3. Russian, Ukrainian, Jewish and minority women from the European part of the Soviet Union were all interchangeably dubbed "Russian" or "European." Tatars from Russia were differentiated; Central Asians did not regard them as Russian or European, but not as Turkestani, either.

4. Biographies of Women's Division leaders are found in the collections Finkel'shtein, *Probuzhdennye velikim Oktiabrem*; Kh. T. Tursunov, ed., *Khudzhum znachit nastuplenie* (Tashkent: Fan, 1987); and in Azizzoda, *Yangi hayot kurashchilari*.

5. Azizzoda identified Oiposho Jalilova as a translator for Serafima Liubimova, the Russian head of the CAB Women's Division from 1923 to 1926. Jalilova came from a Tashkent Uzbek *ziyoli*/Jadid family, was an early unveiler, a teacher and activist. Azizzoda, *Yangi hayot kurashchilari*, 109–13.

6. Although what Russians wrote about Uzbek women was important in shaping Party policies, it cannot be assumed that Uzbeks were familiar with Party discourses that took place in Russian or that the All-Union Women's Division paid much attention to what Uzbeks wrote about themselves. Massell's work relies heavily on *Kommunistka*, while Northrop's work regarding the 1920s relies heavily on the Russian-language CAB newspaper, *Pravda Vostoka*, and Party documents in Russian. These approaches are successful for learning what outsiders thought about Central Asians, but not for learning how Central Asians discussed issues among themselves.

7. The socialist critique of feminism was that the latter unites all women without attention to social class, emphasizing gender solidarity at the expense of class interests. The Women's Division existed from 1919 to 1930, and by 1922 there was discussion within the Communist Party about dissolving it. Stites, *Women's Liberation Movement in Russia*; Wood, *Baba and the Comrade*; Gurevich, "Rabota sredi zhenshin," *Kommunistka*, no. 3–5 (1922): 46–47. In 1930 the Women's Division was dissolved and its tasks parceled out to other agencies. Massell attributes its dissolution to the Party's suspicion that "the growth of an exclusively female-oriented organizational network could easily turn into a spontaneous and uncontrolled process." Massell, *Surrogate Proletariat*, chapter 6 and 356.

8. I do not doubt the sincerity of the Women's Division's workers' concern for Central Asian women. The selective and propagandistic presentations in *Kommunistka*, though, were similar to missionary reports ("We are on the verge of a breakthrough in enlightening the heathen; send money").

9. Class conflict was important in Bolshevik ideology and in *Kommunistka*, but Central Asian Communists had to be pushed to embrace class conflict in 1928.

10. From 1924 to 1929, issue no. 11–12, *Yangi Yo'l* called itself the "organ of the Women's Division of the Communist Party of Uzbekistan (CPUz)." From 1929, no. 11–12, to 1930, no. 3, it was the "propaganda organ of the Division of Women Workers and Peasants of the CPUz." From 1930, no. 5, after the Women's Division had dissolved, until 1934, when *Yangi Yo'l* was closed down, the journal became the "propagandist of the CPUz Central Committee of Agitation and Mass Campaigns." *Yangi Yo'l* was no longer a women's journal, and the staff of regular writers changed. Women dominated the lists of named authors until 1930; after 1930, the named authors were mainly men.

11. O'ktam, "Xotinlar masalasi (musabaha yo'li bilan basiladir)," *Turkiston*, Feb. 14, 1924, 3–4.

12. Comments on the need to learn Uzbek were directed at Russians and other

Europeans. Central Asian writers assumed that all Central Asian peoples could more or less understand one another. The Communist Party's policy of *korennizatsiia* (nativization) stressed that in Uzbekistan, Uzbeks should occupy the majority of Party and state positions and that Russians in Uzbekistan should learn Uzbek. See Martin, *Affirmative Action Empire*, on *korenizatsia*. But Russians refused to learn Uzbek (Russian State Archive of Sociopolitical History [hereafter RGASPI], F. 62, op. 2, d. 662, l. 77) and Uzbeks who pressed the issue were accused of nationalism. Even Zelenskii, the long-serving chairman of the CAB, did not learn to read Uzbek (RGASPI, F. 62, op. 2, d. 469, l. 73), though an article published in his name urged others to learn. Zelenskii and Muratova, "8inchi Mart natijalarini mustahkamlash to'g'risida," *Yangi Yo'l*, no. 4–5 (1928): 30–31. *Yangi Yo'l* articles criticized Russians who did not learn Uzbek and presented positive images of those who did: A. Ye., "Xotin-qizlar mamlakat mudafa'a ishida," no. 8 (1928): 8–9; Sherbek, "Ferg'ona ipachilik fabrikasida," no. 9 (1928): 13–15; Zubaida, "Lenin solg'on yo'lda," no. 10 (1928): 20–21; Rahima, "Zarafshan viloyati xotin-qizlari," no. 10 (1926): 18; Amala Xonim, "Xarob qilar qilai," no. 4 (1929): 14–16; Z. Bashiri, "Erk Yo'lida," no. 2 (1928): 11–13.

13. *Yangi Yo'l* normally listed seven to eight editors per issue. The women mentioned here appeared often in the journal's pages throughout the 1920s and for each there is substantial biographical information available.

14. Krupskaia was married to Lenin, was a long-term Communist Party member, and wrote extensively about women's issues and education.

15. Sobira Xoldarova's memoir, "Moi put' v pechati" appeared in *Partiinyi Rabochik*, April 28, 1962, and is quoted in Marhamat Alimova, *Ular birinchilardan edilar* (Toshkent: O'zbekiston, 1983), 12. She appeared as Sobira Nazirova in 1925, when she was using her husband's last name. In Russian works her name is Sabira Khal'darova.

16. Biographical information on Xoldarova comes from M. Alimova, *Ular birinchilardan edilar*; Finkel'shtein, *Probuzhdennye velikim Oktiabrem*, 219–33; and from my interview with Saodat Shamsieva, a friend of Xoldarova's, and Timur Valiev, Xoldarova's son-in-law. Xoldarova's articles are found in *Yangi Yo'l*, *Qizil O'zbekiston*, and *Yer Yuzi*.

17. Oidin's name appeared in publications in many forms: Manzura Sobira Qori qizi, Manzura Sobirova, Manzura Sobir-Qorieva, and Manzura Karieva. Her pen name, Oidin, means "brightness" or "light," and appears in Russian sources as Aidin. Her biographer wrote that she took a pen name under the influence of her girlfriends because she "understood that showing one's name openly in the press was dangerous." M. Alimova, *Ular birinchilardan edilar*, 30–35. On the conflicts among Uzbekistan's writers, see Edward Allworth, *Uzbek Literary Politics* (The Hague: Mouton, 1964); and William Fierman, *Language Planning and National Development: The Uzbek Experience*, Contributions to the Sociology of Language 60 (Berlin: Mouton de Gruyter, 1991). There are scattered mentions of Oidin in other sources, but nothing about whether she married.

18. Robiya Nosirova in Finkel'shtein, *Probuzhdennye velikim Oktiabrem*, 149–54, where the Russian form of her name is Rabiia Nasyrova.

19. Azizzoda, *Yangi hayot kurashchilari*, 115–19.

20. Finkel'shtein, *Probuzhdennye velikim Oktiabrem*, 149–54. The postwar mood of 1961 in the Soviet Union emphasized a politics of "friendship of peoples," and autobiographies carefully depicted moments when Uzbeks came into helpful and enlightening contact with Russians. Some of these stories are genuine and some are formulaic. On Nasirova's 1924 unveiling, see Azizzoda, *Yangi hayot kurashchilari*, 115–19. Azizzoda was a Tatar intellectual and Party member who personally knew many of Tashkent's intellectuals and interacted with women teachers. The reader is left to wonder whether to believe the story Nosirova told about herself in 1961 or the one Azizzoda told about her. Possibly both are true. Many women tried unveiling several times before abandoning the veil altogether.

21. None of Nosirova's published biographical information mentions Party membership.

22. Salimxon Tillaxon was a member of Ko'mak, a group of intellectuals and Turkestani nationalists who raised funds to send sixty-three Turkestani students to study in Europe between 1922 and 1928. Other Ko'mak members included Munavvar Qori (also executed in 1929), Cho'lpan, Faizulla Xo'jaev, and Turar Ryskulov. A few of the students who studied in Germany did not return, and they became involved in expatriate Turkestani nationalist groups. Sherali Turdiev, "Germaniyada o'qiganlar izidan," *O'qituvchilar Gazetasi*, Apr. 6, 1991, 3. Munavvar Qori's group may indeed have been plotting some nationalist course of action in 1929, but the Soviet Union's internal spying organization, the OGPU, considered almost all Uzbek political leaders, including Xo'jaev, Akmal Ikromov, and Yo'ldosh Oxunboboev, to be nationalists and potential traitors. For example, RGASPI F. 62, op. 2, d. 884, l. 8 ff.; d. 1284, l. 52.

23. Sources on Tillaxonova include M. Alimova, *Ular birinchilardan edilar*, 17–26; Finkel'shtein, *Probuzhdennye velikim Oktiabrem*, 195–201, where the Russian form of her name is Khasiiat Tilliakhanova; and my interview with Saodat Shamsieva and Timur Valiev (Tillaxonova's son). Valiev stated that his mother worried about arrest because of her association with Salimxon's nationalist colleagues, but she died of a terminal illness.

24. Tojixon Shodieva was born in the city of Skoblev, which later was renamed Fargana.

25. Biographies of Shodieva include Tojixon Shodieva, "Shodievaning qisqacha tarjima-i holi," *Yangi Yo'l*, no. 10–11 (1927): 28; Fannina Halle, *Women in the Soviet East*, trans. Margaret M. Green (New York: Dutton, 1938), 310–15; Finkel'shtein, *Probuzhdennye velikim Oktiabrem*, 211–15; Tursunov, *Khudzhum znachit nastuplenie*, 158–62; and M. Mahmudov, "Tojixon Shodieva," in *Barhayot siymolar* (Toshkent: O'zbekiston, 1991), 157–65. Only Mahmudov discusses Shodieva's arrest and exile.

26. Liubimova wrote for Russian women readers that before the revolution, none of the non-European nationalities in the Russian Empire even had schools

that taught in their own languages. She also asserted that Uzbek women were almost completely illiterate. Liubimova, *Kak zhivut i rabotaiut zhenshchiny srednei Azii* (Moskva: Gos. Izdat., 1925), 3.

27. Sobira [Xoldarova], "Xotin-qizlar ma'orifi taraqqida," *Qizil O'zbekiston*, Mar. 8, 1926, 5; Rahimi, "Xotin-qizlar Bilim Yurtiga"; Nosir qizi [Robiya Nosirova], "Toshkent o'lka xotin-qizlar Bilim Yurti," *Yangi Yo'l*, no. 8 (1927): 19–20; Nosirova, "Xotin-qizlar Bilim Yurtining o'n yiligi"; "Xotin-qizlar ma'orifini kuchaytiraylik," *Yangi Yo'l*, no. 7 (1929): 3–4.

28. In 1925, while she was teaching at a girls' school and also in a women's literacy course in Tashkent, Xoldarova arranged regular public readings of *Yangi Yo'l* and began holding "conferences" for women readers. M. Alimova, *Ular birinchilardan edilar*, 9–10.

29. Both *Yangi Yo'l* and *Qizil O'zbekiston* tended to use simpler phrasing, while *Ma'orif va O'qituvchi* and *Yer Yuzi* used a more complex, literary Uzbek language.

30. The name I expected to find, but did not, was Hamza Hakimzoda Niyoziy. Later Soviet histories depicted Hamza as a great proponent of women's liberation, and indeed he did write on the topic. But his work did not appear in *Yangi Yo'l* and neither did anything about his life or death.

31. "Ishga," *Yangi Yo'l*, no. 1 (1925): 10–13.

32. Sharofat, "O'ziga yo'l ochdi," *Yangi Yo'l*, no. 5 (1926): 10–12. Establishing cooperatives for work and for purchasing was one of the Soviet government's ways of competing with, and eventually ending, the free market. It was also a way to establish communal forms of economic life that would provide the basis for collectivization of agriculture. One article noted that 10,151 Uzbek women became members of cooperative stores in 1927. Ibrohim, "Xotin-qizlar O'zbekistonda kapiratsiaya qatnashi," *Yangi Yo'l*, no. 8 (1928): 9–11. Other articles about women's co-ops include "Ona va bola burchaklarining ishlari," *Yangi Yo'l*, no. 10–11 (1927): 41; and Butuzova, "Zhenskie lavki v Uzbekistane," *Kommunistka*, no. 9 (1917): 62–67. Butuzova's description of women's shops included workers reading to shoppers from *Yangi Yo'l*.

33. For example, "Xotin-qiz ozodlig'ida bo'shangliq bo'lmasin," *Yangi Yo'l*, no. 7 (1928): 2; and Saida, "Adolat oining qotili," *Yangi Yo'l*, no. 8 (1928): 19. Russian journals identified themselves as coming from the Division of Russian Women Workers and Peasants. *Yangi Yo'l* simply said it represented the Women's Division. *Yangi Yo'l*'s class references became stronger late in 1928 and throughout 1929.

34. "Islam i imushchestvennoe polozhenie zhenshchin i sirot v dorevoliutsionnoi sredei Azii (po materialam Khivinskogo Khanstva XIX v.)," in Khairullaev, *Islam i zhenshchiny vostoka*, 62–66. For a fuller view of the reasons why Islamic law, in spite of its apparent guarantees, does not mean that women necessarily wind up as property owners, see Annelies Moors, *Women, Property and Islam: Palestinian Experiences, 1920–1990*, Cambridge Middle East Studies (Cambridge: Cambridge University Press, 1995).

35. Goldman, *Women, the State, and Revolution*, 145–63.

36. Michurina, "Sho'ralar qonuni xotinlarg'a nima beradir," *Yangi Yo'l*, no. 3

(1926): 29–30. Michurina wrote her article in Russian and it appeared in print elsewhere; *Yangi Yo'l* translated it into Uzbek.

37. "O zemel'noi reforme," Vtoroi s'ezd KP(b) Uzbekistana, Samarkand, 22–30 Noiabria 1925 g., in *Kommunisticheskaia Partiia Uzbekistana v resoliutsiakh*, 135–39.

38. Lazakat, "Xotinlarg'a ham yer," *Yangi Yo'l*, no. 9 (1926): 11–12.

39. For more on this topic, see Marianne Kamp, "Land for Women, Too" (paper presented at Women in Central Asia: The Politics of Change, Columbia University, New York, Apr. 15, 1998), archived at http://www.sipa.columbia.edu/RESOURCES/CASPIAN/wom_p12.html (access via http://www.archive.org).

40. Uz. St. Arch., F. R-35, op. 2, d. 24, l. 740b, May 14, 1918.

41. Uz. St. Arch., F. R-38, op. 2, d. 317, l. 5–50b; d. 289, ll. 66, 68. See also Pal'vanova, *Emantsipatsiia musul'manki*, 31–34.

42. Karryeva, *Ot bespraviia*, 36.

43. Uz. St. Arch., F. R-86, op. 1, d. 4932, ll. 2, 4, 110b., 34–390b, 48–50. The meetings were held at workplaces and run by state representatives; attendees probably did not include clergy. For a fuller description of civil marriage laws, see Massell, *Surrogate Proletariat*, 210, 267ff.

44. This argument, that girls' bodies mature faster in hot climates, was also used to slip a line permitting marriage at age thirteen for girls in the Transcaucasus into the December 1917 decree on civil marriage in revolutionary Russia. Uz. St. Arch., F. R-38, op. 2, d. 28, l. 9. This opinion was also used by Russian lawmakers in discussions about civil marriage laws in Turkestan. Izzeddin Seifulmuluk apparently found it easy to imagine that the bodies of girls in Arabia underwent exotic early development, just as Russian lawmakers imagined about the bodies of girls from Turkestan and the Transcaucasus. Seifulmuluk, "Oila ham bola tarbiyasi," *Yangi Yo'l*, no. 11–12 (1926): 20.

45. Aminova, *October Revolution*, 52. Typically, local government committees gave out documents that falsified younger girls' ages so that the marriage could be registered legally. Russian-language reports tended to focus on egregious cases, in which eight- or nine-year-old girls were given in marriage, but these were very unusual cases. More typically, marriages were arranged for girls between ages fourteen and seventeen.

46. Bashiri, "Erk Yo'lida," *Yangi Yo'l*, no. 1 (1928): 14–15, 18, and no. 2 (1928): 11–13. The hadith this story implicitly refers to concerns a woman who "offered herself as a wife to the Prophet. Then, one of the men present asked the Prophet to give her in marriage to him if the Prophet had no wish for her." The Prophet asked what the man could give to the woman as mahr, but he had nothing. However, he knew some of the Quran, so the Prophet told him, "I hereby give you in marriage to her for what you know [and hence can teach her] of the Qur'an." Susan A. Spectorsky, *Chapters on Marriage and Divorce: Responses of Ibn Hanbal and Ibn Rahwayh* (Austin: University of Texas Press, 1993), 17. This version of the story is Spectorsky's translation of Ibn Hanbal, *Musnad* 5:330.

47. Rahbar-oi Olimova (b. 1908, Tashkent). A sovchi can be male or female,

but is usually a relative of the prospective husband. A woman sovchi visits homes where there are marriageable daughters, and after finding one she deems acceptable, makes her recommendations to the prospective husband or his relatives. After this, men sovchis are delegated to make the official proposal to men of the prospective wife's family, and to negotiate marriage conditions. New-style weddings varied considerably in Uzbekistan in the 1920s. New-style did not necessarily mean that the couple had a legal wedding registration or that they did not have an Islamic ceremony. Rather, it usually meant that men and women attended a wedding feast (*toi*) together instead of attending separate feasts.

48. Interviews with Bahriniso I. (b. 1910, Namangan region); Habibi Sh.(b. 1921, Kokand); Humoira H. (b. 1913, Kokand); Mafrat-xon M. (b. 1914, Kokand); Muhobat H. (b. 1917, Kokand); Shamsiyat B. (b.1918, Bukhara).

49. Saodat Shamsieva (b. 1908, To'rtqo'l); Bahriniso Y. (b. 1909, Kokand); Aisha B. (b. 1909, Ufa).

50. Sulaimanova gives a thorough treatment of family law in *Istoriia Sovietskogo gosudarstva i pravo Uzbekistana*, vol. 1, 253–76, and throughout vol. 2. See also Pal'vanova, *Emantsipatsiia musul'manki*, 27–29. Until the mid-1920s, Russian documents refer to Kazakhs as "Kirgiz," and to Kyrgyz as "Kara-Kirgiz."

51. G'afur G'ulom, "Gam tuguni," *Yangi Yo'l*, no. 11–12 (1928): 12–14. The judicial system had a policy of considering class as a mitigating factor in crime, with the wealthy deemed more culpable than the poor. "Yosh qizlarni erga berish bilan kurashamiz," *Yangi Yo'l*, no. 1 (1929): 24; Hakima, "Xotinlar huquqini pomol [*sic.*, poimol] qilg'uchi," *Yangi Yo'l*, no. 2 (1929): 5. The sum of money offered in one story, 270 rubles, equaled four or five times the monthly salary of a silk factory worker in Uzbekistan in 1929. In 1989, seeking to explain the persistence of qalin, Liushkevich argued that qalin forms one element in a life-long system of gift exchange and mutual obligation, and that to see it as the equivalent of medieval European bride-price is a false analogy. Liushkevich, "Traditsii mezhsemeninykh sviazei." Northrop documents the persistence of qalin and the Party's interest in charging its own members for their complicity in this "crime of everyday life," in *Veiled Empire*, especially chapter 7.

52. Mahbuba Rahim qizi, "Eski turmushning ikki maraziga qarshi: sho'ra qonuni yosh qizlarni erga berish va qalin bilan kurashadi," *Yangi Yo'l*, no. 6 (1929): 13; X. Obid, "Qalin molning kelib chiqishi," *Yangi Yo'l*, no. 6 (1929): 16–17.

53. Kisliakov, *Sem'ia i brak*, 145.

54. Interviews with Saodat A. (b. 1906, Xo'jand region, Tajikistan); Bahriniso I. (b. 1910, Namangan region); Mag'ruba Q. (b. 1929, Tashkent). In Central Asia, a *xoja* is one who claims descent from either the family of the Prophet Muhammad or from the Arabs who conquered Central Asia in the eighth century. Traditionally they were an endogamous group that prided themselves on purer Islamic practice and greater knowledge of Islam than other Central Asians. See Bruce Privratsky, *Muslim Turkistan: Kazak Religion and Collective Memory* (Richmond, Surrey: Curzon Press, 2001), 37–39. Faizulla Xo'jaev's surname indicated his membership in this social category. Before the revolution, some urban, educated

Muslims made a point of noting that mahr, as they practiced it, was Quranic and that they did not practice qalin, which was Central Asian, non-Quranic, and not regulated by Islamic law.

55. *Kommunisticheskaia Partiia Uzbekistana v resoliutsiiakh*, 210. In the Jadid period, critiques of Russian vices were direct, while in the 1920s they were veiled. In a story about women in Morocco, a *Yangi Yo'l* contributor wrote of Arab girls lured into Casablanca brothels for work, and commented, "The French brought to their own colony the corruption of European civilization, liquor, [and] syphilis." Toshkent-lik, "Quvnoq qizlar mahalasi," *Yangi Yo'l*, no. 7 (1928): 13–14.

56. Habiba, "Ikki g'uncha," *Yangi Yo'l*, no. 7 (1927): 14–15.

57. RGASPI, F. 62, op. 2, d. 883, ll. 51–55, 60.

58. Q. Karlieva, "Farg'ona viloyatidagi ishchi xotin-qizlar," *Yangi Yo'l*, no. 11–12 (1926): 19.

59. Oidin, "Fa'oliyat oldida to'suqlar bir pul," *Yangi Yo'l*, no. 11–12 (1928): 23–24. Obviously, an organization like the Women's Division, when it encouraged children to have their parents arrested, was going to face opposition and have image problems.

60. "Sud va ma'ishat," *Yangi Yo'l*, no. 11–12 (1928): 23–24.


6. UNVEILING BEFORE THE HUJUM

1. Saodat Shamsieva (b. 1908, To'rtqo'l). I was taken to the interview by Timur Valiev, who was the son of Saodat's deceased friend, Hosiyat Tillaxonova, and the son-in-law of the late Sobira Xoldarova, whose stories appear in chapter 5. Valiev participated in the interview. When I went to talk with Saodat, I had not yet read her published autobiography, "Na Sluzhbu dela Partii," in Finkel'shtein, *Probuzh-dennye velikim Oktiabrem*, 186–91, or her life-story interview, Zulhumor Solieva, "Sao-datli zamonda yashaimiz," *Saodat*, no. 11 (1988): 20–22. I knew that she had edited the Uzbek women's magazine, *Jarqin Turmuş*, in the 1930s and had suddenly dis-appeared from its list of editors in 1937. For a comparison of three versions of Sao-dat's life, see Kamp, "Three Lives of Saodat." This transcript eliminates most of my questions, Saodat's repetitions, and several topics that diverge from the themes of this volume.

2. Saodat's father had died, so her brother had responsibility for arranging her marriage.

3. The house was divided into *ichkari*—the inner court, where women stayed—and *tashkari*—the outer court, where male guests were entertained in the guest room, *mehmonxona*. Although this arrangement, in theory, kept women from being seen by nonfamily men, Saodat saw this young man when she cooked and served food to her brother and his guest. However, for a nonfamily male to hold conver-sation with a young woman of his host's family would have been considered improper.

4. In Uzbek, the expression used when a girl marries is that she "touches a husband" (*erga tegadi*).

5. In 1929–1930, Batu, chief of cultural affairs in the Uzbekistan Education Commissariat, and Ramiz, chief of the Scientific Research Institute of Uzbekistan and associated with the Education Commissariat, were purged from the Party and presumably shot. See Allworth, *Uzbek Literary Politics*, 77–78, nn. 17, 18, and 124–25, n. 14.

6. The CPUz Women's Division published *Yangi Yo'l* from late 1925 until 1930, when it became the journal of the Division of Agitation and Propaganda, closing in 1934. A magazine for women was revived in 1936 under a new name, *Jarqin Turmuş* (in 1937 Latin orthography). The name means "bright life," using a word encompassing existence, lifestyle, and family life. For the first few issues, Saodat was listed as an editor, but then her name disappeared. In 1938, *Jarqin Turmuş* became *Jarqin Hayat*, also meaning "bright life." *Jarqin Hayat* continued into the 1940s, was suspended, and then was revived in the 1950s under the name *O'zbekiston Xotin-Qizlar* (Uzbekistan Women and Girls). In 1970, the journal's name changed again, to *Saodat* (Contentment, or Happiness); it continues under this name to the present. Throughout this interview, Saodat used all the names of the women's journal somewhat interchangeably.

7. See chapter 5 for a discussion of who Oidin was.

8. Fotima Yo'ldoshbaeva had served with Saodat on the Uzbekistan Komsomol committee in 1929. Yo'ldoshbaeva was not purged in 1937; rather, she was one of the beneficiaries of vacancies resulting from the purge.

9. Saodat refers to the Party's effort to clear the accusations made against many Party members in the 1937 purge. Being cleared meant that she could reenter the Party and take higher-profile employment. In her 1988 interview, she mentioned that when she applied for clearance, the clerk expressed surprise, because according to her record she had been sentenced to execution. Solieva, "Saodatli zamonda."

10. The CPUz was dissolved shortly after Uzbekistan's independence (September 1, 1991). Some members, like Saodat, formally quit, while others still claimed to be members in 1993.

11. By "old" I meant a Muslim service, performed by a mullah (domla); by "new," a Komsomol or Red wedding—a nonreligious, government process, and mixed-gender feasting.

12. See chapter 5 for a discussion of the ZAGS. Saodat was about fifteen at the time of this marriage; evidently the Russian woman enabled the registration of her marriage without Saodat presenting herself at the ZAGS office.

13. In Uzbek, the term *yetim*, or orphan, is used when a child loses one parent or both parents.

14. In her 1960 autobiography, Saodat was more forthcoming about her Hujum activities. One of her public speeches for unveiling is discussed in chapter 7. See also Finkel'shtein, *Probuzhdennye velikim Oktiabrem*, 186–91.

15. Valiev gave more information about Sobira Xoldarova and Hosiyat Tillaxonova.

16. Ahmed, *Women and Gender in Islam*, 165. On unveiling movements in

various countries, see Badran, *Feminists, Islam, and Nation*; Minault, *Secluded Scholars*; Göle, *Forbidden Modern*; Camron Amin, *The Making of the Modern Iranian Woman: Gender, State Policy, and Popular Culture, 1865–1946* (Gainesville: University of Florida Press, 2002); and in the Soviet Union, Farideh Heyat, *Azeri Women in Transition: Women in Soviet and Post-Soviet Azerbaijan*, Central Asia Research Forum (London: Routledge/Curzon: 2002), chapter 5.

17. On the meaning of hijab for Islamists, see Arlene Macleod, *Accomodating Protest: Working Women, the New Veiling, and Change in Cairo* (New York: Columbia University Press, 1991). The fifteenth-century traveler, Roy Clavijo, observed that women in Timur's court wore black horsehair face veils. Cited in G. A. Pugachenkova, "K istorii parandzhi," *Sovetskaia Etnografiia*, no. 3 (1952): 194. Images of veiling with paranji and chachvon from the fifteenth through seventeenth centuries are found in Thomas W. Lentz and Glenn D. Lowrey, *Timur and the Princely Vision: Persian Art and Culture in the Fifteenth Century* (Washington, D.C.: Smithsonian Institution Press, 1989), 61, cat. no. 17; 163, cat. no. 32.; 186, cat. nos. 84 and 85. See also E. Iu. Iusupov, *Nizomiy "Xamsa" siga ishlagan rasmlar* (Toshkent: Fan, 1985), nos. 200, 201. The fifteenth-century evidence contradicts Northrop's assertion that the "ensemble of the paranji and chachvon . . . appeared only in the mid-nineteenth century." Northrop, *Veiled Empire*, 44.

18. Schuyler, *Turkistan*, 124; A. F. Middendorf, *Ocherki Ferganskoi Doliny* (St. Petersburg, 1882), 365.

19. Meakin, *In Russian Turkestan*, 55.

20. Humoira H. (b. 1913, Kokand).

21. Nalivkin and Nalivkina, *Ocherk byta zhenshchiny*, 31, 97–98, 118; Grebenkin, "Uzbeki," 64; Manzura H. (b. 1921, Tashkent); Manzura H.'s mother (b. 1902, Tashkent); Bahriniso I. (b. 1910, Namangan region). Northrop's reading of archival documents suggests that veiling may have become more common in villages in the 1920s and 1930s, even as it was decreasing in cities. My oral history research does not confirm this; most of those who lived through the 1930s in rural villages reported either radical or gradual decreases in paranji wearing (see chapter 9). Only one informant noted that the paranji first appeared in his village in the 1920s and remained until after World War II. I am instead inclined to believe that pressure on OGPU (Soviet secret police) staffers to report anti-Soviet phenomena prompted them to take increased note of existing paranji wearers and that Northrop's extensive reliance on these sources shapes his interpretation.

22. M. A. Bikdzhanova, "Odezhda Uzbekchek Tashkenta XIX-nachala XX v.," in *Kostium narodov srednei Azii*, ed. O. A. Sukhareva (Moskva: Iz. Nauka, 1979), 140–41.

23. Interviews, with particular reference to Aziza-xon I. (b. 1914, Marg'ilon), Humoira H. (b. 1913, Kokand), Muattar S. (b. 1899, Bukhara), To'xfa P. (b. 1928, Bukhara). Many visitors to Bukhara prior to the revolution noted that Jewish women observed the same veiling practices as Muslim women. M. V. Sazonova, "Zhenskii kostium Uzbekov Khorezma," in *Traditsionnaia odezhda narodov srednei Azii i Kazakhstana*, ed. N. P. Lobacheva, M. Sazonova, and I. V. Zakharova (Moskva: Nauka,

1989), 96; Bikdzhanova, "Odezhda Uzbekchek Tashkenta XIX-nachala XX v," 141; Sukhareva, *Istoriia sredneaziatskogo kostiuma*, 44; Nalivkin and Nalivkina, *Ocherk byta zhenshchiny*, 92, 95.

24. Grebenkin, "Uzbeki," 64.

25. Graf K. K. Palen, *Otchet po revisii Turkestanskago kraia, proizvedennoi po Vysochaishemu poveleniiu senatorom K. K. Palenom*, vol. 1, *Naronye sud'i* (St. Peterburg: Senatskaia Tip, 1909), 122. Palen's description of the work of "people's courts" in Central Asia, meaning Sharia and Adat (customary) courts, was uniformly critical, negative, and anecdotal. Palen was uninterested in the reasoning of qazis, who imprisoned Sarts for drinking beer, visiting brothels, or unveiling. He found it unreasonable that such religiously based decisions were made by judges who served the "cultured," "modern government" of Russia (123).

26. Nalivkin and Nalivkina, *Ocherk byta zhenshchiny*, 3.

27. Halle, *Women in the Soviet East*, 104.

28. `Abdulla ibn `Abdulla, *Izhar al-ta'asuf* (Kazan: Ikhar Shationof Matbu'asi, 1907); Mu'allima Kamila bint `Azatulla Qasimova, *Khanumlar islahi* (Kazan: Beraderan Karimilar, 1908), 28–30; Jemaladdin Validov, "Hijab mas`alasi," *Suyum Bike*, no. 8 (1914): 4–6.

29. Rorlich, *Volga Tatars*, 63 and nn.

30. Hasanov, "Qayuv hijab zararli?" *Alem-i Nisvan*, no. 7 (1907): 3–4.

31. Some Tatar women in Central Asia veiled. Two Tatar interviewees, Sara G. (b. 1916, Tashkent) and Sofia M. (b. 1920, Kokand), reported that some Tatar women, including Sara G.'s mother, wore chopans on their heads and that many abandoned wearing *yashmaks* (half-face veils) around the time of the revolution.

32. Khairullaev, *Islam i zhenshchiny vostoka*, 42; Abdugafurov was a proponent of more intrusive Russian rule in Turkestan. See A. Savitskii, *Sattarkhan Abdugafurov* (Tashkent: Uzbekistan, 1965); Azizzoda, *Yangi hayot kurashchilari*, 109–13; and Hamza Hakimzoda Niyoziy, "Tuhmatchilar jazosi," in *Boy ila xizmatchi: P'esalar* (1918; Toshkent: O'qituvchi, 1988), 82–83.

33. O'ktam, "Xotinlar masalasi."

34. Rahim Berdi, "Xotinlar ozodlig'i kommunistlar," *Turkiston*, Feb. 21, 1924, 3.

35. Azizzoda, *Yangi hayot kurashchilari*, 109–13.

36. Finkel'shtein, *Probuzhdennye velikim Oktiabrem*, 102.

37. "Ozodliq qaldirg'ochlari," *Turkiston*, Mar. 15, 1924, 3. G'azi Yunus and Mir Mashriq were both Turkestani authors, Jadids, and then Communists.

38. Rahbar-oi Olimova, "'Hujum' ishtirokchisi ekanimdan faxrlanaman . . ." *Guliston*, no. 5 (1988): 22–23. A number of these women are mentioned in chapter 5.

39. Putilovskaia, "Rabota kommunisticheskikh partii sredi zhenshchin narodov vostoka," *Kommunistka*, no. 12–13 (1921): 52–54; "Rezoliutsii 1 Vserossiskogo soveshshaniia organizatorov po rabote sredi zhenshchin narodov vostoka," *Kommunistka*, no. 12–13 (1921): 62–64; Hamit Yunusup, "Sharq xotin-qizlarning jihadi," *Qizil Bairoq*, May 22, 1921. According to Liubimova, "Eastern" was a relative term. Being oriental was a matter of "specific cultural and economic back-

wardness," not geography or ethnicity. Serafima Liubimova, *Rabota Partii sredi truzhen-its vostoka* (Moskva: Gos. Izdat, 1928), 3.

40. Tursunov, *Khudzhum znachit nastuplenie*, 139–43, 156–58; Finkel'shtein, *Probuzhdennye velikim Oktiabrem*, 22–42.

41. Vaian Kutur'e [Marie Vailliant-Couturier], "Vuali podnialis'," *Kommunistka*, no. 14–15 (1921): 16–17. The author was a French Communist intellectual and sister of Paul Vailliant-Couturier who published several books about Central Asia. She is identified as the author of the *Kommunistka* article in Tursunov, *Khudzhum znachit nastuplenie*, 141.

42. On Shamsikamar G'oibjonova's career, see Tursunov, *Khudzhum znachit nastuplenie*, 155–58; Finkel'shtein, *Probuzhdennye velikim Oktiabrem*, 101, 143, 223–27.

43. Badran, *Feminists, Islam, and Nation*, 92.

44. Bahriniso Y. (b. 1909, Kokand); Finkel'shtein, *Probuzhdennye velikim Oktiabrem*, 144. Kalinin appears often in Uzbek women's narratives, asking them to unveil. Stalin's remark shows his understanding of the manners of a hierarchical society. Among Uzbeks, refusing a request, especially one made by an elder, brings a serious loss of face. As with Hosiyat Tillaxonova, whose similar story appears in chapter 5, Ibrohimova could not refuse. Following the revolution, Ibrohimova created her own women's organization in Kokand; it became part of the Women's Division when the Communists created a branch in Kokand.

45. Manzura H. (b. 1921, Tashkent); Manzura H.'s mother (b. 1902, Tashkent).

46. Ch., "Xotinlar ozodlig'ig'a qarshi bo'lg'an shahslarga yaxshilab jazo berish lozim," *Ishchi Batraq maktublari*, Oct. 15, 1926, 3; Chernisheva, "Firqaning xotin-qizlarni ozodliqqa chiqarish ishiga imlar to'siqliq qiladur," *Yangi Yo'l*, no. 10 (1926): 17–18.

47. N., "Paranjidan qizil bo'yinboqqa," *Qizil O'zbekiston*, Mar. 6, 1925, 1.

48. Oidin [Manzura Sobir Qori qizi], *Yangilikka qadam (O'zbek to'rmishidan olingan 3 pardalik piyassa)* (1925; Toshkent: Ozbekiston Davlat Nashriioti, 1926).

49. Interview with Mafrat-xon M. (b. 1914, Kokand).

50. Malika-xon J. (b. 1912, Namangan); Uz. St. Arch., Namangan Filial, F. 302, personal file for Hadicha Kunasheva.

51. There are two accounts of the 1926 International Women's Day unveiling. One has Karomat Xonim as the second unveiler, and the other names Salomat Shamsieva. S. A., "Eski Toshkentda," *Qizil O'zbekiston*, Mar. 11, 1926, 2; M. Yaqubof, "8inchi Martg'a bir sovg'a," *Yangi Yo'l*, no. 3 (1927): 11. Bashorat Jalilova also appears in accounts as Jalolova. She appears in numerous memoirs, including that of Rahbar-oi Olimova, collecting Tashkent's daughters for education in either new-method or Soviet schools.

52. Massell explains the law-based approach in *Surrogate Proletariat*.

53. Massell, *Surrogate Proletariat*, xxxiii. I have noted above the peculiar use in Uzbek of the term "orphan." In conditions of premodern health care, many children lost at least one parent during childhood, and were thus "orphans." While the term turns up in a great many Uzbek biographies, it only rarely correlates to children becoming dependent on the state or brought up in orphanages.

# 7. THE HUJUM

1. Rahbar-oi Olimova (b. 1908, Tashkent). I was taken to interview Rahbar-oi by her daughter, Dilarom Alimova, an Uzbek historian who has written extensively about women (Olimova is the Uzbek spelling of her name, but she has published mainly as Alimova). Present at the interview were Alimova, her son and daughter (Nodira), and her brother. My understanding of Rahbar-oi's life is also based on an autobiographical article that she wrote, "Hujum ishtiroqchisi ekanimdan faxrlanaman . . . ," which translates to "I take pride that I happened to be a Hujum participant." I have removed most of my questions, dropped some parts of the interview, and reordered some material chronologically.

2. *Atlas* is woven, silk cloth with ikat dyed patterns.

3. A *ming-boshi* was a district administrative head, responsible for local tax collection and infrastructure.

4. Throughout this section, Rahbar-oi interspersed Russian words for bank, government, passport, and even grandmother. As noted in the introduction, in the Russian colonial period (1865–1917), Turkestanis were treated as unequal colonial subjects and passports were granted to them only on an exceptional basis, usually connected with government service.

5. A *fuzalo* was one who had composed his own scholarly treatise in one of the Islamic sciences. To be regarded as an olim (whence came Rahbar-oi's family name), a man had to successfully complete numerous years of study in the madrasa.

6. G'afur G'ulom became a famous Uzbek poet.

7. A *bek* was a wealthy landowner whose ancestors had obtained land through a grant from the ruler for military service.

8. See chapter 6, notes 13 and 53 on the Uzbek use of the term "orphan."

9. The older sister, presumably, was married and out of the house.

10. Prisoners of war from Germany, Austro-Hungary, and the Ottoman Empire who had been held in Tashkent were allowed out of prison to earn a living. See, for example, Fritz Willfort, *Turkestanisches Tagebuch: Sechs Jahre in russisch-Zentralasien* (Wien: Wilhelm Braumüller, 1930).

11. Bashorat Jalilova (see chapter 6) was one of the founders of the Bilim Yurt (see chapter 4). Rahbar-oi used an honorific form of her name, adding Xonim. Rahbar-oi called the school by another of its names, Dar al-Mu'allimot, or Abode of Women Teachers.

12. In a traditional Uzbek wedding, a band made up of drum, *nai*, and *surnai* would accompany the groom and his friends to the bride's family home for an evening feast; modernists substituted a brass band.

13. Uzbeks use "Marusa," a Russian name, as a condescending name for all Russian women who tie their headscarves under their chins. It suggests "hick."

14. As mentioned earlier, Massell draws on this analysis, which appears in several Russian activist accounts, for the title of his scholarly work, *Surrogate Proletariat*, and for his understanding of the Party's motivation for the campaign. Northrop extends this analysis, arguing that Party leaders pursued women's liberation

because their other strategies for creating the equivalent of a proletariat in Central Asia had failed. He notes in particular that the land reform campaign had not divided the rural poor from the rich to the extent that the Party desired. Northrop, *Veiled Empire*, 75–76. This sounds like an argument that some activists may have made in order to persuade the Party to take on another large campaign, but it had very little to do with the basic Party analysis of social structures in Uzbekistan; the Party continued with land reform and other measures designed to induce class conflict, and as I argue in the next chapter, placed far more emphasis on those programs than on women's liberation. The Party as a whole was not expecting that women would become a surrogate proletariat. The idea that women would become the Party's foot soldiers played no role at all in the arguments that Uzbeks used to convince their fellow Uzbeks to unveil.

15. I. A. Zelenskii, "Xotin-qizlar arasidagi ishlarda firqaning asosi vazifalari," *Qizil O'zbekiston*, Oct. 15, 1926, 2; Robiya Nosir [Nosirova], "Amaliy hujum," *Yangi Yo'l*, no. 1 (1927): 29. Pinar Vanderlippe pointed out to me the difference between *tajovuz* and *hujum*.

16. Aminova, *October Revolution*, 41–42; Serafima Liubimova, *Teoriia i praktika rabota Partii sredi zhehshchin* (Tashkent/Moskva: Turkpechat, 1926), 35. Northrop discusses at length the arguments among Russian Women's Division workers concerning unveiling and notes that several important figures in the Women's Division, like Liubimova and Zhukova, changed their positions in the course of the Hujum. Northrop, *Veiled Empire*, 284–301.

17. Nosir, "Amaliy Hujum."

18. Pal'vanova, *Emantsipatsiia musul'manki*, 178; Tursunov, *Khudzhum znachit nastuplenie*, 153; M. Mahmudov, "Tojixon Shodieva"; Shodieva, "Shodievaning qisqacha tarima-i holi."

19. *Yangi Yo'l*, no. 2 (1927): 16.

20. A'zam, "Satang taklifi," *Qizil O'zbekiston*, Feb. 8, 1927, 2.

21. B. H., "Sakuchilar paranjini o'tib tashladilar," *Qizil O'zbekiston*, Mar. 6, 1927, 2.

22. Aisha B. (Tatar, b. Ufa, 1909).

23. Bahriniso I. (b. 1910, Namangan region).

24. Interview with O'lmas-oi H. (b. 1912, Kokand).

25. Mafrat-xon M. (b. 1914, Kokand).

26. Interview with Milli-xon Ibrohimova (b. 1911, Kokand region). Ibrohimova was a retired city mayor.

27. Manzura H. (b. 1921, Tashkent); Manzura H.'s mother (b. 1902, Tashkent).

28. RGASPI, F. 62, op. 2, d. 883, ll. 31, 42–48, 60, accounts from Kokand, Samarkand, Andijon, Xo'jand; d. 1691, l. 68, ff, Andijon.

29. C. Amin, *Making of the Modern Iranian Woman*, 83.

30. Photos of women from the late 1920s frequently show them wearing a large, silky, crocheted scarf that was made in Kokand and became widely fashionable among the unveiled. Halle, in *Women in the Soviet East*, describes Jahon Obidova in the early 1930s: "Abidova pulled the Orenburg shawl from her shoulders to her

head with an accustomed gesture that seemed almost automatic . . . she had doubt-less been in the habit of pulling up her paranja with exactly the same gesture not long ago." (304). Orenburg shawls of crocheted cashmere became popular throughout the Soviet Union. In Uzbekistan, they are still worn as a secondary cov-ering; a thinner scarf covers the hair and is tied at the back of the neck, and the Orenburg shawl is drapped overtop and hangs loosely, except when women cover their mouths with it. In other countries this might be called veiling. In Uzbekistan it is not.

31. Yelena G'lazqova [Glazkova], "Ochilg'an o'zbek xotin-qizlarg'a ko'makga," *Yangi Yo'l*, no. 8 (1928): 5–6; Halida, "Tutning mevasi pishdi," *Yangi Yo'l*, no. 2 (1928): 12.

32. Sobira [Xoldarova], "Yangilik," *Yer Yuzi*, no. 20 (1927): 8–10; *Chachvon* was reviewed in *Yer Yuzi*, no. 28–29 (1927): 12–13; M. Sh., "Paranji," *Yangi Yo'l*, no. 2 (1929): 7–8.

33. *Pravda Vostoka*, May 23, 1929, 3.

34. Miyon Bo'zruk [Solixov], "Paranjining chiqishi," *Yangi Yo'l*, no. 7 (1927): 8–10. Miyon Bo'zruk's thought here is a clear continuation of Jadid thought, shar-ing Fitrat's concern over unsuitable and ignorant mothers. Miyon Bo'zruk stud-ied at Istanbul University for six years, returning to Uzbekistan in 1927, hence his close links with Turkish thought on women and unveiling.

35. G'azi Yunus, "Paranji va uning kelib chiqishi," *Qizil O'zbekiston*, Feb. 3, 1927, 2. G'azi Yunus and other Jadids in the Communist Party persisted in understand-ing the Party's antireligious policy as an opportunity to "purify" Islam by eradi-cating "superstitious" practices.

36. Hamza Hakimzoda Niyoziy, "Bu kun 8–Mart," in *Hamza Hakimzoda Niyoziy, Mukammal asarlar to'plami*, vol. 3 (Toshkent: Fan, 1981), 67–68. The poem was first published in the newspaper *Yangi Farg'ona* on March 8, 1927. Although Hamza is understood as an antireligious activist, an OGPU analysis of his death linked him instead to the continuing Jadid understanding that certain forms of Islam were oppressive and superstitious and needed to be "purified." For Hamza, "fanaticism" was a distortion of true religion, and that was why he led the attack on the Shah-i Mardon shrine, an action that proved fatal. RGASPI, F. 62, op. 2, d. 1741, ll. 246–253, compiled June to Oct. 1929.

37. Humoira H. (b. 1913, Kokand); Sottiba-xon M. (b. 1920, Namangan); Muat-tar S. (b. 1899, Bukhara).

38. Saodat A. (b. 1906, Nai, Tajikistan). Similar comments came from Bahri-niso I. (b. 1910, Namangan region), and Mafrat-xon M. (b. 1914, Kokand) as well as from many interviewees in the collectivization oral history project, whose com-ments are noted in chapter 9.

39. Interview with Mahtab-oi A. (b. 1901, Charjui). She said that at the store, her husband was forced to deny God's existence and he came home weeping.

40. Interview with Havo-xon Ataqulova (b. 1923, Kokand region). Ataqulova was a locally famous Communist. When she was thirteen, her Pioneer organi-zation's leadership arranged for her to attend a Komsomol meeting in Moscow.

They forged documents to make her appear old enough to be a Komsomol member. In Moscow, she met Stalin, and her photo and articles about her appeared in local newspapers.

41. Aziza-xon I. (b. 1914, Marg'ilon).

42. Interviews with Muattar S. (b. 1899, Bukhara); Halima M. (b. 1922, Bukhara). Shamsiyat B. (b. 1918, Bukhara) also said women did not veil after 1928. Zhukova, a Women's Division worker in Bukhara, reported on the quick and thorough unveiling in Bukhara in 1928 and attributed the Hujum's success to the Bukharan Communist Party's careful preparations. "Mestnye Rabotniki ob izdanii dekreta," *Kommunistka*, no. 1 (1929): 34–35; RGASPI, F. 62, op. 2, d. 1503, l. 46, report on Mar. 8, 1928.

43. Ho'shvaqt I. (b. 1916, Bukhara region).

44. RGASPI, F. 62, op. 2, d. 1503, ll. 42–49.

45. Aminova, *October Revolution*, 93.

46. Ho'shvaqt I. (b. 1916, Bukhara region).

47. Dilarom Alimova, "Istoriografiia: Zhenskii vopros v sovetskoi istoriografii srednei Azii 20–x godov," *Obshchestvennye nauki v Uzbekistan*, no. 11 (1989): 53–54.

48. RGASPI, F. 62, op. 2, d. 1691, l. 43. These files are OGPU reports from 1928 on the "national intelligentsia" understanding of unveiling in Turkey.

49. Göle, *Forbidden Modern*, 71–74, 77–78.

50. Emelie Olson, "Muslim Identity and Secularism in Contemporary Turkey: 'The Headscarf Dispute,'" *Anthropological Quarterly* 58, no. 6 (1985): 162, 164–65.

51. C. Amin, *Making of the Modern Iranian Woman*, 82.

52. Z. Arat, "Kemalism and Turkish Women," 62, 63.

53. Göle, *Forbidden Modern* 14.

54. There were no Communist Party policies regarding men's dress. If anything, some male Party members who had been interested in European dress during the Jadid period placed new emphasis on national "authenticity." Hamza, who was photographed in European, dandy-style suit and haircut in 1915, appeared in his 1920s portaits dressed in a chopan and a do'ppi.

55. Douglas Northrop, "Languages of Loyalty: Gender, Politics, and Party Supervision in Uzbekistan, 1927–1941," *Russian Review* 59, no. 2 (2000): 179–200.

56. Rali, "Afg'on xotinlarning taqdiri yechilmakda," *Yangi Yo'l*, no. 2 (1929): 7.

57. C. Amin, *Making of the Modern Iranian Woman*.

58. The pervasive violence against women in Uzbekistan over unveiling does raise the question: why did Turkey and Iran, where there were also unpopular, state-supported unveiling campaigns, not see similar violence against women? The question may reveal flawed logic, an assumption that the Uzbek case was somehow a normal social response to unveiling, and thus such violence might be expected elsewhere. I address this in chapter 8. However, violence against women appears to loom large in statistics, not necessarily because violence itself increases but because reporting increases. For example, there was a strong rise in rape statistics in America after the 1960s, but many analysts attribute this not to a rise in instances of

rape, but to a rise in the acceptability and encouragement of reporting by the victims. A similar rise in reports of "honor killings" in Jordan also cannot be interpreted to mean that there are more such murders, only that more are reported. In Soviet Uzbekistan, the Women's Division and the Communist Party, as well as the OGPU, actively sought reports, promoted prosecution, and collected statistics on murders, rapes, assaults, and verbal attacks on women who unveiled. One might question whether in Turkey and Iran the lack of agencies to collect such information, and perhaps the lack of media promotion of the idea that instances should be reported, compounded by a lack of archivally based historical research about this period, leads to an unfounded impression that unveiling was carried out without violent attacks on the unveiled.

59. Pal'vanova, *Emantsipatsiia musul'manki*, 196.

60. Karryeva, *Ot bespraviia*, 120–21.

61. Husain, "Yana xotinlarni ochish to'g'risida," *Qizil O'zbekiston*, Feb. 7, 1927, 2–3.

62. Hadicha, "Hujumimiz muvaffaqiyatlik," *Yangi Yo'l*, no. 4 (1927): 3–4. The article was for the May 1, 1927, May Day holiday, which, like International Women's Day, was celebrated in Uzbekistan with mass unveilings.

63. VI Plenum Ts. K. KP(b) Uzbekistana, Samarkand, 13–15 Iunia 1927 g., in *Kommunisticheskaia Partiia Uzbekistana v rezoliutsiiakh*, 302.

64. Aminova, *October Revolution*, 101.

65. D. Alimova, *Zhenskii vopros v srednei Azii*, 31–32.


## 8. THE COUNTER-HUJUM: TERROR AND VEILING

1. There is no complete account of numbers of women killed during this period. Niurina, of the CAB Women's Division, set the number of Uzbek women killed from November 1927 to May 1928 at 235. F. Niurina, "Usilit' podgotovku kul'turnykh kadrov vostoka," *Kommunistka*, no. 5–6 (1929): 25. Sulaimanova cited 270 as an "incomplete" figure for the number murdered in 1928 alone, in *Gosudarstvo i prava*, vol. 2, 329. Babakhodzhaeva put the figure for 1927 and 1928 at "more than 400," in Tursunov, *Khudzhum znachit nastuplenie*, 76. None of the Soviet historians cites data for 1929 and later years, though the murder wave continued. Pal'vanova, on the basis of archival research, cites higher figures: 300 women murdered in Samarkand province between 1926 and 1928, and more than 2,500 in Uzbekistan, "women activists—members of village and regional Councils, leaders of women's clubs and libraries, participants in the arts." Pal'vanova, *Emantsipatsiia musul'manki*, 197.

2. The former approach characterizes Aminova, *October Revolution*, while the latter describes Pal'vanova, *Emantsipatsiia musul'manki*.

3. Soviet historians like Aminova, in *October Revolution*, and Karryeva, in *Ot bespraviia*, regarded the murders as evidence that the Party and government pushed the campaign in inappropriate ways—launched it too soon, with too many errors—and did not fulfill their duties to protect women. Alimova concurs with

Party analysts from the late 1920s who considered male Uzbek Party members inadequately prepared for the unveiling campaign. D. Alimova, *Zhenskii vopros v srednei Azii*, 25, 76. The editors of *Ozbekistonning Yangi Tarixi* argue that the campaign sparked violence because it was carried out in a hurried way, with many injustices, such as forced unveilings, that provoked the people whose whole worldview was challenged by this Communist effort. M. Jo'raev, ed., *O'zbekistonning yangi tarixi*, vol. 2, *O'zbekiston Soviet mustamlakachiligi davrida* (Toshkent: Sharq, 2000), 379–84. In *Veiled Empire*, Northrop echoes Party analysts from the 1920s who tabulated murders of women in a long list of "crimes in everyday life," lumping violent crimes (murder and rape) in with continuing traditional practices, such as polygyny, qalin, and the marriage of minors—as though murdering women was just as ordinary a practice as arranging marriage.

4. Shirin Akiner, "Contemporary Central Asian women," in *Post-Soviet Women: From the Baltic to Central Asia*, ed. Mary Buckley (Cambridge: Cambridge University Press, 1997), 271.

5. My interpretation of this violence is influenced by Sulaimanova, who discusses the murders of women within a context of other violent crimes in *Gosudarstvo i prava*, vol. 2, 318–32.

6. Carroll Smith-Rosenberg, *Disorderly Conduct: Visions of Gender in Victorian America* (New York: Knopf, 1985), 48–49. Smith-Rosenberg builds on Mary Douglas, *Natural Symbols: Explorations of Cosmology* (New York: Pantheon, 1970).

7. Basic works on the topic of collectivization in Uzbekistan include Aminova, *Agrarnye preobrazovaniia*; and Rakhima Aminova, *Osushchestvlenie kollektivizatsii v Uzbekistane (1929–1932 gg.)* (Tashkent: Iz. Fan Uzbekskoi SSR, 1977).

8. "Laqlaqa qotillari sud mahkamasida," *Yer Yuzi*, no. 8 (1926): 14–15.

9. RGASPI, F. 62, op. 2, d. 1813, ll. 4–5, June to Nov. 1929.

10. Hosiyat Tillaxonova, "O'zbekistonda ipakchilik ishining ravnaqi," *Yangi Yo'l*, no. 6 (1928): 6–7.

11. Keller, *To Moscow, Not Mecca*, 171–74.

12. Bahriniso I. (b. 1910, Namangan region).

13. RGASPI, F. 62, op. 2, d. 1691, ll. 3–4.

14. Druzhinina, "Probuzhdennye zhenshchiny vostoka," *Kommunistka* 1, no. 18 (1922): 19.

15. Karlieva, "Vakila Shermatovaning o'ldirishi," *Yangi Yo'l*, no. 1 (1927): 36. The trial news appeared in *Qizil O'zbekiston*, Mar. 18, 1927.

16. The Communist Party of the Soviet Union expanded dramatically in 1924 in what was known as the Lenin levy. In the Turkestan ASSR, the party expanded from about 1,700 members and candidates in 1923 to 7,538 members and candidates in 1924. During 1924 it grew to 14,623, and of those members 6,254 were Uzbek. Between October 1924, the founding of the Uzbekistan Communist Party, and 1926, the Party again increased to 24,383. In 1928, the Party numbered 31,133, with 14,285 Uzbek members, 379 of whom were women. *Kommunisticheskaia Partiia Uzbekistana v tsifrakh: Sbornik statisticheskikh materilov, 1924–1977 gg.* (Tashkent: Uzbekistan, 1979), tables 2, 3, 13, 21, 26, 37, 42. A set of notes on land reform

contains fascinating characterizations of the kinds of people the Party relied on to carry out its reforms, depicting many bases for their unreliablity. RGASPI, F. 62, op. 2, d. 1266, ll. 58–68, Feb. 1928.

17. The OGPU was one of the predecessors to the KGB. In the late 1920s, the OGPU was becoming a strong force, operating at the behest of Party leadership and apart from local law enforcement officials. The OGPU collected information on political activities within villages and reported to the head of the CAB.

18. There is an interesting contrast with Iran, where prostitutes apparently veiled like other women and were forbidden to unveil when Iran's unveiling campaign was underway in the 1930s. Officials were told "that if the prostitutes would take husbands, they could then remove their veils like other respectable women." C. Amin, *Making of the Modern Iranian Woman*, 99.

19. RGASPI, F. 62, op. 2, d. 883, ll. 52–53 (an OGPU report); "Sharixonda yana bir yavvoiliq," *Qizil O'zbekiston*, Mar. 22, 1927, 2. Kassansoi and Shahrixon are in the Fargana Valley. Northrop interprets Party members re-veiling their wives in Shahrixon as evidence of their "primary loyalty" to "Uzbek Muslim culture." Northrop, *Veiled Empire*, 224. I would suggest that, in response to this murder, their main motivation was to protect life and reputation.

20. "G'alabani qo'ldan bermaimiz," *Qizil O'zbekiston*, Apr. 7, 1927, 4.

21. RGASPI, F. 62, op. 2, d. 1503, ll. 47–48. Repeated use of the number sixty suggests approximation.

22. Bahriniso I. (b. 1910, Namangan region).

23. RGASPI, F. 62, op. 2, d. 1691, ll. 7–10.

24. RGASPI, F. 62, op. 2, d. 1503, l. 49, 1928.

25. RGASPI, F. 62, op. 2, d. 1391, ll. 9–10.

26. RGASPI, F. 62, op. 2, d. 1691, ll. 13–16.

27. "Yavvoiy burgut Qumrini changallamokchi," *Qizil O'zbekiston*, Mar. 20, 1927.

28. RGASPI, F. 62, op. 2, d. 1691, ll. 5–15; F. 62, op. 2, d. 883, ll. 39–40, 61.

29. RGASPI, F. 62, op. 2, d. 883, l. 33, June 1927.

30. RGASPI, F. 62, op. 2, d. 1691, ll. 6–8, 75–85, Jan. to Aug. 1928.

31. Saodat in Solieva, "Saodatli zamonda."

32. RGASPI, F. 62, op. 2, d. 1503, ll. 49–50.

33. RGASPI, F. 62, op. 2, d. 1691, ll. 5–13, 68–93.

34. RGASPI, F. 62, op. 2,. d. 1691, l. 109.

35. Rahbar-oi Olimova (b. 1908, Tashkent); Mafrat-xon M. (b. 1914, Kokand); Aziza-xon I. (b. 1914, Marg'ilon); RGASPI F. 62, op. 2, d. 1691, l. 50.

36. For example, Oidin, "Fa'oliyat oldida tusuqlar bir pul."

37. "O'zbekiston sho'ralarining 2inchi qurultayi tarafidan butun mehnatkash-larga murojaat," *Yangi Yo'l*, no. 4 (1927): 3–5.

38. Rahbar-oi Olimova (b. 1908, Tashkent); Shimko, "Yangi turmushga ko'chich oldida," *Yangi Yo'l*, no. 4 (1927): 9–11.

39. Hosiyat Tillaxonova, "Hujum masalsini mustahkamlash kerak," *Yangi Yo'l*, no. 9 (1927): 5.

40. T. Sa'adi, "Ozodliq qurboni (voqe'i hikoya)" *Yangi Yo'l*, no. 12 (1927): 18.

41. Zarif Bashir, "Ozodliq qurbonsiz bo'lmaidi," *Yangi Yo'l*, no. 3 (1928): 18–20; O'gay, "Qanli sahifalar (sud zalidan)," *Yangi Yo'l*, no. 7 (1928): 4; "Ozodliq dushmanlari ulum va `azob," *Yangi Yo'l*, no. 2 (1929): 16; G'afur G'ulom, "Hulkar tole'i," *Yangi Yo'l*, no. 4 (1928): 18–19.

42. Maqsud qizi, "Zainab Qurbon qizi," *Yangi Yo'l*, no. 8 (1928): 8; "Zainab Qurbonova," *Yangi Yo'l*, no. 9 (1928): 23. The incident took place in a Lokai village in Tajikistan. Similar stories include Saida, "Adolat oining qotili"; Maya, "Ozod xotinlar himoya talab,"*Yangi Yo'l*, no. 10 (1928): 23; "Ozodliq dushmanlariga ramdillik bo'lmasin," *Yangi Yo'l*, no. 2 (1929): 6; N., "Shuro sudining sinfi siyosati to'g'rimi?" *Yangi Yo'l*, no. 3 (1929): 9–10; and A. Qobili, "Hujumchilar jallodlari," *Yangi Yo'l*, no. 4 (1929): 21.

43. W. Fitzhugh Brundage, introduction to *Under Sentence of Death: Lynching in the South*, ed. Brundage (Raleigh: University of North Carolina Press, 1997), 11.

44. Fatima Mernissi, *Beyond the Veil: Male-Female Dynamics in a Muslim Society*, rev. ed. (Bloomington: Indiana University Press, 1987).

45. See, for example, the story of Nurxon Yo'ldoshxo'jaeva later in this chapter.

46. Yotam Feldner, "'Honor Murders'—Why the Perps Get Off Easy," *Middle East Quarterly* 7, no. 4 (Dec. 2000): 41–50.

47. "Honor killing" is a term that I borrow from wider literature on the topic; it is not a term that I have found in Uzbek documents or in other Uzbek usage. I explore this aspect of the murder wave in Marianne Kamp, "Femicide as Terrorism: The Case of Uzbekistan's Unveiling Murders," in *Religions and Violence across Time and Tradition*, ed. James Wellman (Lanham, MD: Rowan and Littlefield, 2007).

48. Northrop, *Veiled Empire*, 186.

49. RGASPI, F. 62, op. 2, d. 883, ll. 51–52; d. 1391, ll. 9–10.

50. Northrop, "Languages of Loyalty."

51. Muratova, like prior CAB Women's Division leaders, was sent to Central Asia from assignments elsewhere in the Soviet Union in June 1927. She stayed until 1931. Her biography suggests she was a Cossack from Ukraine. She was appointed due to her expertise in Women's Division work; she was not familiar with Central Asian languages or culture before arriving. Tursunov, *Khudzhum znachit nastuplenie*, 131–36.

52. Interestingly, Kalianova's xo'ja identity was used as evidence of her alien class, but Zakir Xo'ja's membership in the same hereditary group did not provoke questions about his status as a landless peasant, the officially trusted class.

53. RGASPI, F. 62, op. 2, d. 1741, ll. 3–117, July to Oct. 1929. I have left most names from this report in their Russian transliteration form. Kalianova is the Russian transliteration; the Uzbek transliteration would probably be Kalonova.

54. Jahon Obidova's memoir in Finkel'shtein, *Probuzhdennye velykim Oktiabrem*, 118–19. Obidova was involved as a prosecutor in a number of show trials in 1929. The Kasimovshchina trials were covered extensively in *Qizil O'zbekiston* from March until May of 1930. Before March, court cases against murderers of women were frequently reported. After the Kasimovshchina began, that coverage stopped.

55. As Northrop documents in *Veiled Empire*, 333–35, violence against the unveiled continued through the 1930s. However, evidence suggests that the numbers of victims dropped from their peak in the late 1920s.

56. Yo'ldoshbaeva, *Moia sud'ba*, 66–68. The account, written for the Komsomol press, used colorful imagery; case files for the murders of actresses show complex and widespread investigations and arrests.

57. RGASPI, F. 62, op. 2, d. 1691, l. 93.

58. RGASPI, F. 62, op. 2, d. 1691, ll. 20, 85.

59. Serafima Liubimova, "Dekret o chadre i obshchestvo 'doloi kalym i mnogozhenstvo,'" *Kommunistka*, no. 8 (1928): 73.

60. See chapter 5. The power of age hierarchy and social hierarchy in Uzbek culture is such that younger Uzbeks normally assent verbally to any request made by someone who is significantly older, and those in weaker social positions normally assent to whatever those in stronger positions demand. Of course, verbal assent does not ensure actual compliance in action. Another revealing example appears in Fotima Yo'ldoshbaeva's memoir, Iuldashbaeva, *Moia sud'ba*, 44–47.

61. Liubimova, "Dekret o chadre i obshchestvo 'doloi kalym i mnogozhenstvo,'" 74.

62. Liubimova, "Dekret o chadre i obshchestvo 'doloi kalym i mnogozhenstvo,'" 74–75.

63. "Nuzhno li izdat' dikret, zapreshchaiushchii noshenie chadry," *Kommunistka*, no. 8 (1928): 79–81.

64. "Mestnye rabotniki ob izdanii dekreta," *Kommunistka*, 32–34. Oxunboboev was the only leading Uzbek Communist who actually had a poor peasant background. Northrop notes that later Zhukova changed her mind and supported a decree. Northrop, *Veiled Empire*, 296–97.

65. Massell, *Surrogate Proletariat*, 350; Vakila, "Faranjiga qirg'in! Sharq xotin-qizlari arasida ishlovchilar 4inchi maslahat majlisi to'g'risida," *Yangi Yo'l*, no. 1 (1929): 2–3; "Nima uchun dekret chiqarilmadi?" *Yangi Yo'l*, no. 6 (1929): 2–3.

66. Typical stories include Rali, "Dekret chiqarilsin!," *Yangi Yo'l*, no. 2 (1929): 4; "Xotinlar majlislari nima deydi," *Yangi Yo'l*, no. 5 (1929): 25; "Paranji yopinishni man' qiladurg'on qonun chiqarilsin," *Qizil O'zbekiston*, Apr. 2, 1929, 4; and "Xotin-qizlar paranjiga qarshi," *Qizil O'zbekiston*, Apr. 11, 1929, 3. Also, Rahbar-oi Olimova (b. 1908, Tashkent); and Saodat Shamsieva in Finkel'shtein, *Probuzhdennye velikim Oktiabrem*, 186–91, for a translation, see Kamp, "Three Lives of Saodat."

67. "Xotin qizlar ozodliq haqida," *Qizil O'zbekiston*, Apr. 17, 1929, 3.

68. In the 1929–1930 purge, documents regarding the Kasimovshchina featured Uzbek Party members denouncing one another for association with nationalist, anti-Soviet groups. Members of the group of eighteen, connected with Munavvar Qori, were also said to oppose the liberation of women. Those named included Batu, Salimxon Tillaxon, and Laziz Azizzoda, all of whom had track records as strong proponents of women's education and public roles. RGASPI, F. 62, op. 2, d. 2199, 2338, from 1930.

69. "Nima uchun dekret chiqarilmadi?" The writer's information was incorrect; Turkey did not enact a law against veiling broadly, but did ban veils from certain public places. Another article dismissed Afghanistan's failed attempts at unveiling women not as "liberation" but as "bourgeois Europeanization." Rali, "Afg'on xotinlarining taqdiri yechilmokda."

70. French Muslim feminists who support the 2004 French ban on veiling in schools make the same argument. Jane Kramer, "Taking the Veil," *New Yorker*, Nov. 11, 2004, 59–71.

71. "Xotinqizlarni himoya qilish yo'lida," *Qizil O'zbekiston*, Apr. 3, 1929, 1; Uz. St. Arch., F. R-86, op. 1, d. 4450, l. 14, on sentences for murderers of women, 1927, Fargana.

72. Karryeva, *Ot bespraviia*, 126.

73. Sulaimanova, *Gosudarstvo i prava*, vol. 2, 541–42. This law also allowed anonymous denunciation, which was permitted throughout the Soviet Union during the 1930s purges; its genesis probably had nothing to do with murders of women in Uzbekistan, but the application was useful for prosecution.

74. RGASPI, F. 62, op. 2, d. 2541 lists numerous collectivization-related murders, as well as some murders of women activists, in an OGPU file titled "On Antisoviet and Terrorist Acts," 1931. Rustambek Shamsutdinov gives a figure of 113 murders related to collectivization from January to August 1930. Shamsutdinov, *O'zbekistonda Sovetlarnin quloqlashtirish siyosati va uning fojeali oqibatlari* (Toshkent: Sharq, 2001), 12.

75. RGASPI, F. 62, op. 2, d. 1691, l. 113.

## 9. CONTINUITY AND CHANGE IN UZBEK WOMEN'S LIVES

1. Soviet historians like Aminova, in *October Revolution*, focus solely on the successes; Northrop, by contrast, paints a bleak portrait of ongoing failure in *Veiled Empire*.

2. Clements suggests that the Women's Division's demise was in part related to the Hujum. Clements, *Bolshevik Women*, 272. Massell sees the end of the Women's Division as consistent with the Party's "self-liquidating" policy for many organizations. Massell, *Surrogate Proletariat*, 257–59. Wood considers the threat of dissolution as almost inherent in the idea of having a separate women's division within the Communist Party, and notes that the 1930 dissolution was officially linked to the idea that women had been "brought up" to men's level. Wood, *Baba and the Comrade*, 221. Northrop details the internal Party conflict over the Hujum's apparent failure in 1928 and 1929. Northrop, *Veiled Empire*, 284–301.

3. On the creation and dispersal of the Party's Muslim Bureau and Jewish Section, as well as the Party's turn against nationalists, see Martin, *Affirmative Action Empire*, and Bennigsen and Wimbush, *Muslim National Communism in the Soviet Union*.

4. Şirin Tekeli, "Introduction: Women in Turkey in the 1980s," 13.

5. Like their male comrades, women activists were charged with nationalism and with sinister efforts to undermine the Soviet state. Northrop argues that accu-

sations of gender infractions "figured . . . as a justification for purges," linking these implicitly with the vast purge of 1937. Northrop, *Veiled Empire*, 240. A broader reading of purge documents shows that the NKVD targeted Uzbeks based on class affiliation, role in the economy, connections with disfavored elites, as well as on more far-fetched accusations of having foreign connections and conspiring to overthrow Soviet rule. In the litany of crimes, having a veiled wife was probably raised whereever it would stick, but was not the state's primary reason for purging or arresting a Party member in 1937.

6. Northrop, in *Veiled Empire*, follows efforts to unveil women and to enforce Soviet laws, as well as popular opposition to these programs, through the 1930s and 1940s.

7. Abdumalik Razzoqov, *O'zbekistonda paxtachlik tarixi* (Toshkent: O'zbekistan, 1994), 160.

8. For example, RGASPI, F. 62, op. 2, d. 2541, Dec. 1931.

9. Interviews with B. U. (b. 1913); T. D. (b. 1917); P. B. (b. 1915); M. T. (b. 1921); Q. T. (b. 1906); R. X. (b. 1922); U. X. (b. 1919); X. A. (b. 1919); one of the guests at the interview of B. X. (b. c. 1900).

10. Interviews with F. S. (b. 1915); R. Sh. (b. 1917); N. B. (b. 1916); Raj. Sh. (b. 1912); N. J. (b. 1921); U. M. (b. 1922); A. J. (b. 1912).

11. Interviews with O. X. (b. 1903); S. M. (b. 1913); R. S. (b. 1924); Z. A. (b. 1916); Z. X. (b. 1922); E. S. (b. 1923).

12. Interviews with L. U. (b. 1919); O. B. (b. 1922); B. Sh. (b. 1907).

13. Interviewees spoke about being forced to join the kolkhoz, and women about being forced to work on the kolkhoz. When remembering unveiling, most gave very little attention to the moment and simply said, "There was a meeting, and we threw it off." By comparison with their memories of the experience of collectivization, memories of unveiling seemed insignificant.

14. Milli-xon Ibrohimova (b. 1911, Kokand); Hojiraxon Kirgizbaeva (b. 1918, Namangan). Kirgizbaeva was a retired prosecutor.

15. Northrop, *Veiled Empire*, 314–34, quotation 325.

16. Northrop, *Veiled Empire*, 347–51.

17. Tsentral'noe Statisticheskoe Upravlenie, *Itogi vsesoiuznoi perepisi naselenii 1959*, 42, table 25.

18. Rates of schooling are taken from 1959 census tables that show numbers per cohort with completed higher education, numbers with incomplete higher and complete or incomplete middle-school education, and numbers with complete and incomplete primary education. The numbers rise for the age twenty to twenty-four cohort, where in rural communities 899 men of 1,000 had some education, as did 765 women per 1,000. Thus the statistics for the age ten to nineteen group may reflect that many children began school late, well after age ten, and that adult courses were still significantly contributing to mass education. Tsentral'noe Statisticheskoe Upravlenie, *Itogi vsesoiuznoi perepisi naselenii 1959*.

19. There are problems with comparability. By leaving out the over-fifty population, Uzbekistan could ignore that the majority of that group were illiterate,

thus skewing their statistics upward. Nonetheless, Soviet mass education policies made literacy widely available, and while Soviet gender policies did not do all they aspired to do, they mainly overcame a social prejudice against education for girls. William Fierman notes that numbers of children in schools dropped in 1945 and were stagnant through much of the 1950s. Fierman, "The Soviet 'Transformation,'" in *Soviet Central Asia: The Failed Transformation* (Boulder, CO: Westview, 1991), 31.

20. Tsentral'noe Statisticheskoe Upravlenie, *Itogi vsesoiuznoi perepisi naselenii 1959*, 46–47, table 31. In 1939, women were 47 percent of those working in the agricultural sphere; in 1959, women were 53 percent of the agricultural labor force and 60 percent of all nonspecialized workers in agriculture. Ibid., 83, 92, 114, 120, figures from tables 42, 43, 47, 48, 49.

21. Tsentral'noe Statisticheskoe Upravlenie, *Itogi vsesoiuznoi perepisi naselenii 1959*, 119–23, table 48.

22. *O'zbekiston xotin-qizlar 1 s'ezdi, 1958, 7–8 Mart. Stenographik hisobat* (Toshkent: O'zbekiston SSR Davlat Nashriyoti, 1960), 31. Infant mortality rates in some parts of Central Asia in the 1920s were judged to be around 40 percent. There are serious problems with reliability of infant mortality statistics for the Soviet Union. Ellen Jones and Fred W. Grupp, *Modernization, Value Change and Fertility in the Soviet Union* (Cambridge: Cambridge University Press, 1987), 39–44, 100–102.

23. Uzbeks in the Party grew from 49 percent in 1927 to 61 percent in 1933, but breakdowns of women by nationality are not given in published statistics for most years.

24. In 1937, Uzbeks were reduced to 52 percent of Party members and candidates and in 1938 to 48 percent, while the percentage of Russians increased from 20 percent in 1933 to 26 percent in 1938. Given the absolute and dramatic drop in membership in these years, it is clear that Russian growth was only proportional.

25. I discuss the continuity of this understanding of gender roles in Marianne Kamp, "Between Women and the State: Mahalla Committees and Social Welfare in Uzbekistan," in *The Transformation of Central Asia: States and Societies from Soviet Rule to Independence*, ed. Pauline Jones Luong (Ithaca, NY: Cornell University Press, 2004), 44–47, 51–54.

26. Donald Carlisle, "Power and Politics in Soviet Uzbekistan," in Fierman, *Soviet Central Asia*, 100.

27. Sergei Poliakov, *Everyday Islam: Religion and Tradition in Rural Central Asia*, trans. Anthony Olcott (Armonk, NY: M. E. Sharpe, 1992).

28. One year before the end of the Soviet Union, Fierman edited *Soviet Central Asia: The Failed Transformation*, a volume that in large part sums up this approach to scholarship: if the Soviet Union did not succeed in producing utopia in Central Asia, then it was a failure. It may be fair to charge politicians with promoting unfulfillably grand dreams, but Central Asia did change tremendously in the Soviet period, and I would argue that efforts at transformation succeeded more than they failed.

29. Martha Olcott, "Women and Society," in Fierman, *Soviet Central Asia*, 251.

30. Latifot T. (b. 1931, Bukhara region).

## 10. CONCLUSIONS

1. Iman Bibars, *Victims and Heroines: Women, Welfare and the Egyptian State* (London: Zed Books, 2001), 164.

2. Bibars, *Victims and Heroines*, 171, 174.

3. Kandiyoti, "Bargaining with Patriarchy," 274–90.

4. In 1993, I purchased a paranji that dates to the early twentieth century from an antique dealer; such garments now appear in tourist antique shops. New paranjis were available in the bazaar: in Uzbek funeral rites, the corpse of a woman is placed on a bier with arched endposts, one of which is draped with a paranji. Thus, although women long since stopped wearing them, paranjis continued to be a culturally necessary item. Elderly women purchased them not to wear, but to prepare for their own funerals.

5. With the revival of open religious expression in Uzbekistan came an awareness for many Uzbeks that their knowledge of Islam was quite limited. In the early 1990s, they wanted help and education in Islam from Muslims elsewhere and were flooded with missionaries from Pakistan and Saudi Arabia. Donations of money and Qurans from abroad contributed to Uzbeks' appreciation of, respect for, and deference to the words of these missionaries. Uzbeks would often bewail their lack of knowledge, and a great many availed themselves of new opportunities to study. Muslim missionaries from elsewhere were dismissive of Central Asian and Soviet practices, including shrine worship, portraits of the deceased on tombstones, and so on, and Central Asians often deferred to outsiders' judgments about what constituted true Islam. Apparently, wearing dull colors was deemed important to Islamic practice, and thus the differences between modestly dressed women in Uzbek clothing and modestly dressed hijab wearers was especially striking. Most interesting was the color selection: a white headscarf with a blue or black robe, typical of international hijab, put young women in colors traditionally associated with widowhood in Uzbekistan.

6. Human Rights Watch, "Uzbekistan, 1999," http://www.hrw.org/reports/1999/uzbekistan/uzbek-02.htm, p. 2. Scholars have pointed out many differences between the Wahhabi movement of Saudi Arabia and the various religious revival movements in Uzbekistan, and on that basis have questioned the appellation. But Uzbeks routinely refer to the groups as Wahhabis.

7. There were Uzbeks who left Uzbekistan in the early 1990s to join the IRP in Tajikistan and Afghanistan. According to Ahmed Rashid, one of these, Juma Namangani, formed the Islamic Movement of Uzbekistan in 1997 with the purpose of attacking the government of Uzbekistan. Rashid, *Jihad: The Rise of Militant Islam in Central Asia* (New Haven, CT: Yale University Press, 2002). The Namangan murders were attributed to Namangani and his followers. Many analysts of the situation in Uzbekistan stress that repression and poverty make Uzbekistan a fertile territory for the spread of antigovernment and Islamist ideas, arguing that the government should change its repressive, anti-human rights practices and launch economic reforms that might bring greater prosperity. Clearly the government of

Uzbekistan needs to change both its economic policy and its undemocratic methods of governing. But I do not think that these measures alone, even if they could be successful in the short term, will make militant Islam magically disappear. Militant Islam and nonmilitant political Islam are spread by networks and promote ideas that people find attractive and convincing, even in circumstances of political freedom and relative prosperity.

8. Human Rights Watch, "Uzbekistan, 1999."

# GLOSSARY

**Basmachi.** In Central Asia between 1918 and the 1930s, an anti-Soviet militant. In the early Soviet period, there were some armed Central Asian groups who were led by the Kurbashi, or "generals." As the groups divided and were defeated, the term Basmachi came to mean bandit or raider. Uzbek: Bosmochi.

**bek.** A wealthy landowner whose ancestors had obtained land through a grant from the ruler for military service.

**beshik.** Central Asian–style cradle, in which the infant lies on his back and is strapped down.

**Bilim Yurt.** House of Knowledge. The main Women's Bilim Yurt was established in Tashkent in 1919 to train Turkestani women as teachers. More Bilim Yurts were opened elsewhere in Uzbekistan. The Tashkent Bilim Yurt went by several additional names in the 1920s, including Dar al-Mu'allimot and the Uzbek Women's Boarding School.

**boi.** Wealthy person. In Soviet descriptions of social class in Uzbekistan, there are the boi (rich), the o'rta (middle), and the kambag'al (poor).

**CAB.** Central Asian Bureau of the Soviet Communist Party.

**CPUz.** Communist Party of Uzbekistan.

**chachvon.** Black, horsehair face veil that drapes from the top of the head to the waist, at least. Worn with a paranji.

**chopan.** Padded outer robe. Uzbek men wore them as exterior clothing; many women wore them in place of the paranji as a veiling robe.

**dehqon.** Farmer or peasant. Russian: dekhkan.

**domla.** Male Muslim religious teacher in a maktab. Also mullah.

**do'ppi.** Embroidered skull cap. Russian: tubiteika.

**faranji.** See paranji.

**fatwa.** Legal decision or order pronounced by a qualified Islamic legal scholar.

**fuzalo.** A Muslim scholar who completed the madrasa curriculum and composed treatises on religious topics.

**gap.** Conversation; or a group of friends that meets regularly for conversation and feasting.

**hijab.** Arabic for either curtain or modest dress. In the early twentieth century, Muslims in the Russian empire used the term to refer generally to women's practices of veiling. In the late twentieth century, the term became closely associated with international trends in revivalist Islam, denoting especially headscarves that covered the hair and neck.

**Hujum.** Attack or assault. A Communist Party campaign to liberate Central Asian and Azerbaijani women from "tradition." The campaign began in 1927 and continued into the 1930s. Its main symbol in Uzbekistan was unveiling. Russian: Khudzhum.

**ichkari.** The inner courtyard of a home. Where the family lived, and where women would remain out of the sight of male visitors, who enter only the tashkari, or outer courtyard.

**ishon.** Member of the Muslim clergy who either holds a significant position as head of a Friday mosque, due to Islamic learning, or one who leads a Sufi order. Russian: ishan.

**Jadid.** New or modernizer. The term was short for usul-i jadid, or new method in education, a method that emphasized transferrable literacy skills and modern subjects. It became the name of a broader movement among Muslims in Russia who were concerned with political, social, and religious reform.

**kolkhoz.** Collective farm.

**Komsomol.** Communist Youth League.

**madrasa.** School of higher Islamic education.

**mahalla.** Traditional urban neighborhood.

**mahr.** Gift of money or other wealth given by the groom to the bride. Governed by Sharia, mahr also provides some security for a wife against divorce.

**maktab.** School of Islamic education, where boys studied Quran recitation, prayers, proper behavior, and basic literacy.

**millat.** Originally a term denoting minority religious community, in the early twentieth century, Jadids used it to mean nation, ethnic group, or religious group.

**ming-boshi.** Until the Soviet period, a district administrative head, responsible for local tax collection and infrastructure.

**mu'allima.** Woman teacher, trained in modern methods. The term came into use when the Tatar Jadid movement established modern teacher training schools for women.

**Navruz.** Central Asian New Year holiday, March 21.

**NKVD.** Narodnyi Kommissariat Vnutrennikh Del (People's Commissariat for Internal Affairs). The political or secret police of the Soviet Union, reorganized between 1930 and 1934. Successor to OGPU, predecessor to KGB.

**OGPU.** Ob'edinennoe Gosudarstvennoe Politicheskoe Upravlenie (Unified State Political Directorate). The political or secret police of the Soviet Union, reorganized in 1922. Successor to the Cheka.

**olim.** Scholar. A man must successfully complete numerous years of study in the madrasa to become an olim. Plural: ulama. Arabic: `alim

**otin.** Woman teacher who instructs girls in basic Islamic education. The otin teaches girls Quran, prayers, proper behavior, and perhaps some literacy. The otin is also a religious leader for Muslim women's celebrations and rituals. Also buvotin, otin-bibi, oi-mullo.

**paranji.** Robe worn by women to conceal the body from head to toe. The paranji drapes from the head and has decorative sleeves that hang down a woman's back. Worn with a chachvon, it afforded anonymity to its wearer when she went out of her courtyard. The word *paranji* is derived from the Arabic *farajiyyat* through the Persian *feranj*, both indicating a wide shirt or robe. Russian: parandzha. Uzbek: faranji, especially in Samarkand publications.

**perestroika.** Restructuring. Soviet reform of the political and economic system, under the leadership of Mikhail Gorbachev from 1987 to 1991.

**qalin.** Bridewealth. Money or gifts given by the groom to the bride's family. Not governed by Sharia, but stemming instead from Central Asian practices, qalin could be seen as brideprice or purchase of the bride. Russian: kalym.

**qazi.** Islamic judge, trained in the madrasa to interpret Islamic law (Sharia). Russian: kazi. Arabic: qadi.

**qizi / -ova.** Qizi means "daughter of." In the early 1920s, most Central Asian women used this form as a family name. Hosiyat Rahim qizi means Hosiyat, daughter of Rahim. By the late 1920s, many Central Asians were using the Russian ending -ova instead, making Rahim qizi into Rahimova. The male version, "son of," is o'g'li / -ov.

**qori.** Quran reciter.

**qori-xona.** Muslim school for training Quran reciters.

**Quran.** Islamic scriptures, believed to be God's word as revealed to and recited by Muhammad. Also Koran.

**RGASPI.** Rossiiskii Gosudarstvennyi Arkhiv Sotsial'no-politicheskoi Istorii (Russian State Archive of Sociopolitical History), formerly the Communist Party Archive, Moscow.

**Sharia.** Islamic law. Shariat is both the Uzbek and the Russian version of the word, taken from its Persian spelling.

**sovchi.** Family representative who makes marriage arrangements.

**toi.** Wedding feast or a feast for another life-cycle celebration, such as birth or circumcision.

**Turkestan.** Central Asian territory conquered by the Russian empire between the 1850s and 1880s, ruled as a colony by the tsar's appointed governor-general.

The same territory became the Turkestan Autonomous Soviet Socialist Republic from 1918 to 1924, before being divided into "national" republics. Turkestani refers to a native of this region, as opposed to a Russian colonial in Turkestan. The Uzbek spelling, which appears in this book in some titles, is Turkiston. Turkistan (i, rather than e) designates a broader geographical region from western China to northern Afghanistan.

**Uz. St. Arch.** Uzbekistan State Archive, Tashkent.

**vakila.** Woman representative. The Women's Division of the Communist Party held local women's elections for delegates to district conferences. The conferences were designed to spread basic political education, knowledge of the law and of women's rights, and to raise women's enthusiasm for a variety of social transformation programs. Russian: delegatka.

**ulama.** Plural of olim / `alim. Muslim religious scholars, collectively.

**waqf.** Islamic charitable endowment. A donation of land in perpetuity for the support of an institution such as a madrasa or a mosque. Large tracts of land in Central Asia were in waqf, which meant they could not be sold or taxed. The dehqons who farmed waqf land did so as tenants, not owners. Waqf is the common English transliteration. Russian: vakf. Uzbek: vaqf.

**Women's Division.** A section of the Communist Party that developed in the second decade of the twentieth century under the leadership of Aleksandra Kollontai, aimed at drawing women into the Party. The Moscow-based All-Union Women's Division oversaw all Women's Division activity in the Soviet Union. The Central Asian Bureau Women's Division answered to Moscow and oversaw all Women's Division activity in Central Asia. The Women's Division of the Uzbekistan Communist Party answered to the CPUz and the CAB Women's Division. In Central Asia, the Women's Division was led by Russians. Its purposes in Central Asia were to promote women's equality and to urge social transformation that would bring women out of seclusion and into public places and activities. Russian: Zhenotdel'. Uzbek: Xotin-Qizlar Shuba'si.

**xo'ja.** Member of hereditary social group in Central Asia, purportedly the descendents of saintly missionaries who converted Central Asians to Islam. Xo'jas were endogamous and were associated with Islamic learning and other elements of social prestige.

**-xon, -xonim.** Honorific form added to a woman's name. Xon can be used as an honorific after a man's name as well.

**xotin-qizlar.** Women and girls or, more precisely, females who are married and have children; and virgins. In Uzbek, the two terms were consistently used together to indicate all females.

*Yangi Yo'l.* New Path, a magazine for Uzbek women published from 1925 to 1930. After 1930, *Yangi Yo'l* continued publication until 1934, but was no longer primarily a women's magazine. The Russian form of the Uzbek name, *Iangi Iul,* obscures the difference between two Uzbek vowels, and leads to a mixup between New Path and New Year.

**yashmak.** Partial face veil, covering the face below the eyes. It was commonly worn by Turkish women in the late Ottoman period and by Tatar women in Russia in the late imperial period.

**yetim.** Orphan. A child who has lost either one or both parents to death.

**yopinchik.** A scarf used to cover the head, hair, neck, and possibly also the mouth.

**ZAGS.** (Otdel') Zapisi Aktov Grazhdanskogo Sostoianiia (Division of Registry of Citizens' Life Events, or civil registry). Soviet citizens were supposed to register birth, marriage, divorce, and death at the ZAGS; most importantly the division functioned to give the state, rather than religious institutions, control over marriage and divorce.

**ziyoli.** In Turkestan and Uzbekistan, a person of learning. In the early twentieth century, the ziyoli families of Turkestan, Bukhara, and Khiva were the literary class, those that had maintained a tradition both of religious knowledge and literature. In the Soviet period, ziyoli became equivalent to intelligentsia. Ziyolilar is plural and refers to the whole social class.

# BIBLIOGRAPHY

## PERIODICALS

### Pre-1917

Alem-i Nisvan
Din va Ma`ishat
Mir Islama
Oina
Sado-i Farg'ona
Sado-i Turkiston
Suyum Bike
Terjuman
Turkiston Viloyatining Gazetasi


### Soviet Period

Guliston
Ishchi Batraq Maktublari
Kommunistka
Novyi Vostok
Obshchestvennye Nauki v Uzbekistane
O'qituvchilar Gazetasi

*Pravda Vostoka*
*Qizil Bairoq*
*Qizil O'zbekiston*
*Sadoi Sharq*
*Saodat*
*Turkiston*
*Yangi Yo'l*
*Yer Yuzi*

## ARCHIVES

Russian State Archive of Sociopolitical History (RGASPI), formerly the Communist Party Archive, Moscow. Fond 62, Central Asian Bureau.
Uzbekistan State Archive (Uz. St. Arch.), Tashkent. Fonds 32, 34, 38, and 86.
Uzbekistan State Archive, Namangan.
Uzbekistan State Archive, Bukhara.

## ORAL HISTORIES

### *1992–1993 Interviews*

Marianne Kamp carried out all interviews except with Saodat A. In most cases, interviewees are identified by first name and last initial, birth date, and city of birth, unless that was such a small town that to name it would remove anonymity. In cases where women were public figures or published their memoirs, I have used full names, because these women clearly chose not to be anonymous.

Aisha B., b. 1909, Ufa, raised in Bukhara, interviewed 1993, Tashkent. Tatar.
Bahriniso I., b. 1910, Namangan region, interviewed 1993, Tashkent. Uzbek.
Bahriniso Y., b. 1909, Kokand, interviewed 1993, Tashkent. Uzbek.
Habibi Sh., b. 1921, Kokand, interviewed Jan. 1993, Tashkent, with husband
    J. Saidov, b. 1909, Kokand. Uzbek.
Halima M., b. 1922, Bukhara, interviewed 1993, Bukhara. Uzbek.
Havo-xon Ataqulova, b. 1923, Kokand region, interviewed 1993, Kokand.
    Uzbek.
Hojiraxon Kirgizbaeva, b. 1918, Namangan, interviewed 1992, Namangan.
    Interview conducted in Uzbek and Russian; taping was not allowed so I took
    notes. Probably Uzbek, possibly Kyrgyz.
Ho'shvaqt I., born 1916, Bukhara region, interviewed 1993, Bukhara. Tajik.
Humoira H., b. 1913, Kokand, interviewed 1993, Kokand. Uzbek
Latifot T., b. 1931, Bukhara region, interviewed 1993, Bukhara region. Irani
    (Tajik-speaking Shia, descended from Iranian immigrants).
Mafrat-xon M., b. 1914, Kokand, interviewed 1993, Kokand. Uzbek.
Mag'ruba Q., b. 1929, Tashkent, interviewed 1992, Tashkent. Uzbek.

Mahtab-oi A., b. 1901, Charjui, interviewed Bukhara,1993. Uzbek.

Malika-xon J., b. 1912, Namangan, interviewed 1993 Namangan. Uzbek.

Manzura H., b. 1921, Tashkent, interviewed 1992, Tashkent, with her mother, b. 1902, Tashkent. Uzbek.

Milli-xon Ibrohimova, b. 1911, Kokand, interviewed 1992, Namangan. Uzbek.

Muattar S., b. 1899, Bukhara, inteviewed 1993, Tashkent. Tajik.

Muhobat H., b. 1917, Kokand, interviewed Apr. 1993, Kokand. Uzbek.

O'lmas-oi H., b. 1912, Kokand, interviewed Apr., 1993, Kokand. Uzbek.

Rahbar-oi Olimova, b. 1908, Tashkent, interviewed 1993, Tashkent. Uzbek.

Saodat A., b. 1906, Xo'jand region, Tajikistan, interviewed 1992, Tajikistan, by Ikrom Nugmanxo'jaev. Uzbek

Saodat Shamsieva, b. 1908, To'rtqo'l, interviewed 1993, Tashkent, with Timur Valiev, the son of Hosiyat Tillaxonova, b. c. 1923. Uzbek.

Sara G., b. 1916, Tashkent, interviewed 1993, Tashkent. Tatar.

Shamsiyat B., b. 1918, Bukhara, interviewed 1993, Bukhara. Uzbek.

Sofia M., b. 1920, Kokand, interviewed 1993, Kokand. Tatar.

To'xfa P., b. 1928, Bukhara, interviewed 1993, Bukhara. Bukharan Jew.

### *2001–2004 Collectivization Interviews*

Aziza-xon I., b. 1914, Marg'ilon, interviewed May 2003, Tashkent, by Marianne Kamp. Uzbek.

Sottiba-xon M., b. 1920, Namangan, interviewed 2001, Namangan region, by Marianne Kamp and Russell Zanca. Uzbek.

The following interviews were carried out between April and December 2003 by interviewers from Yo'sh Olimlar Jamiyati, Tashkent, including H. Jabbarova, E. Halilov, U. Abdurasulov, K. Kolonov, and Sh. Gayupova. Interviewees are identified only by initials and by the province of their residence; almost all of them lived in very small rural communities, which, if named, would reveal identities. Most interviewees identified themselves as Uzbek, but a few were Kyrgyz or Tajik.

A. J., b. 1912, Bukhara.

B. Sh., b. 1907, Qashqa Daryo.

B. U., b. 1913, Tashkent.

B. X., b. c. 1900, Tashkent.

E. S., b. 1923, Qashqa Daryo.

F. S., b. 1915, Bukhara.

L. U., b. 1919, Qashqa Daryo.

M. T., b. 1921, Tashkent.

N. B., b. 1916, Bukhara.

N. J., b. 1921, Bukhara.

O. B., b. 1922, Qashqa Daryo.

O. X., b. 1903, Qashqa Daryo.
P. B., b. 1915, Tashkent.
Q. T., b. 1906, Tashkent.
R. S., b. 1924, Xorazm.
R. Sh, b. 1917, Bukhara.
R. X., b. 1922, Tashkent.
Raj. Sh., b. 1912, Bukhara.
S. M., b. 1913, Xorazm.
T. D., b. 1917, Tashkent.
U. M., b. 1922, Bukhara.
U. X., b. 1919, Tashkent.
X. A., b. 1919, Tashkent.
Z. A., b. 1916, Xorazm.
Z. X., b. 1922, Qashqa Daryo.

## Other Informants (no formal interview)

Saodat X., b. c. 1958, Namangan region. Uzbek.

## BOOKS AND ARTICLES

Abadan-Unat, Nermin. "The Modernization of Turkish Women." *Middle East Journal* 32, no. 3 (1978): 291–306.
———. "Social Change and Turkish Women." In *Women in Turkish Society*, edited by Nermin Abadan-Unat, 5–31. Leiden, Netherlands: Brill, 1981.
'Abdulla ibn 'Abdulla. *Izhar al-ta'asuf.* Kazan: Ikhar Shationof Matbu'asi, 1907.
Abu-Lughod, Lila, ed. *Remaking Women: Feminism and Modernity in the Middle East.* Princeton, NJ: Princeton University Press, 1998.
Afary, Janat. *The Iranian Constitutional Revolution, 1906–1911: Grassroots Democracy, Social Democracy, and the Origins of Feminism.* New York: Columbia University Press, 1996.
Ahmed, Leila. *Women and Gender in Islam: Historical Roots of a Modern Debate.* New Haven, CT: Yale University Press, 1992.
Akhunova, M. A., Kh. Z. Ziiaev, and G. R. Rashidov. *Istoriia Kokanda.* Tashkent: Fan, 1984.
Akiner, Shirin. "Contemporary Central Asian Women." In *Post-Soviet Women: From the Baltic to Central Asia*, edited by Mary Buckley, 261–304. Cambridge: Cambridge University Press, 1997.
al-Azimi, Mulla Abd al-Salam. "Ta'lim va Tarbiya." *Oina*, no. 13 (1915): 346–49.
Alimhanov, Tahir. "Yana to'i masalasi." *Sado-i Farg'ona*, no. 28 (June 18, 1914): 2.
Alimova, Dilarom. "Istoriografiia: Zhenskii vopros v sovetskoi istoriografii srednei Azii 20-x godov." *Obshchestvennye Nauki v Uzbekistan*, no. 11 (1989): 51–56.

———. *Zhenskii vopros v srednei Azii: Istoriia izucheniia i sovremennye problemy*. Tashkent: Fan, 1991.

Alimova, Marhamat. *Ular birinchilardan edilar*. Toshkent: O'zbekiston, 1983.

Allione, Constanzo, producer. *Where the Eagles Fly: Habiba; a Sufi Saint from Uzbekistan*. New York: Mystic Fire Video, 1997.

Allworth, Edward, ed. *Central Asia: 120 Years of Russian Rule*. Durham, NC: Duke University Press, 1989.

———. *The Modern Uzbeks: From the Fourteenth Century to the Present; A Cultural History*. Stanford, CA: Hoover Institution Press, Stanford University, 1990.

———. *Uzbek Literary Politics*. The Hague: Mouton, 1964.

al-Qadiri, Zakir. *Qizlar Dunyasi*. Kazan: Yefremov, 1911.

*Al-Qur'an: A Contemporary Translation*. Revised ed. Translated by Ahmed Ali. Princeton, NJ: Princeton University Press, 1988.

Amala Xonim. "Xarob qilar qilai." *Yangi Yo'l*, no. 4 (1929): 14–16.

Amin, Camron. *The Making of the Modern Iranian Woman: Gender, State Policy, and Popular Culture, 1865–1946*. Gainesville: University of Florida Press, 2002.

Amin, Qasim. *The Liberation of Women; and The New Woman: Two documents in the history of Egyptian Feminism*. 1898, 1899. Translated by Samiha Sidhom Peterson. Cairo: American University in Cairo Press, 2000.

———. *Novaia Zhenshchina*. Supplement to *Mir Islama*. Translated by I. Iu. Krachkovskii. St. Petersburg, 1912.

Aminova, Rakhima. *Agrarnye preobrazovaniia v Uzbekistane nakanune sploshnoi kollektivizatsii (1925–1929)*. Tashkent: Iz. Fan Uzbekskoi SSR, 1969.

———. *The October Revolution and Women's Liberation in Uzbekistan*. Translated by B. M. Meerovich. Moscow: Nauka, 1977.

———. *Osushchestvlenie kollektivizatsii v Uzbekistane (1929–1932 gg.)*. Tashkent: Iz. Fan Uzbekskoi SSR, 1977.

Anderson, Benedict. *Imagined Communities: Reflections on the Origin and Spread of Nationalism*. Revised ed. London: Verso, 1991.

Aqchurina, Zaynab, et al. "Musulman khatun-qizlarinda harakat." *Suyum Bike*, no. 14 (1914): 17–18.

Arat, Yeşim. "From Emancipation to Liberation." *Journal of International Affairs* 54, no. 1 (2000): 107–24.

Arat, Zehra. "Kemalism and Turkish Women." *Women and Politics* 14, no. 4 (1994): 57–80.

———. "Turkish Women and the Republican Reconstruction of Tradition." In *Reconstructing Gender in the Middle East: Tradition, Identity, and Power*, edited by Fatma Müge Göçek and Shiva Balaghi, 57–78. New York: Columbia University Press, 1994.

Aslan, Canan. "The Legacy of a European-Oriented Transformation: Gender Relations in Contemporary Turkey." *European Legacy* 1, no. 3 (1996): 981–87.

Astapovich, Z. A., ed. *Velikii Oktiabr' i raskreposhcheniie zhenshchin srednei Azii i Kazakhstana (1917–1936 gg): Sbornik dokumentov i materialov*. Moskva: Mysl', 1971.

Attwood, Lynne. *Creating the New Soviet Woman: Women's Magazines as Engineers of Female Identity, 1922–53.* Studies in Russian and East European History and Society. New York: St. Martin's Press, 1999.

Ayni, Sadriddin. *Yoddoshtho.* Vol. 1. Dushanbe: Adib, 1990.

A'zam. "Satang taklifi," *Qizil O'zbekiston,* Feb. 8, 1927, 2.

A'zamxo'jaev, Saidakbar. *Turkiston Muxtoriyati: Milliy-demokratik davlatchilik qurulishi tajribasi.* Toshkent: Manaviyat, 2000.

Azizzoda, Laziz. *Yangi hayot kurashchilari.* Toshkent: Fan, 1977.

Badran, Margot. *Feminists, Islam, and Nation: Gender and the Making of Modern Egypt.* Princeton, NJ: Princeton University Press, 2004.

Badran, Margot, and Miriam Cooke, eds. *Opening the Gates: A Century of Arab Feminist Writing.* Bloomington: Indiana University Press, 1990.

Baron, Beth. *The Women's Awakening in Egypt: Culture, Society, and the Press.* New Haven, CT: Yale University Press, 1994.

Bartol'd, V. V. "Istoriia kul'turnaia zhizn' Turkestana VII: Shkoly." In *Sochineniia,* vol. 2, part 1, 297–318. Moskva: Izd-vo Nauka, 1964.

Bashir, Zarif. "Ozodliq qurbonsiz bo'lmaidi." *Yangi Yo'l,* no. 3 (1928): 18–20.

Bashiri, Z. "Erk Yo'lida." *Yangi Yo'l,* no. 1 (1928): 14–15, 18; no. 2 (1928): 11–13.

Baykan, Aysegul. "The Turkish Woman: An Adventure in Feminist Historiography." *Gender and History* 6, no.1 (1994): 101–16.

Becker, Seymour. *Russia's Protectorates in Central Asia: Bukhara and Khiva, 1865–1924.* Cambridge, MA: Harvard University Press, 1968.

[Behbudi], Mahmud Xo'ja. "Beshiklarimiz miyamizni uyaldur." *Oina,* no. 8 (1915): 181–183.

Behbudi, Mahmud Xo'ja [Selected by M., pseud.]. "Erkak ila ayol na tashrihan farqi?" *Oina,* no. 10 (1915): 256–58.

Behbudi, Mahmud Xo'ja. "Hifz-i sihat-i ayla." *Oina,* no. 47 (1914): 1126–28; no. 48 (1914): 1148–52; no. 49 (1914): 1171–74.

Bennigsen, Alexandre, and S. Enders Wimbush. *Muslim National Communism in the Soviet Union: A Revolutionary Strategy for the Colonial World.* Chicago: University of Chicago Press, 1979.

Bernstein, Laurie. *Sonia's Daughters: Prostitutes and Their Regulation in Imperial Russia.* Berkeley: University of California Press, 1995.

Bibars, Iman. *Victims and Heroines: Women, Welfare and the Egyptian State.* London: Zed Books, 2001.

Bikdzhanova, M. A. "Odezhda Uzbekchek Tashkenta XIX-nachala XX v." In *Kostium narodov srednei Azii,* edited by O. A. Sukhareva, 133–51. Moskva: Iz. Nauka, 1979.

bint Ismatulla, Hanifa Khanim. *Targhib mu'allimalarga maktab ravshanda yazilmishdir.* Kazan: Dombrovskii, 1898.

"Birdan artuq khatun aluv haqinda." *Suyum Bike,* no. 18 (1917): 280.

Brower, Daniel. *Turkestan and the Fate of the Russian Empire.* New York: Routledge/Curzon, 2003.

Brundage, W. Fitzhugh. Introduction to *Under Sentence of Death: Lynching in the*

*South*, edited by W. F. Brundage. Raleigh: University of North Carolina Press, 1997.

Burton, Antoinnette. *Burdens of History: British Feminists, Indian Women, and Imperial Culture, 1865–1915*. Durham: University of North Carolina Press, 1994.

Buttino, Marco. "Study of the Economic Crisis and Depopulation in Turkestan, 1917–1920." *Central Asian Survey* 9, no. 4 (1990): 59–74.

Butuzova. "Zhenskie lavki v Uzbekistane." *Kommunistka*, no. 9 (1917): 62–67.

Carlisle, Donald. "Power and Politics in Soviet Uzbekistan." In *Soviet Central Asia: The Failed Transformation*, edited by William Fierman, 93–130. Boulder, CO: Westview, 1991.

Carrère d'Encausse, Hélène. *Islam and the Russian Empire: Reform and Revolution in Central Asia*. Berkeley: University of California Press, 1988.

Ch. "Xotinlar ozodlig'ig'a qarshi bo'lg'an shahslarga yaxshilab jazo berish lozim." *Ishchi Batraq Maktublari*, Oct. 15, 1926, 3.

Chatterjee, Partha. *The Nation and its Fragments: Colonial and Post-Colonial Histories*. Princeton, NJ: Princeton University Press, 1993.

Chernisheva. "Firqaning xotin-qizlarni ozodliqqa chiqarish ishiga imlar to'siqliq qiladur." *Yangi Yo'l*, no. 10 (1926): 17–18.

———. "O'zbekistonda xotinlar ma'orifi." *Yangi Yo'l*, no. 6 (1928): 3–5.

Clements, Barbara Evans. *Bolshevik Women*. Cambridge: Cambridge University Press, 1997.

David-Fox, Michael, Peter Holquist, and Marshall Poe, eds. *The Resistance Debate in Russian and Soviet History*. Kritika Historical Studies 1. Bloomington, IN: Slavica Publishers, 2003.

Dinikaeva, Zaineb. "Bukharada uyg'atuv asrlari." *Suyum Bike*, no. 12 (1914): 9–10.

Douglas, Mary. *Natural Symbols: Explorations of Cosmology*. New York: Pantheon, 1970.

Druzhinina. "Probuzhdennye zhenshchiny vostoka." *Kommunistka* 1, no. 18 (1922): 19.

Engelstein, Laura, "Culture, Culture Everywhere: Interpretations of Modern Russia, across the 1991 Divide." *Kritika: Explorations in Russian and Eurasian History* 2, no. 2 (2001): 363–93.

Faiziev, T. *Buxoro feodal jamiyatida qullardan foydalanishga doir hujjatlar (XIX asr)*. Toshkent: O'zbekiston SSR "Fan" Nashriyoti, 1990.

Fakhriddin, Rizauddin. *Aila*. 1905. Uzbek reprint, Rizouddin ibn Fakhriddin, *Oila*. Toshkent: Meros, 1991.

Fathiddin-zade, Zuhriddin. "Huquq-i nisvan." *Sado-i Turkiston*, no. 47 (1914): 3; and no. 51 (1914): 2–3.

Feldner, Yotam, "'Honor Murders'—Why the Perps Get Off Easy." *Middle East Quarterly* 7, no. 4 (Dec. 2000): 41–50.

Fierman, William. *Language Planning and National Development: The Uzbek Experience*. Contributions to the Sociology of Language 60. Berlin: Mouton de Gruyter, 1991.

————. "The Soviet 'Transformation.'" In *Soviet Central Asia: The Failed Transformation*, edited by William Fierman, 11–35. Boulder, CO: Westview, 1991.

Finkel'shtein, I., ed. *Probuzhdennye velikim Oktiabrem.* Tashkent: Gos. Izdat. Uzbekskoi SSR, 1961.

Fitrat, Abdurauf. *Oila, yoki oila boshqarish tartiblari.* 1916. Reprint edited by Dilarom Alimova. Toshkent: Manaviyat, 1998.

————. *Rahbar-i najat.* 1915. Tajik reprint, "Rohbari najot," edited by Muhabbat Jalilova, *Sadoi Sharq* 9 (1992): 8–53.

Fitzpatrick, Sheila. "Ascribing Class: The Construction of Social Identity in Soviet Russia." *Journal of Modern History* 65, no. 4 (Dec. 1993): 745–70.

Fleischmann, Ellen. "The Other 'Awakening': The Emergence of Women's Movements in the Modern Middle East, 1900–1940." In *Social History of Women and Gender in the Modern Middle East*, edited by Margaret Meriwether and Judith Tucker, 89–139. Boulder, CO: Westview, 1999.

Forbes, Andrew. *Warlords and Muslims in Chinese Central Asia.* Cambridge: Cambridge University Press, 1986.

Fotima. "Holida Adiba Xonum ma'orif naziri." *Turkiston*, Mar. 9, 1924, 3.

Fraser, Glenda. "Enver Pasha's Bid for Turkestan." *Canadian Journal of History* 23, no. 2 (1988): 197–213.

Frierson, Elizabeth. "Unimagined Communities: State, Press, and Gender in the Hamidian Era." Ph.D. dissertation, Princeton University, 1996.

"G'alabani qo'ldan bermaimiz." *Qizil O'zbekistan*, Apr. 7, 1927, 4.

Garcia, Jerry. "The Measure of a Cock: Mexican Cockfighting, Culture and Masculinity." In *I am Aztlán: The Personal Essay in Chicano Studies*, edited by Chon Noriega and Wendy Belcher, 109–38. Los Angeles: UCLA Chicano Studies Research Press, 2004.

Gazulo, P. G. *Vosstanie 1916 goda v srednei Azii: Sbornik dokumentov.* Tashkent: Gosizdat UzSSR, 1932.

Geraci, Robert. *Window on the East: National and Imperial Identities in Late Tsarist Russia.* Ithaca, NY: Cornell University Press, 2001.

Gh., A. "Khatunlar." In *Khanumlar islahi*, edited by Mu'allima Kamila bint `Azatulla Qasimova, 47–49. Kazan: Beraderan Karimilar, 1908.

G'lazqova [Glazkova], Yelena. "Ochilg'an o'zbek xotin-qizlarg'a ko'makga." *Yangi Yo'l*, no. 8 (1928): 5–6.

Goldman, Wendy Z. *Women, the State, and Revolution: Soviet Family Policy and Social Life, 1917–1936.* Cambridge: Cambridge University Press, 1993.

Göle, Nilüfer. *The Forbidden Modern: Civilization and Veiling.* Critical Perspectives on Women and Gender. Ann Arbor: University of Michigan Press, 1996.

Grebenkin, A. D. "Uzbeki." In *Russkii Turkestan: Sbornik izdannyi po povodu politekhnicheskoi vystavki*, vol. 2, edited by N. A. Maev. Moskva: Universitetskaia Tipografiia, 1872.

G'ulom, G'afur. "Gam tuguni." *Yangi Yo'l*, no. 11–12 (1928): 12–14.

————. "Hulkar tole'i." *Yangi Yo'l*, no. 4 (1928): 18–19.

Gurevich. "Rabota sredi zhenshin." *Kommunistka*, no. 3–5 (1922): 46–47.

H., B. "Sakuchilar paranjini o'tib tashladilar," *Qizil O'zbekiston*, Mar. 6, 1927, 2.

Habiba. "Ikki g'uncha." *Yangi Yo'l*, no. 7 (1927): 14–15.

Hablemitoğlu, Şengül, and Necip Hablemitoğlu. *Şefika Gaspıralı ve Rusya'da Türk Kadın Hareketi (1893–1920)*. Ankara: Ajans-Türk Matbaacılık Sanayii, 1998.

Hadicha. "Hujumimiz muvaffaqiyatlik." *Yangi Yo'l*, no. 4 (1927): 3–4.

Hakima. "Xotinlar huquqini pomol [*sic.*, poimol] qilg'uchi." *Yangi Yo'l*, no. 2 (1929): 5.

Halida. "Tutning mevasi pishdi." *Yangi Yo'l*, no. 2 (1928): 12.

Hall, Jacquelyn Dowd. *Revolt Against Chivalry: Jesse Daniel Ames and the Women's Campaign against Lynching*. New York: Columbia University Press, 1993.

Halle, Fannina. *Women in the Soviet East*. Translated by Margaret M. Green. New York: Dutton, 1938.

Hamza. *See* Niyoziy, Hamza Hakimzoda.

Hasanov. "Qayuv hijab zararli?" *Alem-i Nisvan*, no. 7 (1907): 3–4.

Hellbeck, Jochen. "Working, Struggling, Becoming: Stalin-Era Autobiographical Texts." *Russian Review* 60, no. 3 (2001): 340–59.

Heyat, Farida. *Azeri Women in Transition: Women in Soviet and Post-Soviet Azerbaijan*, Central Asia Research Forum. London: Routledge/Curzon, 2002.

Hilali, I. "Maskav muslimalari kamiteti tarafindan khitabname." *Suyum Bike*, no. 11 (1917): 165–74.

Hirsch, Francine. "Toward an Empire of Nations: Border-Making and the Formation of Soviet National Identities." *Russian Review* 59 (Apr. 2000): 201–26.

Hoffman, David. *Stalinist Values: The Cultural Norms of Soviet Modernity (1917–1941)*. Ithaca, NY: Cornell University Press, 2003.

Hoffman, David, and Yanni Kotsonis, eds. *Russian Modernity: Politics, Knowledge, Practices*. New York: St. Martin's Press, 2000.

Hourani, Albert. *Arabic Thought in the Liberal Age, 1798–1939*. Cambridge: Cambridge University Press, 1983.

Human Rights Watch. "Uzbekistan, 1999." http://www.hrw.org/reports/1999/uzbekistan/uzbek-02.htm

Husain. "Yana xotinlarni ochish to'g'risida." *Qizil O'zbekiston*, Feb. 7, 1927, 2–3.

I., S. "Eski Toshkentda Ta'rixi Majlis." *Qizil O'zbekiston*, Mar. 5, 1926, 1.

Ibrohim. "Xotin-qizlar O'zbekistonda kapiratsiaya qatnashi." *Yangi Yo'l*, no. 8 (1928): 9–11.

Icduygu, Ahmet, Yilmaz Colak, and Nalan Soyarik. "What is the Matter with Citizenship? A Turkish Debate." In *Seventy-five Years of the Turkish Republic*, edited by Sylvia Kedourie, 187–208. London: Frank Cass, 2000.

Ignatiev, N. P. *Mission of N. P. Ignat'ev to Khiva and Bukhara in 1858*. Translated by John Evans. Newtonville, MA: Oriental Research Partners, 1984.

"Ishga." *Yangi Yo'l*, no. 1 (1925): 10–13.

"Islam i imushchestvennoe polozhenie zhenshchin i sirot v dorevoliutsionnoi sredei Azii (po materialam Khivinskogo Khanstva XIX v.)." In *Islam i zhenshchiny vostoka: Istoriia i sovremennost'*, edited by M. M. Khairullaev et al., 62–70. Tashkent: Fan, 1990.

Ismeti, A.. "Shariat qashunda khatun qizlar." *Suyum* Bike, no. 1 (1913): 4.

Ismoilova, D. "Farg'ona Viloyatida 1916 yil halq qo'zg'oloni." *Obshchestvennye nauki v Uzbekistan*, no. 8 (1991): 26–33.

Iusupov, E. Iu. *Nizomiy "Xamsa"siga ishlagan rasmlar*. Toshkent: Fan, 1985.

Ivanov, N. P. *Khivinskaia ekspeditsiia, 1839–1840*. Sanktpeterburg: Tip-a Obshch-estvennaia Pol'za, 1873.

Jalilov, A. K. "Vasiqalar namunalari haqidagi qo'lyozma (XIX asr)." *Obshchestven-nye nauki v Uzbekistane*, no. 1 (1991): 48–54.

Jones, Ellen, and Fred W. Grupp. *Modernization, Value Change, and Fertility in the Soviet Union*. Cambridge: Cambridge University Press, 1987.

Jo'raev, M., ed. *O'zbekistonning yangi tarixi*. Vol. 2, *O'zbekiston Soviet mustamlakachiligi davrida*. Toshkent: Sharq, 2000.

Kamp, Marianne. "Between Women and the State: Mahalla Committees and Social Welfare in Uzbekistan." In *The Transformation of Central Asia: States and Societies from Soviet Rule to Independence*, edited by Pauline Jones Luong, 1–58. Ithaca, NY: Cornell University Press, 2004.

———. "Femicide as Terrorism: The Case of Uzbekistan's Unveiling Murders." In *Religion and Violence across Time and Tradition*, edited by James Wellman. Lanham, MD: Rowan and Littlefield, 2007.

———. "Land for Women, Too." Paper presented at Women in Central Asia: The Politics of Change, Columbia University, New York, Apr. 15, 1998. Archived at http://www.sipa.columbia.edu/RESOURCES/CASPIAN/wom_p12.html (access via http://www.archive.org)

———. "Remembering the Hujum: Uzbek Women's Words." *Central Asia Monitor* 1 (2001): 1–13.

———. "Three Lives of Saodat: Communist, Uzbek, Survivor." *Oral History Review* 28, no. 2 (2001): 21–58.

Kandiyoti, Deniz. "Bargaining with Patriarchy." *Gender and Society* 2, no. 3 (1988): 274–90.

———. "Emancipated but Unliberated? Reflections on the Turkish Case." *Feminist Studies* 13, no. 2 (1987): 317–38.

Kangas, Roger. "Faizulla Khodzhaev: National Communism in Bukhara and Uzbekistan, 1896–1938." Ph.D. dissertation, Indiana University, 1992.

Kappeler, Andreas. "Czarist Policy toward the Muslims of the Russian Empire." In *Muslim Communities Reemerge: Historical Perspectives on Nationality, Politics, and Opposition in the Former Soviet Union and Yugoslavia*, Central Asian Book Series, edited by Andreas Kappeler, Gerhard Simon, Georg Brunner, and Edward Allworth, 141–56. Durham, NC: Duke University Press, 1994.

———. *The Russian Empire: A Multiethnic History*. Translated by Alfred Clayton. New York: Longman, 2001.

Karlieva, Q. "Farg'ona viloyatidagi ishchi xotin-qizlar." *Yangi Yo'l*, no. 11–12 (1926): 19.

Karlieva. "Vakila Shermatovaning o'ldirishi." *Yangi Yo'l*, no. 1 (1927): 36.

Karryeva, Roza. *Ot bespraviia k ravenstvu*. Tashkent: Uzbekistan, 1989.

Kasparova, V., and Ye. Ralli. "Probuzhdennye trudiashchiisia zhenshchiny vostoka." *Novyi Vostok*, no. 2 (1922): 400–420.

Keller, Shoshana. *To Moscow, Not Mecca: The Soviet Campaign against Islam in Central Asia, 1917–1941.* Westport, CT: Praeger, 2001.

———. "Trapped between State and Society: Women's Liberation and Islam in Soviet Uzbekistan." *Journal of Women's History* 10, no. 1 (1998): 20–44.

Khairullaev, M. M. et. al., eds. *Islam i zhenshchiny vostoka: Istoriia i sovremennost'.* Tashkent: Fan, 1990.

Khalid, Adeeb. "Nationalizing the Revolution in Central Asia: The Transformation of Jadidism, 1917–1920." In *A State of Nations: Empire and Nation-Making in the Age of Lenin and Stalin*, edited by Ron Suny and Terry Martin, 145–62. Oxford: Oxford University Press, 2001.

———. *The Politics of Muslim Cultural Reform: Jadidism in Central Asia.* Berkeley: University of California Press, 1998.

———. "Tashkent 1917: Muslim Politics in Revolutionary Turkestan." *Slavic Review* 55, no. 2 (1996): 270–96.

Kisliakov, N. A. *Patriarkhal'no-feodal'nye otnosheniia sredi osedlogo sel'skogo naseleniia Bukharskogo Khanstva v kontse XIX-nachale XX v.* Moskva: Izd-vo Ak. Nauk SSSR, 1962.

———. *Sem'ia i brak u Tadzhikov.* Trudy Instituta Etnografii: New Series, vol. 44. Moskva: Ak. Nauk SSSR, 1959.

*Kommunisticheskaia Partiia Uzbekistana v rezoliutsiiakh i resheniiakh s'ezdov i plenumov Ts. K.* Vol. 1, *1925–1937.* Tashkent: Uzbekistan, 1987.

*Kommunisticheskaia Partiia Uzbekistana v tsifrakh: Sbornik statisticheskikh materilov, 1924–1977 gg.* Tashkent: Uzbekistan, 1979.

Kotkin, Stephen. "Modern Times: The Soviet Union and the Interwar Conjuncture." *Kritika: Explorations in Russian and Eurasian History* 2, no. 1 (2001): 111–64.

Koven, Seth, and Sonya Michaels, eds. *Mothers of a New World: Maternalist Politics and the Origins of Welfare States.* New York: Routledge, 1993.

Krämer, Annette. *Geistliche Autorität und islamische Gessellschaft im Wandel: Studien über Frauenälteste (otin und xalfa) im unabhängigen Usbekistan.* Islamkundliche Untersuchungen, Band 246. Berlin: Klaus Schwarz Verlag, 2002.

Kramer, Jane. "Taking the Veil." *New Yorker*, Nov. 11, 2004, 59–71.

Krylova, Anna. "The Tenacious Liberal Subject in Soviet Studies." In *The Resistance Debate in Russian and Soviet History*, Kritika Historical Studies 1, edited by Michael David-Fox, Peter Holquist, and Marshall Poe, 168–207. Bloomington, IN: Slavica Publishers, 2003.

"Laqlaqa qotillari sud mahkamasida." *Yer Yuzi*, no. 8 (1926): 14–15.

Lazakat. "Xotinlarg'a ham yer." *Yangi Yo'l*, no. 9 (1926): 11–12.

Lazreg, Marnia, ed. "Making the Transition Work for Women in Europe and Central Asia." Europe and Central Asia Gender and Development Series, Discussion Paper No. 411. Washington D.C.: The World Bank, 2000.

Lentz, Thomas W., and Glenn D. Lowrey. *Timur and the Princely Vision: Persian Art and Culture in the Fifteenth Century.* Washington, D.C.: Smithsonian Institution Press, 1989.

Levin, Theodore. *The One Hundred Thousand Fools of God: Musical Travels in Central Asia.* Bloomington: Indiana University Press, 1996.

Liubimova, Serafima. "Dekret o chadre i obshchestvo 'doloi kalym i mnogozhenstvo.'" *Kommunistka*, no. 8 (1928): 73–75.

———. *Kak zhivut i rabotaiut zhenshchiny srednei Azii.* Moskva: Gos. Izdat., 1925.

———. "K itogi soveshchaniia po rabote sredi zhenshchin vostochnykh narodnostei." *Kommunistka*, no. 5 (1923): 11–12.

———. *Rabota Partii sredi truzhenits vostoka.* Moskva: Gos. Izdat, 1928.

———. *Teoriia i praktika rabota Partii sredi zhehshchin.* Tashkent/Moskva: Turkpechat, 1926.

Liushkevich, F. E. "Traditsii mezhsemeinykh sviazei Uzbeksko-Tadzhikskogo naseleniia srednei Azii (k probleme bytovaniia *kalyma* i drugikh patriarkhal'nykh obychaev)." *Sovetskaiia Etnografiia*, no. 4 (1989): 58–68.

Lorenz, Richard, "The Economic Bases of the Basmachi Movement in the Farghana Valley." In *Muslim Communities Reemerge: Historical Perspectives on Nationality, Politics, and Opposition in the Former Soviet Union and Yugoslavia*, Central Asian Book Series, edited by Andreas Kappeler, Gerhard Simon, Georg Brunner, and Edward Allworth, 277–303. Durham, NC: Duke University Press, 1994.

Lummis, Trevor. *Listening to History: The Authenticity of Oral Evidence.* Totowa, NJ: Barnes and Noble, 1988.

Lykoshin, N. S. *Pol' zhizni v Turkestane: Ocherki byta tuzemnago naseleniia.* Petrograd: Sklad T-va "V. A. Berezovskii," 1916.

Macleod, Arlene. *Accomodating Protest: Working Women, the New Veiling, and Change in Cairo.* New York: Columbia University Press, 1991.

Mahmudov, M. "Tojixon Shodieva." In *Barhayot Siymolar*, 157–65. Toshkent: O'zbekiston, 1991,

Mani, Lata. "Contentious Traditions: The Debate on SATI in Colonial India." *Cultural Critique* 7 (1987): 118–56.

Maqsud qizi. "Zainab Qurbon qizi." *Yangi Yo'l*, no. 8 (1928): 8

Martin, Terry. *The Affirmative Action Empire: Nations and Nationalism in the Soviet Union, 1923–1939.* Ithaca, NY: Cornell University Press, 2001.

Martin, Virginia. *Law and Custom in the Steppe: The Kazakhs of the Middle Horde and Russian Colonialism in the Nineteenth Century.* Richmond, Surrey: Curzon Press, 2001.

Massell, Gregory. *The Surrogate Proletariat: Moslem Women and Revolutionary Strategies in Soviet Central Asia, 1919–1929.* Princeton, NJ: Princeton University Press, 1974.

Maya. "Ozod xotinlar himoya talab." *Yangi Yo'l*, no. 10 (1928): 23

Meakin, Annette M. B. *In Russian Turkestan: A Garden of Asia and its People.* New York: Charles Scribner's Sons, 1915.

Medlin, William K., William M. Cave, and Finley Carpenter. *Education and Devel-*

opment in Central Asia: A Case Study on Social Change in Uzbekistan. Leiden,
Netherlands: Brill, 1971.

Mernissi, Fatima. Beyond the Veil: Male-Female Dynamics in a Muslim Society. Revised
ed. Bloomington: Indiana University Press, 1987.

"Mestnye rabotniki ob izdanii dekreta." Kommunistka, no. 1 (1929): 32–35.

Michaels, Paula. Curative Powers: Medicine and Empire in Stalin's Central Asia. Pittsburgh: Pittsburgh University Press, 2003.

Michurina. "Sho'ralar qonuni xotinlarg'a nima beradir." Yangi Yo'l, no. 3 (1926):
29–30.

Middendorf, A. F [A. Th. von Middendorf]. Ocherki Ferganskoi Doliny. St. Petersburg, 1882.

Minault, Gail. Secluded Scholars: Women's Education and Muslim Social Reform in
Colonial India. Oxford: Oxford University Press, 1998.

Mirza, Yusufxon. "Iz Kokanda." Turkiston Viloyatining Gazetasi, Jan. 11 1915, 1–2.

Moors, Annelies. Women, Property and Islam: Palestinian Experiences, 1920–1990.
Cambridge Middle East Studies. Cambridge: Cambridge University Press,
1995.

Mufti Zade, S. "Bir jama badalida fahshg'a rivoj." Turkiston Viloyatining Gazetasi,
Jan. 12, 1916.

"Musliman khatunlarining tavushlari." Suyum Bike, no. 9 (1917): 142.

"Musulman khatun-qizlarinda harakat." Suyum Bike, no. 14 (1914): 17–18.

Muzafiriya, Kamila. "Aidingiz birga!" Suyum Bike, no. 2 (1914): 11–13.

Muzafiriya, Sara. "Aib uzimizda." Sado-i Turkiston, Aug. 14, 1914, 1.

N. "Paranjidan qizil bo'yinboqqa." Qizil O'zbekiston, Mar. 6, 1925, 1.

N. "Shuro sudining sinfi siyosati to'g'rimi?" Yangi Yo'l, no. 3 (1929): 9–10.

Najie. "Khatunlar tarafindan Musulman Duma a'zalarina." Alem-i Nisvan, no. 7
(1907): 1–2, reprinted from the Tatar periodical Vaqt.

Najmabadi, Afsaneh. "Crafting an Educated Housewife in Iran." In Remaking
Women: Feminism and Modernity in the Middle East, edited by Lila Abu-Lughod,
91–125. Princeton, NJ: Princeton University Press, 1998.

Nalivkin, Validimir Petrovich, and M. Nalivkina. Ocherk byta zhenshchiny osedlago
tuzemnago naseleniia Fergany. Kazan': Tipografiia Imperatorskago Universiteta,
1886.

Nerazik, E. E., and A. N. Zhilina, eds. Zhilishche narodov srednei Azii i Kazakhstana.
Moskva: Izd-vo Nauka, 1982.

"Nima uchun dekret chiqarilmadi?" Yangi Yo'l, no. 6 (1929): 2–3.

Niurina, F. "Usilit' podgotovku kul'turnykh kadrov vostoka." Kommunistka, no. 5–6
(1929): 25.

Niyoziy, Hamza Hakimzoda. "Bu kun 8-Mart." In Hamza Hakimzoda Niyoziy,
Mukammal asarlar to'plami, vol. 3, 67–68. Toshkent: Fan, 1981. Originally
appeared in Yangi Farg'ona, Mar. 8, 1927.

———. "Tuhmatchilar jazosi." In Boy ila xizmatchi: P'esalar, 79–90. 1918.
Toshkent: O'qituvchi, 1988.

Northrop, Douglas. "Languages of Loyalty: Gender, Politics, and Party Supervision in Uzbekistan, 1927–1941." *Russian Review* 59, no. 2 (2000): 179–200.

———. "Nationalizing Backwardness: Gender, Empire, and Uzbek Identity." In *A State of Nations: Empire and Nation-Making in the Age of Lenin and Stalin*, edited by Ronald Suny and Terry Martin, 191–220. Oxford: Oxford University Press, 2001.

———. "Subaltern Dialogues: Subversion and Resistance in Soviet Uzbek Family Law." *Slavic Review* 60, no. 1 (2001): 115–39.

———. *Veiled Empire: Gender and Power in Stalinist Central Asia*. Ithaca, NY: Cornell University Press, 2004.

Nosir [Nosirova], Robiya. "Amaliy hujum." *Yangi Yo'l*, no. 1 (1927): 29.

Nosir qizi [Robiya Nosirova]. "Toshkent o'lka xotin-qizlar Bilim Yurti." *Yangi Yo'l*, no. 8 (1927): 19–20.

Nosirova, [Robiya]. "Xotin-qizlar Bilim Yurtining o'n yiligi." *Yangi Yo'l*, no. 5 (1929): 4–5.

"Nuzhno li izdat' dikret, zapreshchaiushchii noshenie chadry?" *Kommunistka*, no. 8 (1928): 79–81.

Obid, X. "Qalin molning kelib chiqishi." *Yangi Yo'l*, no. 6 (1929): 16–17.

O'gay. "Qanli sahifalar (sud zalidan)." *Yangi Yo'l*, no. 7 (1928): 4.

O'Hanlon, Rosalind. "Issues of Widowhood: Gender and Resistance in Colonial Western India." In *Contesting Power: Resistance and Everyday Social Relations in South Asia*, edited by Douglas Haynes and Gyan Prakash, 62–108. Berkeley: University of California Press, 1992.

Oidin. "Fa'oliyat oldida to'suqlar bir pul." *Yangi Yo'l*, no. 11–12 (1928): 23–24.

Oidin [Manzura Sobir Qori qizi]. *Yangilikka qadam (O'zbek turmishidan olingan 3 pardalik piyassa)*. 1925. Toshkent: O'zbekiston Davlat Nashriyoti, 1926.

O'ktam. "Xotinlar masalasi (musabaha yo'li bilan basiladir)." *Turkiston*, Feb. 14, 1924, 3–4.

Oldenburg, Veena Talwar. "Lifestyle as Resistance: The Case of the Courtesans Lucknow." In *Contesting Power: Resistance and Everyday Social Relations in South Asia*, edited by Douglas Haynes and Gyan Prakash, 23–62. Berkeley: University of California Press, 1992.

Olcott, Martha. "Women and Society." In *Soviet Central Asia: The Failed Transformation*, edited by William Fierman, 235–54. Boulder, CO: Westview, 1991.

Olimova, Rahbar-oi. "'Hujum' ishtirokchisi ekanimdan faxrlanaman . . ." *Guliston*, no. 5 (1988): 22–23.

Olson, Emelie. "Muslim Identity and Secularism in Contemporary Turkey: 'The Headscarf Dispute.'" *Anthropological Quarterly* 58, no. 6 (1985): 161–71.

"O'lka O'zbek xotin-qizlar Bilim Yurtining xozirgi holda." *Qizil Bairoq*, Dec. 17, 1921, 1.

"Ona va bola burchaklarining ishlari." *Yangi Yo'l*, no. 10–11 (1927): 41.

Ortner, Sherry. "Theory in Anthropology since the Sixties." *Comparative Studies in Society and History* 26, no. 1 (Jan. 1984): 126–67.

Ostroumov, Nikolai Petrovich. *K 50ti letiu Tashkenta: Tashkentskie Sarty pod Russkim upravleniem.* 1915.

*O'zbek Soviet entsiklodepiyasi.* Toshkent: O'zbek Soviet Entsiklopediyasi Bo'sh Redaktsiyasi, 1973.

"O'zbekiston sho'ralarining 2inchi qurultayi tarafidan butun mehnatkashlarga murojaat." *Yangi Yo'l,* no. 4 (1927): 3–5.

*O'zbekiston xotin-qizlar 1 s'ezdi, 1958, 7–8 Mart. Stenographik hisobat.* Toshkent: O'zbekiston SSR Davlat Nashriyoti, 1960.

"Ozodliq dushmanlari ulum va `azob." *Yangi Yo'l,* no. 2 (1929): 16.

"Ozodliq dushmanlariga ramdillik bo'lmasin." *Yangi Yo'l,* no. 2 (1929): 6.

"Ozodliq qaldirg'ochlari." *Turkiston,* Mar. 15, 1924, 3.

Paksoy, H. B. "The Basmachi from Within: An Account of Zeki Velidi Togan." *Nationalities Papers* 23, no. 2 (1995): 373–99.

Palen, Graf K. K. *Otchet po revisii Turkestanskago kraia, proizvedennoi po Vysochaishemu povelieniiu senatorom K. K. Palenom.* Vol. 1, *Naronye sud'i.* St. Peterburg: Senatskaia Tip., 1909.

Pal'vanova, Bibi. *Emantsipatsiia musul'manki: Opyt raskreposhcheniia zhenshchiny sovetskogo vostoka.* Moskva: Idz-vo Nauka, 1982.

"Paranji yopinishni man' qiladurg'on qonun chiqarilsin." *Qizil O'zbekiston,* Apr. 2, 1929, 4.

Park, Alexander. *Bolshevism in Turkestan, 1917–1927.* New York: Columbia University Press, 1957.

Patek-Salom, Gaye, and Pina Hukum. "Women's Emancipation after the Ataturk Period." In *Women of the Mediterranean,* edited by Monique Gadant, 92–109. London: Zed, 1986.

*Pervaia vseobshchaia perepis' naseleniia rossiiskoi imperii, 1897 g.* Vol. 83, *Samarkandskaia oblast'.* Vol. 86, *Syrdarinskaia oblast'.* Vol. 89, *Ferganskaia oblast'.* St. Peterburg: Izd. Tsentral'nago Statisticheskago Komiteta Ministerstva Vnutrennikh Del, 1897.

Piakovskii, A. V., ed. *Vosstanie 1916 goda v srednei Azii i Kazakhstane: Sbornik dokumentov.* Moskva: Akademiia Nauk, 1960.

Pierce, Richard. *Russian Central Asia: A Study in Colonial Rule, 1865–1917.* Berkeley: University of California Press, 1960.

Poliakov, Sergei. *Everyday Islam: Religion and Tradition in Rural Central Asia.* Translated by Anthony Olcott. Armonk, NY: M. E. Sharpe, 1992.

Privratsky, Bruce. *Muslim Turkistan: Kazak Religion and Collective Memory.* Richmond, Surrey: Curzon Press, 2001.

Pugachenkova, G. A. "K istorii parandzhi." *Sovetskaia Etnografiia,* no. 3 (1952): 191–95.

Putilovskaia. "Rabota kommunisticheskikh partii sredi zhenshchin narodov vostoka." *Kommunistka,* no. 12–13 (1921): 52–54.

Qaramiqef [*sic*]. "Maktublar." *Suyum Bike,* no. 11 (1915): 20.

Qasimova, Mu'allima Kamila bint `Azatulla. *Khanumlar islahi.* Kazan: Beraderan Karimilar, 1908.

Qobili, A. "Hujumchilar jallodlari."*Yangi Yo'l*, no. 4 (1929): 21.

Rahim qizi, Mahbuba. "Eski turmushning ikki maraziga qarshi: sho'ra qonuni yosh qizlarni erga berish va qalin bilan kurashadi." *Yangi Yo'l*, no. 6 (1929): 13.

Rahima. "Zarafshan viloyati xotin-qizlari." *Yangi Yo'l*, no. 10 (1926): 18.

Rahim, Hosiyat. "Xotin-qizlar Bilim Yurtiga ta'rixi bir qarash." *Yangi Yo'l*, no. 5 (1927): 5–8.

Rali. "Afg'on xotinlarining taqdiri yechilmokda." *Yangi Yo'l*, no. 2 (1929): 7.

———. "Dekret chiqarilsin!" *Yangi Yo'l*, no. 2 (1929): 4.

Rashid, Ahmed. *Jihad: The Rise of Militant Islam in Central Asia.* New Haven, CT: Yale University Press, 2002.

Razzoqov, Abdumalik. *O'zbekistonda paxtachlik tarixi.* Toshkent: O'zbekistan, 1994.

"Rezoliutsii 1 Vserossiskogo soveshschaniia organizatorov po rabote sredi zhenshchin narodov vostoka." *Kommunistka*, no. 12–13 (1921): 62–64.

Rorlich, Azade-Ayşe. *The Volga Tatars: A Profile in National Resistance.* Stanford, CA: Hoover Institution Press, Stanford University, 1986.

S., A. "Eski Toshkentda." *Qizil O'zbekiston*, Mar. 11, 1926, 2.

Sa'adi, T. "Ozodliq qurboni (voqe'i hikoya)." *Yangi Yo'l*, no. 12 (1927): 18.

Safarov, Georgii. *Kolonial'naia Revoliutsiia (Opyt Turkestana).* Moskva: Gos. Izd-vo., 1921.

Sahadeo, Jeffrey. "Creating a Russian Colonial Community: City, Nation, and Empire in Tashkent, 1865–1923." Ph.D. dissertation, University of Illinois, 2000.

Saida. "Adolat oining qotili." *Yangi Yo'l*, no. 8 (1928): 19.

Said Rasul Xo'ja Domla Said Aziz Xo'ja Mahdum Mufti o'g'li. *Ustod-i avval.* Reprint of a 1909 lithograph. Toshkent: Meros, 1990.

Savitskii, A. *Sattarxan Abdugafurov.* Tashkent: Uzbekistan, 1965.

Sazonova, M. V. "Zhenskii kostium Uzbekov Khorezma." In *Traditsionnaia odezhda narodov srednei Azii i Kazakhstana*, edited by N. P. Lobacheva, M. Sazonova, and I. V. Zakharova, 90–106. Moskva: Nauka, 1989.

Schoeberlein-Engel, John. "Identity in Central Asia: Construction and Contention in the Conceptions of 'Özbek,' 'Tâjik,' 'Muslim,' 'Samarqandi' and Other Groups." Ph.D. dissertation, Harvard University, 1994.

Schuyler, Eugene. *Turkistan: Notes of a Journey in Russian Turkistan, Kokand, Bukhara, and Kuldja.* Vol. 1. New York: Scribner, Armstrong and Co., 1877.

Scott, Joan. "The Evidence of Experience." *Critical Inquiry* 17 (1991): 773–97.

Seifulmuluk, Izzeddin. "Oila ham bola tarbiyasi." *Yangi Yo'l*, no. 11–12 (1926): 20.

Sh., M. "Paranji." *Yangi Yo'l*, no. 2 (1929): 7–8.

Shamsutdinov, Rustambek. *O'zbekistonda Sovetlarnin quloqlashtirish siyosati va uning fojeali oqibatlari.* Toshkent: Sharq, 2001.

Shaniiazov, K. Sh. *Etnograficheskie ocherki material'noi kul'tury Uzbekov konets XIX-nachalo XX v.* Tashkent: Fan, 1981.

"Sharixonda yana bir yavvoiliq." *Qizil O'zbekiston*, Mar. 22, 1927, 2.

Sharofat. "O'ziga yo'l ochdi." *Yangi Yo'l*, no. 5 (1926): 10–12.

Shaw, Stanford, and Ezel Kural Shaw. *History of the Ottoman Empire and Modern Turkey*. Vol. 2. Cambridge: Cambridge University Press, 1977.

Sherbek. "Ferg'ona ipachilik fabrikasida." *Yangi Yo'l*, no. 9 (1928): 13–15.

Shimko. "Yangi turmushga ko'chich oldida." *Yangi Yo'l*, no. 4 (1927): 9–11.

Shodieva, Tojixon. "Shodievaning qisqacha tarjima-i holi." *Yangi Yo'l*, no. 10–11 (1927): 28.

Sibghatulla qizi, Fakhr ul-Banat. *Aila Sabaqlari*. 1913. Uzbek reprint, *Oila Saboqlari*, edited by Teshaboi Ziyoyev. Toshkent: Yozuvchi, 1992.

Sirman, Nükhet. "Feminism in Turkey: A Short History." *New Perspectives on Turkey* 3, no. 1 (Fall 1989): 1–34.

Skallerup, Thomas. "Artisans between Guilds and Cooperatives: A History of Social and Economic Change in Russian Turkestan and Soviet Central Asia." Ph.D. dissertation, Indiana University, 1990.

Skocpol, Theda. *Protecting Soldiers and Mothers: The Political Origins of Social Policy in the United States*. Cambridge, MA: Harvard University Press, 1992.

Smith-Rosenberg, Carroll. *Disorderly Conduct: Visions of Gender in Victorian America*. New York: Knopf, 1985.

Sokol, Edward. *The Revolt of 1916 in Russian Central Asia*. Baltimore: Johns Hopkins, 1953.

Solieva, Zulhumor. "Saodatli zamonda yashaimiz." *Saodat*, no. 11 (1988): 20–22.

[Solixov], Miyon Bo'zruk. "Paranjining chiqishi." *Yangi Yo'l*, no. 7 (1927): 8–10.

Spectorsky, Susan A. *Chapters on Marriage and Divorce: Responses of Ibn Hanbal and Ibn Rahwayh*. Austin: University of Texas Press, 1993.

Stansell, Christine. *City of Women: Sex and Class in New York, 1789–1860*. Urbana: University of Illinois Press, 1982.

Stites, Richard. *The Women's Liberation Movement in Russia: Feminism, Nihilism, and Bolshevism, 1860–1917*. 2nd ed. Princeton, NJ: Princeton University Press 1990.

"Sud va ma'ishat." *Yangi Yo'l*, no. 11–12 (1928): 23–24.

Sukhareva, O. A. *Bukhara XIX-nachalo XX v.* Moskva: Nauka, 1962.

———. *Islam v Uzbekistane*. Tashkent: Izd-vo Akademii Nauk Uzbekskoi SSR, 1960.

———. *Istoriia sredneaziatskogo kostiuma, Samarkand, 2-ia polovina XIX-nachalo XX vek.* Moskva: Izd-vo Nauka, 1982.

Sulaimanova, Kh. S. *Istoriia Sovetskogo gosudarstva i prava Uzbekistana*. Vol. 1, *1917–1924*. Tashkent: Izd-vo Akademiia Nauk Uzbekskoi SSR, 1960.

———. *Istoriia Sovetskogo gosudarstva i prava Uzbekistana*. Vol. 2, *1924–1937*. Tashkent: Izd-vo Ak. Nauk Uzbekskoi SSR, 1963.

Suny, Ron. "The Empire Strikes Out: Imperial Russia, 'National Identity,' and Theories of Empire." In *A State of Nations: Empire and Nation-Making in the Age of Lenin and Stalin*, edited by Ron Suny and Terry Martin, 23–66. Oxford: Oxford University Press, 2001.

Tekeli, Şirin. "Introduction: Women in Turkey in the 1980s." In *Women in Modern Turkish Society*, edited by Şirin Tekeli, 1–21. London: Zed, 1995.

Thompstone, Stuart. "Russian Imperialism and the Commercialization of the Central Asian Cotton Trade." *Textile History* 26 (1995): 233–58.

Tillaxonova, Hosiyat. "Hujum masalsini mustahkamlash kerak." *Yangi Yo'l*, no. 9 (1927): 5.

———. "O'zbekistonda ipakchilik ishining ravnaqi." *Yangi Yo'l*, no. 6 (1928): 6–7.

Tokhtakhodjaeva, Marfua [To'xtaxo'jaeva]. "Women and Law in Uzbekistan." In *Assertions of Self: The Nascent Women's Movement in Central Asia*, 5–22. Lahore, Pakistan: Shirkat Gah, 1995.

———. *Between the Slogans of Communism and the Laws of Islam*. Translated from Russian by Sufian Aslam. Lahore, Pakistan: Shirkat Gah Women's Resource Centre, 1992.

Toshkentlik. "Quvnoq qizlar mahalasi." *Yangi Yo'l*, no. 7 (1928): 13–14.

Toshkentlik bir Mu'allima, "Turkiston mu'allimalari tarafindan bir sado," *Sado-i Turkiston*, no. 11 (1914): 1–2

Tsentral'noe Statisticheskoe Upravlenie. *Itogi vsesoiuznoi perepisi naselenii 1959: Uzbekskaia SSSR*. Moskva: Gosizdat, 1962.

Tsentral'noe Statisticheskoe Upravlenie Turkestanskoi Respubliki. *Materialy Vserossiiskikh sel'sko-khoziaistvennykh perepisei*. Vol 1, *Samarkandskoi oblasti*. Tashkent: Izdaniie TEU Turkrespubliki, 1924.

———. *Materialy Vserossiiskikh sel'sko-khoziaistvennykh perepisei*. Vol. 3, *Syrdariinskoi oblasti*. Samarkand: Ts.S.U, UzSSR, 1925.

Tufagan Xojim. "Hamshiralar tilindan." *Sado-i Turkiston*, no. 53 (1914): 3.

Tuncay, Mete. "Kadınlar halk firkasi." *Tarih ve Toplum* 9, no. 51 (1989): 158.

Turdiev, Sherali. "Germaniyada o'qiganlar izidan." *O'qituvchilar Gazetasi*, Apr. 6, 1991, 3.

Turkistonlik Noghai Mullah. "Yangi fikrchi, eski fikrchi." *Turkiston Viloyatining Gazetasi*, Jan. 7, 1910, 2.

Tursunov, Kh. T., ed.. *Khudzhum znachit nastuplenie*. Tashkent: Fan, 1987.

United Nations. *Demographic Yearbook*. New York: Statistical Office, United Nations, 1960, 1979.

Vaian Kutur'e [Marie Vailliant-Couturier]. "Vuali podnialis'." *Kommunistka*, no. 14–15 (1921): 16–17.

Vakila. "Faranjiga qirg'in! Sharq xotin-qizlari arasida ishlovchilar 4inchi maslahat majlisi to'g'risida." *Yangi Yo'l*, no. 1 (1929): 2–3.

Validov, Jemaladdin. "Hijab mas'alasi." *Suyum Bike*, no. 8 (1914): 4–6.

Vambery, Arminius. *Travels in Central Asia*. New York: Harper Brothers, 1865.

Viadyanath, R. *Formation of the Soviet Central Asia Republics: A Study in Soviet Nationalities Policy, 1917–1936*. New Delhi, India: People's Publishing House, 1967.

Virskii, M. ed. *Spravochnaia knizhka Samarkandskoi Oblasti na 1895 g.* Vypusk' 3. Samarkand: Tipografiia Shtaba Voisk, 1895.

Voronina, A. N. *Narodnye traditsii arkhitektury Uzbekistana*. Moskva: Gos. Izd-vo Arkhitektury i Gradostroitel'stv, 1951.

*Vsesoiuznaia perepis' naseleniia: Okanchatel'nye itogi*. Vol. 15, *Population, UzSSR*. Moskva: Tsentral'naia Upravleniia Statistiki, 1926.

Willfort, Fritz. *Turkestanisches Tagebuch: Sechs Jahre in russisch-Zentralasien*. Wien: Wilhelm Braumüller, 1930.

Wood, Elizabeth. *The Baba and the Comrade: Gender and Politics in Revolutionary Russia*. Bloomington: Indiana University Press, 1997.

Xaidarova, N. X., ed. *Sovet O'zbekiston kitobi/kniga Sovetskogo Uzbekistana, 1917–1927: Bibliografik ko'rsatkich*. Toshkent: O'zbekiston SSR Davlat Kitob Palatasi, 1976.

[Xoldarova], Sobira. "Xotin-qizlar ma'orifi taraqqida." *Qizil O'zbekiston*, Mar. 8, 1926, 5.

———. "Yangilik." *Yer Yuzi*, no. 20 (1927): 8–10.

Xo'qandli Ashraf ul-Banat Tajie. Letter to the editor. *Alem-i Nisvan* 35 (1906): 572–74.

"Xotinlar majlislari nima deydi." *Yangi Yo'l*, no. 5 (1929): 25.

"Xotin-qiz ozodlig'ida bo'shangliq bo'lmasin." *Yangi Yo'l*, no. 7 (1928): 2.

"Xotin-qizlar ma'orifini kuchaytiraylik." *Yangi Yo'l*, no. 7 (1929): 3–4.

"Xotinqizlarni himoya qilish yo'lida." *Qizil O'zbekiston*, Apr. 3, 1929, 1.

"Xotin qizlar ozodliq haqida." *Qizil O'zbekiston*, Apr. 17, 1929, 3.

"Xotinqizlar paranjiga qarshi." *Qizil O'zbekiston*, Apr. 11, 1929, 3.

Yamauchi, Masayuki. *The Green Crescent under the Red Star: Enver Pasha in Soviet Russia, 1919–1922*. Tokyo: Institute for Study of Languages and Cultures of Asia and Africa, 1991.

Yaqubof, M. "8inchi Martg'a bir sovg'a." *Yangi Yo'l*, no. 3 (1927): 11.

Yaroshevskii, Dov. "Empire and Citizenship." In *Russia's Orient: Imperial Borderlands and Peoples, 1700–1917*, edited by Daniel Brower and Edward Lazzerini, 58–79. Bloomington: Indiana University Press, 1997.

"Yavvoiy burgut Qumrini changallamokchi." *Qizil O'zbekiston*, Mar. 20, 1927.

Ye., A. "Xotin-qizlar mamlakat mudafa'a ishida." *Yangi Yo'l*, no. 8 (1928): 8–9.

Yo'ldoshbaeva, Fotima [Fatima Iuldashbaeva]. *Moia sud'ba*. Tashkent: Yosh Gvardiia, 1972.

"Yosh qizlarni erga berish bilan kurashamiz." *Yangi Yo'l*, no. 1 (1929): 24.

Yunus, G'azi. "Paranji va uning kelib chiqishi." *Qizil O'zbekiston*, Feb. 3, 1927, 2.

Yunusup, Hamit. "Sharq xotin-qizlarning jihadi." *Qizil Bairoq*, May 22, 1921.

Yusuf, Khass-Hajib. *Wisdom of Royal Glory (Kutadgu Bilig): A Turko-Islamic Mirror for Princes*. 11th century. Translated by Robert Dankoff. Chicago: University of Chicago Press, 1983.

"Zainab Qurbonova." *Yangi Yo'l*, no. 9 (1928): 23.

Zelenskii, I. A. "Xotin-qizlar arasidagi ishlarda firqaning asosi vazifalari." *Qizil O'zbekiston*, Oct. 15, 1926, 2.

Zelenskii and Muratova. "8inchi Mart natijalarini mustahkamlash to'g'risida." *Yangi Yo'l*, no. 4–5 (1928): 30–31.

Ziiaev, Kh. Z. "Natsional'no-osvoboditel'noe vosstanie 1916 god v Turkestane."
  *Obshchestvennye nauki v Uzbekistan*, no. 7 (1991): 27–36.
Ziyad. "Taraqqiiparvar fida`i yaki `anqa shimali." *Din va Ma`ishat*, no. 4 (1909):
  83–84.
Zubaida. "Lenin solg'on yo'lda." *Yangi Yo'l*, no. 10 (1928): 20–21.

# INDEX

Backwardness, 8, 14, 22, 32, 35, 66–
67, 74–75, 94, 99, 109–10, 137,
149–50, 162, 182, 241n16, 242n29
Bahriniso I., 83, 90, 116, 119, 167,
176, 190, 195, 265n54, 275n21,
280n38
Basmachi, 60–62, 85, 158, 164, 180,
187, 189–91, 200, 256n23, 256n25
Behbudi, Mahmud Xo'ja, 41, 43, 46,
52, 252n42, 253n57, 262n23
Bibars, Iman, 231, 290nn1–2
Bilim Yurt (Women and Girls' House
of Knowledge), 86–90, 93, 100,
102–5, 116, 126, 141, 148, 154,
157, 263–64nn38–39, 264n41,
264nn44–45, 278n11
body, 33, 44, 114, 119, 179, 187–88,
197, 200, 203, 234, 236, 271n44
*boi* (wealthy landowner), 111, 113,
115, 182, 188–89, 191, 195, 198,
200, 203, 205, 212, 231, 266n64,
278n7
Bolshevik, 5, 12–14, 32–33, 51, 59–
61, 63, 69, 73, 88, 152, 154, 157,
183–84, 229, 256n25, 267n9. *See
also* Communist Party member
Bukhara (city and province), xiv–xvi,
9, 12, 17, 45, 50, 62, 80, 134–36,
176–78, 192, 194–95, 208–9
Bukharan Emirate, 19–23, 28–31, 78, 80
Bukharan People's Republic (BPR),
61, 64
Burnasheva, Zahida, 48, 86, 88,
253n66, 264n39

Census (*perepis'*), 27, 43, 62, 80,
222, 224, 239n6, 243n39, 248n8,
249n14, 249n18, 251n41, 261n14,
288n18, 289n20. *See also* population statistics
Central Asian Bureau (CAB), 5, 16–
17, 74, 92, 98–100, 150, 162, 203–
5, 207, 213
*chachvon*, 3, 11, 29, 42, 110, 132pl,

135, 143, 145, 171–72, 275n17,
280n32
citizenship, 9, 67, 181, 258n41; Russian, 23, 26, 28, 49–50, 58,
241n28, 254n2; Soviet 13–14,
53–54, 63, 66–67, 75, 114, 117,
146, 212
class, 9, 12–13, 15, 58, 61–62, 73, 93,
99, 107, 111–12, 115, 118, 127,
133–34, 159, 167, 184, 191, 200,
203, 208–10, 217, 228; enemies,
71, 202–3, 209; warfare, 189–90
clergy, 39, 48, 56, 71, 91–92, 120,
135, 150–51, 169, 175, 181–85,
188, 190–91, 194–98, 200, 207,
229, 231, 237, 271n43. *See also
domla; mullah*
clothing, modern and traditional, 19,
21, 27, 45, 118–19, 124, 134–36,
141, 145, 155, 157, 159, 161pl,
178, 179–80, 194–95, 220, 225–
26, 233–37, 281n54, 290n5
clubs, women's, 90, 97, 107, 111, 140,
144–45, 163pl, 172, 196, 282n1
coercion, 3, 10, 12, 22, 70, 74, 115,
118–19, 133, 145, 170, 176, 178,
180, 184, 188, 213. *See also*
unveiling
collective farm, 106, 128, 218–20,
223–25
collectivization, 14, 57, 72, 104, 113,
127, 176, 190–92, 212–14, 218–
19, 221–23, 233
colonialism (Russian, Soviet), xiv, 4,
6–9, 11, 13, 19–29, 31, 33, 53–
54, 59–61, 63, 65, 81, 133, 135,
138, 222, 231, 240n10, 242n28,
245n14, 247n32, 254n4, 258n35,
278n4; comparative, 7–9, 11, 22,
27–28, 33, 39, 65, 133, 241n23,
250n21, 273n55. *See also* anticolonialism
colonized (Central Asians), 5, 9, 14,
22, 28–29, 54

colonizers (Russian), 5, 19, 22, 25–
26, 28–29, 57, 63, 123, 247n32,
250n21, 255n11
Commissars: education, 85–88, 90,
126, 265n45; justice, 113;
nationalities, 21, 62, 64, 256n26;
peoples, 64, 164
Communism, 4, 17, 66, 74, 94, 97,
107, 109, 120, 158, 173–74, 180,
182, 193, 257n28, 283n4
Communist Party (all-Union), 4–5,
10–11, 14, 17, 32, 53, 62, 66, 68,
76, 90, 141, 150, 209–12, 217,
232; Central Executive Committee,
98, 184
Communist Party member, 11, 14, 16,
33, 65, 76, 86–87, 92–94, 97–102,
105, 107, 118, 119, 125, 127, 129–
31, 134, 138–39, 142–44, 148–51,
157, 159, 161pl, 162–64, 166–67,
169–70, 172–73, 175, 178–79,
183, 193–96, 198, 202–4, 207–8,
210, 217, 220, 225–26, 230–231
Communist Party of Uzbekistan
(CPUz), xi, 3, 9, 11, 17, 61, 63–64,
72, 85, 91, 93, 97, 105–7, 109,
114, 119–20, 123, 132–33, 143,
146, 148, 149, 151, 164, 166,
180–84, 187, 190, 193–94, 199,
218, 225, 230; central committee,
92, 106, 126–27, 164–65, 204
community, 12, 34, 38, 47, 65, 69, 84,
150, 171, 183, 186–88, 191, 194,
196, 201, 211, 213–14, 219–20,
233. See also millat (nation); rural
compliance, 12, 72, 233, 286n60
conscription, military, 23, 54–55, 75,
103, 242n28, 254n2
conservatives (Muslim), 5, 34–35, 40,
42–43, 46, 52, 59, 120, 137, 172,
174, 184, 229–230, 237, 250n27
constraint, 12, 213, 231
continuity, 4, 17, 19, 31–32, 47, 78,
215, 240n10, 242n34, 289n25

cotton, 22, 26–27, 30, 38, 45, 113,
135, 190, 204, 218, 224,
246nn20–21
courts: Islamic, 25, 69, 122, 190,
252n51, 276n25; Peoples/Soviet,
69, 71, 113–14, 121–22, 160, 196,
199–200, 202, 205; Russian, 23–
24, 245n14; Turkish 71
courtyard (*ichkari* and *tashkari*), 29–
30, 40, 78, 92, 94, 121, 124, 135,
169, 176, 228, 273n3
crime, 46, 55, 117, 187, 197, 200, 207,
218, 221, 245n14, 272n51; counterrevolutionary, 211–12; of everyday life (*byt'*), 212, 231, 272n51,
283n3, 283n5, 288n5

Death sentence, 24, 193, 200, 206,
211, 236, 245n14
*dehqon*, 26–27, 38, 112, 118, 182, 189,
191, 197, 203, 246n22
dekulakization, 130, 191, 203, 218,
266n64
demonstration, 3, 55–58, 75, 103,
147pl, 149, 162, 166, 176, 180,
187, 191, 199, 209–10, 219, 221,
255n11, 256n19
divorce: Islamic, 24, 34, 45–47,
66, 69, 183, 195, 245nn12–13,
252n52; Soviet, 69–71, 100, 106,
159, 169, 193, 196–97, 259n50
divorcée, 5, 113, 148, 250n20
*domla*, 77, 79, 81, 83–84, 90, 93,
103, 129, 152, 157, 169, 175, 233,
266n58, 274n11
dowry, 44–45, 119. See also *mahr*; *qalin*

Eastern (Oriental), 14, 99, 137, 141–
42, 155, 207, 210, 242n29, 276n39
Edip, Halide, 70, 73–74
editor, 17, 37, 44, 123, 127, 137,
248n11; of *Yangi Yo'l*, 94, 97–
98, 100–107, 110, 112, 122, 200,
209–10, 268n13, 274n6, 283n3

education, 7–8, 17, 21, 45, 65, 93, 107,
153, 217; Islamic, 21, 34, 38, 40,
76–77, 79–82, 84–86, 88, 90–93,
103–4, 234–35, 246n27, 261n10,
265n55; modern, 33–35, 40, 42,
65, 77, 83–84, 102–3, 153, 169,
176, 211, 262n20, 290n5; Russian,
28, 84; Soviet, 4, 76, 81, 85–88,
90, 92–93, 107, 126, 149, 158, 176,
220, 222–24, 227, 230, 266n64,
288n18, 289n19; of women and
girls, 4, 11, 17, 32, 34–36, 38, 40–
43, 49–52, 66, 75, 77, 79–84, 86,
88, 92, 97, 100, 103, 106–12, 115–
16, 120, 122, 129–31, 137, 139,
144–45, 153, 155, 178, 181, 215,
219, 222–23, 226, 229, 235–36,
250n27, 253n63, 262n23, 264n45,
287n68. *See also otin;* schools
Egypt, 8, 12, 34, 38, 41, 46, 49, 51,
131, 133, 143, 174, 231
emancipation, women's, 67, 70, 130,
146, 178, 184
Empire: Russian, xiv, 6, 8, 13–14,
21–23, 25–26, 34, 36, 38, 42, 47,
49, 51, 54, 58–59, 82, 241n28;
Soviet, 4–5, 12, 14, 63, 227. *See also*
imperialism
enemy, 182, 190; of the people, 126,
128, 130. *See also* class enemies
equality, male-female, 25, 32, 43, 49,
51–53, 59, 66, 68, 71, 73, 75, 79,
109, 113, 122, 131–32, 138, 150,
171, 180–81, 186, 217, 219–20,
226–27, 229–30, 232–33, 236,
254n74, 258n46, 260n70
ethnicity, 21, 30, 34, 53–54, 62–63,
87, 248n8, 257nn28–29
European, 8, 10, 16, 22, 28, 73, 125,
133, 144, 153, 217, 224, 227–28,
266n3, 268n12, 287n69; thought,
33, 43, 46, 51, 253n57
exile, 20–21, 28, 101, 106, 189, 191,
203, 206, 218, 234, 245n14, 269n25

Fakhriddin, Rizauddin, 42, 45–47
family: ideas about, 6, 25, 29–31, 33,
40–43, 45–46, 49, 52, 66, 99, 137,
178, 187, 195, 211–12, 215, 227,
241n23, 252n52, 253n63; law, 24,
67–72, 74, 113–14, 150, 176,
272n50
family evening, 109, 196–98
Fargana, ix, xiv–xvi, 21, 25–27, 55–
57, 192, 195–96, 205–6, 244n7,
269n24, 284n19
farmer, 21, 24, 26, 112–13, 176, 182,
190–91, 196, 212, 244n10, 246n22;
collective, 191, 203, 219, 224,
242n32; landless farm worker, 111,
118, 191, 285n52; poor, 144, 190–
92, 195, 203–5, 217, 286n64
*fatwa*, 48, 182, 183–85
feminist ideas, 12, 25, 41, 44, 131,
133, 287n70; and Communism,
98, 111, 216–17; scholars and
activists, 6, 13, 143, 231, 249n13
fire, 94–97, 121, 158, 166, 171, 177,
192pl, 220, 266n1
Fitrat, Abdurauf, 40–45, 47, 50, 52,
250nn27–28, 252n42, 252n48,
252n52, 253nn62–63, 254n74,
280n34

G'azi Yunus, 140, 173–75, 276n37,
280n35
gender, 5, 12, 14, 27, 53, 73, 75, 99,
111, 215, 217, 224, 230, 233,
267n7, 288n5
gender relations, 7, 11, 188, 204,
214–15, 226–27, 230, 289n25
gender segregation, 14, 21, 29–30,
52, 77, 79, 109, 111, 120, 122,
136–37, 196, 220, 274n11
G'oibjonova, Shamsikamar, 142–43, 148
Göle, Nilüfer, 66, 68
Grebenkin, A. D., 26, 135–36
G'ulom, G'afur, 109, 116, 118, 152–53,
278n6

*H*adith, 50, 115, 119, 254n75, 271n46

Haft-yak, 80, 83, 124, 152

Hajj, 49, 81, 136, 175

Hamza Hakimzoda Niyoziy, 138, 174–75, 252n44, 270n30, 276n32, 280n36, 281n54

hegemony, 13, 231–32, 236

*hijab*, 134, 137, 139, 174, 183–84, 233–37, 275n17, 290n5

historians, 4, 8, 10–12, 15–17, 54, 58, 60, 67, 71, 98, 174, 178, 182, 184, 186, 212–13, 227, 231, 239n2, 242n34, 258n44, 270n30, 278n1, 281n58, 282n1, 282n3, 287n1

honor, 24, 29, 42, 119–22, 186, 195, 197–98, 201, 211, 217, 219, 230, 282n58

Hujum (attack campaign, 1927), 3, 5, 10–12, 17–18, 100, 106, 123, 130, 132, 134, 146, 148, 150–51, 162, 164–65, 167–71, 174, 177, 180–81, 183–89, 191–94, 196–99, 201–03, 205, 207, 210–13, 215, 217–21, 225–27, 230, 233, 236, 242n30, 279n16, 281n42, 287n2; Hujum Commission, 164–65, 167, 194

human rights, 118, 130, 258n46, 291n7

Humoira-xon H., 80–81, 116, 175–76, 260n1, 261n12, 265n58

*I*brohimova, Milli-xon, 169, 178, 220–21, 279n26; To'raxon, 140, 143, 148, 277n44

*ichkari*. See courtyard

identity, 21, 53, 65, 97, 234, 285n52; Muslim, 51, 234, 237, 249n15; Turkestani, 23, 33–34, 87, 248n5; Uzbek, 4, 6, 62, 13–14, 53, 64, 99, 166–67, 171, 221–22, 241n26, 242n30

Ikromov, Akmal, 158, 164, 166, 179, 205, 269n22

illiteracy, 7, 16, 81, 83, 88, 90, 112, 129, 152, 160, 182, 194, 215, 222, 265n54, 270n26, 289n19. *See also* literacy

imperialism, 12, 14, 21–24, 26, 63, 65, 69, 79, 142, 191, 254n2; economic, 22–25; subjects of, 23, 241n24. *See also* Empire

incitement, 187, 194, 196–201, 214, 232

intelligentsia. See *ziyolilar*

International Women's Day (March 8), 108, 140, 144–46, 152, 165–66, 194, 197, 199, 277n51, 282n62

interviews, ix, 6, 14–16, 19, 48, 79, 81, 123, 135, 138, 149, 151, 198, 218–19, 228, 242n32; subjects of, 300–302

Iran, 4, 7, 10, 48, 131, 133, 151, 172, 174, 178–79, 181, 210, 223, 251n39, 255n19, 262n20, 266n1, 281n58, 284n18

ishon, 56, 120, 153–54, 182, 195–96. *See also* clergy

Islam, xi, 6–8, 34, 41, 47, 51, 94, 110, 131, 183–85, 220, 227–28, 233–36, 260n4, 266n1, 272n54, 280n36, 290n5, 290n7; and veiling, 137, 173–75, 178, 194–95, 201, 232, 234. *See also* piety

Islamic institutions, 10, 76, 79, 83, 85, 91, 136, 189–90

Islamic society, 7, 9–10, 34, 38, 58–59, 116, 131, 133

Islamists, 34, 134, 235–37, 275n17, 291n7

*J*adid movement, 17, 20–21, 27–28, 33, 42, 52, 82, 87, 162, 229, 261n11, 248n7

Jadid thought: on women's education, 4, 17, 28, 32–33, 37–43, 51, 53, 76–77, 82–84, 87, 93, 97 103, 107, 119–20, 122, 152, 229, 250n27; on marriage, 42–49, 51–52, 113, 118–19, 229, 253n63; on reform of women, 8, 9,17, 28, 32–33, 35–39, 42, 51–52, 229; on veiling, 33, 136–37, 146, 148–49, 173–75, 183–84, 211; on women's rights, 3, 49, 51–52, 59, 164. *See also* schools

Jadids (reformers), 5, 13, 17, 20–21, 23, 28, 31, 39–40, 57, 59, 62, 75–76, 82, 93–94, 103–7, 109, 148, 164, 173–75, 184, 210–11, 226, 229–30, 246n27, 280nn34–36

Jalilova, Bashorat, 88, 140, 146, 148, 154, 264n45, 277n51

judge, 19, 28, 42, 69, 71, 113, 121, 136, 199, 202, 205, 244n9, 276n25

Kalianova, 202–5, 285n52

Kalinin, Mikhail, 104, 143, 158, 277n44

Kamp, Marianne, 242n33, 242n36, 271n39, 273n1, 285n47, 289n25

Kandiyoti, Deniz, 67, 232, 258n40, 258n44

Karryeva, Roza, 58, 182, 282n3

Kasimovshchina, 205, 285n54, 286n68

Kazakh, 21, 26, 56, 62, 84, 117–18, 135, 137, 139, 241n26, 255n4, 257n29, 263n31, 272n50

Kazakhstan, xv–xvi, 22, 54, 244n7, 254n1, 257n26

Keller, Shoshana, x, 11–12, 256n25

Khalid, Adeeb, x, 9, 33, 79, 82, 243n4, 248n5, 248n8, 252n44, 261n10

Khiva, ix, xiv, 9, 13, 25, 91, 247n32; khanate of, 22–23, 29, 31, 61, 245n14, 256n26, 261n16; People's Republic of, 61–62, 257n33. *See also* Xorazm

Kokand, xi, xiv–xv, 14, 38–39, 55, 59–60, 125, 145, 166–69, 234, 247n32,

248n8, 249n11, 249nn14–16; khanate of, 22–23, 36, 78; Turkestan Autonomy in, 59–60

*Kommunistka* (Woman Communist, journal), 98–99, 111, 142, 174, 193, 266n61, 267nn6–9, 277n41, 281n42, 282n1

Komsomol (Communist Youth League), 97, 119, 126–28, 146, 156–59, 162, 166, 194, 219, 274n8

Kotkin, Stephen, 8, 75

Krämer, Annette, 260n2, 261n4, 261n13, 262n25

Krupskaia, Nadezhda, 100–101, 147, 210, 268n14

kulak. See *boi* (wealthy landowner); dekulakization

Kunasheva, Hadicha, 145, 148, 277n50

Kyrgyz, 56, 62, 87, 118, 135, 137, 139, 241n26, 244n9, 272n50

Kyrgyzstan, xvi, 54, 137, 244n7, 254n1, 257n26, 257n29

Land: confiscation, 26, 57, 60, 112–13, 189, 204, 218, 231, 255n4; ownership, 22–24, 56, 109, 112–13, 176, 244n10, 246n22; reform, 146, 181–82, 189–93, 197, 199–200, 204–5, 279n14, 283n16

Latifot T., 80, 228, 260n1, 261n12, 262n19

law: changes in, 6, 22–26, 34, 39, 48, 51–52, 54, 66–71, 73–74, 112–14, 198, 205, 207–8, 211, 244n10, 245n14, 258n46, 271n44, 287n73; enforcement of, 72–73, 116–19, 121–22, 150–51, 162–63, 200, 202, 206, 212, 215, 217, 233, 288n6; and veiling, 106, 137, 176–77, 179–80, 206–11, 235, 287n69. *See also* family law; Sharia

liberation, women's, 3–5, 11, 17, 32, 39–40, 100, 102, 118, 122, 130–31, 139, 150, 160, 165, 167, 178,

183–85, 191, 198, 202–5, 207, 209, 211–12, 227, 230, 270n30, 278n14, 286n68, 287n69

life stories, ix, 15, 19, 273n1

literacy, 7, 16, 38, 40, 42, 76, 78, 80–83, 88–90, 92–93, 97, 107, 108pl, 112, 122, 124, 146, 150, 152, 182, 222–24, 249n14, 261n14, 261n18, 289n19; courses, 90, 97, 111, 172, 176, 178, 212, 215, 222, 265n54, 270n58

Liubimova, Serafima, 92, 100, 164, 179, 207–8, 267n5, 269n26, 276n39, 279n16

lynching, 187, 201–2, 232

*Madrasa*, 38, 69, 77–79, 82–85, 91, 93, 152, 175, 181, 189, 261n12, 265n58

Mafrat-xon M., 116, 145, 168–69, 178, 198

*mahalla* (urban neighborhood), 78, 80, 103, 117, 143, 160, 162, 166, 168, 177, 197, 224

*mahr*, 24, 45, 119, 245n13, 252n52, 271n46, 273n54

*maktab*, 37–38, 77–83, 85–86, 189, 262n24, 265n55; curriculum of, 79–80, 82, 93, 261n10

male authority, 44, 77–78, 173, 188, 201, 211, 232; and guardianship of women, 43–44, 50

male spaces, 22, 27–30, 39, 97, 273n3

Malika-xon J., 79, 83, 89, 145, 263n36

Manzura H., 92–93, 143, 170–71, 252n53, 266n63

*Ma'orif va O'qituvchi* (Education and Teacher, newspaper), 16, 104, 243n40, 270n29

marriage: age of, 21, 36, 43–44, 46, 66, 69–70, 72, 89–90, 100, 105, 109, 113–14, 116–19, 124, 129, 149, 155, 169, 175, 203, 215, 221, 226, 252n42, 271n44, 271n45,

283n3; arranged/coerced, 19, 30, 43–45, 69–70, 100, 105, 107, 115–19, 124, 149, 155–56, 175–76, 204, 219, 227, 247n37, 250n20, 252n44, 272n47, 273n2; companionate, 36, 44, 51, 109, 115, 117, 156, 226, 229–30; ideas about, 6, 24, 33–35, 40, 42–52, 69–70, 81, 97, 107, 109, 113–17, 252n48; men's opportunities for, 43–46, 119, 252n52, 253n57; polygynous, 19, 21, 38–39, 44, 46–48, 51–52, 66, 69–70, 72, 105, 114–18, 124, 150, 169, 193, 215, 221, 226, 231, 252n42, 253n59, 253n62, 254n68, 283n3

Martin, Terry, 63, 240n10, 242n37, 268n12, 287n3

Massell, Gregory, 3, 5, 11, 68–69, 148, 191, 208, 239nn1–3, 247n1, 258n40, 258n42, 260n70, 267n6, 267n7, 277n52, 278n14, 287n2

Middle East, 7–9, 27, 228, 234, 237, 251n32

*millat* (nation), 34, 41, 44, 51, 55

mobilization, 8, 53, 63, 67, 75, 146, 222, 232

modernists, 4, 6, 34, 41, 43, 104, 113, 151, 173, 211

modernization, 4, 7, 9, 18, 33, 54, 59, 63, 66, 73–75, 94, 97, 120, 131, 176, 178–79, 180, 224, 227, 229–30, 233; and women, 4, 10, 43, 66–68, 70, 73–75, 83, 94, 97, 102, 106, 110, 131–33, 137, 179, 180–81, 185, 211, 215, 224, 227, 233, 260n70

modesty, 42, 155, 178, 180, 225, 234, 236, 290n5

morality, 40–44, 46, 50, 99, 119–21, 144–45, 155, 169, 173, 226, 273n55

Moscow, 13, 59, 68, 74, 87, 98, 100–103, 106, 126–27, 141–43, 170–71, 191, 230, 258n35

*Qizil O'zbekiston* (Red Uzbekistan, newspaper), 16, 103–4, 127, 164–65, 179–80, 183, 194, 199, 209, 243n40, 270n29, 285n54

Quran, xii, 19, 30, 37–38, 40, 44–48, 59, 76–77, 79–81, 86, 92–93, 102, 119, 124, 131, 152, 182, 194, 206, 233, 253n62, 266n58, 271n46, 273n54, 290n5

*Rabotnitsa* (Woman Worker, journal), 97, 109, 111, 127

Rahbar-oi Olimova, vii, 76, 79, 88–89, 116, 140, 152–60, 162, 166, 168, 171, 173, 178, 198–99, 209, 260n1, 262n19, 265n46, 277n51, 278n1, 278nn4–5, 278n11

railroad, xiv, 22, 26, 28, 38, 61, 177

Ramiz, 109, 126, 264n45, 274n5

rape, 72, 118, 170, 186, 188, 194–96, 202–4, 281n58, 283n3

rapist, 122, 196, 207

Red Army, 59–62, 64, 85, 187, 222, 257n34; Russian, 21–23, 39, 54–56, 242n28; Uzbek national division, 64, 146, 166, 257n34

religious practice, 7, 30, 40, 44, 50, 70, 77, 80, 92, 119, 129, 131, 157, 191, 196, 227, 234–35, 280n35; veiling as, 18, 136, 146, 159, 165, 168–72, 177, 182, 201, 207, 220, 234–35, 276n25. *See also* Islam; piety

resistance, 5, 10–13, 18, 27, 68, 171, 179, 181, 186–87, 191, 202, 213, 230–33, 241n23

revolution, 5, 21, 149, 158, 211, 215; cultural, 17, 149, 189, 211; Russian, February 1917, 13–14, 51–52, 57, 58–59, 73; Russian 1905, 49, 57, 71, 149; social, 71. *See also* Bolshevik; October Revolution

revolutionary, 49, 51, 58, 61, 66, 68, 110, 158, 191, 200, 208, 247n1, 260n70

Reza Shah, 10, 133, 179, 181

rights: women's, 3, 13–14, 35–38, 41, 49–51, 58–59, 67, 70, 74–75, 97, 102, 107, 109, 112–13, 118, 121, 138–39, 141, 146, 150, 171, 178, 181, 212, 215, 217, 230, 233, 235; to education, 34, 41, 43; Islamic, 24, 41, 44, 49–51; to own land, 112; to vote, 49, 71, 73–74, 217

riots, 54–55, 57–58

rural: communities, 18, 60, 188–89, 220, 222, 243n39, 275n21, 279n14, 288n18; Uzbek women, 14, 16, 18, 27, 29–30, 112, 135, 218–26; Uzbeks, 16, 26, 243n38

Russian language, xi, 4–6, 11, 15–16, 35, 46, 84, 87, 97–98, 111, 131, 164, 167, 174, 193, 242nn29–30, 243n40, 246n22, 247n30, 257n28, 258n35, 271n45, 272n50; Uzbek knowledge of, 16–17, 28, 33, 100, 123, 126, 130, 138, 142, 155, 222, 243n38, 267n6, 278n4

Russian women, 15–16, 38, 57–58, 98–100, 108, 115, 122, 125, 138, 140–41, 143, 148, 160–61, 163, 193, 208, 226, 247n1, 249n13, 254n69, 266n3, 269n26, 274n12, 278n13

Russians, 5, 15–16, 22–23, 26–28, 32, 34–35, 38–39, 49, 59–60, 84, 98, 103, 112, 120, 123–24, 134–35, 138, 155, 157, 162, 166, 188, 191, 195, 202, 205, 222, 229, 230–31, 242n37, 243n39, 244n7, 245n17, 255n4, 267n12, 269n20, 273n55, 289n24; administrators, 24, 39, 55, 59, 80–81, 248n8

Russification, 33, 87, 144, 157, 159, 166, 201, 237

Samarkand, xiv, xv, 21, 55–56, 60, 62, 126, 177, 192, 205, 207, 209–10

Saodat A., 119, 176

Sart, 13, 36–37, 40, 62, 64–65, 81, 248n8, 250n21, 263n31, 264n41, 276n25

schools: gymnasia, 28, 84, 124; Islamic, 77–79, 82, 85–86, 91, 93, 123–24, 129, 190, 197, 233, 235, 263n34, 265n56; Jadid, 38, 40, 76–77, 85–86, 91–92, 249n16, 262n24; Jadid schools for girls, 32, 35, 37–38, 76–77, 80, 82–84, 86–90, 93, 103, 129, 137–38, 153–54, 179, 229, 248n10, 253n66, 263n30, 263n36, 264n45; Russian-Native, 27–28, 82, 84–85, 130, 152, 155; Soviet, 63, 66, 76–77, 85–93, 97, 109, 120–21, 126, 140, 143–46, 152, 154–55, 157–58, 162, 166–67, 175, 179–80, 190, 210, 220, 222–24, 228, 233, 239n6, 263n37, 264n41, 266n64, 288–89n18–19. *See also* education; *madrasa*; *maktab*

seclusion, 4, 18, 21, 29, 43, 49, 57, 135–37, 162–65, 175–77, 180, 201–2, 207, 211, 214, 215, 219, 221, 226–27, 229–33. *See also* gender segregation

secularism, 67–70, 72, 74, 77, 82, 236–37

sexuality, 24, 29, 39, 42–44, 46–47, 69, 119, 164, 188, 193, 196, 201, 215–16, 230, 250n21, 252n42

Shahrixon (Fargana valley), 194, 284n19

Shamsieva, Saodat, 83, 117, 123–31, 138, 140–41, 148–49, 178, 197, 209–11, 218, 268n16, 269n23, 273n1

Sharia (Islamic law), xi–xii, 23–24, 29, 34, 41–45, 47–51, 59, 67–70, 74, 113–14, 136–37, 150, 182–83,

244n9, 245nn13–14, 254n76, 270n34, 273n54

Shodieva, Tojixon, 100, 105–6, 122, 165, 269nn24–25

Sibghatullah qizi, Fakhr ul-Banat, 44, 46–47, 51

silk, 26–27, 29, 115, 145, 148, 190, 220, 224, 226, 246n20, 272n51, 278n2, 279n30

slavery, 23, 25, 39, 173; as metaphor for women's status, 25, 50, 118, 138–39, 142, 146, 158, 164–65, 174, 180, 193, 210, 245nn17–18

Smith-Rosenberg, Carroll, 188, 214

socialism, 7, 51, 62–64, 76, 98, 164, 180, 224, 267n7; state, 32, 212, 226

Solixov, Miyon Bo'zruk, 109, 173–74, 280n34

*sovchi*, 116, 124, 156, 271n47

soviet (council), 59–61, 71, 74, 118, 189, 195–97, 199, 204, 208–11, 212, 259n61, 282n1; all-Russian, 143

Soviet government, 3–4, 7, 11, 13, 17, 33, 48, 59–61, 63, 67–68, 72, 75, 81, 85, 93, 97, 104, 110, 117, 122, 130, 133, 143, 164, 181, 183, 185, 187, 189–91, 195, 201, 211–13, 217, 219, 230–33, 258n42, 270n32, 288n5, 289n28

Soviet Union, 4–13, 16, 21, 53–54, 64, 66, 74, 90–91, 98–99, 109, 113, 178, 210, 217–18, 222–28, 240n14, 242n34, 254n1, 258n35, 259n50, 260n70, 266n3, 269n20, 275n16, 280n30, 285n51, 287n73

Stalin, 21, 143, 220, 222, 224, 277n44, 281n40

Stalinism, 3, 216, 227, 242n34

state: as agent of change, 33, 75, 133, 231–32; control, 74, 179, 190, 212, 218, 233, 236; and individual/

state (continued)
  citizen, 53, 146; intervention by,
    8, 63, 66, 146, 176, 187, 196, 214,
    217; surveillance, 72
  subject: as agent, 11–13, 53, 242n34;
    colonial, 5, 14, 23–24, 54, 63,
    179, 241n28, 278n4; liberal, 15,
    242n34; oral history, 14–15
  subordination, 3; women's, 13, 18,
    139, 165, 211, 231–32
  suicide, 195, 227, 266n1
  superstition, 33–34, 77, 94, 96–97,
    109, 174, 280nn35–36
  surrogate proletariat, 5, 68, 75, 164,
    191–92, 247n1, 260n70, 278n14
  Suyum Bike (journal), 35, 44, 47–48,
    51, 122, 137, 254n69

Tajie, Ashraf ul-Banat of Kokand,
  36–40
Tajik, 15, 62, 64, 87, 134, 205
Tajikistan, 62, 235, 248nn9–11
tashkari. See courtyard
Tashkent, xi, xiv–xvi, 16, 21–22, 55–
  56, 58–62, 65, 84–90, 98, 125,
  127–28, 134–36, 138–44, 146,
  152–53, 158, 166, 170–71, 192,
  207–10, 219, 233, 236
Tatars, xii, 8, 15, 27, 32–33, 35–36,
  38, 40–42, 44, 46, 50–51, 55, 78,
  82–84, 117, 122, 136–37, 139,
  243n40, 246n27, 248nn7–10,
  249n15, 251n34, 254n69, 254n76,
  262n20, 266n3, 269n20, 276n31;
  and education, 82–84, 87–88, 90,
  123, 154, 263nn30–31, 264n41,
  265n46; relations with Uzbek
  women, 35–36, 48, 52, 83, 87–
  88, 90, 98–99, 123–24, 136, 138,
  149, 163, 166, 264n39
teacher, 16, 37, 41, 77, 84, 87, 89, 91–
  92, 104, 116, 146, 157–58, 167,
  195–96, 207, 216pl, 243n40; training, 79, 82, 84, 86, 88–90, 93, 103,

  125–26, 154, 157–58, 169, 177,
  264n39. See also domla; mu'allima;
  otin
terror, 18, 158, 186–87, 201, 211, 285n47
Tillaxonov, Salimxon, 105, 148, 154,
  264n45, 269nn22–23, 286n68
Tillaxonova, Hosiyat, 100, 104–7,
  105pl, 122, 126–27, 140, 148, 154,
  190, 199, 269n23, 273n1, 274n15,
  277n44
To'xtaxo'jaeva (Tokhtakhodjaeva),
  Marfua, 6, 75
translation, xi, 16, 33, 80, 98, 108,
  164, 230, 267n5
Turkestan, xiv, 9, 13–14, 17, 19–31,
  33–41, 43–51, 53–63, 75–77, 79–
  84, 134–38, 229, 244n7, 244n10,
  246n21, 249n13, 256n26, 257n28;
  Autonomous Soviet Socialist
  Republic (TASSR), 61–62, 68,
  69, 73, 85–88, 90, 113, 117,
  141–43, 257n33
Turkestani, 9, 21–36, 42–43, 46–47,
  49, 51–64, 76–77, 81–84, 87, 93,
  137–38, 227, 229, 244nn9–10,
  245n14, 248n8, 255n4, 255n11,
  264n42, 264n45, 266n3, 269n22,
  278n4; women, 29, 35, 37–39,
  43, 51–54, 57–59, 75, 81, 83–84,
  86–87, 97, 99, 136, 143, 262n23.
  See also Uzbek women
Turkey, 4, 7, 10, 17, 54, 66–75, 131,
  133, 151, 172–74, 178–84, 189,
  210, 217, 234, 237, 258n40,
  258n44, 260n2, 281n48, 281n58,
  287n69; unveiling in, 179
Turkic: custom, 45, 78, 266n1; languages, x, xii, 13, 16, 21, 34–36,
  38–39, 49, 80, 124, 245n15,
  246n27, 248n8, 248n10, 252n48;
  unity, 62
Turkiston Viloyatining Gazetasi (Turkestan Provincial Newspaper), 39,
  42, 245n15

Veiling (continued)
    not face, 167, 169, 172, 176–78,
        220, 226, 233–36; reveiling, 141,
        160, 162, 166, 169–70, 172, 194,
        196, 199, 201–2, 207–8, 212, 220–
        21, 232, 269n20; as symbol, 22,
        28, 131, 180, 184, 242n30. See also
        paranji
    victim, 11, 13, 39, 94, 96, 109, 181,
        187, 198, 207, 211, 231, 250n21,
        282n58, 286n55
    violence, 3–4, 11, 13, 28, 55, 58–
        59, 66–67, 144–45, 148–49, 158–
        60, 164–66, 170, 177, 181, 186–
        200, 205, 213–14, 217, 230–33,
        281n58, 283n3, 283n5, 286n55

Waqf, 23, 60, 79, 81, 85, 190, 204,
    246n22
wedding, 42, 70, 95, 116, 129, 156–
    57; feast, 44, 46, 220, 272n47,
    278n12
widow, 5, 100, 110, 112–13, 148,
    250n20, 290n5
women representatives, 71, 74, 111,
    118, 141, 144–46, 160, 169, 225
Women's Division, CPUz, 16–17,
    35, 40, 56, 71, 73–74, 90, 94,
    97–99, 101, 106–7, 110–11, 120,
    140, 142, 144–51, 163pl, 165,
    169, 172, 178, 184, 193–94, 198–
    200, 202–9, 215, 217–18, 225,
    230, 267n4, 267n10, 273n59,
    277n44
Women's Division of the Communist
    Party (all-Union and CAB), 5,
    11, 14, 32, 92, 98–100, 108, 122,
    141–42, 148, 150, 162–64, 171,
    174, 178, 193, 199, 203, 207–8,
    211–17, 226, 230, 247n1, 260n70,

    267nn5–8, 279n16, 285n51,
        287n2
women's work, 26–27, 29–30, 109,
    111, 121, 128, 169, 176, 191, 209,
    215, 216pl, 219–20, 222–25, 228,
    234, 247n37, 262n23, 270n32,
    289n20
World War II, 116, 128, 169, 176,
    219–23, 228, 243n38

Xo'jaev, Faizulla, 61, 64, 130, 158,
    164, 166, 257n28, 257n33,
    269n22, 272n54
Xoldarova, Sobira, 100–101pl, 106–8,
    122, 140, 147, 172, 218, 268n15,
    268n16, 273n1
Xorazm, xv, 13, 16, 123, 126, 129–30,
    134, 192, 198, 209, 220

Yangi Yo'l (New Path, journal), 16,
    17, 94, 97, 99–122, 127, 144, 148,
    165, 172–73, 179, 183, 200, 209–
    10, 217, 267n10, 268nn12–13,
    270nn28–30, 270n33, 274n6. See
    also editor
Yer Yuzi (Face of the Earth, journal),
    16, 104, 179, 243n40, 270n29
Yo'ldoshbaeva (Iuldashbaeva),
    Fotima, 80, 128, 205–6, 249n17,
    274n8

ZAGS (civil registry), 69, 116–17,
    129, 156–57, 203, 234, 274n12
Zelenski, I. A., 162, 164, 205, 268n12,
    279n15
Zhukova, 208, 210, 279n16, 281n42,
    286n64
ziyolilar (intelligentsia), 89, 92, 101,
    103–4, 107, 124–26 159, 203,
    208, 210, 265n38, 267n5, 281n48

www.ingramcontent.com/pod-product-compliance
Ingram Content Group UK Ltd.
Pitfield, Milton Keynes, MK11 3LW, UK
UKHW010306240525
458861UK00002B/263